German
DeMYSTiFieD®

DeMYSTiFieD® Series

Accounting Demystified
Advanced Calculus Demystified
Advanced Physics Demystified
Advanced Statistics Demystified
Algebra Demystified
Alternative Energy Demystified
Anatomy Demystified
asp.net 2.0 Demystified
Astronomy Demystified
Audio Demystified
Biology Demystified
Biotechnology Demystified
Business Calculus Demystified
Business Math Demystified
Business Statistics Demystified
C++ Demystified
Calculus Demystified
Chemistry Demystified
Circuit Analysis Demystified
College Algebra Demystified
Corporate Finance Demystified
Databases Demystified
Data Structures Demystified
Differential Equations Demystified
Digital Electronics Demystified
Earth Science Demystified
Electricity Demystified
Electronics Demystified
Engineering Statistics Demystified
Environmental Science Demystified
Everyday Math Demystified
Fertility Demystified
Financial Planning Demystified
Forensics Demystified
French Demystified
Genetics Demystified
Geometry Demystified
German Demystified
Home Networking Demystified
Investing Demystified
Italian Demystified
Java Demystified
JavaScript Demystified
Lean Six Sigma Demystified
Linear Algebra Demystified
Logic Demystified
Macroeconomics Demystified
Management Accounting Demystified
Math Proofs Demystified
Math Word Problems Demystified
MATLAB® Demystified
Medical Billing and Coding Demystified
Medical Terminology Demystified
Meteorology Demystified
Microbiology Demystified
Microeconomics Demystified
Nanotechnology Demystified
Nurse Management Demystified
OOP Demystified
Options Demystified
Organic Chemistry Demystified
Personal Computing Demystified
Philosophy Demsytified
Pharmacology Demystified
Physics Demystified
Physiology Demystified
Pre-Algebra Demystified
Precalculus Demystified
Probability Demystified
Project Management Demystified
Psychology Demystified
Quality Management Demystified
Quantum Mechanics Demystified
Real Estate Math Demystified
Relativity Demystified
Robotics Demystified
Sales Management Demystified
Signals and Systems Demystified
Six Sigma Demystified
Spanish Demystified
sql Demystified
Statics and Dynamics Demystified
Statistics Demystified
Technical Analysis Demystified
Technical Math Demystified
Trigonometry Demystified
uml Demystified
Visual Basic 2005 Demystified
Visual C# 2005 Demystified
xml Demystified

German DeMYSTiFieD®

2nd edition

Ed Swick

New York Chicago San Francisco Lisbon London Madrid Mexico City
Milan New Delhi San Juan Seoul Singapore Sydney Toronto

The **McGraw·Hill** Companies

1 2 3 4 5 6 7 8 9 10 11 12 13 14 15 16 17 QFR/QFR 1 9 8 7 6 5 4 3 2 1

ISBN 978-0-07-175588-7 (book and CD set)
MHID 0-07-175588-8 (book and CD set)

ISBN 978-0-07-175579-5 (book for set)
MHID 0-07-175579-9 (book for set)

e-ISBN 978-0-07-175587-0
e-MHID 0-07-175587-X

Library of Congress Control Number 2010935978

Maps created by Douglas Norgord, Geographic Techniques.

This book is printed on acid-free paper.

Contents

Part Three Lots More About Verbs

Introduction

You've decided to learn German. Or you want to refresh the German skills you learned in the past. Or perhaps you're currently in a German class and you need some extra help with difficult concepts. Whatever your goal might be for learning German, *German Demystified* will efficiently guide you on your way.

Taking the mystery out of German is an important step in the learning process. Students need to know that the study of German is not as formidable a challenge as they might have thought. For one thing, English and German are sister languages that were separated in the early years by the migration of one Germanic group—the Anglo-Saxons—from the Continent to England. In the centuries that have passed since that migration, the Continental language and the language spoken in England evolved in two different ways. But, despite the separation of the two languages by geography and the passage of time, much in them remains similar.

There are many words in both German and English that are identical or that show an obvious kinship. The spelling of the words or even their modern pronunciation may be somewhat different, but the fact that they belong to the same family is quite clear. Here are just a few examples:

German	**English**
braun	*brown*
bringen	*to bring*
Bruder	*brother*
finden	*to find*

Haus	*house*
kommen	*to come*
Kuh	*cow*
Mann	*man*

Much of the grammar is also similar. All European languages have irregularities, especially with verbs. However, learning the irregularities of German verbs can be less of a task, because German and English have some similarities in how verbal irregularities occur. For example, both languages often have the same irregular vowel change from the present to the past tense.

German	**English**
kommen—kam	*to come—came*
sehen—sah	*to see—saw*
trinken—trank	*to drink—drank*

This alone is an enormous advantage for the English speaker who wishes to learn German.

How to Use This Book

Demystifying German goes beyond recognizing the similarities between German and English. This book will provide a clear and straightforward approach to understanding German grammatical concepts, including uncomplicated explanations of new material, a variety of examples that illustrate that material, and numerous vehicles for practicing what is learned. In this book you will also find key vocabulary. Vocabulary terms are presented both in short lists and in context within example phrases and sentences.

German Demystified can be used in two ways. You can begin with Chapter 1 and work your way through the chapters in progression. You can also use this book in a modular way by using the Table of Contents and Index to locate particular areas of German that you want to study.

This book features two kinds of practice: oral and written. It's important to understand that one form of practice is no more important than the other. They are different in form but function together in the development of German skills. Language is both a spoken and written entity; therefore, oral practice is obviously necessary when learning a new language, but written practice provides time to think about grammatical concepts and vocabulary meaning. Written practice allows the student time to ponder and analyze what is being learned and is the way in which one records knowledge and evaluates progress. Both forms of practice will be important for you as you proceed through this book.

Below is an illustration of how the oral practices in this book are structured. They are not merely lists of words or of random sentences to be practiced aloud. Instead, the oral practices contain paradigms that illustrate a concept important to the language. Let's look at an example of an oral practice in English providing paradigms that illustrate pronouns used as direct objects.

> Practice saying the following list of sentences out loud.
>
> *We visited them in March.*
>
> *We visited her in March.*
>
> *We visited him in March.*
>
> *I visited you in March.*
>
> *She visited us in March.*
>
> *You visited me in March.*

The written practices will appear in various forms. In some instances you will be asked to complete a sentence by inserting new words. For example, an English exercise with pronouns changing from their subjective form to their objective form would look like this:

> Rewrite the following sentence using the correct forms of the pronouns provided in parentheses.
>
> Thomas met ______ at the theater.
>
> (I) *Thomas met me at the theater.*
>
> (she) *Thomas met her at the theater.*
>
> (he) *Thomas met him at the theater.*
>
> (we) *Thomas met us at the theater.*

Other forms of written practice include verb conjugations, multiple-choice exercises, and writing original sentences.

You will occasionally find tables in this book. They are used to highlight special information and to remind you of a concept that is important to keep in mind. For example:

German does not capitalize adjectives that refer to a country:

die **deutsche** Fahne	the ***German*** flag
der **amerikanische** Tourist	the ***American*** tourist
der **italienische** Wagen	the ***Italian*** car

Each chapter ends with a quiz that will help you to evaluate your understanding of the material covered. The quizzes are open-book quizzes—you should use the content of the chapter as a resource for determining the correct answers. A good suggestion is to achieve a score of at least 80 percent before going on to the next chapter.

After every five chapters, you will have a Part Test. There are four parts to the book, and the Part Tests are, therefore, named Part One Test, Part Two Test, Part Three Test, and Part Four Test. It is suggested that you consider these tests closed-book tests in order to check your comprehension of the concepts in each part. You should get a score of at least 75 percent in a Part Test before moving on to the next part.

The last test in this book is the Final Exam. It consists of questions that are drawn from all four parts of the book. This exam contains 50 questions, and a good score on the Final Exam would be 75 percent or above.

At the end of the book, there is an Answer Key, which provides the correct answers for all Quizzes, Part Tests, and the Final Exam. In the case of questions that require you to provide an original sentence as your answer, you will be provided with sample answers for comparison.

This edition of *German Demystified* is accompanied by an important tool—an audio CD. The contents of this CD are comprised of both individual words and complete sentences. The new words are often isolated to provide for clarity and ease of pronunciation. But German, like English, is a language of complete thoughts. Therefore, learning to pronounce complete sentences is essential, and an abundance of practice with complete sentences is included on the CD. Some of the sentences on the CD are from dialogues, and others are found in the Oral Practices of the chapter text. The voices on the CD are of native Germans speaking naturally and at a normal rate.

If you work diligently but at a pace that is comfortable for you, your efforts will result in success and the language of German will be demystified.

Übung macht den Meister. *Practice makes perfect.*

Acknowledgment

With much gratitude to Stefan Feyen for all his help and suggestions.

Part One

Getting Started

chapter 1

German Pronunciation

In this chapter you will learn how to pronounce the German alphabet and use its special characters. You will discover the sounds of individual letters and how they differ when combined with other letters.

CHAPTER OBJECTIVES

In this chapter you will learn about:

- German Alphabet
- Special Characters
- Consonant Combinations
- Vowel Combinations
- Some Special Pronunciation Rules
- German Cognates

German Alphabet

There really isn't a German alphabet just like there really isn't an English alphabet. The Germans do what English speakers do: They use the Latin alphabet and add a few extra characters of their own for good measure. There are only four extra characters in German, and all the other letters are the same as used in the English language. However, there is a difference between German and English pronunciation of the letters.

You must remember that the letters of the alphabet are merely signals of pronunciation possibilities. In all languages there are nuances of the same sound, and often one letter stands for all those nuances. Consider the English vowel *a*. Its name is *ay*, but it is pronounced differently in various words. For example: f*a*ther, b*a*d, b*a*ll, and t*a*pe. Unlike *a*, sometimes the name of a letter gives absolutely no clue as to its pronunciation, such as the English consonant *w*. It is called *double u*, but makes a sound completely different from that. You'll discover that there are a few instances when the German name of a letter does the same thing.

There are various pronunciations for single letters in German as well. Fortunately, they are not as numerous as in English, and, for the most part, German spelling consistently gives the information needed to pronounce words accurately.

Following is the complete alphabet with the German name of each letter, the sound each letter makes, and a sample German word using that letter with its pronunciation and meaning.

Track 1

Letter	Name	Sounds Like	German Example Word (German Pronunciation)	English Meaning
A a	ah	mama	las (lahss)	*read*
B b	bay	Bob	Boot (bote)	*boat*
C c	tsay	its	Cent (tsent)	*cent*
D d	day	dad	dann (dunn)	*then*
E e	ay	say	Tee (tay)	*tea*
F f	eff	fife	finden (fin-den)	*to find*
G g	gay	goggle	geben (gay-ben)	*to give*
H h	hah	hope	Haus (house)	*house*
I i	ee	keep	Igel (ee-gel)	*hedgehog*
J j	yawt	yawn	ja (yah)	*yes*

K k	**kah**	kick	kalt (kult)	*cold*
L l	**ell**	lull	Laus (louse)	*louse*
M m	**emm**	mom	Maus (mouse)	*mouse*
N n	**enn**	noon	nein (nine)	*no*
O o	**oh**	only	oder (oh-duh)	*or*
P p	**pay**	pipe	parken (par-ken)	*to park*
Q q	**koo**	quite	Quark (kvahrk)	*curd cheese*

(When pronounced in a German word, the **k** sound of the letter **q** is followed by the **v** sound.)

R r	**air**	roar	Ruhm (room)	*fame*

(There is no English equivalent for this pronunciation of **r**. See "Some Special Pronunciation Rules" in this chapter for further explanation.)

S s	**ess**	zealous	Sessel (zes-sel)	*armchair*

(At the beginning of a word **s** is pronounced like a **z**.)

T t	**tay**	tot	Teil (tile)	*part*
U u	**oo**	moon	U-Bahn (oo-bahn)	*subway*
V v	**fow**	for	Volkswagen (fohlks-vah-gen)	*Volkswagen*
W w	**vay**	vivid	wild (villt)	*wild*
X x	**ix**	taxi	Taxi (tahk-see)	*taxi*
Y y	**uepsilon**	mystic	physisch (fuez-ish)	*physical*

(With this letter, the lips are pursed to say **oo**, but the voice is saying **ee**. The result is this special vowel sound **ue**. For further explanation, see the explanation for **Ü ü** later in this chapter.)

Z z	**tset**	its	Zelt (tsellt)	*tent*

Oral Practice

Track 2

Say each word out loud. Look at the pronunciation on the right to check your accuracy.

German	English	German Pronunciation
1. faul	*lazy*	(fowl)
2. Sau	*sow*	(zow)
3. Mauer	*wall*	(mow-uh)

4. Eisen	*iron*	(eye-zen)
5. Meister	*master*	(my-stuh)
6. schnell	*fast*	(shnell)
7. stellen	*to put*	(shtel-len)
8. sterben	*to die*	(shtair-ben)
9. Sitz	*seat*	(zits)
10. sitzen	*to sit*	(zit-sen)
11. Spiel	*game*	(shpeel)
12. spielen	*to play*	(shpee-len)
13. wiegen	*to weigh*	(vee-gen)
14. Wagen	*car*	(vah-gen)
15. schlagen	*hit*	(shlah-gen)
16. Zeit	*time*	(tsite)
17. Zimmer	*room*	(tsim-muh)
18. Donner	*thunder*	(dawn-uh)
19. Tanne	*fir tree*	(tuh-neh)
20. Tante	*aunt*	(tahn-teh)

Special Characters

The next three special characters in the German alphabet have an umlaut over them. These dots over the vowels indicate a shift in the normal pronunciation of those letters.

The first letter is very much like the letter **E e** illustrated previously.

Ä ä	**ay**	say	spät (shpayt)	*late*

The following letter does not have an English equivalent sound. It is similar to the vowel **e** as it is pronounced in the English word *her*. The letter combination er will stand for its pronunciation here.

Ö ö	**er**	were	schön (shern)	*nice, pretty*

The next letter is pronounced like the sound **oo** with the lips tightly pursed, but the voice is saying **ee**. It is the same pronunciation for the letter **Y y** illustrated previously. The vowel combination **ue** will stand for its pronunciation. It is similar to a French **u** as in **sud** (*south*).

Ü ü	**ue**	sure	über (ue-buh)	*over*

Vowel with Umlaut	Sound	Vowel with No Umlaut	Sound
Ä ä	ay	A a	ah
Ö ö	er	O o	oh
Ü ü	ue (like French)	U u	oo

The following letter is a combination of an **s** and a **z** treated as a single letter. It does not have a capitalized form and is used in place of a double **s** (**ss**) after long vowel sounds, and diphthongs.

ß	**ess-tset**	less	weiß (vice)	*white*

Compare the use of the **ß** following a long vowel and **ss** following a short vowel.

aß (ahs—long *ah*) *ate*   passen (puhs-sen—short *uh*) *to fit*

Oral Practice

 Track 3

Say each word out loud. Look at the pronunciation on the right to check your accuracy.

	German	English	German Pronunciation
1.	älter	*older*	(el-tuh)
2.	fällt	*falls*	(fellt)
3.	löst	*solves*	(lerst)
4.	böse	*angry*	(ber-zeh)
5.	Flüsse	*rivers*	(flues-eh)
6.	klug	*smart*	(klook)
7.	lügen	*to lie*	(lue-gen)
8.	groß	*big*	(gross)
9.	Grüße	*greetings*	(grue-seh)
10.	Kasse	*cashier*	(kuhs-eh)

Consonant Combinations

The following letter combinations stand for a specific sound different from a single consonant. You will notice that some have an English equivalent.

1. **Ch** stands for the sound of the friction of air at the back of the throat much like the **ch** sound in the Scottish word *loch*. For example: **ich** means *I* and is pronounced **eech**. The italicized consonants ***ch*** will stand for this sound.
2. **Chs** in the middle of a word is pronounced like English *x*. For example, **Sachsen** means *Saxony* and is pronounced **zahx-en**.
3. **Ck** is pronounced like the English *ck*. For example, **schicken** means *to send* and is pronounced **shick-en**.
4. A final **g** is pronounced as a **k** or the guttural ***ch*** (see Number 1, in this list). For example, **klug** means *smart* and is pronounced **klook**. The word for *king* is **König** and is pronounced **ker-ni*ch*** or **ker-nik**.
5. **H** that follows a vowel at the end of a syllable is not pronounced. For example, **gehen** means *to go* and is pronounced **gay-en**.
6. With **pf**, both the **p** and the **f** are sounded in the pronunciation. For example, **pfiff** means *whistle* and is pronounced **pfiff**.
7. **Sch** is like the English combination *sh*. For example: **Schule** means *school* and is pronounced **shoo-leh**.
8. Two consonant combinations—**sp** and **st**—add the sound **sh** to their pronunciation. For example, **Sport** means *sports* and is pronounced **shport**. **Still** means *quiet* and is pronounced **shtill**.
9. **Th** exists in German, but it is pronounced like a **t**. For example, the German noun **Theater** means *theater*, but it is pronounced **tay-ah-tuh**.
10. **Tsch** sounds like the English combination *ch*. For example, **Tschechien** means *Czech Republic* and is pronounced **che*ch*-ee-en**.
11. **Tz** is pronounced as it is in English. For example, **letzte** means *last* and is pronounced **letz-teh**.

Oral Practice

Track 4

Say each word out loud. Look at the pronunciation on the right to check your accuracy.

	German	English	German Pronunciation
1.	sprechen	*to speak*	(shpre***ch***-en)
2.	Stadt	*city*	(shtaht)
3.	setzen	*to set*	(zet-zen)
4.	schrecken	*to scare*	(shreck-en)
5.	Thema	*topic*	(tay-mah)
6.	Tisch	*table*	(tish)
7.	Käfig	*cage*	(kay-fi***ch***)
8.	sehen	*to see*	(zay-en)
9.	Pförtner	*doorman*	(pfert-nuh)
10.	sechs	*six*	(zex)

Vowel Combinations

The following vowel combinations stand for a single sound but, in most cases, have a sound different from a single vowel.

1. **Aa** is pronounced as a long **ah**. For example, **Haar** means *hair* and is pronounced **hahr**.
2. **Au** is pronounced together as **ow**. For example, **kaufen** means *to buy* and is pronounced **cow-fen**.
3. **Äu** is pronounced **oi**. For example, **Fräulein** means *miss/young lady* and is pronounced **froi-line**.
4. **Ee** has a long **ay** sound. For example, **Tee** means *tea* and is pronounced **tay**.
5. **Ei** is pronounced **eye**. For example, **mein** means *my* and is pronounced **mine**.
6. **Eu** is also pronounced **oi**. For example, **Freude** means *joy* and is pronounced **froi-deh**.

7. **Ie** is pronounced **ee**. For example, **sieht** means *sees* and is pronounced **zeet**.
8. **Oo** has a long **oh** sound. For example, **Boot** means *boat* and is pronounced **bote**.

Oral Practice

 Track 5

Say each word out loud. Look at the pronunciation on the right to check your accuracy.

	German	English	German Pronunciation
1.	Eule	*owl*	(oi-leh)
2.	teilen	*to share*	(ty-len)
3.	schrieb	*wrote*	(shreep)
4.	Kaufmann	*businessman*	(cowf-munn)
5.	Seemann	*seaman*	(zay-munn)
6.	Säule	*column*	(zoi-leh)
7.	fährt	*drives*	(fairt)
8.	Saar	*the Saar*	(zahr)
9.	Freundin	*girlfriend*	(froin-din)
10.	Boote	*boats*	(bote-eh)

Some Special Pronunciation Rules

The final **-e** on a German word is pronounced **eh**. Be careful not to pronounce it **ah** or **uh**. For example, **Tante** means *aunt* and is pronounced **tahn-teh**. **Beste** means *best* and is pronounced **bess-teh**.

In the German-speaking world of Germany, Austria, and Switzerland, there are two distinct ways of pronouncing **r**. One way is the rolled **r** as is heard in Italian or Russian. The other is the so-called guttural **r** that is a sound made near the back of the tongue. In German the guttural sound is used when the **r** is located at the beginning of a word. For example, **rot** means *red* and is pronounced **rote**, with a guttural sound distinctly similar to a French **r**. When this letter is at the end of a syllable or word, particularly in the combination **er**, it sounds more like **uh** and does not resemble an **r**. It is similar to a final **r** in British English. For example, **Zucker** means *sugar* and is pronounced **tsoo-kuh**.

When a **b** or a **d** is located at the end of a prefix or word, they are pronounced **p** and **t** respectively. For example, **starb** means *died* and is pronounced **shtahrp**. The word **abfahren** means *to depart* and is pronounced **ahp-fahr-en**. The noun **Land** means *country* and is pronounced **lunt**. The word **Kind** means *child* and is pronounced **kint**.

Short and Long Vowels

Vowels tend to be pronounced short before a double consonant and long before a single consonant or a consonant preceded by **h**. Let's look at some examples.

Track 6

German	German Pronunciation	English
lassen	(luhs-sen) long	*to let*
lasen	(lah-zen) short	*read*
stehlen	(shtay-len) long	*to steal*
stellen	(shtel-len) short	*to put*
gib	(geep) long	*give*
Mitte	(mit-teh) short	*middle*
Hof	(hofe) long	*court, yard*
hoffen	(haw-fen) short	*to hope*
tun	(toon) long oo	*to do*
Suppe	(zoo-peh) short oo	*soup*

In English the combination *oo* may look the same in many words, but that vowel combination has two pronunciations. For example, long *oo—moon, soon*; and short *oo—look, shook*. When learning German, however, English speakers tend to use the long **oo** sound for all words that have the vowel **u**. But the short and long **oo** sounds must be distinguished in German, as well.

Oral Practice

 Track 7

Say each word out loud. Look at the pronunciation on the right to check your accuracy.

	German	English	German Pronunciation
1.	stören	*to disturb*	(ster-ren)
2.	gelacht	*laughed*	(geh-lah***ch***t)

3. Kaffee	*coffee*	(kah-fay)
4. Brötchen	*roll*	(brert-***ch***en)
5. Schlange	*snake*	(shlahng-eh)
6. jünger	*younger*	(y**ue**ng-uh)
7. floh	*fled*	(flow)
8. Sprüche	*sayings*	(shpr**ue*ch***-eh)
9. gelb	*yellow*	(gelp)
10. Band	*ribbon*	(bunt)

German Cognates

Cognates are words that are identical or very similar in two languages. And that can be problematic, because English speakers sometimes pronounce the German cognate with the English pronunciation. Here are some example words in German with their pronunciations and the English equivalents. Take special note of the German pronunciations.

German	German Pronunciation	English
Auto	(ow-toe)	*auto*
Adresse	(ah-dres-seh)	*address*
effektiv	(ay-feck-teef)	*effective*
Konflikt	(kone-flickt)	*conflict*
minus	(mee-noos)	*minus*
Präsident	(pray-zee-dent)	*president*
Problem	(proe-blame)	*problem*
Service	(zare-veese)	*service*

Many words that end in *-tion* in English also do in German. But that syllable is pronounced **-tsee-own** in German.

Position	(poe-zee-tsee-own)	*position*
Konstitution	(kone-stee-too-tsee-own)	*constitution*

Perhaps you have already noticed that all German nouns—whether proper or common—are capitalized. Here are a few more examples:

German	German Pronunciation	English
Name	(nah-meh)	*name*
Berlin	(bare-leen)	*Berlin*
Kapitalist	(kah-pee-tah-leest)	*capitalist*
Amerika	(ah-mare-ee-kah)	*America*

Oral Practice

 Track 8

Pronounce the following German words out loud without looking at the pronunciations. Then check the correct pronunciation that is provided.

	German	English	German Pronunciation
1.	Pilot	*pilot*	(pee-lote)
2.	Professor	*professor*	(pro-fes-suh)
3.	attraktiv	*attractive*	(ah-trahk-teef)
4.	komisch	*funny*	(koe-mish)
5.	Tür	*door*	(tuer)
6.	Kanada	*Canada*	(kah-nah-dah)
7.	halten	*to hold*	(hul-ten)
8.	blind	*blind*	(blint)
9.	Dialekt	*dialect*	(dee-ah-lekt)
10.	Alpen	*Alps*	(ahl-pen)
11.	Fenster	*window*	(fenn-stuh)
12.	schreiben	*to write*	(shry-ben)
13.	Diplomat	*diplomat*	(dee-ploh-maht)
14.	laufen	*to run*	(low-fen)
15.	Bier	*beer*	(beer)

QUIZ

In the blanks provided, write the letter of the pronunciation on the right that matches the German word on the left. For example:

spielen *to play*	B	A. (frow)
Frau *woman*	A	B. (shpee-len)
1. **Grüße** *greetings*	______	A. (poe-zee-tsee-own)
2. **Position** *position*	______	B. (lunt)
3. **Tür** *door*	______	C. (tsih-muh)
4. **Land** *country*	______	D. (tish)
5. **sehen** *to see*	______	E. (shpre***ch***-en)
6. **Tisch** *table*	______	F. (gr***ue***-seh)
7. **sprechen** *to speak*	______	G. (klook)
8. **böse** *angry*	______	H. (b**e**r-zeh)
9. **klug** *smart*	______	I. (zay-en)
10. **Zimmer** *room*	______	J. (t**ue**r)

chapter 2

People and Names

In this chapter you will learn about German names and how the German definite articles are used. In addition you will encounter the basic conjugation of verbs. This chapter will also include ways to say hello and good-bye.

CHAPTER OBJECTIVES

In this chapter you will learn about:

- German Names
- People
- Definite Articles
- Conjugation of German Verbs
- Places
- Greetings

German Names

The United States consists of people from many lands, and one of those lands is Germany. For over two centuries Germans have come to this country with their culture, their traditions, and their names. Consequently, you may find that you already know many German names.

Some names are considered traditional or maybe even called old-fashioned. But just like in English, as time goes by, old-fashioned names come back into vogue. Here are just a few:

Für Jungen *For Boys*	**Für Mädchen *For Girls***
Gerhardt	Luise
Reinhardt	Gretchen
Helmut	Angelika
Werner	Frieda
Heinrich	Waltraud

In Germany today you will encounter a variety of names, some that come from other cultures, and some that are currently in fashion but will gradually lose their popularity and be replaced by a new trend. For example:

Für Jungen *For Boys*	**Für Mädchen *For Girls***
Erik	Gudrun
Boris	Tanja
Christoph	Natascha
Felix	Angela
Nils	Iris

Oral Practice

 Track 9

Practice saying the following list of sentences out loud. Then for the last sentence, fill in the blank with your own name.

Mein Name ist Gerhardt.	*My name is Gerhardt.*
Mein Name ist Frieda.	*My name is Frieda.*
Mein Name ist Boris.	*My name is Boris.*
Mein Name ist Tanja.	*My name is Tanja.*
Mein Name ist ______.	*My name is ______.*

Asking Someone's Name

When you ask for someone's name, you say:

Was ist Ihr Name?	*What is your name?*

Interestingly, German has another way of asking for or for giving someone's name. The verb **heißen** is used in these sentences. This verb means *to be called*. When you use it in a sentence, it will have the same translation as **Mein Name ist** ______.

What is your Name?	***My name is Marianne.***
Was ist Ihr Name?	Mein Name ist Marianne.
Wie heißen Sie?	Ich heiße Marianne.

Oral Practice

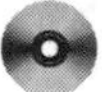 Track 10

Practice asking someone's name and telling what your name is.

Wie heißen Sie?	*What is your name?*
Ich heiße Helmut.	*My name is Helmut.*
Ich heiße Luise.	*My name is Luise.*
Ich heiße Werner.	*My name is Werner.*
Ich heiße Gudrun.	*My name is Gudrun.*
Ich heiße ______.	*My name is* ______.

Notice that in the question **Wie heißen Sie?** the verb has an **-en** ending. In the answer **Ich heiße...**, the verb has an **-e** ending. This difference is important and will be explained fully a little later. For now, use **heißen** in the question and **heiße** in the answer.

German Titles

Just as in English, Germans use a title with their last names in formal situations or when providing official information about themselves. The word for *Mr.* before a man's last name is **Herr**, and the word for *Ms., Mrs.,* or *Miss* before a woman's last name is **Frau**. There is another feminine title: **Fräulein** (*Miss*). German tends to shy away from using this title, and all women, married or single, are addressed with **Frau**. Let's look at some example sentences in the following Oral Practice section.

Oral Practice

 Track 11

Practice saying the following list of sentences out loud. At the end of the series of sentences, provide your own last name.

Wie heißen Sie, bitte?	*What is your name, please?*
Ich heiße Braun. Werner Braun.	*My name is Braun. Werner Braun.*
Guten Tag, Herr Braun.	*Hello, Mr. Braun.*
Ich heiße Schiller. Tanja Schiller.	*My name is Schiller. Tanja Schiller.*
Guten Tag, Frau Schiller.	*Hello, Ms. Schiller.*
Ich heiße Schneider. Friedrich Schneider.	*My name is Schneider. Friedrich Schneider.*
Guten Tag, Herr Schneider.	*Hello, Mr. Schneider.*
Ich heiße Keller. Marianne Keller.	*My name is Keller. Marianne Keller.*
Guten Tag, Frau Keller.	*Hello, Mrs. Keller.*
Ich heiße ______. ______ ______.	*My name is ______. ______ ______*
Guten Tag, (Herr/Frau) ______.	*Hello, (Mr./Mrs.) ______.*

Written Practice 1

Using the names in parentheses, write the two ways you can give your name. For example:

(Albert)	Ich heiße Albert.	Mein Name ist Albert.
1. (Martin)	______.	______.
2. (Tina)	______.	______.
3. (Herr Schäfer)	______.	______.
4. (Frau Kamps)	______.	______.
5. (Boris Becker)	______.	______.
6. (Maria Schell)	______.	______.
7. (Professor Bach)	______.	______.
8. (Doktor Berg)	______.	______.
9. (Iris)	______.	______.
10. (*your own name*)	______.	______.

People

Since English and German are related languages, it's no surprise that there are many words in both languages that resemble one another. These words are called cognates. English and German share a variety of cognates absorbed from other sources as well.

Many cognates refer to people. For example:

Track 12

der Artist	*artist; performer*	der Mechaniker	*mechanic*
der Boss	*boss*	der Pilot	*pilot*
der Diplomat	*diplomat*	der Professor	*professor*
der Clown	*clown*	der Reporter	*reporter*
der Kapitalist	*capitalist*	der Student	*student*
der Mann	*man*	der Vater	*father*

The German words in this list are used only to describe men. English speakers tend to avoid using words that specify a gender role, but German is different. The makeup of the language requires specifying gender, therefore many nouns add the suffix **-in** to signal that the person described is female. Let's look at some feminine nouns or nouns that refer to women. Some of them will have the suffix **-in**.

die Artistin	*artist; performer*	die Mutter	*mother*
die Dame	*lady*	die Pilotin	*pilot*
die Frau	*woman*	die Professorin	*professor*
die Kapitalistin	*capitalist*	die Reporterin	*reporter*
die Lehrerin	*teacher*	die Sängerin	*singer*
die Mechanikerin	*mechanic*	die Studentin	*student*

If you know the feminine form of a word ends in **-in**, simply remove the suffix and you will have the masculine form of that word. For example:

Feminine	**Masculine**
die Lehrerin	der Lehrer
die Sängerin	der Sänger

Written Practice 2

Change each of the following masculine nouns to feminine nouns and include the definite article.

1. der Diplomat ______
2. der Student ______
3. der Artist ______
4. der Kommunist ______
5. der Mechaniker ______
6. der Optimist ______
7. der Pilot ______
8. der Manager ______

Definite Articles

Feminine nouns use **die** (*the*) as their definite article, and masculine nouns use **der** (*the*). German also has a third gender: neuter. The definite article for neuter nouns or inanimate objects is **das** (*the*), for example, **das Haus** (*the house*). But many German nouns are considered masculine, feminine, or neuter even though they are not referring to males, females, or inanimate objects. For example:

 Track 13

Masculine		**Feminine**		**Neuter**	
der Wagen	*car*	die Lampe	*lamp*	das Baby	*baby*
der Schuh	*shoe*	die Schule	*school*	das Kind	*child*
der Arm	*arm*	die Hand	*hand*	das Mädchen	*girl*

This concept of gender, although not difficult, is new to English speakers and requires some getting used to. Be patient with it, and it will gradually fall in line for you. Just accept the fact that you have to be aware of three forms of the definite article (**der**, **die**, **das**) and not just one as in English (*the*).

When you ask *who* someone is, you use **wer** (**Wer ist das?** *Who is that?*). The answer always begins with **Das ist...** (*That is . . .*).

Das ist...	der Lehrer.
	die Lehrerin.
	das Kind.
	das Mädchen.
	der Professor.
	die Mutter.
	Erik.
	Frau Schneider.

Oral Practice

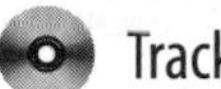
Track 14

Practice saying the following list of sentences out loud.

Wer ist das?	*Who is that?*
Das ist der Lehrer.	*That is the teacher.*
Wer ist das?	*Who is that?*
Das ist die Professorin.	*That is the professor.*
Wer ist das?	*Who is that?*
Das ist der Student.	*That is the student.*
Wer ist das?	*Who is that?*
Das ist der Pilot.	*That is the pilot.*
Wer ist das?	*Who is that?*
Das ist die Mutter.	*That is the mother.*
Wer ist das?	*Who is that?*
Das ist der Vater.	*That is the father.*
Wer ist das?	*Who is that?*
Das ist Professor Schäfer.	*That is Professor Schäfer.*
Wer ist das?	*Who is that?*
Das ist Frau Kamps.	*That is Frau Kamps.*

Now practice saying these sentences out loud.

Wie heißt der Herr?	*What is the gentleman's name?*
Der Herr heißt Schneider.	*The gentleman's name is Schneider.*
Konrad Schneider.	*Konrad Schneider.*
Wie heißt die Dame?	*What is the lady's name?*
Die Dame heißt Bauer.	*The lady's name is Bauer.*
Angela Bauer.	*Angela Bauer.*

Wie heißt die Studentin?	*What is the student's name?*
Die Studentin heißt Tanja.	*The student's name is Tanja.*
Wie heißt der Reporter?	*What is the reporter's name?*
Der Reporter heißt Herr Bach.	*The reporter's name is Mr. Bach.*
Wie heißt das Baby?	*What is the baby's name?*
Das Baby heißt Gudrun.	*The baby's name is Gudrun.*
Wie heißt das Kind?	*What is the child's name?*
Das Kind heißt Felix.	*The child's name is Felix.*

Conjugation of German Verbs

You have probably noticed that **heißt** in the previous sentences looks a little different from what it looked like in earlier examples (**heiße**). When it is used with a word that describes a person other than the speaker, its form is **heißt**. For example:

Track 15

Sie heißen	*you are called (your name is)*
ich heiße	*I am called (my name is)*
das Kind heißt	*the child is called (the child's name is)*
der Mann heißt	*the man is called (the man's name is)*
die Dame heißt	*the lady is called (the lady's name is)*
der Lehrer heißt	*the teacher is called (the teacher's name is)*

This change of endings on a verb is called a conjugation. There are conjugations in English, but they are simpler in form than German conjugations. Most English verbs add an *-s* in the third person singular of the present tense, and the plural forms of other persons have no added ending.

I speak, you speak, he speak**s**, we speak, they speak
I learn, you learn, he learn**s**, we learn, they learn

Only the verb *to be* is more complicated:

I am, you are, he is, we are, they are

The difference of the endings on **heißen** is part of the German conjugation. Verb conjugations will be taken up fully later in this book.

Oral Practice

Track 16

Practice saying the following list of sentences out loud.

Wie heißen Sie?	*What is your name?*
Ich heiße Tina.	*My name is Tina.*
Mein Vater heißt Karl.	*My father's name is Karl.*
Wie heißen Sie?	*What is your name?*
Ich heiße Robert.	*My name is Robert.*
Mein Vater heißt Gerhardt.	*My father's name is Gerhardt.*
Wie heißen Sie?	*What is your name?*
Ich heiße Wilhelm.	*My name is Wilhelm.*
Mein Vater heißt Wilhelm.	*My father's name is Wilhelm.*

Written Practice 3

Write the question that asks a person's name. Then write responses to that question with the names shown in parentheses. For example:

(Karl) Wie heißen Sie?

Ich heiße Karl.

1. (Angela) ______________________________?
   ______________________________.
2. (Herr Bauer) ______________________________?
   ______________________________.
3. (Thomas) ______________________________?
   ______________________________.
4. (Frau Kamps) ______________________________?
   ______________________________.
5. (Gudrun Klein) ______________________________?
   ______________________________.

Places

 Track 17

Many cities and countries have similar names in both English and German. Let's look at a few.

German	**English**
Amerika	*America*
Berlin	*Berlin*
Dänemark	*Denmark*
England	*England*
Hamburg	*Hamburg*
Hannover	*Hanover*
Kanada	*Canada*
Mexiko	*Mexico*
Paris	*Paris*
Polen	*Poland*
Rom	*Rome*
Warschau	*Warsaw*

The word for *German* is **Deutsch**. The English word *Dutch* is a similar word but refers to the Netherlands and not to Germany. The word for *Germany* is **Deutschland**. And a German city that may not be recognized by its German spelling is **München** (*Munich*).

German words for two general locations are **hier** and **da** (or **dort**), which mean respectively *here* and *there*. A sentence that gives someone's location is composed of a subject, the verb **ist**, and the location, usually following the preposition **in**.

Herr Bauer ist...	in Berlin.
	in Mexiko.
	in Frankfurt.
	in Amerika.
	hier.
	dort.

Now that you know some countries and cities, you can begin to ask where (**wo**) someone is.

Oral Practice

 Track 18

Practice saying the following list of sentences out loud.

Wo ist Herr Schneider?	*Where is Mr. Schneider?*
Herr Schneider ist in Deutschland.	*Mr. Schneider is in Germany.*
Wo ist Professor Gelb?	*Where is Professor Gelb?*
Professor Gelb ist in Amerika.	*Professor Gelb is in America.*
Wo ist der Lehrer?	*Where is the teacher?*
Der Lehrer ist in Paris.	*The teacher is in Paris.*
Wo ist die Studentin?	*Where is the student?*
Die Studentin ist in Berlin.	*The student is in Berlin.*
Wo ist das Kind?	*Where is the child?*
Das Kind ist hier.	*The child is here.*
Wo ist der Vater?	*Where is the father?*
Der Vater ist da.	*The father is there.*
Wo ist die Reporterin?	*Where is the reporter?*
Die Reporterin ist in Warschau.	*The reporter is in Warsaw.*
Wo ist Frau Bauer?	*Where is Mrs. Bauer?*
Frau Bauer ist in Dänemark.	*Mrs. Bauer is in Denmark.*

Written Practice 4

Use the nouns in parentheses that refer to a person to ask where someone is. Then use the noun that refers to a place to answer the question. For example:

(Martin/Berlin) Wo ist Martin?
Martin ist in Berlin.

1. (das Kind/hier) ____________________?
____________________.
2. (mein Vater/dort) ____________________?
____________________.
3. (Erik/Deutschland) ____________________?
____________________.

4. (Thomas/da) ______________________________?

______________________________.

5. (Iris/München) ______________________________?

______________________________.

Greetings

You now know three interrogative words: **wer** (*who*), **wie** (*how*), and **wo** (*where*). In the expression **Wie heißt der Mann?** we translate **wie** as *what* (*What is the man's name?*). Actually, in German you're saying: ***How** is the man called?*

The phrase **Wie geht's?** (*How are you?*) is a very common expression in German. For example:

Guten Tag, Thomas. Wie geht's?	*Hello, Thomas. How are you?*
Gut, danke.	*Fine, thanks.*
Guten Tag, Tanja. Wie geht's?	*Hello, Tanja. How are you?*
Gut, danke.	*Fine, thanks.*
Guten Tag, Felix. Wie geht's?	*Hello, Felix. How are you?*
Gut, danke.	*Fine, thanks.*
Guten Tag, Gudrun. Wie geht's?	*Hello, Gudrun. How are you?*
Gut, danke.	*Fine, thanks.*

Although **Guten Tag** means literally *good day*, it is also used during the day to say *hello*. In the morning, you say **Guten Morgen** (*good morning*). In the evening, you say **Guten Abend** (*good evening*). And late at night, when you're about to go to bed, you say **Gute Nacht** (*good night*).

Oral Practice

 Track 19

In the following section you'll find some common exchanges between two people meeting on the street. Practice saying these brief dialogues out loud.

Guten Tag, Herr Schneider.	*Good day, Mr. Schneider.*
Guten Tag, Wilhelm. Wie geht's?	*Hello, Wilhelm. How are you?*
Gut, danke.	*Fine, thanks.*

And two more people:

Guten Morgen, Frau Benz.	*Good morning, Ms. Benz.*
Guten Morgen, Karl. Wie geht's?	*Hello, Karl. How are you?*
Gut, danke.	*Fine, thanks.*

And two more people:

Guten Abend, Doktor Bauer.	*Good evening, Dr. Bauer.*
Guten Abend, Tina. Wie geht's?	*Hello, Tina. How are you?*
Gut, danke.	*Fine, thanks.*

At bedtime you say:

Gute Nacht, Herr Dorf.	*Good night, Mr. Dorf.*
Gute Nacht, Nils.	*Good night, Nils.*

Written Practice 5

Write a greeting to the people whose names are given in parentheses. Note the time of day indicated. For bedtime, write the appropriate phrase.

1. in the morning (Onkel Peter) ____________________.
2. in the evening (Herr Schneider) ____________________.
3. in the afternoon (Frau Keller) ____________________.
4. bedtime (Martin) ____________________.

When saying good-bye to someone, use the phrase **Auf Wiedersehen** (*till I see you again*). It is sometimes said without **auf**: just **Wiedersehen**. And occasionally you'll hear **Auf Wiederschauen**. In casual conversation, you can use the word **Tschüs** (*so long*).

Oral Practice

 Track 20

Practice saying the following brief dialogues out loud.

Guten Tag, Frau Bach.	*Hello, Ms. Bach.*
Guten Tag, Felix. Wie geht's?	*Hello, Felix. How are you?*
Gut, danke.	*Fine, thanks.*

Auf Wiedersehen, Felix.	*Good-bye, Felix.*
Auf Wiedersehen, Frau Bach.	*Good-bye, Ms. Bach.*

Two more people:

Guten Morgen, Helmut.	*Good morning, Helmut.*
Guten Morgen, Luise. Wie geht's?	*Good morning, Luise. How are you?*
Gut, danke.	*Fine, thanks.*
Auf Wiederschauen, Luise.	*Good-bye, Luise.*
Auf Wiederschauen, Helmut.	*Good-bye, Helmut.*

Two more people:

Guten Abend, Karl.	*Good evening, Karl.*
Guten Abend, Natascha. Wie geht's?	*Good evening, Natascha. How are you?*
Gut, danke.	*Fine, thanks.*
Tschüs, Natascha.	*So long, Natascha.*
Tschüs, Karl.	*So long, Karl.*

Written Practice 6

Greet each person and ask how he or she is. Translate the English expressions in parentheses into German to form your sentences. For example:

(good day/Karl) Guten Tag, Karl.
Wie geht's?

1. (good day/Helga) ______________________.
______________________?

2. (good morning/Thomas) ______________________.
______________________?

3. (good evening/Tanja) ______________________.
______________________?

4. (good day/Herr Bach) ______________________.
______________________?

5. (good morning/Rita) ______________________.
______________________?

6. (good evening/Frau Kamps) ______________________.
______________________?

QUIZ

Write the feminine form of the masculine nouns provided, using the definite articles. For example:

der Professor *die Professorin*

1. **der Mechaniker** ________________
2. **der Lehrer** ________________

Using the names provided in parentheses, write the two ways that you tell someone your name. For example:

(Karl) *Mein Name ist Karl.*

Ich heiße Karl.

3. **(Werner)** ________________

____

4. **(Tanja)** ________________

____

Using the name in parentheses, ask who someone is and give the answer. For example:

(Martin) *Wer ist das?*

Das ist Martin.

5. **(Tina)** ________________

____

6. **(Herr Keller)** ________________

____

Use the nouns in parentheses that refer to a person to ask where someone is. Then use the nouns that refer to a place to answer the questions. For example:

(der Mann/London) *Wo ist der Mann?*

Der Mann ist in London.

7. (Frau Schneider/Berlin) ______________________

____

8. (der Lehrer/Deutschland) ______________________

____

Circle the letter of the word or phrase that best completes each sentence.

9. Das ______________ heißt Angela.

A. Frau
B. Felix
C. Mädchen
D. Mann

10. Wie ______________? Gut, danke.

A. wer
B. ist
C. heißt
D. geht's

chapter 3

Asking Questions

In this chapter you will learn how to ask and answer questions, including questions that require a yes or no response. In addition, you will encounter the function of the German indefinite articles and the possessive adjective **mein**.

CHAPTER OBJECTIVES

In this chapter you will learn about:

- Asking Questions with *Wer*
- Indefinite Articles
- Possessive Adjective *Mein*
- Yes or No Questions
- Using *Oder* for Differentiation
- Asking Questions with *Was*
- Asking Questions with *Wo*
- Possessive Adjective *Ihr*
- About the German-Speaking World

Asking Questions with *Wer*

Wer ist das? You already know what that question means: *Who is that?* The answer will always be a person. Let's meet some new people, so you can begin forming questions about them.

der Bruder	*brother*	der Junge	*boy*
die Schwester	*sister*	das Mädchen	*girl*
der Freund	*friend*	der Onkel	*uncle*
die Freundin	*friend; girlfriend*	die Tante	*aunt*
der Großvater	*grandfather*	der Sohn	*son*
die Großmutter	*grandmother*	die Tochter	*daughter*

Notice the gender of the previous nouns and the use of the definite articles **der**, **die**, and **das**. Except for **das Mädchen**, the masculine and feminine nouns happen to conform to the sexual gender of the person. Remember that that will not always be the case.

Indefinite Articles

Just as in English, German has indefinite articles. In English, the indefinite articles are *a* and *an*. In German, they are **ein** and **eine**. Use **ein** with all masculine and neuter nouns, and use **eine** with all feminine nouns. For example:

der Lehrer	*the teacher*	ein Lehrer	*a teacher*
das Haus	*the house*	ein Haus	*a house*
die Lehrerin	*the teacher*	eine Lehrerin	*a teacher*

Possessive Adjective *Mein*

The same endings are used with the possessive adjective **mein** (*my*). Use **mein** with all masculine and neuter nouns, and use **meine** with all feminine nouns. For example:

der Wagen	*the car*	mein Wagen	*my car*
das Kind	*the child*	mein Kind	*my child*
die Lampe	*the lamp*	meine Lampe	*my lamp*

In a response to the question **Wer ist das?** (*Who is that?*), the definite article, indefinite article, or the possessive adjective **mein** can be used.

Wer ist das? Das ist die Lehrerin.
Das ist ein Freund.
Das ist meine Tante.

Oral Practice

 Track 22

Practice asking who someone is and answering each question out loud.

Wer ist das?	*Who is that?*
Das ist ein Freund.	*That is a friend.*
Wer ist das?	*Who is that?*
Das ist eine Freundin.	*That is a friend.*
Wer ist das?	*Who is that?*
Das ist mein Bruder.	*That is my brother.*
Wer ist das?	*Who is that?*
Das ist meine Schwester.	*That is my sister.*
Wer ist das?	*Who is that?*
Das ist mein Onkel.	*That is my uncle.*
Wer ist das?	*Who is that?*
Das ist meine Tante.	*That is my aunt.*
Wer ist das?	*Who is that?*
Das ist mein Großvater.	*That is my grandfather.*
Wer ist das?	*Who is that?*
Das ist meine Tochter.	*That is my daughter.*

Yes or No Questions

You can respond to many questions with **ja** or **nein** (*yes* or *no*). Notice that the questions that require a **ja** or **nein** answer begin with a verb and the verb is followed by a subject (**das**). In the following examples the verb used is **ist**, followed by **das**. It's the same word order we use in English for such questions. For example:

Ist das ein Professor?	*Is that a professor?*
Ja, das ist ein Professor.	*Yes, that is a professor.*

Ist das eine Schule? — *Is that a school?*
Ja, das ist eine Schule. — *Yes, that is a school.*

When you negate an answer with **nein**, you must use the negative **kein** (*not a, not any, none*), which follows the verb **ist** in the sentence. Use the following pattern when answering questions in the positive (**ja**) or in the negative (**nein**).

Ist das ein ______? Ja, das ist ein ______. Nein, das ist kein ______.

For example:

Ist das ein Haus? — *Is that a house?*
Nein, das ist kein Haus. — *No, that is not a house.*
Das ist ein Museum. — *That is a museum.*
Ist das eine Lampe? — *Is that a lamp?*
Nein, das ist keine Lampe. — *No, that is not a lamp.*
Das ist eine Vase. — *That is a vase.*

However, if a definite article (**der**, **die**, **das**) or a possessive pronoun precedes a noun that is negated, **nicht** is used in place of **kein**.

Ist das der Lehrer?
Ja, das ist der Lehrer. — *Yes, that is the teacher.*
Nein, das ist nicht der Lehrer. — *No, that is not the teacher.*

Ist das Ihr Bruder?
Ja, das ist mein Bruder. — *Yes, that is my brother.*
Nein, das ist nicht mein Bruder. — *No, that is not my brother.*

Written Practice 1

Answer each question in the negative using **nein** and **nicht**. For example:

Ist der Mann zu Hause? Nein, der Mann ist nicht zu Hause.

1. Ist Werner in der Schweiz? ______.
2. Ist der Junge Ihr Bruder? ______.
3. Ist das Mädchen Ihre Schwester? ______.
4. Ist die Bibliothek hier? ______.
5. Ist der Park weit von hier? ______.

Oral Practice

 Track 23

Practice saying each question and answer out loud.

Ist das der Onkel?	*Is that the uncle?*
Ja, das ist der Onkel.	*Yes, that is the uncle.*
Nein, das ist nicht der Onkel. Das ist der Großvater.	*No, that is not the uncle. That is the grandfather.*
Ist das ein Freund?	*Is that a friend?*
Ja, das ist ein Freund.	*Yes, that is a friend.*
Nein, das ist kein Freund. Das ist mein Bruder.	*No, that is not a friend. That is my brother.*
Ist das die Großmutter?	*Is that the grandmother?*
Ja, das ist die Großmutter.	*Yes, that is the grandmother.*
Nein, das ist nicht die Großmutter. Das ist meine Tante.	*No, that is not the grandmother. That is my aunt.*
Ist das eine Freundin?	*Is that a friend?*
Ja, das ist eine Freundin.	*Yes, that is a friend.*
Nein, das ist keine Freundin. Das ist meine Schwester.	*No, that is not a friend. That is my sister.*

Using *Oder* for Differentiation

When you add the word **oder** (*or*) to questions, you can ask for a differentiation between two people or things.

Ist das eine Schule oder ein Museum?	*Is that a school or a museum?*
Das ist ein Museum.	*That is a museum.*
Ist das der Bruder oder der Sohn?	*Is that the brother or the son?*
Das ist der Bruder.	*That is the brother.*
Ist das Gudrun oder Tanja?	*Is that Gudrun or Tanja?*
Das ist Tanja.	*That is Tanja.*
Ist das eine Professorin oder eine Lehrerin?	*Is that a professor or a teacher?*
Das ist eine Lehrerin.	*That is a teacher.*

Written Practice 2

For each of the pairs of words in parentheses, write a question asking to differentiate between the two people or things. Answer with either one of the words in the pair. For example:

(Karl/Helmut) Ist das Karl oder Helmut?

Das ist Karl.

1. (ein Professor/ein Lehrer) ____________________?

____________________.

2. (der Vater/der Großvater) ____________________?

____________________.

3. (eine Lampe/eine Vase) ____________________?

____________________.

4. (Frau Bauer/Frau Schäfer) ____________________?

____________________.

Asking Questions with *Was*

Was ist das? (*What is that?*) This question asks *what* something is and, therefore, inquires about inanimate objects. Let's become acquainted with some objects, so you can begin forming questions with **was** (*what*).

das Auto	ein Auto	*car*
das Buch	ein Buch	*book*
das Gymnasium	ein Gymnasium	*secondary school*
das Heft	ein Heft	*notebook*
das Sweatshirt	ein Sweatshirt	*sweatshirt*
der Bleistift	ein Bleistift	*pencil*
der Computer	ein Computer	*computer*
der Fluss	ein Fluss	*river*
der Kuli	ein Kuli	*ballpoint pen*
der Park	ein Park	*park*
die Bibliothek	eine Bibliothek	*library*
die Stadt	eine Stadt	*city*

die Uhr	eine Uhr	*clock*
die Wohnung	eine Wohnung	*apartment*
die Zeitung	eine Zeitung	*newspaper*

The response to the question **Was ist das?** (*What is that?*) will follow **Das ist...** and can be composed of a noun modified by a definite article, indefinite article, or the possessive adjective **mein**, as shown here:

Das ist... der Park.
die Zeitung.
ein Sweatshirt.
eine Uhr.
mein Kuli.
meine Wohnung.

Oral Practice

Track 24

Practice asking these questions and giving the answers out loud.

Ist das ein Buch oder ein Heft?	*Is that a book or a notebook?*
Das ist ein Buch.	*That is a book.*
Ist das eine Bibliothek oder ein Gymnasium?	*Is that a library or a secondary school?*
Das ist eine Bibliothek.	*That is a library.*
Was ist das?	*What is that?*
Das ist mein Computer.	*That is my computer.*
Was ist das?	*What is that?*
Das ist meine Zeitung.	*That is my newspaper.*
Was it das?	*What is that?*
Das ist ein Fluss.	*That is a river.*
Was ist das?	*What is that?*
Das ist eine Uhr.	*That is a clock.*
Ist das eine Wohnung?	*Is that an apartment?*
Ja, das ist eine Wohnung.	*Yes, that is an apartment.*
Nein, das ist keine Wohnung. Das ist ein Haus.	*No, that is not an apartment. That is a house.*
Ist das ein Bleistift?	*Is that a pencil?*

Ja, das ist ein Bleistift.	*Yes, that is a pencil.*
Nein, das ist kein Bleistift.	*No, that is not a pencil.*
Das ist ein Kuli.	*That is a ballpoint pen.*
Ist das eine Stadt?	*Is that a city?*
Ja, das ist eine Stadt.	*Yes, that is a city.*

Asking Questions with *Wo*

Wo ist...? (*Where is . . . ?*) When asked *where* someone or something is, you can respond with a city or country name. Or you might use the expression **weit von hier** (*far from here*). In its negated form it's **nicht weit von hier** (*not far from here*). You can use **zu Hause** to say that someone is *at home*. In its negated form you say **nicht zu Hause** (*not at home*). For example:

Wo ist Herr Weber?	*Where is Mr. Weber?*
Herr Weber ist in Deutschland.	*Mr. Weber is in Germany.*
Wo ist das Gymnasium?	*Where is the secondary school?*
Das Gymnasium ist weit von hier.	*The secondary school is far from here.*
Wo ist der Park?	*Where is the park?*
Der Park ist nicht weit von hier.	*The park is not far from here.*
Wo ist Frau Bach?	*Where is Ms. Bach?*
Frau Bach ist zu Hause.	*Ms. Bach is at home.*

A response to the question **Wo ist...?** (*Where is . . .?*) consists of any phrase that shows location. Many such phrases begin with the preposition **in**.

Die Frau ist...	in Amerika.
	in London.
	zu Hause.
	nicht zu Hause.
	dort.
Mein Haus ist...	in Berlin.
	hier.
	da.
	weit von hier.
	nicht weit von hier.

Oral Practice

 Track 25

Practice asking these questions and giving the answers out loud.

Wo ist der Pilot?	*Where is the pilot?*
Der Pilot ist in Hannover.	*The pilot is in Hanover.*
Wo ist die Bibliothek?	*Where is the library?*
Die Bibliothek ist weit von hier.	*The library is far from here.*
Wo ist das Museum?	*Where is the museum?*
Das Museum ist nicht weit von hier.	*The museum is not far from here.*
Wo ist Professor Kamps?	*Where is Professor Kamps?*
Professor Kamps ist zu Hause.	*Professor Kamps is at home.*
Ist Frau Kamps zu Hause?	*Is Ms. Kamps at home?*
Ja, Frau Kamps ist zu Hause.	*Yes, Ms. Kamps is at home.*
Nein, Frau Kamps ist nicht zu Hause. Frau Kamps ist in Berlin.	*No, Ms. Kamps is not at home. Ms. Kamps is in Berlin.*
Ist Ihre Tante zu Hause?	*Is your aunt at home?*
Ja, meine Tante ist zu Hause.	*Yes, my aunt is at home.*
Nein, meine Tante ist nicht zu Hause. Meine Tante ist in Polen.	*No, my aunt is not at home. My aunt is in Poland.*

Written Practice 3

Write a question asking about the word or phrase in parentheses. Remember that **Wer ist das?** is used when referring to a person, **Was ist das?** refers to an object, and **Wo ist ______?** is used when referring to a place. For example:

(mein Vater) Wer ist das?

(das Haus) Was ist das?

(Berlin) Wo ist Berlin?

1. (der Pilot) ____________________?
2. (mein Bruder) ____________________?
3. (die Bibliothek) ____________________?

4. (Tante Ingrid) ______________ ______________?

5. (München) ____________________________?

Possessive Adjective *Ihr*

Until now you have used only the possessive adjective **mein**. Use the possessive adjective **Ihr** to say *your*. Notice that **Ihr** is always written with a capital **i**. And like **eine** and **meine**, **Ihr** will have an **-e** ending with feminine nouns (**Ihre Mutter**).

Masculine	Feminine	Neuter
der Sohn	die Schwester	das Heft
ein Sohn	eine Schwester	ein Heft
mein Sohn	meine Schwester	mein Heft
Ihr Sohn	Ihre Schwester	Ihr Heft

Let's look at some example sentences with **Ihr**.

Ist das Ihr Wagen oder mein Wagen?	*Is that your car or my car?*
Das ist Ihr Wagen.	*That is your car.*
Ist das Ihre Zeitung oder meine Zeitung?	*Is that your newspaper or my newspaper?*
Das ist Ihre Zeitung.	*That is your newspaper.*
Ist das Ihr Heft oder mein Heft?	*Is that your notebook or my notebook?*
Das ist Ihr Heft.	*That is your notebook.*

Oral Practice

 Track 26

Practice asking these questions and giving the answers out loud.

Wo ist Ihr Vater?	*Where is your father?*
Mein Vater ist zu Hause.	*My father is at home.*
Wo ist Ihre Schwester?	*Where is your sister?*
Meine Schwester ist in Hamburg.	*My sister is in Hamburg.*
Wo ist Ihre Großmutter?	*Where is your grandmother?*
Meine Großmutter ist in Rom.	*My grandmother is in Rome.*
Ist Ihr Onkel in Berlin?	*Is your uncle in Berlin?*

Nein, mein Onkel ist nicht in Berlin. Mein Onkel ist in Heidelberg.	*No, my uncle is not in Berlin. My uncle is in Heidelberg.*
Ist Ihre Freundin zu Hause?	*Is your girlfriend at home?*
Nein, meine Freundin ist nicht zu Hause. Meine Freundin ist in Amerika.	*No, my girlfriend is not at home. My girlfriend is in America.*
Ist Ihr Auto hier?	*Is your car here?*
Nein, mein Auto ist weit von hier.	*No, my car is far from here.*

Written Practice 4

Ask the question whether something or someone is here with each of the words in parentheses. Use **Ihr** or **Ihre** appropriately. For example:

(Haus) Ist Ihr Haus hier? (Is your house here?)

(Lampe) Ist Ihre Lampe hier? (Is your lamp here?)

1. (Schwester) ______________________________?
2. (Vater) ______________________________?
3. (Tante) ______________________________?
4. (Wagen) ______________________________?
5. (Schule) ______________________________?

About the German-Speaking World

The three major countries that use German as the official language or one of the official languages are:

Deutschland *Germany* Österreich *Austria* die Schweiz *Switzerland*

Notice that **die Schweiz** is always said with the definite article much the same way that English says *the Netherlands* or *the Ukraine*. When you say that you are in Switzerland, the definite article changes: **in der Schweiz**. This does not occur with Germany and Austria: **in Deutschland** and **in Österreich**.

As German speakers travel about the three German-speaking countries, they communicate with little difficulty. There are regional pronunciations and local dialects, but since everyone is taught **Hochdeutsch** (*High German*) in the educational system, everyone has command of the standard language. Dialects are usually limited to a community or small region.

If someone comes from Germany, his or her nationality is described like this:

Der Mann ist Deutscher.	*The man is German.*
Die Frau ist Deutsche.	*The woman is German.*

If someone comes from Austria, you say:

Mein Onkel ist Österreicher.	*My uncle is Austrian.*
Meine Tante ist Österreicherin.	*My aunt is Austrian.*

If someone comes from Switzerland, you say:

Der Lehrer ist Schweizer. Die Lehrerin ist Schweizerin.	*The teacher is Swiss.*

If someone comes from the United States, he or she is called **Amerikaner**:

Ihr Freund ist Amerikaner.	*Your friend is an American.*
Ist Ihre Freundin Amerikanerin?	*Is your girlfriend an American?*

Oral Practice

 Track 27

Practice asking these questions and giving the answers out loud.

Wo ist Ihr Freund?	*Where is your friend?*
Mein Freund ist in der Schweiz.	*My friend is in Switzerland.*
Ist Ihr Freund Schweizer?	*Is your friend Swiss?*
Nein, mein Freund ist kein Schweizer. Mein Freund ist Deutscher.	*No, my friend is not Swiss. My friend is German.*
Wo ist Ihre Lehrerin?	*Where is your teacher?*
Meine Lehrerin ist in Österreich.	*My teacher is in Austria.*
Ist Ihre Lehrerin Österreicherin?	*Is your teacher Austrian?*
Ja, meine Lehrerin ist Österreicherin.	*Yes, my teacher is Austrian.*
Wo ist Ihre Tante?	*Where is your aunt?*
Meine Tante ist in Bern.	*My aunt is in Bern.*
Ist Ihre Tante Schweizerin?	*Is your aunt Swiss?*
Nein, meine Tante ist keine Schweizerin. Meine Tante ist Deutsche.	*No, my aunt is not Swiss. My aunt is German.*

Written Practice 5

Complete each sentence with any appropriate word or phrase. For example:

Mein Freund ist Schweizer.

1. Ist das ein Museum oder __________?
2. Wo ist __________?
3. Der Mann ist mein __________?
4. __________ ist das?
5. Ist die Frau Ihre Mutter oder __________?
6. Die Dame ist eine __________.

7. Mein Bruder ist in ______ ______.
8. ______ ist nicht weit von hier.
9. ______ heißt Professor Schmidt.
10. Ist das Ihre ______?

QUIZ

Write each noun with **ein**, **mein**, and **Ihr**. For example:

das Haus *ein Haus* *mein Haus* *Ihr Haus*

1. **der Wagen** ______ ______ ______
2. **die Schule** ______ ______ ______
3. **das Heft** ______ ______ ______

Write two answers to each question, one with **ja** and the other with **nein** and **nicht**, or **nein** and **kein**. For example:

Ist der Mann Deutscher?

Ja, der Mann ist Deutscher.

Nein, der Mann ist kein Deutscher.

4. **Ist die Lehrerin in Berlin?**

______

______

5. **Ist Ihr Vater Amerikaner?**

______

______

Using **wer**, **was**, **wie**, or **wo**, write a question about the word or phrase in bold print in each of the sentences. For example:

Der Mann heißt **Helmut**.

Wie heißt der Mann?

6. **Meine Tante ist in der Schweiz.**

____

7. **Das ist der Bleistift.**

____

8. **Meine Freundin** ist in Deutschland.

____

Circle the letter of the word or phrase that best completes each sentence.

9. **Der _______________ ist mein Freund.**
   A. Dame
   B. Lehrerin
   C. Mädchen
   D. Junge

10. **Herr Keller ist _______________.**
   A. Österreicher
   B. Schule
   C. wer
   D. kein

chapter 4

Describing People and Things

In this chapter you will learn how to conjugate the verbs **sein** and **heißen**. In addition, you will discover the use of the German pronouns and some helpful adjectives. There will be more information on forming questions, and the first of the cardinal numbers will be introduced.

CHAPTER OBJECTIVES

In this chapter you will learn about:

- Using the Verb *Sein*
- Pronouns
- Using the Verb *Heißen*
- Some Useful Adjectives
- Asking Questions with *Wann* and *Warum*
- Asking *Wie geht's?*
- Cardinal Numbers One to Ten

Using the Verb *Sein*

An infinitive is the unconjugated form of a verb that expresses the action of the verb but does not indicate the person (first, second, or third) or number (singular or plural) doing the action. The English infinitive for **sein** is *to be*. The German infinitive for *to be* is **sein**.

In Chapter 2, you were introduced to the third person singular conjugation (**ist**) of the infinitive **sein** (*to be*).

Was ist das? *What is that?* Das ist mein Buch. *That is my book.*

But just like English, German has other conjugations of that verb. In English they are:

	Singular	**Plural**
First person	I am	we are
Second person	you are	you are
Third person	he is	they are
		she is
		it is

Pronouns

The German pronouns fall into the categories of singular and plural like English, and they likewise are distinguished by being first, second, or third person pronouns. Let's look at the conjugation of **sein** to see what happens to this verb when conjugated with the various pronouns.

Conjugation of the verb **sein** in the present tense:

	Singular		**Plural**	
First person	ich bin	*I am*	wir sind	*we are*
Second person	du bist	*you are*	ihr seid	*you are*
	Sie sind	*you are*	Sie Sind	*you are*
Third person	er ist	*he is*	sie sind	*they are*
	sie ist	*she is*		
	es ist	*it is*		

After looking at this chart, you are undoubtedly aware of the frequent use of the pronoun *you*. Long ago, English included *thou* and *ye* among the words that mean *you*. Today, English speakers use only the pronoun *you* as both the singular and plural forms of the word and make no distinctions between formal or informal usage. German is different.

German makes a distinction between people with whom you are on a formal basis (strangers, your boss, a store clerk, a police officer, and so on), and those with whom you are on an informal basis (children, family members, friends).

When you are on a formal basis with one person or a group of people, you use the pronoun **Sie**. For example, when asking a stranger's name, you say:

Wie heißen Sie?	*What is your name?*

When you are speaking to two or more strangers, you ask:

Wie heißen Sie?	*What are your names?*

There is no difference between the singular and the plural for **Sie** in German.

But when you speak to children, family members, or friends, use the pronoun **du** (this is actually the counterpart of the old English word *thou*). **Du** is singular. You use it when speaking to one person:

Wie heißt du?	*What is your name?*

The plural of **du** is **ihr**. Use this pronoun when speaking informally to two or more people:

Wie heißt ihr?	*What are your names?*

The verb **sein** functions much like the English verb *to be* within sentences. Let's look at some example questions and answers using **sein** conjugated with the three forms of the pronoun *you*.

Sind Sie zu Hause?	*Are you at home?*
Ja, ich bin zu Hause.	*Yes, I am at home.*

or

Ja, wir sind zu Hause.	*Yes, we are at home.*
Bist du in Berlin?	*Are you in Berlin?*
Nein, ich bin nicht in Berlin.	*No, I am not in Berlin.*
Seid ihr in der Schweiz?	*Are you in Switzerland?*
Ja, wir sind in der Schweiz.	*Yes, we are in Switzerland.*

Oral Practice

 Track 28

Practice saying the following list of sentences out loud.

Ich bin Amerikaner.	*I am an American.*
Ich bin Amerikanerin.	*I am an American.*
Bist du Deutscher?	*Are you German?*
Sind Sie Deutsche?	*Are you German?*
Wo seid ihr?	*Where are you?*
Wir sind in Deutschland.	*We are in Germany.*
Sie sind nicht weit von hier.	*They are not far from here.*
Wo ist Ihr Vater?	*Where is your father?*
Er ist in Hamburg.	*He is in Hamburg.*
Wo ist Ihre Freundin?	*Where is your girlfriend?*
Sie ist in Österreich.	*She is in Austria.*
Wo ist Ihr Heft?	*Where is your notebook.*
Es ist zu Hause.	*It is at home.*

Written Practice 1

Provide the conjugated forms for the verb **sein** with the pronouns and nouns below.

1. ich ____________________
2. sie (*they*) ____________________
3. du ____________________
4. sie (*she*) ____________________
5. ihr ____________________
6. Ihr Bruder ____________________
7. die Studentin ____________________
8. er ____________________
9. es ____________________
10. wir ____________________

Using the Verb *Heißen*

Let's look at the conjugation of the verb *heißen* in the present tense. As discussed in Chapter 2, this verb is used to tell what someone's name is. It literally means *to be called* but is most often translated as *one's name is*. For example:

Track 29

Ich heiße Martin.	*My name is Martin.*
ich heiße	wir heißen
du heißt	ihr heißt
Sie heißen	Sie heißen
er, sie, es heißt	sie heißen

Notice that the pronouns **er**, **sie**, and **es** are used like their English counterparts (*he*, *she*, and *it*) to refer, respectively, to a male, a female, and an inanimate object. In German you also use **er** with all masculine nouns, **sie** with all feminine nouns, and **es** with all neuter nouns. For example:

Ist der Wagen neu?	*Is the car (masculine) new?*
Ja, **er** ist neu.	*Yes, **it** is new.*
Ist die Lampe neu?	*Is the lamp (feminine) new?*
Ja, **sie** ist neu.	*Yes, **it** is new.*
Ist das Kind krank?	*Is the child (neuter) sick?*
Ja, **es** ist krank.	*Yes, **he/she** is sick.*

The plural of **er**, **sie**, and **es** is **sie** (*they*). Perhaps it seems confusing at first that **sie** (*she, it*) and **sie** (*they*) look identical. But Germans have no trouble distinguishing these two pronouns: One is singular, and the other is plural, so the verb conjugations are different, making it clear which pronoun is being used.

In addition, there is the pronoun **Sie** (formal, singular, or plural *you*). Once again, there is no confusion in using this pronoun, because the context of a conversation or a text tells how it is being used.

Oral Practice

Practice saying the following list of sentences out loud.

Ist sie eine Freundin?	*Is she a friend?*
Sind sie in der Schweiz?	*Are they in Switzerland?*
Sind Sie Deutscher, Herr Bauer?	*Are you German, Mr. Bauer?*

Sie ist zu Hause.	*She is at home.*
Sie sind in Heidelberg.	*They are in Heidelberg.*
Sie sind der Professor.	*You are the professor.*
Die Vase? Wo ist sie?	*The vase? Where is it?*
Der Kuli? Wo ist er?	*The ballpoint? Where is it?*
Das Buch? Wo ist es?	*The book? Where is it?*

To avoid any possibility of confusion in this book, the pronoun **sie** will be identified as either **sie** *s.* (singular = *she; it*) or **sie** *pl.* (plural = *they*) where necessary. The pronoun **Sie** (*you*) is always capitalized and is, therefore, easily identifiable.

Remember, if you use a singular noun as the subject of the verb **sein**, use the conjugation form **ist**: **mein Vater ist**, **das Mädchen ist**, and so on.

Written Practice 2

Change the phrases in bold print below to the appropriate pronouns: **er**, **sie** *s.*, **es**, or **sie** *pl.* For example:

Der Mann ist mein Freund. Er ist mein Freund.

1. **Mein Wagen** ist hier. ______________________.
2. Ist **die Wohnung** da? ______________________?
3. **Das Haus** ist weit von hier. ______________________.
4. Wo ist **Ihr Kind**? ______________________?
5. **Thomas und Karl** sind zu Hause. ______________________.
6. Wo ist **meine Mutter**? ______________________?

Write the appropriate pronoun substitution using **er**, **sie** *s.*, **es**, or **sie** *pl.* for the following nouns.

7. Ihre Tante ______________
8. Ihr Haus ______________
9. mein Bleistift ______________
10. mein Sohn ______________
11. ein Onkel ______________
12. eine Vase ______________
13. ein Mädchen ______________

14. das Wetter ______________________

15. Martin und Tanja ______________________

Some Useful Adjectives

 Track 30

Now that you've learned how to conjugate the verb **sein**, it's time to add some adjectives to your vocabulary. Adjectives modify or describe nouns and are useful in telling what someone or something is like. Here are some examples:

alt	*old*	krank	*sick*
gesund	*healthy*	kurz	*short*
glücklich	*happy*	lang	*long*
groß	*big, large*	neu	*new*
gut	*good*	rot	*red*
interessant	*interesting*	schlecht	*bad*
jung	*young*	schwarz	*black*
klein	*little, small*	weiß	*white*

When using words like these as predicate adjectives (adjectives that follow the verb) in German, place the adjective at the end of the sentence. For example:

Ist Ihr Haus groß?	*Is your house big?*
Nein, mein Haus ist klein.	*No, my house is little.*
Ist der Bleistift kurz oder lang?	*Is the pencil short or long?*
Der Bleistift ist kurz.	*The pencil is short.*

The rule is the same when adjectives describe pronouns.

Ich bin alt.	*I am old.*
Du bist jung.	*You are young.*
Er ist krank.	*He is sick.*
Sie ist interessant.	*She is interesting.*
Es ist neu.	*It is new.*
Wir sind glücklich.	*We are happy.*
Ihr seid gesund.	*You are healthy.*
Sie Sind schön.	*They are pretty.*

Oral Practice

 Track 31

Practice saying the following list of sentences out loud.

Der Lehrer ist gut.	*The teacher is good.*
Die Professorin ist interessant.	*The professor is interesting.*
Meine Großmutter ist alt.	*My grandmother is old.*
Mein Wagen ist rot.	*My car is red.*
Ist Ihr Haus weiß?	*Is your house white?*
Sind sie jung?	*Are they young?*
Das Wetter ist schlecht.	*The weather is bad.*
Der Kuli ist neu.	*The ballpoint is new.*
Ist das Museum alt?	*Is the museum old?*
Ich bin jung.	*I am young.*
Du bist klein, Felix.	*You are little, Felix.*

Written Practice 3

Rewrite the sentences with the adjectives provided in parentheses.

1. Ist Ihr Vater alt?
   (jung) ______________________________?
   (krank) ______________________________?
   (gesund) ______________________________?
2. Das Buch ist alt.
   (interessant) ______________________________.
   (neu) ______________________________.
   (schwarz) ______________________________.
3. Wir sind alt.
   (klein) ______________________________.
   (groß) ______________________________.
   (krank) ______________________________.

Written Practice 4

Rewrite the questions filling in the first blanks with the words in parentheses and the second with their opposites. For example:

(alt) Ist er ___alt___ oder ___jung___?

1. (neu) Ist das Haus ______ oder ______?
2. (krank) Ist sie ______ oder ______?
3. (schlecht) Ist das Wetter ______ oder ______?
4. (kurz) Ist mein Bleistift ______ oder ______?
5. (jung) Sind Karl und Max ______ oder ______?
6. (groß) Ist das Museum ______ oder ______?
7. (weiß) Ist Ihr Haus ______ oder ______?
8. (gesund) Ist meine Schwester ______ oder ______?
9. (lang) Ist der Kuli ______ oder ______?
10. (klein) Ist das Kind ______ oder ______?

Asking Questions with *Wann* and *Warum*

You have learned how to form questions with **wer**, **was**, **wie**, and **wo**. Two more useful interrogatives are **wann** (*when*) and **warum** (*why*). They function the same as the other interrogatives do: A question begins with the interrogative and is followed by the verb.

Wer ist das?	***Who is*** *that?*
Was ist das?	***What is*** *that?*
Wie geht's?	***How are*** *you?*
Wo sind Gudrun und Sonja?	***Where are*** *Gudrun and Sonja?*
Wann ist die Party?	***When is*** *the party?*
Warum bist du zu Hause?	***Why are*** *you at home?*

The answer to a question beginning with **wann** will provide a moment in time.

heute	*today*	nächste Woche	*next week*
morgen	*tomorrow*	am Montag	*on Monday*

Oral Practice

Practice saying the following list of sentences out loud.

Wann ist die Party?	*When is the party?*
Die Party ist heute.	*The party is today.*
Die Party ist morgen.	*The party is tomorrow.*
Die Party ist nächste Woche.	*The party is next week.*
Die Party ist am Montag.	*The party is on Monday.*
Wann ist das Examen?	*When is the exam?*
Das Examen ist heute.	*The exam is today.*
Das Examen ist morgen.	*The exam is tomorrow.*
Das Examen ist nächste Woche.	*The exam is next week.*
Das Examen ist am Montag.	*The exam is on Monday.*

The answer to a question beginning with **warum** will provide a reason for an action and will begin with the conjunction **denn** (*because*). For example:

Warum ist Erik zu Hause?	*Why is Erik at home?*
Erik ist zu Hause, **denn** er ist krank.	*Erik is at home, because he is sick.*

Written Practice 5

Change each sentence into a question. Use the word or phrase in bold print as a guide for which interrogative word to use (**wann**, **warum**, or **wer**). For example:

Mein Professor ist in Mannheim.

Wer ist in Mannheim?

1. Das Examen ist **nächste Woche**.

_______________________________________?

2. **Meine Tochter** ist in der Schweiz.

_______________________________________?

3. Die Party ist **morgen**.

_______________________________________?

4. Thomas und Helga sind in Bonn, **denn sie sind krank**.

_______________________________________?

5. Mein Großvater ist zu Hause, **denn er ist alt**.

____?

6. **Ich** bin morgen in Deutschland.

____?

7. Wir sind **am Montag** in Leipzig.

____?

8. **Ihr** seid gesund.

____?

9. Das Examen ist **heute**.

____?

10. Das Kind ist zu Hause, **denn es ist sehr klein**.

____?

Oral Practice

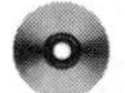 Track 32

Practice saying the following list of sentences out loud.

Warum ist Iris zu Hause?	*Why is Iris at home?*
Iris ist zu Hause, denn sie ist krank.	*Iris is at home, because she is sick.*
Warum bist du zu Hause?	*Why are you at home?*
Ich bin zu Hause, denn ich bin krank.	*I am at home, because I am sick.*
Warum ist er zu Hause?	*Why is he at home?*
Er ist zu Hause, denn er ist krank.	*He is home, because he is sick.*
Warum ist das Mädchen zu Hause?	*Why is the girl at home?*
Das Mädchen ist zu Hause, denn es ist krank.	*The girl is at home, because she is sick.*
Warum sind wir zu Hause?	*Why are we at home?*
Ihr seid zu Hause, denn ihr seid krank.	*You are at home, because you are sick.*
Thomas! Erik! Warum seid ihr zu Hause?	*Thomas! Erik! Why are you at home?*
Wir sind zu Hause, denn wir sind krank.	*We are at home, because we are sick.*

Warum sind Sie zu Hause, Herr Brenner?	*Why are you at home, Mr. Brenner?*
Ich bin zu Hause, denn ich bin krank.	*I am at home, because I am sick.*

Written Practice 6

Write an answer to each question, using the information provided in parentheses. For example:

(sein krank) Warum ist Martin zu Hause?

Martin ist zu Hause, denn er ist krank.

1. (sein krank) Warum sind Tanja und Maria in Berlin?

   ________________________________.

2. (nächste Woche) Wann ist das Examen?

   ________________________________.

3. (sein krank) Warum bist du zu Hause, Erik?

   ________________________________.

4. (am Montag) Wann ist das Konzert?

   ________________________________.

Asking *Wie geht's?*

The expression **Wie geht's?** contains a contraction. The verb **geht** is followed by an apostrophe and the letter **s**. That apostrophe and **s** are the contraction of the pronoun **es**. In its full form you would say: **Wie geht es?**

A response to this question might be: **Gut, danke.** But if you're not feeling well, you can say: **Schlecht** (*bad*). And you ask: **Und Ihnen?** (*And you?*) to inquire about someone else's health. In a conversation between two people, the phrases may look like this:

Track 33

Guten Abend, Herr Meier.	*Good evening, Mr. Meier.*
Guten Abend, Frau Keller. Wie geht's?	*Hello, Mrs. Keller. How are you?*
Gut, danke. Und Ihnen?	*Fine, thanks. And you?*
Sehr gut.	*Very well.*

Or the conversation could look like this:

Guten Morgen, Frau Benz.	*Good morning, Mrs. Benz.*
Guten Morgen, Professor Braun. Wie geht's?	*Hello, Professor Braun. How are you?*
Schlecht. Und Ihnen.	*Bad. And you?*
Sehr gut. Danke.	*Very well. Thanks.*

Oral Practice

Practice saying the following list of sentences out loud.

Guten Tag, Herr Bauer. Wie geht's?	*Hello, Mr. Bauer. How are you?*
Sehr schlecht.	*Very bad.*
Nicht schlecht.	*Not bad.*
Nicht gut. Und Ihnen?	*Not well. And you?*
Sehr gut. Und Ihnen?	*Very well. And you?*

Cardinal Numbers One to Ten

Cardinal numbers express the numerical value of a number: one, two, ten, one hundred, and so forth. In German the first ten cardinal numbers, including zero, are:

null	*zero*	sechs	*six*
eins	*one*	sieben	*seven*
zwei	*two*	acht	*eight*
drei	*three*	neun	*nine*
vier	*four*	zehn	*ten*
fünf	*five*		

In mathematical equations, use the following words:

+	plus *or* und	*plus; and*
−	minus *or* weniger	*minus; less*
=	ist	*is*
?	wie viel	*how much*

In sentences they look like this:

Wie viel ist zwei plus drei?	*How much is two plus three?*
Zwei plus drei ist fünf.	*Two plus three is five.*
Wie viel ist acht und eins?	*How much is eight and one?*
Acht und eins ist neun.	*Eight and one is nine.*
Wie viel ist zehn minus vier?	*How much is ten minus four?*
Zehn minus vier ist sechs.	*Ten minus four is six.*
Wie viel ist sieben weniger fünf?	*How much is seven minus five?*
Sieben weniger fünf ist zwei.	*Seven minus five is two.*

Oral Practice

 Track 34

Practice saying the following list of sentences out loud.

Drei plus eins ist vier.	*Three plus one is four.*
Acht und zwei ist zehn.	*Eight and two is ten.*
Neun minus neun ist null.	*Nine minus nine is zero.*
Sechs weniger fünf ist eins.	*Six minus five is one.*
Wie viel ist drei und sieben?	*How much is three and seven?*

Now change the following equations into words out loud. The correct version is shown on the right.

$8 - 7 = 1$	Acht weniger (minus) sieben ist eins.
$3 + 3 = ?$	Wie viel ist drei plus (und) drei?
$9 - 5 = 4$	Neun weniger (minus) fünf ist vier.
$10 + 0 = ?$	Wie viel ist zehn plus (und) null?
$6 + 1 = 7$	Sechs plus (und) eins ist sieben.
$4 + 2 = ?$	Wie viel ist vier plus (und) zwei?

Written Practice 7

Change the following equations into words.

1. $4 + 5 = 9$ ______________________________.
2. $8 - 6 = ?$ ______________________________?
3. $10 - 3 = 7$ ______________________________.

QUIZ

Write the appropriate form of **heißen** and **sein** for the subjects provided. For example:

Sie *heißen* *sind*

1. **ich** __________ __________
2. **du** __________ __________
3. **er** __________ __________
4. **wir** __________ __________
5. **ihr** __________ __________

In the blanks provided, replace the nouns given with the pronoun **er**, **sie** (*s.*), or **es**. For example:

der Mann *er*

6. **die Schule** __________
7. **das Mädchen** __________
8. **der Lehrer** __________

Circle the letter of the word or phrase that best completes each sentence.

9. **Warum __________ Sie heute zu Hause?**
   A. sein
   B. seid
   C. ist
   D. sind

10. **__________ ist die nächste Party?**
   A. Wer
   B. Denn
   C. Wann
   D. Sehr

chapter 5

Indicating Possession

In this chapter you will learn to use the verb **haben** as well as the feminine definite article. In addition, possessive adjectives will be introduced together with negation by means of the word **kein**.

CHAPTER OBJECTIVES

In this chapter you will learn about:

- Using the Verb *Haben*
- Definite Article *Die*
- Possessive Adjectives *Dein* and *Euer*
- Using *Kein*
- Household Objects

Using the Verb *Haben*

Another important German verb is **haben** (*to have*). And like **sein** and **heißen**, **haben** requires special conjugational endings with the various pronouns. Let's see what these endings look like.

The conjugation of **haben** in the present tense:

ich habe	*I have*	wir haben	*we have*
du hast	*you have*	ihr habt	*you have*
Sie haben	*you have*	Sie haben	*you have*
er hat	*he has*	sie haben	*they have*
sie hat	*she has*		
es hat	*it has*		
wer hat	*who has*		
der Mann hat	*the man has*		

Written Practice 1

Conjugate the verb **haben** with the nouns and pronouns provided below.

1. Tina und Benno ______________________

2. sie *s.* ______________________

3. sie *pl.* ______________________

4. ihr ______________________

5. meine Tochter ______________________

6. du ______________________

7. die Fahrkarten ______________________

8. Sie ______________________

9. es ______________________

10. mein Schreibtisch ______________________

To use **haben**, one must *have* something. Here are some handy words that a person can have:

das Bier	*beer*	die CD	*CD*
das Brot	*bread*	die CDs	*CDs*
das Geld	*money*	die Fahrkarten	*tickets (bus, train, etc.)*
der Fahrplan	*schedule, timetable*	die Milch	*milk*
die Bluse	*blouse*	die Schlüssel	*keys*

In sentences with **haben**, these nouns can look like this:

Haben Sie das Brot?	*Do you have the bread?*
Thomas hat das Geld.	*Thomas has the money.*
Wir haben eine CD.	*We have a CD.*
Wer hat meine Schlüssel?	*Who has my keys?*

Definite Article *Die*

You'll notice in the previous list of nouns that the plural words (**die CDs**, **die Fahrkarten**, and **die Schlüssel**) are used with the definite article **die**. However, these words may not be feminine nouns. They are plural, and all plural nouns use the definite article **die**—no matter what their gender is in the singular.

Oral Practice

 Track 35

Practice saying the following list of sentences out loud.

Hast du das Geld?	*Do you have the money?*
Ja, ich habe das Geld.	*Yes, I have the money.*
Habt ihr die Fahrkarten?	*Do you have the tickets?*
Ja, wir haben die Fahrkarten.	*Yes, we have the tickets.*
Wer hat das Bier?	*Who has the beer?*
Mein Vater hat das Bier.	*My father has the beer.*
Sie hat meine Bluse.	*She has my blouse.*
Haben Sie die Milch?	*Do you have the milk?*
Robert hat den Fahrplan.	*Robert has the schedule.*

Did you notice that **der Fahrplan** changed to ***den*** **Fahrplan** in the example sentence? This occurs with all *masculine* nouns when they are used as direct objects, in this case following the verb **haben**. This will be explained fully in Chapter 8.

Naturally, the verb **haben** can be used with other nouns that you have learned previously, and they can be used with definite articles, indefinite articles, **mein**, or **Ihr**.

Written Practice 2

Rewrite each sentence, replacing the nouns with the ones in parentheses.

1. Hast du die Bluse?

   (die CDs) ______________________________?

   (das Geld) ______________________________?

   (ein Heft) ______________________________?

2. Ich habe die Bluse.

   (die Fahrkarten) ______________________________.

   (der Fahrplan) ______________________________.

   (das Brot) ______________________________.

Oral Practice

Practice saying the following list of sentences out loud.

Wer hat meine CDs?	*Who has my CDs?*
Haben Sie Ihre Fahrkarten?	*Do you have your tickets?*
Tina hat eine Zeitung.	*Tina has a newspaper.*
Wir haben ein Haus in Berlin.	*We have a house in Berlin.*
Was hat das Kind?	*What does the child have?*
Es hat ein Sweatshirt.	*He/She (The child) has a sweatshirt.*
Herr Benz, ich habe Ihr Buch.	*Mr. Benz, I have your book.*

Written Practice 3

Ask the people shown in parentheses what they have. **Was haben Sie?** is used if the relationship is formal. Use **Was hast du?** if it is informal singular. And if the relationship is informal plural, **Was habt ihr?** is used.

1. (Tante Gerda) ______________________________?
2. (Bruder) ______________________________?
3. (Vater und Mutter) ______________________________?
4. (Professor Keller) ______________________________?

5. (eine Freundin) ____?
6. (Frau Schneider) ____?

Possessive Adjectives *Dein* and *Euer*

You are already quite aware that German has three forms of *you*: **du**, **ihr**, and **Sie**. German also has three forms of the possessive adjective *your*. Until now, you have used only **Ihr**, which is the formal *your* and refers to the pronoun **Sie** (the formal *you*). The pronouns **du** and **ihr** have their own possessive adjectives.

Pronoun (*you*)	Masculine and Neuter	Feminine and Plural
du	dein	deine
ihr	euer	eure
Sie	Ihr	Ihre

Just as you must know which pronoun to use (**du**, **ihr**, or **Sie**), you must also know which possessive adjective to use (**dein**, **euer**, or **Ihr**), depending on the relationship you have with a person—formal or informal. For example:

Formal:

Herr Bauer, haben Sie Ihre Fahrkarten?	*Mr. Bauer, do you have your tickets?*

Informal, singular:

Tanja, hast du dein Heft?	*Tanja, do you have your notebook?*

Informal, plural:

Robert und Tina, habt ihr eure Schlüssel?	*Robert and Tina, do you have your keys?*

Written Practice 4

Using the names of the people in parentheses, ask whether it is their desk. Use **dein**, **euer**, or **Ihr**. For example:

(Herr Bauer) *Herr Bauer, ist das Ihr Schreibtisch?*

1. (Doktor Keller) ____?
2. (Tanja) ____?

3. (Tante Gerda) ____?
4. (Albert und Tina) ____?
5. (Frau Schäfer) ____?

Oral Practice

 Track 36

Practice saying the following list of sentences out loud.

Hast du dein Sweatshirt?	*Do you have your sweatshirt?*
Ja, ich habe mein Sweatshirt.	*Yes, I have my sweatshirt.*
Haben Sie Ihr Buch?	*Do you have your book?*
Ja, ich habe mein Buch.	*Yes, I have my book.*
Habt ihr eure Fahrkarten?	*Do you have your tickets?*
Nein, Thomas hat die Fahrkarten.	*No, Thomas has the tickets.*
Wer hat einen Fahrplan?	*Who has a schedule?*
Er hat einen Fahrplan.	*He has a schedule.*
Wir haben einen Fahrplan.	*We have a schedule.*
Wer hat eine CD?	*Who has a CD?*
Sie hat eine CD.	*She has a CD.*
Sie haben eine CD.	*They have a CD.*

As you probably noticed in the previous sentences, just as **der Fahrplan** changes to ***den*** **Fahrplan** when it follows **haben**, **ein Fahrplan** changes to **ein*en*** **Fahrplan**.

Written Practice 5

Provide the appropriate forms of **dein**, **euer**, and **Ihr** for the nouns provided. For example:

Lehrer	dein	euer	Ihr
1. der Tisch	______	______	______
2. die Treppe	______	______	______
3. das Sofa	______	______	______
4. die CDs	______	______	______
5. der Fahrplan	______	______	______

When you want to know *how many* or *how much* of something someone has, you ask **wie viel**. It's the same expression used in a mathematical equation: ***Wie viel* ist zwei plus sieben?** Let's look at **wie viel** as it's used in sentences with the verb **haben**.

Wie viel Fahrkarten haben Sie?	*How many tickets do you have?*
Ich habe vier Fahrkarten.	*I have four tickets.*
Wie viel CDs hat Marianne?	*How many CDs does Marianne have?*
Marianne hat zehn CDs.	*Marianne has ten CDs.*

You need to be aware that with the English infinitive *to have*, it is most common to form a question with *do*: ***Do you** have your tickets? How many books **does** he **have**?* German forms all such questions with the verb preceding the subject: ***Haben Sie* Ihre Fahrkarten? Wie viel CDs *hat er*?** In German the equivalent of a verb such as *do* is never added to a question.

It is common to use **wie viele** with plural nouns. But **wie viel** is also correct, so this form can be used with both singular and plural nouns.

wie viele Fahrkarten (plural)	*how many tickets*
wie viel Fahrkarten (plural)	*how many tickets*
wie viel Geld (singular)	*how much money*

Oral Practice

 Track 37

Practice saying the following list of sentences out loud.

Wie viel(e) Schlüssel haben Sie?	*How many keys do you have?*
Ich habe vier Schlüssel.	*I have four keys.*
Wie viel Geld hat dein Bruder?	*How much money does your brother have?*
Wie viel(e) Fahrkarten habt ihr?	*How many tickets do you have?*
Wir haben drei Fahrkarten.	*We have three tickets.*
Wie viel(e) CDs haben wir?	*How many CDs do we have?*
Ihr habt neun CDs.	*You have nine CDs.*
Wie viel Brot hat eure Mutter?	*How much bread does your mother have?*
Wie viel Milch hat dein Sohn?	*How much milk does your son have?*
Wie viel Bier hast du?	*How much beer do you have?*

You can use the word **viel(e)** alone. It means *much* or *many* and it answers the question **wie viel**. Use **viel** with singular nouns, use **viele** with plural nouns. For example:

Ich habe viel Geld.	*I have a lot of (much) money.*
Sie hat viele CDs.	*She has a lot of (many) CDs.*

Written Practice 6

With each word provided in parentheses, write a question with **wie viel(e)** and an answer with **viel(e)**. Follow the pattern of the example.

(Brot) Wie viel Brot habt ihr? *How much bread do you have?*

Wir haben viel Brot. We have a lot of bread.

1. (Milch) ____________________?
   ____________________.
2. (CDs) ____________________?
   ____________________.
3. (Geld) ____________________?
   ____________________.
4. (Fahrkarten) ____________________?
   ____________________.
5. (Schlüssel) ____________________?
   ____________________.

Using *Kein*

This is a word that you encountered in Chapter 3 that means *not any*, *not a*, or *no*: **kein Brot** (*no bread*), **keine Fahrkarten** (*not any tickets*). It functions like *mein* or *dein* and is a replacement for **nicht ein** (*not a*). But unlike **ein**, **kein** can be used in the plural (**keine Schlüssel**—*no keys*). Like **nicht** it is a negative.

Masculine and Neuter	**Feminine and Plural**
dein	deine
mein	meine
kein	keine

In sentences, **kein** looks like this:

Hast du ein Auto?	*Do you have a car?*
Nein, ich habe kein Auto.	*No, I have no car. (No, I don't have a car.)*
Hat Benno eine Schwester?	*Does Benno have a sister?*
Nein, er hat keine Schwester.	*No, he has no sister.*

Oral Practice

Practice saying the following list of sentences out loud.

Habt ihr Geld?	*Do you have money?*
Nein, wir haben kein Geld.	*No, we have no money.*
Hast du viel Brot?	*Do you have a lot of bread?*
Nein, ich habe kein Brot.	*No, I have no bread.*
Haben Sie viele Schlüssel?	*Do you have many keys?*
Nein, ich habe keine Schlüssel.	*No, I have no keys.*
Hat dein Bruder viele Fahrkarten?	*Does your brother have many tickets?*
Nein, mein Bruder hat keine Fahrkarten.	*No, my brother has no tickets.*

Written Practice 7

Rewrite the sentences, filling in the blanks with the appropriate forms of the words in parentheses. Remember that the feminine and plural will require an **-e** ending.

1. Wer hat ______ Geld? Who has money? ______

   (mein) ______________________________?

   (viel) ______________________________?

   (kein) ______________________________?

2. Martin hat ______ Schlüssel. *Martin has ______ keys.*

   (euer) ______________________________.

   (viel) ______________________________.

   (kein) ______________________________.

3. Wo ist ______ Freundin? *Where is ______ girlfriend?*
   (dein) ______________________________?
   (Ihr) ______________________________?
   (euer) ______________________________?

Written Practice 8

Using **kein**, write a negative answer to each question. Remember to provide the appropriate endings to **kein** when necessary. For example:

Haben Sie ein Heft? Nein, ich habe kein Heft.

1. Habt ihr Brot? ______________________________.
2. Hat Frau Keller meine Schlüssel? ______________________________.
3. Haben Sie das Geld? ______________________________.
4. Hat das Kind die Milch? ______________________________.
5. Hat deine Schwester die Bluse? ______________________________.
6. Haben Sie viele Zimmer? ______________________________.
7. Hat Robert meine CDs? ______________________________.
8. Hat dein Vater das Bier? ______________________________.

Household Objects

In a German household you'll find many of the same objects that you'd find in a house anywhere. Some of these are:

das Bild	*picture*	der Teppich	*carpet*
der Boden	*floor*	der Tisch	*table*
das Fenster	*window*	die Treppe	*stairway*
der Schreibtisch	*desk*	die Tür	*door*
das Sofa	*sofa*	die Zimmer (*pl.*)	*rooms*
der Stuhl	*chair*		

These words can be used in sentences such as:

Ist die Tür groß oder klein?	*Is the door big or little?*
Wo ist dein Fenster?	*Where is your window?*

Der Boden ist weiß.	*The floor is white.*
Der Tisch und der Stuhl sind dort.	*The table and the chair are there.*
Ist euer Sofa alt?	*Is your sofa old?*
Der Teppich ist rot und lang.	*The carpet is red and long.*
Ist die Treppe kurz?	*Is the stairway short?*
Mein Bild ist schlecht.	*My picture is bad.*
Ist Ihr Schreibtisch neu?	*Is your desk new?*
Wie viele Zimmer habt ihr?	*How many rooms do you have?*

Written Practice 9

Rewrite the sentences, filling in the blanks with the words in parentheses. Change the verbs from singular to plural or plural to singular as needed.

1. Wo ist ______?
   (das Sofa) ________________________?
   (der Stuhl und der Schreibtisch) ________________?
2. Die Zimmer haben ______ Fenster.
   (ein) ____________________________.
   (kein) ___________________________.
3. ______ ist sehr klein.
   (der Tisch) _________________________.
   (die Zimmer) ________________________.

QUIZ

Fill in each blank with the appropriate conjugation of the verb **haben**, using the subject pronouns provided. For example:

der Mann ___*hat*___

1. **wir** __________ **ich** __________
2. **er** __________ **du** __________

Provide the appropriate forms of **dein**, **euer**, **Ihr**, and **kein** for the nouns given. Then place an X on the blank to identify the noun as singular or plural. For example:

					sing.	plur.
Lehrer	*dein*	*euer*	*Ihr*	*kein*	X	______
3. der Tisch	______	______	______	______	______	______
4. die Fahrkarten	______	______	______	______	______	______
5. die Bluse	______	______	______	______	______	______

Using **kein**, write a negative answer to each question. Provide the appropriate ending to **kein** where necessary. For example:

Haben Sie ein Heft? *Nein, ich habe kein Heft.*

6. Hast du ein Sofa? ______________________________

7. Hat Frau Benz eine Schwester? ______________________________

8. Haben Sie ein Bild? ______________________________

Circle the letter of the word or phrase that best completes each sentence.

9. Wie ______________ Geld haben Sie?

A. heißt
B. dort
C. viel
D. Ihr

10. Nein, ______________ sind nicht hier.

A. das Bild
B. ein Sofa
C. die Schlüssel
D. ein Schreibtisch

PART ONE TEST

1. **In the blank provided, write the letter of the pronunciation on the right that matches the German word on the left. For example:**

spielen	*to play*	B	A. (frow)
Frau	*woman*	A	B. (shpee-len)

Flugzeug	______	**A. (hare shay-fuh)**
Herr Schäfer	______	**B. (eer zite)**
Bruder	______	**C. (eer-eh shves-tuh)**
Ihre Schwester	______	**D. (broo-duh)**
ihr seid	______	**E. (flook-tsoik)**

2. **Write the correct form of heißen needed for each of the subject nouns and pronouns provided.**

   ich ______________________

   du ______________________

   Frau Benz ______________________

   wir ______________________

   ihr ______________________

3. **Write the correct form of sein needed for each of the subject nouns and pronouns provided.**

   ich ______________________

   du ______________________

   Erik ______________________

   ihr ______________________

   Sie ______________________

Using the words or phrases in bold print as a signal for which interrogative to use, ask questions with **wer**, **was**, **wann**, **wo**, or **warum**.

4. Das ist **eine Schule.** ______________________?

5. Mein Vater ist **in Deutschland.** ______________________?

6. Er ist zu Hause, **denn er ist krank.** ____________________________?

7. **Meine Tante** ist sehr alt. ____________________________?

8. Die Party ist **am Montag.** ____________________________?

Write the appropriate forms of **ein**, **Ihr**, and **kein** for each of the following nouns.

9. **die Bluse** ____________ ____________ ____________

10. **das Heft** ____________ ____________ ____________

Using **nicht**, answer each question in the negative. For example:

Ist das Ihr Hause? *Nein, das ist nicht mein Haus.*

11. **Ist das Fenster klein?** ____________________________

12. **Sind Karl und Gudrun zu Hause?** ____________________________

In each blank provided, write the pronoun that is the appropriate replacement for the phrase given, using **er**, **sie** (*s.*), **es**, or **sie** (*pl.*).

13. **der Schreibtisch** ____________________________

14. **die Fahrkarten** ____________________________

15. **das Auto** ____________________________

16. **die Lehrerin** ____________________________

Rewrite the sentences, filling in the first blanks with the words in parentheses and the second with the opposites. For example:

(alt) Ist er *alt* oder *jung*?

17. **(groß) Ist die Schule** ____________ **oder** ____________?

18. **(neu) Ist Ihr Bleistift** ____________ **oder** ____________?

Answer each question in the negative, using **kein**. For example:

Haben Sie ein Buch? *Nein, ich habe kein Buch.*

19. Hast du die Schlüssel? ____________________

20. Habt ihr das Brot? ____________________

Circle the letter of the word or phrase that best completes each sentence.

21. Meine Schwester ____________ Marianne.

A. seid C. Angela
B. heißt D. nicht

22. Ist Ihr Vater ____________?

A. zu Hause C. kein
B. nächste Woche D. Name

23. Die Schule ist nicht ____________ von hier.

A. alt C. weit
B. groß D. sehr

24. ____________ ist Ihre Mutter?

A. Warum C. Hat
B. Viel D. Wo

25. Neun weniger sieben ist ____________.

A. zwei C. plus
B. nicht D. fünf

Part Two

Using Verbs

chapter 6

Actions in the Present Tense

In this chapter you will learn the conjugation of the verb **werden** and how the German present tense is formed. In addition, the use of the pronoun **es** will be described and more cardinal numbers will be introduced.

CHAPTER OBJECTIVES

In this chapter you will learn about:

- Using the Verb *Werden*
- Pronoun *Es*
- Present Tense
- Cardinal Numbers Eleven to Twenty

Using the Verb *Werden*

The verb **werden** means *to become* or *to get* and has a unique conjugation that should be learned early, because this verb has a high-frequency use. Its conjugation looks like this:

ich werde	*I become*	wir werden	*we become*
du wirst	*you become*	ihr werdet	*you become*
Sie werden	*you become*	Sie werden	*you become*
er wird	*he becomes*	sie werden	*they become*
sie wird	*she becomes*		
es wird	*it becomes*		
wer wird	*who becomes*		
was wird	*what becomes*		

Werden can be used to tell what profession someone wants to join—what someone whats to *become*. For example:

Mein Bruder wird Professor.	*My brother is becoming a professor.*
Wird Ihre Tochter Lehrerin?	*Is your daughter becoming a teacher?*

Oral Practice

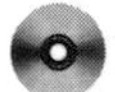 Track 39

Practice saying the following list of sentences out loud.

Ich werde Krankenschwester.	*I am becoming a nurse.*
Wirst du Arzt?	*Are you becoming a physician?*
Er wird Zahnarzt.	*He is becoming a dentist.*
Wird sie auch Ärztin?	*Is she becoming a physician, too?*
Werden Sie Lehrer?	*Are you becoming a teacher?*
Die Kinder werden Fußballspieler.	*The children are becoming soccer players.*

In addition, you can use a variety of adjectives that tell how someone's or something's condition is changing. Some of these adjectives are:

böse	*angry*	kalt	*cold*
dunkel	*dark*	kühl	*cool*
glücklich	*happy*	müde	*tired*

heiß	*hot*	spät	*late*
hell	*bright*	warm	*warm*

Written Practice 1

The words in parentheses describe a person, an occupation, and a second person. Write a sentence that says that the first person is becoming that occupation. Write that the second person is also (**auch**) becoming that occupation. For example:

(Karl/Lehrer/er)

Karl wird Lehrer.

Er wird auch Lehrer.

1. (deine Tochter/Lehrerin/meine Schwester)

 ____________________.

 ____________________.

2. (Erik/Zahnarzt/Sie *pl.*)

 ____________________.

 ____________________.

3. (die Kinder/Fußballspieler/er)

 ____________________.

 ____________________.

Written Practice 2

For each statement on the left, choose a statement on the right that logically follows.

1. Es ist spät. _____	a. Guten Morgen.
2. Es wird hell. _____	b. Nein, ich bin nicht müde.
3. Ich bin müde. _____	c. Ich gehe nach Hause.
4. Der Mann ist sehr krank. _____	d. Nein, ich habe kein Geld.
5. Wie alt ist das Mädchen? _____	e. Er wird wieder gesund.
6. Es wird sehr kalt. _____	f. Deutsch auch.

7. Wir lernen Spanisch. _______ g. Neunzehn Jahre alt.
8. Kaufst du ein Auto? _______ h. Nein, mit dem Zug.
9. Schläfst du? _______ i. Das Wetter ist schlecht.
10. Fährst du mit dem Bus? _______ j. Hier ist ein Bett.

Pronoun *Es*

In English there are impersonal expressions used which have the pronoun *it* as their subject. In these expressions an invisible entity is causing something to happen. That entity is *it*.

It is raining again.
It got dark early.
It was terribly hot yesterday.

The cause for the rain, the darkness, and the heat is *it*. German does the same thing with **es** (*it*) and frequently uses **werden** in such expressions. Let's look at some examples.

Es wird kalt.	*It is getting cold.*
Es wird hell.	*It is becoming bright.*
Es wird spät.	*It is getting late.*

You can also use other subjects with the verb **werden** to tell what a person or thing is becoming.

Mein Onkel wird böse.	*My uncle is becoming angry.*
Ihre Wirtin wird müde.	*Your landlady is getting tired.*
Thomas und Erik werden glücklich.	*Thomas and Erik are becoming happy.*
Der Ofen wird heiß.	*The oven is getting hot.*

Oral Practice

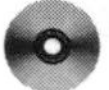 Track 40

Practice saying the following list of sentences out loud.

Wird es wieder kalt?	*Is it getting cold again?*
Ja, es wird wieder sehr kalt.	*Yes, it is getting very cold again.*
Wird es wieder heiß?	*Is it getting hot again?*

Ja, es wird wieder sehr heiß.	*Yes, it is getting very hot again.*
Werdet ihr müde, Kinder?	*Are you getting tired, children?*
Nein, wir werden nicht müde.	*No, we are not getting tired.*
Es wird spät. Es ist zehn Uhr.	*It is getting late. It is ten o'clock.*
Werden Sie krank, Herr Müller?	*Are you getting sick, Mr. Mueller?*
Nein, ich werde gesund.	*No, I am getting healthy.*
Warum wirst du wieder böse?	*Why are you getting angry again?*

Written Practice 3

Complete the sentence with each of the adjectives in parentheses.

Es wird wieder ______________________________.

1. (kalt) ______________________________.
2. (kühl) ______________________________.
3. (hell) ______________________________.
4. (dunkel) ______________________________.
5. (heiß) ______________________________.

Present Tense

You have already encountered the present tense of four verbs: **heißen**, **sein**, **haben**, and **werden**.

	heißen	**sein**	**haben**	**werden**
ich	heiße	bin	habe	werde
du	heißt	bist	hast	wirst
er	heißt	ist	hat	wird
wir	heißen	sind	haben	werden
ihr	heißt	seid	habt	werdet
sie	heißen	sind	haben	werden

Perhaps you can already see the pattern developing in these four conjugations. Except for **sein** and **werden**, these verbs have the same specific ending that occurs with each pronoun. In summary, those endings are:

ich	**-e**	wir	**-en**
du	**-st**	ihr	**-t**
er	**-t**	sie	**-en**

(The pronoun **er** in this list represents the endings required for **sie** *s.* and **es** as well as for all singular nouns. The pronoun **sie** in this list is plural and represents **Sie** and all plural nouns.)

The basic form of a German verb is the infinitive. Most German infinitives end in **-en**. Here are just a few examples:

fragen	*to ask*	lernen	*to learn*
gehen	*to go*	sagen	*to say*
hören	*to hear*	schreiben	*to write*
kaufen	*to buy*	spielen	*to play*
kommen	*to come*	suchen	*to look for*

When you conjugate a verb in the present tense, you remove the infinitive ending **-en** and add the conjugational endings as illustrated above. For example:

	lernen (lern-)	**schreiben (schreib-)**	**kommen (komm-)**
ich	lerne	schreibe	komme
du	lernst	schreibst	kommst
er	lernt	schreibt	kommt
wir	lernen	schreiben	kommen
ihr	lernt	schreibt	kommt
sie	lernen	schreiben	kommen

Written Practice 4

Conjugate each of the following verbs with the subjects provided.

	hören	**suchen**	**fragen**
ich	________	________	________
du	________	________	________
er	________	________	________
wir	________	________	________
ihr	________	________	________
sie	________	________	________
Tina	________	________	________

Oral Practice

Track 41

Practice saying the following list of sentences out loud.

Lernst du Deutsch?	*Are you learning German?*
Ja, ich lerne Deutsch und Spanisch.	*Yes, I am learning German and Spanish.*
Was lernt deine Schwester?	*What is your sister learning?*
Meine Schwester lernt auch Deutsch.	*My sister is learning German, too.*
Die Kinder schreiben auf deutsch.	*The children write in German.*
Wir schreiben auch auf deutsch.	*We are writing in German, too.*
Wer geht nach Hause?	*Who is going home?*
Die Kinder gehen nach Hause.	*The children are going home.*
Spielt ihr Fußball?	*Do you play soccer?*
Ja, wir spielen gut Fußball.	*Yes, we play soccer well.*

Perhaps you've noticed that the English translation of some of the examples is not word for word. This is due in part to the complexity of English. The English present tense has three forms. German has one. Let's take a closer look at this.

A Habit, a Frequent Action:
I write in German. Ich schreibe auf deutsch.

An Action in Progress or Incomplete:
I am writing in German. Ich schreibe auf deutsch.

An Emphatic Statement:
I do write in German. Ich schreibe auf deutsch.

And when you ask a question in English, you begin the question with the verb if it is an action in progress or incomplete. If the question relates to a habit or a frequent action, you begin the question with a form of *do*. In German both types of questions begin with the verb.

Do you write in German?	Schreibst du auf deutsch?
Are you writing in German?	Schreibst du auf deutsch?

These translation differences occur in the other tenses as well.

Using an Umlaut

Some verbs have an irregularity in the present tense: They require the addition of an umlaut in the second person singular (**du**) and the third person singular (**er**). This occurs mostly with verbs that have the vowel **-a-** in the stem. Here are some examples with **fahren** (*to drive; to travel*), **fallen** (*to fall*), **schlafen** (*to sleep*), and **tragen** (*to carry; to wear*).

Track 42

	fahren	**fallen**	**schlafen**	**tragen**
ich	fahre	falle	schlafe	trage
du	fährst	fällst	schläfst	trägst
er	fährt	fällt	schläft	trägt
wir	fahren	fallen	schlafen	tragen
ihr	fahrt	fallt	schlaft	tragt
sie	fahren	fallen	schlafen	tragen

Identifying Location

To say that someone or something is *at home*, use the expression **zu Hause**. Use the expression **nach Hause** (*home, homeward*) to say someone is going home. Use **wo** to ask *where* a location is. And use **wohin** to ask *where* someone is going.

Wo ist er?	*Where is he?*
Er ist zu Hause.	*He is at home.*
Wohin fährt er?	*Where is he driving?*
Er fährt nach Hause.	*He is driving home.*

Oral Practice

 Track 43

Practice saying the following list of sentences out loud.

Wohin fahren Sie?	*Where are you driving?*
Ich fahre nach Hause.	*I am driving home.*
Wohin fährst du, Hans?	*Where are you driving, Hans?*
Ich fahre nach Deutschland.	*I am driving to Germany.*
Wohin fährt Herr Weber?	*Where is Mr. Weber driving?*
Er fährt nach Dortmund.	*He is driving to Dortmund.*
Wir fahren nach Heidelberg.	*We are driving to Heidelberg.*
Fahrt ihr nach Köln?	*Are you driving to Cologne?*

Sie fahren nach Dänemark.	*They are driving to Denmark.*
Ist Hans müde?	*Is Hans tired?*
Ja, er ist sehr müde und fällt ins Bett.	*Yes, he is very tired and falls into bed.*
Sind die Kinder müde?	*Are the children tired?*
Ja, sie sind sehr müde und fallen ins Bett.	*Yes, they are very tired and fall into bed.*
Wer schläft im Park?	*Who is sleeping in the park?*
Ein Freund schläft im Park.	*A friend is sleeping in the park.*
Schläfst du im Park?	*Do you sleep in the park?*
Nein, ich schlafe zu Hause.	*No, I sleep at home.*
Trägst du einen Hut?	*Do you wear a hat?*
Nein, ich trage keinen Hut.	*No, I do not wear a hat.*

Written Practice 5

Using the pronouns or nouns given, write questions that ask whether someone is traveling *by bus* (**mit dem Bus**) or *by train* (**mit dem Zug**). For example:

(Hans) Fährt Hans mit dem Bus oder mit dem Zug?

1. (du) ______________________________?
2. (sie *s.*) ______________________________?
3. (Sie) ______________________________?
4. (Herr Weber) ______________________________?
5. (sie *pl.*) ______________________________?
6. (er) ______________________________?
7. (die Kinder) ______________________________?

Written Practice 6

Answer each of the following questions in the affirmative using **ja**. For example:

Hast du einen Bruder? Ja, ich habe einen Bruder.

1. Schreibt Herr Mann ein Buch? ______________________________.
2. Hört ihr die Musik? ______________________________.
3. Tragen Sie einen Hut? ______________________________.

Now answer each question in the affirmative using **ja** and in the negative using **nein** and **nicht**. For example:

Seid ihr zu Hause? Ja, wir sind zu Hause.

Nein, wir sind nicht zu Hause.

4. Sind wir in Österreich? ______________________.

______________________.

5. Fahren Sie mit dem Bus? ______________________.

______________________.

6. Schläft Onkel Peter im Park? ______________________.

______________________.

7. Fallen die Kinder ins Bett? ______________________.

______________________.

8. Kommt ihr nach Hause? ______________________.

______________________.

Cardinal Numbers Eleven to Twenty

You already know the numbers from zero to ten. Here are the numbers from eleven to twenty.

elf	*eleven*	sechzehn	*sixteen*
zwölf	*twelve*	siebzehn	*seventeen*
dreizehn	*thirteen*	achtzehn	*eighteen*
vierzehn	*fourteen*	neunzehn	*nineteen*
fünfzehn	*fifteen*	zwanzig	*twenty*

Notice that the final **-s** in the number **sechs** is dropped when it becomes **sechzehn**. And the number **sieben** drops the second syllable when it becomes **siebzehn**.

Let's look at these numbers in some example sentences.

Meine Wirtin hat elf Kinder.	*My landlady has eleven children.*
Martin kauft vierzehn Fahrkarten.	*Martin is buying fourteen tickets.*
Mein Bruder ist zwanzig Jahre alt.	*My brother is twenty years old.*

Oral Practice

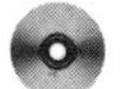 Track 44

Practice saying the following list of sentences out loud.

Wie viel Kinder habt ihr?	*How many children do you have?*
Wir haben zehn Kinder.	*We have ten children.*
Wer hat fünfzehn Kinder?	*Who has fifteen children?*
Herr Benz hat fünfzehn Kinder.	*Mr. Benz has fifteen children.*
Kaufen Sie einen Schlüssel?	*Are you buying a key?*
Ich kaufe zwölf Schlüssel.	*I am buying twelve keys.*
Wie viel CDs kaufst du?	*How many CDs are you buying?*
Ich kaufe neunzehn CDs.	*I am buying nineteen CDs.*
Wie alt bist du?	*How old are you?*
Ich bin sechzehn Jahre alt.	*I am sixteen years old.*
Wie alt sind Karl und Tina?	*How old are Karl and Tina?*
Karl ist elf Jahre alt und Tina ist siebzehn.	*Karl is eleven years old and Tina is seventeen.*
Wie viel ist zwanzig minus sechs?	*How much is twenty minus six?*
Zwanzig minus sechs ist vierzehn.	*Twenty minus six is fourteen.*
Wie viel ist dreizehn plus sieben?	*How much is thirteen plus seven?*
Dreizehn plus sieben ist zwanzig.	*Thirteen plus seven is twenty.*

Written Practice 7

Using the information in parentheses, tell how old someone or something is. For example:

(die Schule/10) Die Schule ist zehn Jahre alt.

1. (die Kinder/13) ______________________________.
2. (das Museum/15) ______________________________.
3. (du/20) ______________________________.

QUIZ

1. **Write the present tense conjugation of the following verbs, using the subjects provided.**

	werden	kommen	lernen
ich	______	______	______
du	______	______	______
er	______	______	______
wir	______	______	______
ihr	______	______	______
Sie	______	______	______
Karl und Tina	______	______	______

In this exercise you will see a person and an occupation, and a second person and second occupation. Write a sentence that says that each person is becoming the accompanying occupation. For example:

(Hans/Lehrer, ich/Pilot) *Hans wird Lehrer.*

Ich werde Pilot.

2. **(meine Schwester/Ärztin, du/ Krankenschwester)** ______

______

3. **(Sie/Mechaniker, er/Zahnarzt)** ______

______

4. **Write the present tense conjugation of the following verbs with the subjects provided.**

	fahren	fallen	schlafen
ich	______	______	______
du	______	______	______
er	______	______	______

wir	________	________	________
ihr	________	________	________
Sie	________	________	________
die Kinder	________	________	________

Answer each question with the number provided in parentheses. For example:

Wie viel Kinder haben Sie? (3) *Ich habe drei Kinder.*

5. **Wie viel Schlüssel hast du? (6)** ________________________

6. **Wie viel Fahrkarten hat Erik? (10)** ________________________

7. **Wie alt ist Ihr Sohn? (18)** ________________________

8. **Wie alt ist Ihre Tochter? (15)** ________________________

Circle the letter of the word or phrase that best completes each sentence.

9. **Wirst du ____________?**

   A. heute
   B. Lehrerin
   C. fährst
   D. Kinder

10. **Es ____________ sehr kalt.**

   A. wird
   B. nicht
   C. hat
   D. kein

chapter 7

Irregularities in Present Tense Verbs

In this chapter you will learn present tense conjugations with irregularities and how the inseparable prefixes function on verbs. In addition, vocabulary dealing with colors and titles will be introduced.

CHAPTER OBJECTIVES

In this chapter you will learn about:

- Present Tense Verb Irregularities
- Inseparable Verb Prefixes
- Colors
- Common/Professional Titles

Present Tense Verb Irregularities

There are a few more unique aspects of the German present tense that must be discussed. You are already aware that some present tense conjugations require an umlaut over the vowel **-a-** in the second and third person singular (**du fährst**,

er fährt). Only one verb requires an umlaut over the vowel **-o-**: **stoßen** (*to punch; to kick*).

Track 45

ich stoße	wir stoßen
du stößt	ihr stoßt
er stößt	sie stoßen

Notice that there is not an **-st** ending on the second person singular **du stößt**. When the stem of a verb ends with **-s**, **-ss**, **-ß**, **-z**, or **-tz**, only a **-t** is added:

heißen	*to be called*	du heißt	*you are called*
passen	*to fit*	du passt	*you fit*
reisen	*to travel*	du reist	*you travel*
reizen	*to annoy*	du reizt	*you annoy*
schützen	*to protect*	du schützt	*you protect*

Some verbs in the present tense have another kind of irregularity in the conjugation of the second and third person singular. Many verbs that have the vowel **-e-** in the stem change that vowel to **-i-** or **-ie-**. Let's look at some examples of verbs that change the stem vowel **-e-** to **-i-**.

Track 45

	essen	**sprechen**	**nehmen**
	(to eat)	***(to speak)***	***(to take)***
ich	esse	spreche	nehme
du	isst	sprichst	nimmst
er	isst	spricht	nimmt
wir	essen	sprechen	nehmen
ihr	esst	sprecht	nehmt
sie	essen	sprechen	nehmen

Now let's look at some examples of verbs that change the stem vowel to **-ie-**.

	lesen	**sehen**	**stehlen**
	(to read)	***(to see)***	***(to steal)***
ich	lese	sehe	stehle
du	liest	siehst	stiehlst
er	liest	sieht	stiehlt
wir	lesen	sehen	stehlen

ihr	lest	seht	stehlt
sie	lesen	sehen	stehlen

Refer to Appendix A for a complete list of irregular verbs.

Oral Practice

 Track 46

Practice saying the following list of sentences out loud.

Was nimmst du?	*What are you taking (having)?*
Ich nehme eine Tasse Kaffee.	*I am taking a cup of coffee.*
Was nimmt Johannes?	*What is Johannes taking?*
Er nimmt eine Tasse Tee.	*He is taking a cup of tea.*
Was nehmen Sie, Herr Müller?	*What are you taking, Mr. Mueller?*
Ich nehme ein Glas Milch.	*I am taking a glass of milk.*
Was essen Sie?	*What are you eating?*
Ich esse ein Butterbrot.	*I am eating a sandwich.*
Was isst dein Sohn?	*What is your son eating?*
Mein Sohn isst Eis.	*My son is eating ice cream.*
Was liest du, Hans?	*What are you reading, Hans?*
Ich lese die Zeitung.	*I am reading the newspaper.*
Was liest Andrea?	*What is Andrea reading?*
Andrea liest einen Brief.	*Andrea is reading a letter.*
Wer sieht den Mann?	*Who sees the man?*
Wir sehen den Mann.	*We see the man.*
Was stiehlt der Mann?	*What does the man steal?*
Er stiehlt eine Tasche.	*He steals a purse.*
Der Mann ist ein Dieb.	*The man is a thief.*

Written Practice 1

Write the present tense conjugation of the following verbs with the pronouns provided.

	sprechen	**sehen**
ich	________________	________________
du	________________	________________
er	________________	________________

	sprechen	**sehen**
wir	______________	______________
ihr	______________	______________
sie	______________	______________

There is another aspect of spelling to be considered. If a verb stem ends in **-d** or **-t**, an **-e-** will follow the stem before the conjugational endings for the second person singular and plural and the third person singular are added. For example:

	finden *(to find)*	**warten** *(to wait)*
ich	finde	warte
du	findest	wartest
er	findet	wartet
wir	finden	warten
ihr	findet	wartet
sie	finden	warten

Inseparable Verb Prefixes

Prefixes alter the meaning of verbs. English does this primarily with verbs that are derived from Latin: *press*—de*press*, com*press*, sup*press*, and so on. But German uses prefixes extensively with a wide variety of verbs. One type of prefix is the inseparable prefix—prefixes that do not separate from the verb when the verb is conjugated. These prefixes are: **be-**, **emp-**, **ent-**, **er-**, **ge-**, **ver-**, and **zer-**. These prefixes change the meaning of the verb.

For example, **kaufen** means *to buy*; ***ver*kaufen** means to *sell*. **Suchen** means *to look for*; ***be*suchen** means *to visit*. The change in meaning, however, does not affect the conjugation of these verbs.

	verkaufen	**besuchen**
ich	verkaufe	besuche
du	verkaufst	besuchst
er	verkauft	besucht
wir	verkaufen	besuchen
ihr	verkauft	besucht
sie	verkaufen	besuchen

Here are a few commonly used verbs that have an inseparable prefix.

bestellen	*to order (food, etc.)*	gehören	*to belong to*
empfinden	*to feel*	verstehen	*to understand*
entsetzen	*to horrify*	zerstören	*to destroy*
erwarten	*to expect, await*		

Oral Practice

 Track 47

Practice saying the following list of sentences out loud.

Sprechen Sie Deutsch?	*Do you speak German?*
Ja, ich spreche und verstehe Deutsch.	*Yes, I speak and understand German.*
Sprichst du Arabisch?	*Do you speak Arabic?*
Nein, ich spreche Italienisch.	*No, I speak Italian.*
Wer spricht Russisch?	*Who speaks Russian?*
Frau Wolkow spricht Russisch.	*Ms. Volkov speaks Russian.*
Was verkaufst du?	*What are you selling?*
Ich verkaufe mein Auto.	*I am selling my car.*
Robert kauft es.	*Robert is buying it.*
Was bestellst du?	*What are you ordering?*
Ich bestelle ein Glas Bier.	*I am ordering a glass of beer.*
Mein Freund bestellt eine Tasse Tee.	*My friend is ordering a cup of tea.*
Der Film entsetzt meine Mutter.	*The movie horrifies my mother.*
Verstehen Sie die Dame?	*Do you understand the lady?*
Nein, ich verstehe sie nicht.	*No, I do not understand her.*

Written Practice 2

Rewrite the following sentences, changing the verb in bold print to the verb provided in parentheses. Note the change in meaning of the sentences.

1. Er **sieht** meine Freundin. (*He sees my girlfriend.*)

   (besuchen *to visit*) ______________________________.

   (erwarten *to expect*) ______________________________.

(verstehen *to understand*) ______________________________.

(finden *to find*) ______________________________.

2. Erik **hat** die Schlüssel. (*Erik has the keys.*)

(sehen *to see*) ______________________________.

(suchen *to look for*) ______________________________.

(stehlen *to steal*) ______________________________.

(verkaufen *to sell*) ______________________________.

Oral Practice

 Track 48

Practice saying the following list of sentences out loud.

Lernen Sie Deutsch?	*Are you learning German?*
Sprechen Sie Deutsch?	*Do you speak German?*
Verstehen Sie Deutsch?	*Do you understand German?*
Lesen Sie Deutsch?	*Do you read German?*
Schreiben Sie Deutsch?	*Do you write German?*
Das Buch gehört Robert.	*The book belongs to Robert.*
Die CDs gehören Robert.	*The CDs belong to Robert.*
Der Hut gehört Tina.	*The hat belongs to Tina.*
Die Schlüssel gehören Tina.	*The keys belong to Tina.*
Was suchst du?	*What are you looking for?*
Ich suche ein Buch.	*I am looking for a book.*
Was schreibst du?	*What are you writing?*
Ich schreibe einen Brief.	*I am writing a letter.*

Colors

You already know the colors **schwarz**, **weiß**, and **rot**. Here are a few more:

braun	*brown*	grün	*green*
gelb	*yellow*	rosa	*pink*
grau	*gray*		

When you use a color as a predicate adjective after **sein** or **werden**, it requires no ending. However, when a color or any other adjective modifies many singular subject nouns directly, it requires an **-e** ending. The only exception is **rosa**. It makes no changes. Adjectives that end in **-el** will also make a change, by dropping the **e** when an ending is added: **dunkel—dunkle**. Let's look at some examples.

Mein Wagen ist rot.	*My car is red.*
Der rote Wagen ist neu.	*The red car is new.*
Ihre Bluse ist grün.	*Her blouse is green.*
Ihre grüne Bluse ist sehr alt.	*Her green blouse is very old.*
Die Tasse ist gelb.	*The cup is yellow.*
Die gelbe Tasse ist nicht hier.	*The yellow cup is not here.*
Die Vase ist rosa.	*The vase is pink.*
Wo ist die rosa Vase?	*Where is the pink vase?*

Oral Practice

 Track 49

Practice saying the following list of sentences out loud.

Die braune Jacke ist neu.	*The brown jacket is new.*
Das weiße Haus ist in Washington.	*The White House is in Washington.*
Der alte Herr ist mein Vater.	*The old gentleman is my father.*
Das kleine Glas ist für Tina.	*The little glass is for Tina.*
Ist der junge Mann ein Freund?	*Is the young man a friend?*
Ist die rosa Bluse für deine Mutter?	*Is the pink blouse for your mother?*
Ist der grüne Hut neu oder alt?	*Is the green hat new or old?*
Das große Buch ist ein Wörterbuch.	*The big book is a dictionary.*

Written Practice 3

Fill in the blanks with the adjectives provided in parentheses.

1. (klein) Das ____________________ Mädchen ist meine Tochter.
2. (weiß) Meine ____________________ Bluse ist nicht alt.
3. (dunkel) Es wird sehr ____________________.
4. (jung) Ist Ihr Onkel ____________________ oder alt?
5. (neu) Wo ist die ____________________ Tasse?

6. (grau) Der ________________ Hut ist nicht hier.
7. (deutsch) Die ________________ Frau kauft eine Tasse Kaffee.

Written Practice 4

Look at each statement on the left. Then place the letter of the statement on the right that logically follows. Not all letters will be used.

1. Wer stiehlt das Geld? ______	a. Er ist elf Jahre alt.
2. Sie kauft eine neue Bluse. ______	b. Ich verstehe sie nicht.
3. Hans spricht Russisch. ______	c. Der Dieb.
4. Was liest du? ______	d. Nein, sie ist weiß.
5. Ist der neue BMW rot? ______	e. Ist sie gelb?
6. Sie bestellt eine Tasse Tee. ______	f. Ich nehme ein Butterbrot.
7. Erik nimmt ein Glas Milch. ______	g. Thomas bestellt Bier.
8. Lesen Sie ein Buch? ______	h. Er versteht es auch.
9. Ist die Tasse grau? ______	i. In der Schweiz.
10. Sie spricht Arabisch. ______	j. Ein Buch.
	k. Nein, ich lese eine Zeitung.
	l. Nein, er ist grün.

Common/Professional Titles

Most titles are similar in both English and German. There are common titles that refer to everyone, and other titles that designate someone's profession. For example:

Common Titles:

Herr Meier	*Mr. Meier*
Frau Meier	*Ms. Meier, Mrs. Meier, Miss Meier*

Professional Titles:

Doktor Bauer ist Arzt.	*Dr. Bauer is a physician.*
Doktor Keller ist Ärztin.	*Dr. Keller is a physician (female).*
Doktor Schmidt ist Zahnarzt.	*Dr. Schmidt is a dentist.*
Professor Benz schreibt ein Buch.	*Professor Benz is writing a book.*

When addressing someone with a common title (**Herr**, **Frau**), just use the title and the last name.

Guten Tag, Herr Schröder.	*Hello, Mr. Schroeder.*
Gute Nacht, Frau Kamps.	*Good night, Ms. Kamps.*

When someone has a professional title, use both the common and professional titles together.

Guten Abend, Herr Doktor.	*Good evening, doctor.*
Auf Wiedersehen, Frau Doktor.	*Good-bye, doctor.*
Guten Tag, Herr Professor.	*Good afternoon, professor.*
Guten Morgen, Frau Professor.	*Good morning, professor.*

And if a doctor or professor has a wife, she, too, can be addressed with the professional title.

Wiederschauen, Frau Doktor.	*Good-bye, ma'am (wife of the doctor).*
Wiedersehen, Frau Professor.	*Good-bye, ma'am (wife of the professor).*

Written Practice 5

Complete each sentence by filling in the blanks with any appropriate word or phrase.

1. Meine Mutter liest ______________________.
2. Die Kinder spielen im ______________________.
3. Der alte Mann ______________________ Englisch und Deutsch.
4. Ich habe kein Geld. Ich kann es nicht ______________________.
5. Der Dieb ______________________ meine Tasche.
6. Ist ______________________ heiß oder kalt?
7. Es ist ______________________. Wo ist die Lampe?
8. Siehst du ______________________?
9. Guten ______________________, Frau Doktor.
10. Der ______________________ Hut ist sehr alt.
11. Ist euer Vater ______________________?
12. Ist der neue Wagen braun oder ______________________?
13. Ich finde ______________________.

14. Martin ______________________ ein Butterbrot und ein Glas Milch.

15. Die ____________________ ____________________ gehören Tina.

Written Practice 6

Form a question about each sentence by changing the words or phrases in bold print to **wer**, **was**, **wann**, **wo**, **wohin**, **wie viel**, **wie alt**, or **warum**. For example:

Martin kauft **ein Heft**.

Was kauft Martin?

1. **Angela** besucht eine Freundin in Berlin.

   ____?

2. Mein Vater fährt **nach Österreich**.

   ____?

3. Die Kinder finden **eine alte Uhr**.

   ____?

4. Sie trägt ein Sweatshirt, **denn es ist sehr kalt**.

   ____?

5. Meine Tochter ist **zwölf Jahre alt**.

   ____?

6. Ich gehe **heute** in die Stadt.

   ____?

7. Zwei Jungen spielen Tennis **im Park**.

   ____?

8. Der Professor hat **achtzehn** Schlüssel.

   ____?

9. Er fährt mit dem Bus **nach Hause**.

   ____?

10. Karin liest **einen Brief**.

    ____?

11. **Die Kinder** warten im Park.

    ____?

12. Erik hat **kein** Geld.

____?

13. Sonja versteht **Russisch und Italienisch**.

____?

14. Ich lese das Buch, **denn es ist sehr interessant**.

____?

15. Onkel Heinz trägt **einen Hut**.

____?

QUIZ

1. Write the present tense conjugation of the following verbs, using the pronouns provided.

	sehen	sprechen	verstehen	reisen
ich	________	________	________	________
du	________	________	________	________
er	________	________	________	________
wir	________	________	________	________
ihr	________	________	________	________
Sie	________	________	________	________

Rewrite each sentence below, changing the italicized verbs to the ones provided in parentheses.

2. Er *findet* einen Brief.

(suchen) ____

(lesen) ____

(sehen) ____

(haben) ____

3. Andrea *sucht* ein Buch.

(kaufen) ____

(verkaufen) ____

(lesen) ____

(stehlen) ____

4. **Die Kinder *lernen* Deutsch.**

   (verstehen) ______________________

   (sprechen) ______________________

5. **Ich *habe* eine Tasse Tee.**

   (nehmen) ______________________

   (bestellen) ______________________

Circle the letter of the word or phrase that best completes each sentence.

6. **Wo ist das neue ____________?**

   A. Brief
   B. Wörterbuch
   C. Fahrkarten
   D. Zug

7. **Der Tourist ____________ mit dem Zug.**

   A. fahrt
   B. lest
   C. liest
   D. fährt

8. **____________ reisen Sie, Herr Bauer?**

   A. Wohin
   B. Sehen
   C. Was
   D. Kann

9. **Angela ____________ eine Tante.**

   A. besucht
   B. siehst
   C. bestellen
   D. trage

10. **Der ____________ Wagen ist sehr alt.**

   A. klein
   B. eine Tasse
   C. rote
   D. gelb

chapter 8

Talking About Location

In this chapter you will learn the use of three important verbs of motion as well as the difference between **wohnen** and **leben**, and **kennen** and **wissen**. Telling time is included here along with the use of coordinating conjunctions. Together with some special verbs and separable prefixes, the accusative case will be introduced in this chapter.

CHAPTER OBJECTIVES

In this chapter you will learn about:

- Using the Verb *Kommen*
- Telling Time
- Using the Verbs *Gehen* and *Fahren*
- Using the Verbs *Wohnen* and *Leben*
- Word Order
- Some Coordinating Conjunctions
- Using the Verbs *Wissen* and *Kennen*
- Infinitives Ending in *-ieren*
- Separable Verb Prefixes
- Accusative Case
- Accusative Pronouns

Using the Verb *Kommen*

The verb **kommen** (*to come*) is a high-frequency verb. In the present tense this verb has no irregularities.

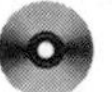 Track 50

ich komme	*I come*	wir kommen	*we come*
du kommst	*you come*	ihr kommt	*you come*
er kommt	*he comes*	sie kommen	*they come*

When you want to know where someone comes from, ask:

Woher kommen Sie?	*Where do you come from?*
Woher kommst du?	*Where do you come from?*
Woher kommt ihr?	*Where do you come from?*
Woher kommt dieser Mann?	*Where does this man come from?*
Woher kommt diese Frau?	*Where does this woman come from?*

Use the preposition **aus** (*out; from*) to reply to this with the name of a city, a country, or a continent.

Wir kommen aus Wien.	*We come from Vienna.*
Ich komme aus England.	*I am from England.*
Er kommt aus Asien.	*He comes from Asia.*

Oral Practice

Practice saying the following list of sentences out loud.

Woher kommen Sie?	*Where do you come from?*
Ich komme aus Amerika.	*I come from America.*
Woher kommt dieser Herr?	*Where does this gentleman come from?*
Er kommt aus Schweden.	*He comes from Sweden.*
Woher kommt diese Dame?	*Where does this lady come from?*
Sie kommt aus Düsseldorf.	*She comes from Düsseldorf.*
Kommt der Student aus China?	*Does the student come from China?*
Nein, er kommt aus Japan.	*No, he comes from Japan.*
Kommen diese Leute aus Asien?	*Do these people come from Asia?*
Nein, sie kommen aus Afrika.	*No, they come from Africa.*

Nein, sie kommen aus Australien.	*No, they come from Australia.*
Nein, sie kommen aus Nordamerika.	*No, they come from North America.*
Nein, sie kommen aus Südamerika.	*No, they come from South America.*

The pronoun **man** means *one* or *you* when it refers to people in general. It is commonly used with **kommen**.

Wie kommt man zum Theater?	*How does one (do you) get to the theater?*
Wie kommt man zum Park?	*How does one get to the park?*

Written Practice 1

Rewrite each sentence, changing the subject in bold print to the pronoun **man**. For example:

Verstehen **Sie** das?

Versteht man das?

1. Warum fahrt **ihr** mit der Straßenbahn?

   ______________________________?

2. Wie kommen **deine Eltern** vom Rathaus zum Bahnhof?

   ______________________________?

3. Wisst **ihr**, wohin Gudrun reist?

   ______________________________?

4. Hier sprechen **die Leute** Deutsch.

   ______________________________?

Oral Practice

Practice saying the following list of sentences out loud.

Wie kommt man zum Bahnhof?	*How do you (does one) get to the train station?*
Man kommt mit dem Bus zum Bahnhof.	*You get to the train station by bus.*

Wie kommt man zum Rathaus?	*How do you get to city hall?*
Man kommt mit der Straßenbahn zum Rathaus.	*You get to city hall by streetcar.*
Wie kommt man zur Kunsthalle?	*How do you get to the art museum?*
Man kommt mit dem Bus zur Kunsthalle.	*You get to the art museum by bus.*
Wie kommt man nach Berlin?	*How do you get to Berlin?*
Man kommt mit dem Zug nach Berlin.	*You get to Berlin by train.*
Wie kommt man nach Kanada?	*How do you get to Canada?*
Man kommt mit dem Flugzeug nach Kanada.	*You get to Canada by airplane.*
Kommst du mit dem Auto nach Paris?	*Are you coming to Paris by car?*
Ja, ich komme mit dem Auto nach Paris.	*Yes, I am coming to Paris by car.*

Written Practice 2

Write the present tense conjugation of **kommen** with the following pronouns and nouns.

ich	__________	wir	__________
du	__________	ihr	__________
er	__________	sie	__________
man	__________	dieser Herr	__________
die Kinder	__________	diese Dame	__________

Written Practice 3

Using the words in parentheses, answer the questions. For example:

Woher kommst du? (Bonn) Ich komme aus Bonn.

1. Woher kommt Herr Braun? (London)

   ______________________________.

2. Woher kommt der Amerikaner? (New York)

   ______________________________.

3. Woher kommt die Österreicherin? (Wien)

____.

4. Woher kommt Frau Benz? (Deutschland)

____.

5. Woher kommt diese Dame? (Italien)

____.

Telling Time

When telling time, place the hour number in front of the word **Uhr**. For example, **Es ist drei Uhr** means *It is three o'clock*. When telling at what time something occurs, precede the phrase with the preposition *um*. For example, **Er kommt um drei Uhr nach Hause** means *He comes home at three o'clock*.

There are numerous phrases that can be used with the verb **kommen**. Let's look at a few of them.

Er kommt spät.	*He comes late.*
Um sechs Uhr kommt er von der Arbeit.	*At six o'clock he comes from work.*
Ich komme in einer halben Stunde.	*I will come in a half hour.*
Wir kommen in zwei Wochen.	*We are coming in two weeks.*
Wer kommt ins Zimmer?	*Who is coming into the room?*
Er kommt in den Himmel.	*He is going to heaven.*
Er kommt in die Hölle.	*He is going to hell.*

Oral Practice

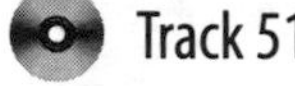

Track 51

Practice saying the following list of sentences out loud.

Kommt er spät zur Party?	*Is he coming to the party late?*
Ja, er kommt sehr spät zur Party.	*Yes, he is coming very late to the party.*
Kommt sie immer spät?	*Does she always come late?*
Ja, sie kommt immer zu spät.	*Yes, she always comes too late.*
Mein Vater kommt immer um sechs Uhr von der Arbeit.	*My father always comes from work at six o'clock.*

Um wie viel Uhr kommst du von der Arbeit?	*What time do you come from work?*
Ich komme sehr spät von der Arbeit.	*I come from work very late.*
Wann kommen Sie zum Bahnhof?	*When are you coming to the train station?*
Ich komme in einer halben Stunde.	*I am coming in a half hour.*
Martin kommt in einer Stunde.	*Martin is coming in an hour.*
Wann kommt ihr zur Party?	*When are you coming to the party?*
Wir kommen um sechs Uhr zur Party.	*We are coming to the party at six o'clock.*
Wann kommst du nach Hause?	*When are you coming home?*
Ich komme in zwei Wochen nach Hause.	*I am coming home in two weeks.*
Wer kommt nächste Woche?	*Who is coming next week?*
Tante Gerda kommt nächste Woche.	*Aunt Gerda is coming next week.*
Kommst du zu Fuß?	*Are you coming on foot?*

Using the Verbs *Gehen* and *Fahren*

Both **gehen** and **fahren** can be translated as *to go*. However, **gehen** is more precisely *to go on foot* and **fahren** *to travel* or *to drive* by some form of transportation (**Bus**, **Zug**, **Straßenbahn**, and so forth). English does not have to be so specific when using the verb *to go*:

What time are you going to school?	(It could be on foot. It could be by bus.)
When are you going to Berlin?	(It could be by train or airplane.)

German prefers to be specific:

Um wie viel Uhr gehst du zur Schule?	*What time are you going to school?* (on foot)
Wann fährst du nach Berlin?	*When are you going to Berlin?* (by a form of motorized transportation)

And when the distance is great and you're going to travel by airplane, you use the verb **fliegen** (*to fly*).

Wohin fliegt ihr nächste Woche?	*Where are you flying (going) next week?*
Wir fliegen nächste Woche nach China.	*We are flying (going) to China next week.*

Using the Verbs *Wohnen* and *Leben*

The verbs **wohnen** and **leben** can be translated as *to live*, but the former means *to reside* somewhere, and the latter means to *be alive*. Let's look at some example sentences.

Wo wohnen Sie, Herr Bauer?	*Where do you live, Mr. Bauer?*
Ich wohne in Hamburg.	*I live in Hamburg.*
Mein Großvater lebt noch.	*My grandfather is still living.*

Oral Practice

Practice saying the following list of sentences out loud.

Wo wohnen Sie jetzt?	*Where do you live now?*
Ich wohne jetzt in Freiburg.	*I live in Freiburg now.*
Wo wohnt Ihre Tochter?	*Where does your daughter live?*
Meine Tochter wohnt jetzt in Bonn.	*My daughter lives in Bonn now.*
Lebt Ihr Großvater noch?	*Is your grandfather still living?*
Ja, er lebt noch, aber er ist sehr alt.	*Yes, he is still living, but he is very old.*
Lebt Ihre Großmutter noch?	*Is your grandmother still living?*
Nein, sie lebt nicht mehr.	*No, she is no longer living.*
Wann gehst du zum Bahnhof?	*When are you going to the train station?*
Ich gehe um neun Uhr zum Bahnhof.	*I am going to the train station at nine o'clock.*
Wann fährt er zum Rathaus?	*When is he going to city hall?*
Er fährt morgen zum Rathaus.	*He is going to city hall tomorrow.*
Fliegt ihr nach Europa?	*Are you flying to Europe?*

Ja, wir fliegen nach Europa.	*Yes, we are flying to Europe.*
Von Frankfurt nach München fahren wir mit dem Auto.	*We are going by car from Frankfurt to Munich.*
Von Hamburg nach Berlin fahren wir mit dem Zug.	*We are going by train from Hamburg to Berlin.*
Vom Bahnhof zum Rathaus fahren wir mit der Straßenbahn.	*From the train station to city hall we are going by streetcar.*
Wohin fahren diese Leute?	*Where are these people going?*

Word Order

When a word or phrase other than the subject begins a sentence, the verb precedes the subject. For example:

Wir fahren nach Hamburg. (subject followed by verb)

but

Heute *fahren wir* nach Hamburg. (verb followed by subject)
Ich fahre mit der Straßenbahn. (subject followed by verb)

but

Vom Bahnhof zum Rathaus *fahre ich* mit der Straßenbahn. (verb followed by subject)

Written Practice 4

Rewrite each sentence, starting it with the word or phrase in parentheses and changing the word order accordingly. For example:

Ich gehe zur Schule. (heute) Heute gehe ich zur Schule.

1. Die Touristen reisen nach Italien. (morgen) ______________.
2. Wir sehen viele Kinder. (im Park) ______________.
3. Ich bestelle ein Glas Bier. (im Restaurant) ______________.
4. Sie fahren mit dem Auto. (vom Rathaus zur Schule) ______________.
5. Mein Vater fliegt nach Australien. (heute) ______________.

Some Coordinating Conjunctions

You have already encountered four important conjunctions: **und** (*and*), **oder** (*or*), **denn** (*because*), and **aber** (*but*). These are called coordinating conjunctions because they combine two sentences (clauses) into one.

Karl liest ein Buch **und** Marianne schreibt einen Brief.	*Karl reads a book, **and** Marianne writes a letter.*
Gehen wir zum Rathaus, **oder** gehen wir zum Bahnhof?	*Are we going to city hall, **or** are we going to the train station?*
Er trägt ein Sweatshirt, **denn** es wird sehr kalt.	*He is wearing a sweatshirt, **because** it is getting very cold.*
Der Mann lebt noch, **aber** er ist sehr alt.	*The man is still living, **but** he is very old.*

NOTE ***The German conjunction* und *does not require a comma to separate the two clauses as do the other coordinating conjunctions.***

Using the Verbs *Wissen* and *Kennen*

These two verbs mean *to know*, but the former means *to have knowledge*, and the latter means *to be acquainted with*. The verb **wissen** has an irregular conjugation in the present tense. Let's compare the conjugations of these two verbs.

	wissen	**kennen**
ich	weiß	kenne
du	weißt	kennst
er	weiß	kennt
wir	wissen	kennen
ihr	wisst	kennt
sie	wissen	kennen

In sentences, these two verbs are used like this:

Wissen Sie, wo Herr Bauer wohnt?	*Do you know where Mr. Bauer lives?*
Nein, das weiß ich nicht.	*No, I do not know that.*
Kennst du Frau Meier?	*Do you know Ms. Meier?*
Ja, ich kenne sie gut.	*Yes, I know her well.*

Oral Practice

 Track 52

Practice saying the following list of sentences out loud.

Weißt du, wo meine Schlüssel sind?	*Do you know where my keys are?*
Nein, das weiß ich nicht.	*No, I do not know.*
Weiß man, wer da wohnt?	*Does anyone know who lives there?*
Ich weiß, wer da wohnt.	*I know who lives there.*
Erik wohnt da. Kennst du Erik?	*Erik lives there. Do you know Erik?*
Nein, ich kenne Erik nicht.	*No, I do not know Erik.*
Kennen Sie diese Frau?	*Do you know this woman?*
Ja, ich kenne sie. Das ist Frau Kamps.	*Yes, I know her. That is Ms. Kamps.*
Sie wohnt in Bonn, aber Herr Kamps wohnt in Leipzig.	*She lives in Bonn, but Mr. Kamps lives in Leipzig.*

Written Practice 5

Complete the sentences by filling in the blanks with the appropriate verbs: **gehen** or **fahren**, **wohnen** or **leben**, **wissen** or **kennen**. Conjugate the verbs accordingly.

1. Meine Eltern ________________ jetzt in Freiburg.
2. ________________ Ihre Großmutter noch?
3. Wir ________________den Mann nicht. Wie heißt er?
4. Er ________________ mit dem Zug nach Rom.
5. Herr Benz ________________ in der Schillerstraße.
6. Wohin ________________ du?
7. ________________ Sie, wo Frau Schneider wohnt?
8. Ich ________________ zum Rathaus. Es ist nicht weit von hier.
9. Warum ________________ ihr zu Fuß?
10. ________________ Sie meine Eltern nicht?

Infinitives Ending in *-ieren*

There is a large category of verbs that end in **-ieren**. These verbs tend to come from foreign sources, and in many instances English speakers can recognize the meanings of such verbs at first glance. For example:

arrangieren	*to arrange*	marschieren	*to march*
diskutieren	*to discuss*	organisieren	*to organize*
fotografieren	*to photograph*	probieren	*to try, to taste*
imitieren	*to imitate*	spazieren	*to stroll*
immigrieren	*to immigrate*	studieren	*to study*

These verbs are always regular in the present tense.

	diskutieren	**studieren**
ich	diskutiere	studiere
du	diskutierst	studierst
er	diskutiert	studiert
wir	diskutieren	studieren
ihr	diskutiert	studiert
sie	diskutieren	studieren

Though you will encounter many such verbs in German, there are a few German verbs that look like **-ieren** verbs but are not. This distinction will become important in the next few chapters when you begin working with other tenses. The present tense of these verbs is conjugated the same, but it is in the various past tenses that the verbs will differ from regular **-ieren** verbs. One such German verb that is not an **-ieren** verb is **verlieren** (*to lose*).

ich verliere	wir verlieren
du verlierst	ihr verliert
er verliert	sie verlieren

Written Practice 6

Combine each string of words as a sentence, conjugating the verbs appropriately. For example:

ich/suchen/mein/Schlüssel Ich suche meine Schlüssel.

1. wir/fotografieren/das Rathaus ________________.
2. Martin/verlieren/das Geld ________________.
3. ich/studieren/Deutsch/und/Russisch ________________.
4. die Kinder/probieren/den Pudding ________________.
5. diese Leute/spazieren/im Park ________________.

Separable Verb Prefixes

In Chapter 7 you were introduced to inseparable prefixes. There are also numerous separable prefixes that are derived from two large groups of words: prepositions and adverbs. Here are some examples of separable prefixes: **an-**, **auf-**, **aus-**, **ein-**, **mit-**, **um-**, **vor-**, and **zu-**. Some example verbs with these prefixes are:

ankommen	*to arrive*	mitgehen	*to go along*
aufmachen	*to open*	umsteigen	*to transfer (to other transportation)*
ausgeben	*to spend*	vorstellen	*to introduce*
einsteigen	*to get on (transportation)*	zumachen	*to close*

There are many other separable prefixes, but you can quickly identify them by the position of the stress in the verb. If the stress is on the prefix (**áufmachen**), the prefix is separable. If the stress is on the stem of the verb (**besúchen**), the prefix is inseparable. When a verb with a separable prefix is conjugated in the present tense, the prefix separates from the verb and is placed at the end of the sentence. For example:

aufmachen *(to open)*

Ich mache das Fenster **auf**.	*I open the window.*
Du machst das Fenster **auf**.	*You open the window.*
Er macht das Fenster **auf**.	*He opens the window.*
Wir machen das Fenster **auf**.	*We open the window.*
Ihr macht das Fenster **auf**.	*You open the window.*
Sie machen das Fenster **auf**.	*They open the window.*
Wer macht das Fenster **auf**?	*Who is opening the window?*

ausgeben *(to spend)*

Ich gebe zu viel Geld **aus**.	*I spend too much money.*
Du gibst zu viel Geld **aus**.	*You spend too much money.*
Er gibt zu viel Geld **aus**.	*He spends too much money.*
Wir geben zu viel Geld **aus**.	*We spend too much money.*
Ihr gebt zu viel Geld **aus**.	*You spend too much money.*
Sie geben zu viel Geld **aus**.	*They spend too much money.*
Wer gibt zu viel Geld **aus**?	*Who spends too much money?*

Written Practice 7

Write the present tense conjugation of each of the following verbs.

	ankommen	**einsteigen**	**vorstellen**
ich	________	________	________
du	________	________	________
er	________	________	________
wir	________	________	________

	ankommen	**einsteigen**	**vorstellen**
ihr	________	________	________
sie	________	________	________

Accusative Case

The subject of a German sentence is in the nominative case. For example:

Der Mann ist alt.	***The man*** *is old.*
Meine Lampe ist neu.	***My lamp*** *is new.*
Wo ist **dein Sweatshirt**?	*Where is* ***your sweatshirt****?*
Ihre Kinder haben keine CDs.	***Your children*** *do not have any CDs.*

Direct objects are in the accusative case. The direct object in a sentence is the word that receives the action of the verb. Ask *what* or *whom* of the verb to identify the direct object. For example:

I buy a new blouse.	(*What* do I buy?) (*a new blouse* = direct object)
I know this woman.	(*Whom* do I know?) (*this woman* = direct object).

It works the same in German.

Ich kaufe eine neue Bluse.	(*Was* kaufe ich?) (**eine neue Bluse** = direct object)
Ich kenne diese Frau.	(*Wen* kenne ich?) (**diese Frau** = direct object)

It's important to be able to identify a direct object, because in German, masculine nouns used as direct objects make a declensional change. Let's compare the nominative and accusative cases of masculine nouns.

Nominative	Accusative
der Mann	den Mann
ein Lehrer	einen Lehrer
kein Freund	keinen Freund
mein Tisch	meinen Tisch
Ihr Wagen	Ihren Wagen

As you can plainly see, the modifier (**der**, **ein**, **kein**, **mein**, **Ihr**) of a masculine noun requires an **-en** ending when it is used in the accusative case, that is, when it is used with a direct object. Now compare masculine nouns used as subjects of sentences and as direct objects of sentences.

Subjects—Nominative Case

Mein Lehrer wohnt in Heidelberg. *My teacher lives in Heidelberg.*
Wo ist Ihr Wagen? *Where is your car?*

Direct Objects—Accusative Case

Kennen Sie meinen Lehrer? *Do you know my teacher?*
Ein Freund kauft Ihren Wagen. *A friend buys your car.*

But with feminine, neuter, and plural nouns, there is no declensional change from the nominative case to the accusative case.

Subjects—Nominative Case

Meine Tante ist sehr alt. *My aunt is very old.*
Wo ist das Heft? *Where is the notebook?*
Die Schlüssel sind in der Tasche. *The keys are in the purse.*

Direct Objects—Accusative Case

Morgen besuche ich meine Tante. *Tomorrow I will visit my aunt.*
Robert verliert das Heft. *Robert loses the notebook.*
Iris findet die Schlüssel. *Iris finds the keys.*

Oral Practice

Practice saying the following list of sentences out loud.

Kennen Sie meine Eltern?	*Do you know my parents?*
Nein, ich kenne sie nicht.	*No, I do not know them.*
Ich stelle meinen Vater und meine Mutter vor.	*I introduce my father and my mother.*
Kennst du den Amerikaner?	*Do you know the American?*
Ja, ich kenne den Amerikaner.	*Yes, I know the American.*
Er wohnt in Cleveland, aber studiert in Hamburg.	*He lives in Cleveland but is studying in Hamburg.*
Ich stelle den Amerikaner vor.	*I introduce the American.*
Wann kommt Herr Schneider an?	*When does Mr. Schneider arrive?*
Ich weiß nicht. Ich frage meinen Mann.	*I do not know. I will ask my husband.*
Wir steigen in den Bus ein und fahren nach Hause.	*We get on the bus and go home.*
In der Schillerstraße steigen wir um.	*We transfer at Schiller Street.*
Wo steigt ihr ein?	*Where do you get on?*
Wir steigen in der Hauptstraße ein.	*We get on on Main Street.*
Wo steigen sie um?	*Where do they transfer?*
Sie steigen in der Waldstraße um.	*They transfer on Wald Street.*
Hans, machst du das Fenster auf?	*Hans, are you opening the window?*
Ja, es ist sehr heiß heute.	*Yes, it is very hot today.*
Wer macht die Tür zu?	*Who closes the door?*
Meine Eltern machen die Tür zu.	*My parents close the door.*
Wir gehen zum Bahnhof.	*We are going to the train station.*
Mein Bruder geht mit.	*My brother is going along.*

Written Practice 8

Rewrite the sentences using the nouns in parentheses. These will be direct objects and will require the accusative case.

1. Kennen Sie ________?

   (mein Onkel) ____?

   (diese Dame) ____?

(der Professor) ______________________________?

(das Mädchen) ______________________________?

2. Dieser Mann kauft ______.

(ein Wagen) ______________________________.

(mein Haus) ______________________________.

(Ihre CDs) ______________________________.

(der Teppich) ______________________________.

Accusative Pronouns

Just as masculine nouns change in the accusative case when they are used as direct objects, so do most pronouns. In English it looks like this, for example:

Subject: He learns German.
Direct Object: Do you know **him**?

German pronouns act in the same way.

Subject Pronouns—Nominative Case	**Direct Object Pronouns—Accusative Case**
ich	mich
du	dich
er	ihn
sie (*s.*)	sie
es	es
wir	uns
ihr	euch
sie (*pl.*)	sie
Sie	Sie
wer	wen
was	was

In sentences they look like this:

Der Mann kennt mich nicht.	*The man does not know me.*
Der Mann kennt dich nicht.	*The man does not know you.*
Der Mann kennt ihn nicht.	*The man does not know him.*

Der Mann kennt sie nicht.	*The man does not know her.*
Der Mann kennt uns nicht.	*The man does not know us.*
Der Mann kennt euch nicht.	*The man does not know you.*
Der Mann kennt sie nicht.	*The man does not know them.*
Der Mann kennt Sie nicht.	*The man does not know you.*
Wen kennt der Mann?	*Whom does the man know?*
Was sieht der Mann?	*What does the man see?*

When you replace a noun with a pronoun, it must be the same gender and case as the noun. For example:

Eine Frau kommt.	*A woman is coming.*
Sie kommt.	*She is coming.*
Sehen Sie den Mann?	*Do you see the man?*
Sehen Sie **ihn**?	*Do you see him?*

Written Practice 9

Rewrite the sentences using the nouns or pronouns in parentheses. These will be direct objects and will require the accusative case.

1. Wer verkauft _______?

(mein Wagen) ____?

(ein Hut) ____?

(die Fahrkarten) ____?

(das Auto) ____?

(es) ____?

2. Kennt ihr _______?

(meine Eltern) ____?

(der Lehrer) ____?

(die Leute) ____?

(mein Freund) ____?

(er) ____?

QUIZ

Rewrite each sentence as a question. Use the phrases in bold print as signals to use **wo**, **wohin**, or **woher**. For example:

Er geht nach Hause. *Wohin geht er?*

1. **Meine Eltern sind zu Hause.** ____________________

2. **Die Touristen gehen zum Bahnhof.** ____________________

3. **Erik und Tina kommen aus der Schweiz.** ____________________

Rewrite each sentence with the correct form of the words in parentheses.

4. **Der alte Mann kennt __________ nicht.**
   (mein Vater) ____________________
   (diese Frau) ____________________
   (der Lehrer) ____________________
   (diese Leute) ____________________
   (er) ____________________

Provide the accusative case form of each word or phrase in parentheses.

5. **(die Kinder)**
   (ich) ____________________
   (du) ____________________
   (mein Freund) ____________________
   (er) ____________________
   (sie *s.*) ____________________
   (ein Hut) ____________________
   (wir) ____________________
   (ihr) ____________________
   (Sie) ____________________

In the blanks provided, write the pronoun that is the correct replacement for the phrases in bold print. For example:

Karl hat **das Buch**. ____es____

6. **Siehst du die Lehrerin? ______________**

   Ich verkaufe meinen Wagen. ______________

   Kennen Sie meine Eltern? ______________

Circle the letter of the word or phrase that best completes each sentence.

7. **Martin ______________ meine Schwester vor.**
   - A. stellt
   - B. steigt
   - C. geht
   - D. kennt

8. **Um ______________ kommt der nächste Zug?**
   - A. diese Leute
   - B. wie viel Uhr
   - C. spät
   - D. vom Bahnhof

9. **______________ besuchen Sie in Heidelberg?**
   - A. Wir
   - B. Der alte Professor
   - C. Wen
   - D. Ein Amerikaner

10. **Meine Großmutter ______________ den Pudding.**
    - A. probiert
    - B. ausgeben
    - C. fotografieren
    - D. wohnt

chapter 9

Talking About the Past

In this chapter you will learn about possessive adjectives. In addition, the past tense will be introduced as well as the use of certain prepositions. The formation of plurals will also be included.

CHAPTER OBJECTIVES

In this chapter you will learn about:

- Possessive Adjectives
- Regular Past Tense
- Irregular Past Tense
- Accusative Case Prepositions
- Plurals
- Neuter Nouns

Possessive Adjectives

You have already encountered some of the possessive adjectives. Each possessive adjective has a subject pronoun counterpart, from which it is derived. Here is a complete list:

Subject Pronoun	**Possessive Adjective**
ich	mein
du	dein
er	sein
sie (*s.*)	ihr
es	sein
wir	unser
ihr	euer
sie (*pl.*)	ihr
Sie	Ihr
wer	wessen

Except for **wessen** (*whose*), a feminine or masculine ending is required in the accusative case: **mein**, **meine**, **meinen/sein**, **seine**, **seinen/unser**, **unsere**, **unseren**, and so forth. In sentences, the possessive adjectives look like this:

Ich verliere mein Buch.	*I lose my book.*
Du verlierst dein Buch.	*You lose your book.*
Er verliert sein Buch.	*He loses his book.*
Sie verliert ihr Buch.	*She loses her book.*
Es (Das Kind) verliert sein Buch.	*He/She (The child) loses his/her book.*
Wir verlieren unser Buch.	*We lose our book.*
Ihr verliert euer Buch.	*You lose your book.*
Sie verlieren ihr Buch.	*They lose their book.*
Sie verlieren Ihr Buch.	*You lose your book.*
Wessen Buch verlieren sie?	*Whose book do they lose?*

Masculine, feminine, and neuter nouns use **sein**, **ihr**, and **sein** (*his*, *her*, *its*) as their possessive adjectives. All plural nouns use **ihr** (*their*).

Der Mann verkauft sein Haus.	*The man sells his house.*
Die Frau verkauft ihren Wagen.	*The woman sells her car.*

Das Mädchen verkauft sein Buch.	*The girl sells her book.*
Diese Leute verkaufen ihre Autos.	*These people sell their cars.*

Oral Practice

 Track 53

Practice saying the following list of sentences out loud.

Wir diskutieren unser Problem.	*We discuss our problem.*
Das ist aber auch mein Problem.	*But that is my problem, too.*
Der Student macht seine Tür auf.	*The student opens his door.*
Die Ärztin macht ihr Fenster zu.	*The physician closes her window.*
Wessen Wagen kaufen Sie?	*Whose car are you buying?*
Ich kaufe seinen Wagen.	*I am buying his car.*
Wessen Haus kauft ihr?	*Whose house are you buying?*
Wir kaufen ihr Haus.	*We are buying her house.*
Wessen Kleider verkauft ihr?	*Whose clothes are you selling?*
Wir verkaufen unsere Kleider.	*We are selling our clothes.*
Wessen Bücher verkauft der Chef?	*Whose books is the boss selling?*
Der Chef verkauft seine Bücher.	*The boss is selling his books.*

Written Practice 1

Answer each question with the possessive adjective provided in parentheses. For example:

Wessen Buch hast du? (mein) Ich habe mein Buch.

1. Wessen Kleider findest du? (sein) ______________________.
2. Wessen Freundin kennst du? (ihr) ______________________.
3. Wessen Wagen kauft ihr? (euer) ______________________.
4. Wessen Kind siehst du? (mein) ______________________.
5. Wessen Milch nimmt er? (dein) ______________________.
6. Wessen Eltern wohnen in Leipzig? (Ihr) ______________________.
7. Wessen Chef weiß nichts? (unser) ______________________.

Written Practice 2

For each sentence, change the possessive adjective in bold print to the one in parentheses. For example:

Er findet **sein** Buch.

(ihr) Er findet ihr Buch.

1. Ich besuche **meine** Eltern in München.

   (Ihr) ______________________________.

   (euer) ______________________________.

   (unser) ______________________________.

2. Wer findet **ihren** Bleistift?

   (mein) ______________________________?

   (sein) ______________________________?

   (unser) ______________________________?

Regular Past Tense

German, just like English, has both a regular past tense formation and an irregular past tense formation. The regular past tense adds the suffix **-te** to the stem of the verb plus the appropriate conjugational endings. This is similar to how English adds the suffix *-ed* to a verb to form the past tense (*look—looked, jump—jumped,* and so forth).

To form the regular past tense in German, drop the infinitive ending **-en** and add the endings **-te**, **-test**, **-te**, **-ten**, **-tet**, and **-ten**. Let's look at some regular verbs in the past tense.

	bestellen *(ordered)*	**studieren** *(studied)*	**lernen** *(learned)*	**zumachen** *(closed)*
ich	bestell**te**	studier**te**	lern**te**	mach**te** zu
du	bestell**test**	studier**test**	lern**test**	mach**test** zu
er	bestell**te**	studier**te**	lern**te**	mach**te** zu
wir	bestell**ten**	studier**ten**	lern**ten**	mach**ten** zu
ihr	bestell**tet**	studier**tet**	lern**tet**	mach**tet** zu
sie	bestell**ten**	studier**ten**	lern**ten**	mach**ten** zu

In the past tense the first person singular (**ich**) and the third person singular (**er**) will always have the same ending. And the rules for using separable and inseparable prefixes apply in the past tense just as they do in the present tense.

Written Practice 3

Conjugate the following verbs in the past tense.

	fragen	**gehören**	**vorstellen**
ich	______________	______________	______________
du	______________	______________	______________
er	______________	______________	______________
wir	______________	______________	______________
ihr	______________	______________	______________
sie	______________	______________	______________
wer	______________	______________	______________

Oral Practice

 Track 54

Practice saying the following list of sentences out loud.

Wo lerntest du Deutsch?	*Where did you learn German?*
Ich lernte in Berlin Deutsch.	*I learned German in Berlin.*
Wohntest du in Berlin?	*Did you live in Berlin?*
Ja, ich wohnte zwei Jahre in Berlin.	*Yes, I lived in Berlin for two years.*
Studiertest du in Berlin?	*Did you study in Berlin?*
Nein, ich studierte an der Universität in Hamburg.	*No, I studied at the university in Hamburg.*
Wo spieltet ihr Tennis?	*Where did you play tennis?*
Wir spielten Tennis im Park.	*We played tennis in the park.*
Wo hörtet ihr Radio?	*Where did you listen to the radio?*
Wir hörten Radio im Wohnzimmer.	*We listened to the radio in the living room.*
Wen fragtest du?	*Whom did you ask?*
Ich fragte den Chef.	*I asked the boss.*
Warum verkauftest du diese Kleider?	*Why did you sell these clothes?*
Ich verkaufte die Kleider, denn sie sind alt.	*I sold the clothes, because they are old.*

Wo arbeiteten Sie?	*Where did you work?*
Ich arbeitete in der Stadt.	*I worked in the city.*

Remember that a verb stem that ends in **-d** or **-t** will add an extra **-e-** before the conjugational endings, as illustrated by **Ich arbeitete** in the previous sentence.

Irregular Past Tense

Some English verbs do not form the past tense with the suffix *-ed*. These verbs are irregular and form the past tense by means of a vowel change. For example, in the case of the verb *to go*, a completely new verb is formed—*went*. Some examples of these English verbs are:

Infinitive	Past Tense
to go	went
to speak	spoke
to stand	stood
to write	wrote

German does the same thing. The irregular past tense is formed by a vowel change, and the appropriate conjugational endings are added to the verb. Here are some commonly used irregular verbs in the third person singular (**er**) past tense.

Infinitive	Past Tense	Meaning
ausgeben	gab aus	*spent*
bleiben	blieb	*stayed*
einsteigen	stieg ein	*got on (transportation)*
essen	aß	*ate*
fahren	fuhr	*drove*

Infinitive	Past Tense	Meaning
finden	fand	*found*
fliegen	flog	*flew*
gehen	ging	*went*
heißen	hieß	*was called*
kommen	kam	*came*
lesen	las	*read*

schreiben	schrieb	*wrote*
sehen	sah	*saw*
sprechen	sprach	*spoke*
stehlen	stahl	*stole*
tragen	trug	*carried; wore*
verstehen	verstand	*understood*

See Appendix A for a complete list of irregular verbs.

When conjugated with the various persons, irregular verbs add the endings **-**, **-st**, **-**, **-en**, **-t**, and **-en** to the stem of the irregular past tense. Notice that the **ich** and **er** forms have no endings added.

	verstehen ***(understood)***	**gehen** ***(went)***	**ausgeben** ***(spent)***
ich	verstand	ging	gab aus
du	verstandest	gingst	gabst aus
er	verstand	ging	gab aus
wir	verstanden	gingen	gaben aus
ihr	verstandet	gingt	gabt aus
sie	verstanden	gingen	gaben aus

Again, take note of **du verstandest** and **ihr verstandet** in this list to see how the extra **-e-** is added when a verb stem ends in **-d** or **-t**.

Written Practice 4

Conjugate the following irregular verbs in the past tense with the subjects provided.

	fahren	**kommen**	**fliegen**
ich	______________	______________	______________
du	______________	______________	______________

	fahren	**kommen**	**fliegen**
er	______________	______________	______________
wir	______________	______________	______________
ihr	______________	______________	______________
sie	______________	______________	______________
dieser Mann	______________	______________	______________

A few verbs not only make a vowel change but also add the **-te**, **-test**, **-tet**, or **-ten** suffixes in the irregular past tense. For example:

	wissen *(knew)*	**kennen** *(was acquainted)*	**nennen** *(named)*
ich	wusste	kannte	nannte
du	wusstest	kanntest	nanntest
er	wusste	kannte	nannte
wir	wussten	kannten	nannten
ihr	wusstet	kanntet	nanntet
sie	wussten	kannten	nannten

Just as in the present tense, the past tense in English begins most *yes* or *no* questions with a form of *to do*. *Did you understand him? Did you see your Friend?* In German such questions begin with the verb. **Verstandest du ihn? Sahen Sie Ihren Freund?** In questions that begin with an interrogative (**wie lange**, **wo**, and so forth), the verb and subject follow the interrogative word. **Wo wohnten diese Leute?** *Where did these people live?*

Oral Practice

Practice saying the following list of sentences out loud.

Wie lange blieben Sie in der Stadt?	*How long did you stay in the city?*
Ich blieb zwei Tage in der Stadt.	*I stayed in the city for two days.*
Wer blieb zu Hause?	*Who stayed home?*
Seine Kinder blieben zu Hause.	*His children stayed home.*
Was schrieb der Chef?	*What did the boss write?*
Der Chef schrieb drei Briefe.	*The boss wrote three letters.*
Wusstet ihr, wo die Leute wohnten?	*Did you know where the people lived?*
Ja, wir wussten, wo sie wohnten.	*Yes, we knew where they lived.*
Wussten Sie, was Thomas sah?	*Did you know what Thomas saw?*
Nein, wir wussten nicht, was er sah.	*No, we did not know what Thomas saw.*
Kamst du mit dem Flugzeug?	*Did you come by airplane?*
Nein, ich kam mit dem Auto.	*No, I came by car.*
Wohin gingen sie?	*Where did they go?*
Sie gingen zum Bahnhof.	*They went to the train station.*

Sie fuhren mit dem Zug nach Bern.	*They went to Bern by train.*
Kannten Sie diese Leute?	*Did you know these people?*
Ja, ich kannte sie gut.	*Yes, I knew them well.*
Kanntest du unseren Chef?	*Did you know our boss?*
Nein, ich kannte ihn nicht.	*No, I did not know him.*

Three important verbs need to be considered individually because of the extensive role they play in the German language. These verbs are **haben**, **sein**, and **werden**. Each one is irregular in the present tense and likewise irregular in the past tense. Their past tense conjugations follow:

Track 55

	haben *(had)*	**sein** *(was/were)*	**werden** *(became)*
ich	hatte	war	wurde
du	hattest	warst	wurdest
er	hatte	war	wurde
wir	hatten	waren	wurden
ihr	hattet	wart	wurdet
sie	hatten	waren	wurden

Oral Practice

Practice saying the following list of sentences out loud.

Hatten Sie ein Problem?	*Did you have a problem?*
Nein, ich hatte kein Problem.	*No, I did not have a problem.*
Was hatten die Leute?	*What did the people have?*
Die Leute hatten viele Fragen.	*The people had a lot of questions.*
Wo warst du gestern?	*Where were you yesterday?*
Ich war gestern in der Stadt.	*I was in the city yesterday.*
Wer war im Restaurant?	*Who was in the restaurant?*
Mein Chef war im Restaurant.	*My boss was in the restaurant.*
Wann wurde es so kalt?	*When did it become (get) so cold?*
Es wurde gestern so kalt.	*It became (got) so cold yesterday.*
Wer wurde die neue Chefin?	*Who became the new boss?*
Frau Benz wurde die neue Chefin.	*Ms. Benz became the new boss.*

Written Practice 5

Write the past tense of the following regular and irregular verbs in the third person singular (**er**) conjugation.

essen	________________	lesen	________________
sagen	________________	sprechen	________________
bleiben	________________	heißen	________________
haben	________________	gehen	________________
sein	________________	warten	________________
arbeiten	________________	werden	________________
finden	________________	wissen	________________
verstehen	________________	ankommen	________________

Written Practice 6

Rewrite the following sentences putting them in the past tense.

1. Ich komme mit dem Bus.

   ____.

2. Es wird heute sehr kalt.

   ____.

3. Warum esst ihr im Wohnzimmer?

   ____?

4. Meine Tochter studiert an einer Universität in Amerika.

   ____.

5. Wo steigen wir um?

   ____?

6. Die Männer zerstören das alte Haus.

   ____.

7. Wen siehst du im Wohnzimmer?

   ____?

8. Der Chef diskutiert die Probleme.

   ____.

9. Ich bin immer krank.

____.

10. Weißt du, wer die Bücher verkauft?

____?

Accusative Case Prepositions

The accusative case of nouns and pronouns is used not only with direct objects but also when a noun or pronoun is the object of an accusative preposition. The accusative prepositions are as follows:

bis	*until; as far as*	ohne	*without*
durch	*through*	wider	*against* (poetic older form)
für	*for*	um	*around*
gegen	*against*		

Prepositions are not always used in the same way in every language. The definitions of the prepositions illustrated above are only their general meanings. But their translations can differ when used in a specific sense. For example, **um** means *around*. However, when using it to express at what time something occurs, **um** then means *at*.

um die Ecke	*around the corner*	um sechs Uhr	*at six o'clock*

The preposition **bis** is used alone with names of places, words that express time, and adverbs. In other sentences **bis** is combined with another preposition. For example:

Er reiste bis Leipzig.	*He was traveling as far as Leipzig.*
Sie blieb bis Montag hier.	*She stayed here until Monday.*
Ich war bis gestern Abend da.	*I was there until last evening.*

but

Er blieb bis **zu** seinem Tod in Bonn.	*He stayed in Bonn until his death.*
Sie gingen bis **zum** Rathaus.	*They went as far as city hall.*

Oral Practice

Practice saying the following list of sentences out loud.

Was hatte Onkel Peter?	*What did Uncle Peter have?*
Er hatte ein Geschenk für seinen Sohn.	*He had a gift for his son.*
Er hatte ein Geschenk für ihn.	*He had a gift for him.*
Er kaufte ein Geschenk für seine Tochter.	*He bought a gift for his daughter.*
Er kaufte ein Geschenk für sie.	*He bought a gift for her.*
Gegen wen sprach der Chef?	*Whom did the boss speak against?*
Er sprach gegen diese Leute.	*He spoke against these people.*
Er sprach gegen sie.	*He spoke against them.*
Er sprach auch gegen mich.	*He also spoke against me.*
Wir fuhren durch einen Tunnel.	*We drove through a tunnel.*
Wir fuhren bis Heidelberg.	*We drove as far as Heidelberg.*
Kamen Sie ohne Ihre Kinder?	*Did you come without your children?*
Ja, ich kam ohne sie.	*Yes, I came without them.*
Die Kunsthalle ist um die Ecke.	*The art museum is around the corner.*

Written Practice 7

Rewrite each section with the words in parentheses.

1. Ich fand eine neue Lampe für ______.

(du) ______________________________.

(mein Freund) ______________________________.

(sie *s.*) ______________________________.

(Ihr Chef) ______________________________.

2. Diese Frau hatte nichts gegen ______. (**nichts** = *nothing*)

(ich) ______________________________.

(wir) ______________________________.

(Ihre Chefin) ______________________________.

(Sie) ______________________________.

3. Robert kam ohne ______.

(das Geld) ______.

(er) ______.

(sie *pl.*) ______.

(sein Vater) ______.

4. Er ging ohne ______ zum Park.

(sein Freund) ______.

(du) ______.

(wir) ______.

(ihr Onkel) ______.

(ihr) ______.

(seine Kinder) ______.

5. Die Amerikaner fuhren bis ______.

(Hamburg) ______.

(München) ______.

(Polen) ______.

(gestern Abend) ______.

(elf Uhr) ______.

Plurals

English plurals are, for the most part, quite simple to form. Most end in *-s*. German has a few plurals that end in **-s** as well. But these are foreign words such as: **die Parks**, **die Hotels**, **die Autos**. The majority of German nouns form their plurals in a variety of patterns. Let's look at some of these patterns.

Masculine Nouns

If a noun ends in **-er**, **-en**, or **-el**, it will not have an added ending but may add an umlaut to a vowel in the word.

der Lehrer	becomes	die Lehrer	*teachers*
der Wagen	becomes	die Wagen	*cars*
der Mantel	becomes	die Mäntel	*coats*

Many other masculine nouns form the plural with an **-e** or **umlaut + -e**.

der Brief	becomes	die Briefe	*letters*
der Bleistift	becomes	die Bleistifte	*pencils*
der Bahnhof	becomes	die Bahnhöfe	*train stations*

Feminine Nouns

Most feminine nouns end in **-(e)n** in their plural forms.

die Stunde	becomes	die Stunden	*hours*
die Frau	becomes	die Frauen	*women*

Feminine nouns formed with the suffix **-in** add **-nen** in the plural.

die Studentin	becomes	die Studentinnen	*students*
die Chefin	becomes	die Chefinnen	*bosses*

Neuter Nouns

If a noun ends in a suffix that forms a diminutive (**-chen** or **-lein**), no ending is added to form the plural.

das Mädchen	becomes	die Mädchen	*girls*
das Röslein	becomes	die Röslein	*little roses*

Many nouns with one syllable form the plural by adding **-er** or **umlaut + -er**.

das Haus	becomes	die Häuser	*houses*
das Kind	becomes	die Kinder	*children*
das Land	becomes	die Länder	*countries*

These rules are generalizations about the formation of plurals. Many nouns break the rules. Some masculine nouns use an **-en** or **-er** ending to form the plural.

der Student	becomes	die Studenten	*students*
der Mann	becomes	die Männer	*men*

Some feminine nouns add an **umlaut** but no suffix to form the plural.

die Mutter	becomes	die Mütter	*mothers*
die Tochter	becomes	die Töchter	*daughters*

Some neuter nouns add the suffix **-e** to form the plural.

das Gedicht	becomes	die Gedichte	*poems*
das Element	becomes	die Elemente	*elements*

The only true way to be certain of the plural formation of a noun is to check it in a dictionary. In time and with experience, you will come to use plurals automatically, just as you know in English that *children* is the plural of *child* or that *geese* is the plural of *goose*.

Written Practice 8

Form the plurals of the following nouns. Write each one with the definite article.

1. das Buch ________________
2. der Arm ________________
3. der Vater ________________
4. die Schwester ________________
5. der Boden ________________
6. das Rathaus ________________
7. der Himmel ________________
8. die Ärztin ________________
9. das Kleid ________________
10. die Tante ________________
11. der Bruder ________________
12. das Heft ________________
13. die Zeitung ________________
14. der Tisch ________________
15. der Teppich ________________
16. die Lampe ________________

Oral Practice

Practice saying the following list of sentences out loud.

Hattest du nur eine Lampe?	*Did you only have one lamp?*
Nein, ich hatte viele Lampen.	*No, I had a lot of lamps.*
Hatten Sie nur einen Wagen?	*Did you only have one car?*
Nein, ich hatte zwei Wagen.	*No, I had two cars.*
Hattet ihr nur einen Bruder?	*Did you only have one brother?*
Nein, wir hatten vier Brüder.	*No, we had four brothers.*
Wie viele Schwestern hattest du?	*How many sisters did you have?*
Ich hatte nur eine Schwester.	*I only had one sister.*
Wie viele Bücher hatte Erik?	*How many books did Erik have?*
Er hatte nur ein Buch.	*He only had one book.*
Wie viele Fahrkarten hatte Tina?	*How many tickets did Tina have?*
Sie hatte nur eine Fahrkarte.	*She only had one ticket.*
Wie viele Briefe hattet ihr?	*How many letters did you have?*
Wir hatten nur einen Brief.	*We only had one letter.*

QUIZ

Answer each question with the possessive adjective in parentheses. For example:

Wessen Haus ist das? (mein) Das ist mein Haus.

1. **Wessen Schlüssel haben Sie? (sein)** ____________________
2. **Wessen Buch las Erik? (mein)** ____________________
3. **Wessen Eltern besuchte Werner? (unser)** ____________________

Rewrite each sentence below, replacing the possessive adjective in bold print with the ones provided in parentheses.

4. **Frau Keller verliert ihren Hut.**
   (mein) ____________________
   (dein) ____________________

5. **Ich besuchte meinen Onkel.**

 (sein) ______________________________

 (unser) ______________________________

6. **Write the past tense conjugations for the following verbs, using the subjects provided.**

	sein	ausgeben	haben
ich	________	________	________
du	________	________	________
er	________	________	________
wir	________	________	________
ihr	________	________	________
sie (*pl.*)	________	________	________
die Leute	________	________	________

Change the following present tense questions into the past tense.

7. **Verkauft er seinen Wagen?**

 ____

 Verstehen Sie, was er sagt?

 ____

Rewrite the sentences below, filling in the blank with the words in parentheses. Make any necessary changes to pronouns or word endings.

8. **Frau Schneider hatte einen Brief für ________.**

 (ich) ______________________________

 (er) ______________________________

 (mein Onkel) ______________________________

 Der Mann sprach gegen ________.

 (Ihr Sohn) ______________________________

 (sie *s.*) ______________________________

 (wir) ______________________________

Circle the letter of the word or phrase that best completes each sentence.

9. Martin kam _______________ das Geld.

A. zum
B. wartete
C. ohne
D. immer

10. Wir _______________ unseren Sohn Hans.

A. nannten
B. lasen
C. verkauften
D. sprachen

chapter 10

Time and Calendar

In this chapter you will learn about the conjugations of certain irregular verbs in the present and past tenses. The dative case will be introduced as well as more of the cardinal numbers. The concept of telling time in German will also be included.

CHAPTER OBJECTIVES

In this chapter you will learn about:

- More Irregular Verbs in the Present and Past Tenses
- Dative Case
- Dative Pronouns
- More About Word Order
- Cardinal Numbers Twenty and Above
- More About Telling Time
- Ordinal Numbers
- Days and Months
- Sports and Hobbies

More Irregular Verbs in the Present and Past Tenses

There are several other important verbs that are irregular. They have a high-frequency use in German and should be identified early. Some of these irregular verbs have a vowel change and add the suffixes **-te**, **-test**, **-ten**, and **-tet**. Look at the examples below (note only the third person singular conjugation is shown here).

Present and Past Tense

Infinitive		Present Tense		Past Tense	
bringen	*to bring*	bringt	*brings*	brachte	*brought*
denken	*to think*	denkt	*thinks*	dachte	*thought*
rennen	*to run*	rennt	*runs*	rannte	*ran*
senden	*to send*	sendet	*sends*	sandte	*sent*

Other irregular verbs are:

Infinitive		Present Tense		Past Tense	
anfangen	*to begin*	fängt an	*begins*	fing an	*began*
anrufen	*to telephone*	ruft an	*telephones*	rief an	*telephoned*
brechen	*to break*	bricht	*breaks*	brach	*broke*
fallen	*to fall*	fällt	*falls*	fiel	*fell*
fressen*	*to eat*	frisst	*eats*	fraß	*ate*
geben	*to give*	gibt	*gives*	gab	*gave*
helfen	*to help*	hilft	*helps*	half	*helped*
laufen	*to run*	läuft	*runs*	lief	*ran*
liegen	*to lay*	liegt	*lies*	lag	*lay*
nehmen	*to take*	nimmt	*takes*	nahm	*took*
schneiden	*to cut*	schneidet	*cuts*	schnitt	*cut*
stehen	*to stand*	steht	*stands*	stand	*stood*
tun	*to do*	tut	*does*	tat	*did*
vergessen	*to forget*	vergisst	*forgets*	vergaß	*forgot*

* This verb is used with animals only.

Oral Practice

Practice saying the following list of sentences out loud.

Der Metzger brachte das Fleisch.	*The butcher brought the meat.*
Der Hund fraß das Fleisch.	*The dog ate the meat.*
Der Ausländer nahm das Fleisch.	*The foreigner took the meat.*
Niemand schnitt das Fleisch.	*No one cut the meat.*
Er dachte an Frau Keller.	*He thought about Ms. Keller.*
Sie rief Frau Keller an.	*She telephoned Ms. Keller.*
Ich sandte Frau Keller ein Geschenk.	*I sent Ms. Keller a gift.*
Wer gab Frau Keller ein Geschenk?	*Who gave Ms. Keller a gift?*
Niemand half Frau Keller.	*No one helped Ms. Keller.*
Niemand vergaß Frau Keller.	*No one forgot Ms. Keller.*
Der Metzger rennt wieder zur Polizei.	*The butcher is running to the police again.*
Wann fängt der Film an?	*When does the movie start?*
Meine Kusine brach sich den linken Arm.	*My cousin broke her left arm.*
Oma fiel auf den rechten Arm.	*Granny fell on her right arm.*
Der Hund liegt unter dem Tisch.	*The dog is lying under the table.*
Was tust du? Warum stehst du hinter der Tür?	*What are you doing? Why are you standing behind the door?*
Ich tue nichts.	*I am not doing anything.*

Written Practice 1

Conjugate the following verbs in the present tense with the pronouns provided.

	denken	**anfangen**	**helfen**
ich	______________	______________	______________
du	______________	______________	______________
er	______________	______________	______________

	brechen	**fallen**	**vergessen**
du	______________	______________	______________
er	______________	______________	______________
wir	______________	______________	______________

Conjugate the following verbs in the past tense with the pronouns provided.

	fallen	bringen	stehen
ich	______	______	______
er	______	______	______
wir	______	______	______

	rennen	anrufen	schneiden
ich	______	______	______
du	______	______	______
ihr	______	______	______

Dative Case

You have already encountered the nominative case, which identifies the subject of a sentence, and the accusative case, which identifies the direct object of a sentence and which is used following accusative prepositions. The dative case identifies the indirect object of a sentence.

When you ask *to whom* or *for whom* with the subject and verb of a sentence, you can identify the indirect object. For example:

I gave Karl a gift. (*To whom* did I give a gift?) The indirect object is *Karl*.
I bought Tina a flower. (*For whom* did I buy a flower?) The indirect object is *Tina*.

The indirect object in a German sentence will be in the dative case. In the accusative case, only masculine nouns make a declensional change. In the dative case, all nouns make a declensional change. Let's compare the nominative, accusative, and dative cases of the three genders and the plural forms.

	Masculine	Feminine	Neuter	Plural
nom	der Mann	die Frau	das Kind	die Kinder
acc	den Mann	die Frau	das Kind	die Kinder
dat	dem Mann	der Frau	dem Kind	den Kindern

Any determiner (**der**, **mein**, **kein**, **dieser**, etc.) used in the dative case will have the same dative endings illustrated above, for example: **einem Mann**, **diesem Mann**, **keinem Mann**; **dieser Frau**, **meiner Frau**, **Ihrer Frau**; **einem Kind**, **deinem Kind**, **unserem Kind**; **diesen Kindern**, **seinen Kindern**, **keinen Kindern**.

Take note that a dative plural noun that does not have an **-n** ending will add that ending: **Kinder*n***. In sentences, the dative case looks like this:

Ich gab **dem Mann** ein Geschenk.	*I gave **the man** a gift.*
Ich kaufte **meiner Frau** eine Blume.	*I bought **my wife** a flower.*

Written Practice 2

Rewrite the nouns provided on the left in the dative case with **ihr**, **mein**, and **dies-**. For example:

der Mann	ihrem Mann	meinem Mann	diesem Mann
der Metzger	________	________	________
die Wohnung	________	________	________
das Land	________	________	________
die Bücher	________	________	________
die Uhr	________	________	________

Oral Practice

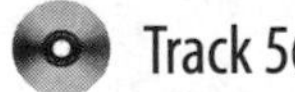

Practice saying the following list of sentences out loud.

Was gibst du dem Ausländer?	*What are you giving the foreigner?*
Ich gebe dem Ausländer eine Fahrkarte.	*I give the foreigner a ticket.*
Was gaben Sie Ihrer Tante?	*What did you give your aunt?*
Ich gab meiner Tante eine Rose.	*I gave my aunt a rose.*
Was kauftet ihr den Männern?	*What did you buy the men?*
Wir kauften den Männern Bier.	*We bought the men beer.*
Wir senden unserem Freund einen Brief.	*We send our friend a letter.*
Wir sandten deiner Tochter ein Paket.	*We sent your daughter a package.*
Wer sandte den Studenten neue Bücher?	*Who sent the students new books?*

Dative Pronouns

German pronouns also have a dative case formation.

Nominative Case	**Dative Case**
ich	mir
du	dir
er	ihm
sie (*s.*)	ihr
es	ihm
wir	uns
ihr	euch
sie (*pl.*)	ihnen
Sie	Ihnen
wer	wem

Use the dative pronouns when the pronouns are indirect objects in a sentence. For example:

Ich gebe **dir** eine Blume.	*I give **you** a flower.*
Ich kaufe **ihr** eine Tasse Tee.	*I buy **her** a cup of tea.*

Oral Practice

Practice saying the following list of sentences out loud.

Wem geben Sie die Bücher?	*To whom are you giving the books?*
Ich gebe ihm die Bücher.	*I give him the books.*
Was bringst du deiner Lehrerin?	*What are you bringing for your teacher?*
Ich bringe ihr ein Geschenk.	*I bring her a gift.*
Wem schreiben Sie diesen Brief?	*To whom are you writing this letter?*
Ich schreibe Ihnen diesen Brief.	*I am writing this letter to you.*
Er sandte mir eine Postkarte.	*He sent me a postcard.*
Er sandte dir eine Ansichtskarte.	*He sent you a picture postcard.*
Er sandte uns ein Telegramm.	*He sent us a telegram.*
Er sandte euch ein Geschenk.	*He sent you a gift.*
Er sandte ihnen vier Briefe.	*He sent them four letters.*

Written Practice 3

Rewrite the sentences below, filling in the blanks with the words in parentheses. Make the appropriate declensional changes.

1. Der Metzger gab ______ ein Geschenk.
   (ich) ______________________________.
   (du) ______________________________.
   (sie *pl.*) ______________________________.
   (mein Sohn) ______________________________.
   (meine Söhne) ______________________________.
   (die Ausländerin) ______________________________.
2. Wer schreibt ______ einen Brief?
   (sie *s.*) ______________________________?
   (wir) ______________________________?
   (Sie) ______________________________?
   (ihr) ______________________________?
   (die Polizei) ______________________________?
   (Ihre Kinder) ______________________________?
3. Was sendet er ______?
   (wir) ______________________________?
   (sie *pl.*) ______________________________?
   (ihr) ______________________________?
   (Sie) ______________________________?
   (ich) ______________________________?

More About Word Order

In German if the indirect object and the direct object of a sentence are both nouns, the indirect object will precede the direct object.

Wir geben dem Lehrer einen Kuli. *We give the teacher a ballpoint pen.*

If the indirect object is a pronoun and the direct object is a noun, the indirect object will precede the direct object.

Wir geben ihm einen Kuli. *We give him a ballpoint pen.*

However, when the direct object is a pronoun, the direct object will precede the indirect object, whether the indirect object is a noun or a pronoun.

Wir geben ihn dem Lehrer. *We give it to the teacher.*
Wir geben ihn ihm. *We give it to him.*

Written Practice 4

Rewrite each sentence twice. In the first sentence, change the indirect object to a pronoun. In the second sentence, change both the indirect object and the direct object to a pronoun. For example:

Sie gab dem Lehrer ein Geschenk.

Sie gab ihm ein Geschenk.

Sie gab es ihm.

1. Robert schrieb seiner Frau einen Brief.

_______________________________.

_______________________________.

2. Ich kaufte meinem Sohn ein Auto.

_______________________________.

_______________________________.

3. Senden Sie Ihren Eltern neue Bücher?

_______________________________?

_______________________________?

4. Gudrun brachte ihrer Freundin ein Heft.

_______________________________.

_______________________________.

5. Wir verkauften den Männern die Kleider.

_______________________________.

_______________________________.

Cardinal Numbers Twenty and Above

In earlier times, the number twenty-four was said as *four and twenty*. (Do you remember the nursery rhyme that begins, "Four and twenty blackbirds baked in a pie . . ."?) That approach to numbers over twenty still exists in German. Let's become familiar with such numbers.

20	zwanzig	21	einundzwanzig
30	dreißig	32	zweiunddreißig
40	vierzig	43	dreiundvierzig
50	fünfzig	54	vierundfünfzig
60	sechzig	65	fünfundsechzig
70	siebzig	76	sechsundsiebzig
80	achtzig	87	siebenundachtzig
90	neunzig	98	achtundneunzig
100	(ein)hundert	900	neunhundert
340	dreihundertvierzig	672	sechshundertzweiundsiebzig
1 000	(ein)tausend	4 000	viertausend
1 000 000	eine Million	3 000 000	drei Millionen
1 000 000 000	eine Milliarde	1 000 000 000 000	eine Billion

German numbers are always written as one word; however, they tend to be shown as numerals and not as words. Notice that the German word **Billion** means *trillion* in U.S. English. **Milliarde** means *billion*.

More About Telling Time

 Track 57

You already know the expression used to tell time on the hour.

Es ist acht Uhr.	*It is eight o'clock.*
Er kommt um neun Uhr.	*He comes at nine o'clock.*

Just as in English, German has a variety of ways to express certain times on the clock. There are three ways of expressing the quarter hour.

3:15 Es ist drei Uhr fünfzehn.
Es ist Viertel nach drei. (**das Viertel** = *quarter*)
Es ist ein Viertel vier.

Notice the third expression, which says that the time is one quarter before the next hour—**vier** (*four*).

On the half hour, you say:

6:30 Es ist sechs Uhr dreißig.
Es ist halb sieben.

Notice the second expression, which says that the time is halfway to the next hour—**sieben** (*seven*).

On the three-quarters of the hour, you say:

9:45 Es ist neun Uhr fünfundvierzig.
Es ist Viertel vor zehn.
Es ist drei Viertel zehn.

Notice the second and third time expressions, which say that the time is on the way to the next hour—**zehn** (*ten*).

Now look at some varied examples of time.

12:05 Es ist zwölf Uhr fünf.
Es ist fünf (Minuten) nach zwölf.
1:10 Es ist ein Uhr zehn.
Es ist zehn (Minuten) nach eins.
2:22 Es ist zwei Uhr zweiundzwanzig.
Es ist zweiundzwanzig (Minuten) nach zwei.
4:35 Es ist vier Uhr fünfunddreißig.
Es ist fünf Minuten nach halb fünf.
10:48 Es ist zehn Uhr achtundvierzig.
Es ist zwölf Minuten vor elf.

German does not use A.M. or P.M. Instead, the twenty-four-hour clock is used. For example:

0.05	null Uhr fünf	*12:05* A.M.
4.15	vier Uhr fünfzehn	*4:15* A.M.
6.30	sechs Uhr dreißig	*6:30* A.M.
13.00	dreizehn Uhr	*1:00* P.M.
15.30	fünfzehn Uhr dreißig	*3:30* P.M.
24.00	vierundzwanzig Uhr	*12:00 midnight*

German uses a period to separate the hour from the minutes: *2.30 two-thirty*.

Written Practice 5

Complete the phrases that express the times shown on the left.

1. (6.30) Es ist ____________________ sieben.
2. (9.35) Es ist neun Uhr ____________________.
3. (12.55) Es ist fünf Minuten vor ____________________.
4. (2.15) Es ist ____________________ nach zwei.
5. (11.30) Es ist halb ____________________.
6. (4.45) Es ist vier Uhr ____________________.
7. (3.55) Es ist fünf
   Minuten ____________________ ____________________.

Ordinal Numbers

Ordinal numbers are those that can be used as adjectives. In English most ordinal numbers end in *-th*: *eighth, sixteenth, hundredth,* and so forth. In German the numbers through nineteen end in **-te**. From twenty and above, they end in **-ste**. For example:

5th	fünfte	*fifth*	20th	zwanzigste	*twentieth*
10th	zehnte	*tenth*	31st	einunddreißigste	*thirty-first*
14th	vierzehnte	*fourteenth*	99th	neunundneunzigste	*ninety-ninth*

Just like English, German has a few irregular ordinals. They are:

1st	erste	*first*
3rd	dritte	*third*
7th	siebte	*seventh*

In sentences German ordinals look like this:

Das erste Gedicht heißt *Rote Rosen.*	*The first poem is called* Red Roses.
Unser dritter Sohn ist in Mannheim.	*Our third son is in Mannheim.*
Sie ist am Dreiundzwanzigsten geboren.	*She was born on the twenty-third.*

When the ordinals are used to express dates, they follow **am** (the contraction of **an** + **dem** = **am**): **am vierten Mai** (*on the fourth of May*).

Days and Months

Let's look at the days of the week and the months of the year in German. Notice how much they resemble their English equivalents. First, **Wochentage** (*days of the week*):

Sonntag	*Sunday*	Donnerstag	*Thursday*
Montag	*Monday*	Freitag	*Friday*
Dienstag	*Tuesday*	Samstag	*Saturday*
Mittwoch	*Wednesday*	(*or*) Sonnabend	*Saturday*

Now, **Monate** (*months*):

Januar	*January*	Juli	*July*
Februar	*February*	August	*August*
März	*March*	September	*September*
April	*April*	Oktober	*October*
Mai	*May*	November	*November*
Juni	*June*	Dezember	*December*

All days of the week and months of the year are masculine: **der Montag**, **der Oktober**.

Use **am** (**an** + **dem**) to say *on* a day of the week: **am Freitag** (*on Friday*). Use **im** (**in** + **dem**) to say *in* a month of the year.

Robert kommt am Sonntag.	*Robert is coming on Sunday.*
Sie ist im Juli geboren.	*She was born in July.*

Oral Practice

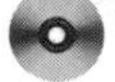 Track 58

Practice saying the following list of sentences out loud.

Wann kommt dein Cousin zu Besuch?	*When is your cousin coming for a visit?*
Er kommt am Dienstag zu Besuch.	*He is coming on Tuesday for a visit.*

Wann seid ihr wieder in Mannheim?	*When are you in Mannheim again?*
Wir sind am Mittwoch wieder in Mannheim.	*We are back in Mannheim again on Wednesday.*
Wann ist das Kind geboren?	*When was the child born?*
Das Kind ist im Februar geboren.	*The child was born in February.*
Wann sind die Zwillinge geboren?	*When were the twins born?*
Die Zwillinge sind im Juni geboren.	*The twins were born in June.*
Wann bist du geboren?	*When were you born?*
Ich bin im Dezember geboren.	*I was born in December.*
Ich bin am elften Mai geboren.	*I was born on the eleventh of May.*
Sie ist am ersten September geboren.	*She was born on the first of September.*
Sie sind am dritten Oktober geboren.	*They were born on the third of October.*
Wer ist am Achtundzwanzigsten geboren?	*Who was born on the twenty-eighth?*
Unsere Tochter ist am Achtundzwanzigsten geboren.	*Our daughter was born on the twenty-eighth.*

Use **im Jahre** to express in what year something occurs.

Er ist im Jahre 1992 geboren. (1812 = achtzehnhundertzwölf)	*He was born in 1992.*
Im Jahre 2000 wohnte sie noch in Bonn. (2000 = zweitausend)	*In 2000 she still lived in Bonn.*

Written Practice 6

Rewrite each sentence, filling in the blank with the dates provided in parentheses. Change the cardinal number to the appropriate ordinal number.

1. Er besuchte uns am ______ März.

(1) ____.

(3) ____.

(9) ____.

(15) ____.

(27) ____.

2. Ihr Sohn ist am ______ Juli geboren.

(30) ____.

(31) ____.

(2) ____.

(7) ____.

(12) ____.

Sports and Hobbies

Germans are very much into fitness. They belong to gyms and athletic leagues and participate in various sports. **Welche Sportart treiben Sie?** (*What sport do you participate in?*) is what is said to ask what sport someone is pursuing. You can answer with: **Ich spiele…** (*I play* . . .) and name the sport.

Oral Practice

Practice saying the following list of sentences out loud.

Welche Sportart treiben Sie?	*What sport do you participate in?*
Ich spiele Fußball.	*I play soccer.*
Welche Sportart treibst du, Monika?	*What sport do you participate in, Monica?*
Ich spiele Basketball.	*I play basketball.*
Welche Sportart treibt ihr?	*What sport do you participate in?*
Wir spielen Eishockey.	*We play hockey.*
Wir spielen Golf.	*We play golf.*
Wir spielen Handball.	*We play handball.*
Wir spielen Tischtennis.	*We play table tennis.*
Was macht ihr gern?	*What do you like to do?*
Wir spielen gern Schach.	*We like to play chess.*
Was machst du gern, Thomas?	*What do you like to do, Thomas?*
Ich schwimme gern.	*I like swimming.*
Was machen Sie gern, Herr Benz?	*What do you like to do, Mr. Benz?*
Ich fahre gern Rad.	*I like biking.*

Ich laufe gern Ski.	*I like skiing.*
Ich lese gern.	*I like reading.*
Ich wandere gern.	*I like hiking.*
Ich sammele Briefmarken.	*I collect stamps.*
Mein Hobby ist Basteln.	*My hobby is doing handicrafts.*

Use the word **gern** after a verb to say what you *like* doing.

Ich spiele gern Tennis.	*I like playing tennis.*
Wir tanzen gern.	*We like dancing.*

Written Practice 7

Using the phrases in parentheses, write sentences that tell what you like to do. For example:

(Briefe schreiben) Ich schreibe gern Briefe.

1. (Schach spielen) ______________________.
2. (wandern) ______________________.
3. (schimmen) ______________________.
4. (Golf spielen) ______________________.
5. (Rad fahren) ______________________.
6. (Ski laufen) ______________________.
7. (lesen) ______________________.

QUIZ

1. **Write the present tense conjugation of the following verbs with the pronouns provided.**

	essen	sehen	laufen
ich	________	________	________
du	________	________	________
er	________	________	________

Write the past tense conjugation of the following verbs with the pronouns provided.

	bringen	anrufen	vergessen
ich	________	________	________
du	________	________	________
er	________	________	________

2. **Rewrite each noun in the dative case using kein, unser, and dies-.**

	unser	sein	dies-
das Rad	________	________	________
der Brief	________	________	________
die Postkarte	________	________	________
die Kinder	________	________	________

3. **Rewrite the following sentence, using the dative case for the pronouns provided in parentheses.**

   Der Lehrer gab ________ einen Kuli.

   (ich) ________________________________

   (du) ________________________________

   (er) ________________________________

   (sie *s.*) ________________________________

   (Sie) ________________________________

4. Rewrite each sentence twice. In the first sentence, change the indirect object to a pronoun. In the second sentence, change both the indirect object and the direct object to pronouns. For example:

Sie gab dem Lehrer ein Geschenk.

Sie gab ihm ein Geschenk.

Sie gab es ihm.

Sie brachte der Frau die Kleider.

____

____

Ich kaufte den Kindern einen neuen Ball.

____

____

Write out the following times in sentences. For example:

3:00 *Es ist drei Uhr.*

5. 10:30 ____________________________________

6. 4:45 ____________________________________

7. 8:15 ____________________________________

8. Rewrite the following sentence, filling in the blank with the date as provided by the numbers in parentheses.

Mein Sohn ist am ____________ März geboren.

(1) ____________________________________

(3) ____________________________________

(16) ____________________________________

(22) ____________________________________

(30) ____________________________________

Circle the word or phrase that best completes each sentence.

9. **Onkel Karl kommt am ________________.**

   A. neunzehn
   B. sieben Uhr
   C. Freitag
   D. Schach spielen

10. **Das Konzert fängt um ________________ Uhr an.**

   A. zweite
   B. im Jahre 2011
   C. Oktober
   D. vier

Still Struggling

The variety of irregular verbs in German can seem a bit overwhelming. But don't forget to use Appendix A: Principal Parts of Irregular Verbs at the end of this book to help you conquer irregularities.

PART TWO TEST

Write the present tense forms of the following verbs with the pronouns provided.

1. **werden**

   ich ______________________________

   du ______________________________

   er ______________________________

   wir ______________________________

2. **sehen**

   ich ______________________________

   du ______________________________

   er ______________________________

   ihr ______________________________

3. **fahren**

   ich ______________________________

   du ______________________________

   er ______________________________

   Sie ______________________________

4. **mitgehen**

   ich ______________________________

   du ______________________________

   er ______________________________

   wir ______________________________

Write the present and past tense conjugations of the following verbs with the pronouns provided.

5. **besuchen**

   ich ______________ ______________

   du ______________ ______________

   er ______________ ______________

   ihr ______________ ______________

6. **helfen**

ich ______________ ______________

du ______________ ______________

er ______________ ______________

Sie ______________ ______________

7. **sein**

ich ______________ ______________

du ______________ ______________

er ______________ ______________

wir ______________ ______________

8. **haben**

ich ______________ ______________

du ______________ ______________

er ______________ ______________

ihr ______________ ______________

Use the words or phrases in bold print as signals for the kind of question you should form from each sentence. Rewrite each sentence as a question, changing the word or phrase in bold print to **wer**, **wen**, **wem**, or **was**. For example:

Martin kauft **ein Heft.**

Was kauft Martin?

9. **Meine Schwester gab mir einen Bleistift.**

____

10. **Die Kinder lesen ein Buch.**

____

11. **Herr Benz besucht seinen Onkel in Hamburg.**

____

12. **Karin** ist im Park.

____

Use the words or phrases in bold print as signals for the kind of question you should form from each sentence. Change the word or phrase in bold print to **wann**, **wo**, or **wohin**.

13. Tina fuhr mit dem Zug **nach Frankreich**.

____

14. Das Konzert fängt **um sechs Uhr** an.

____

15. Die Jungen sind **im Wohnzimmer**.

____

16. Fill in the blanks with the appropriate verb: **gehen** or **fahren**, or **wissen** or **kennen**. Conjugate the verb appropriately in the present tense.

    Ich ______________ den Mann nicht. Wie heißt er?

    Die Kinder ______________ zu Fuß.

    Er ______________ nicht, wo das Restaurant ist.

    Meine Eltern ______________ mit dem Bus nach Berlin.

17. Complete each sentence with the correct form of the direct objects provided in parentheses.

    Ich kaufe ______________________________________.

    (ein Hut) ______________________________________

    (diese Bluse) ______________________________________

    Wir besuchten ______________________________________.

    (dein Lehrer) ______________________________________

    (er) ______________________________________

18. Provide the accusative case and dative case forms of each word or phrase.

	Accusative Case	Dative Case
meine Mutter	__________	__________
dein Auto	__________	__________
der Zahnarzt	__________	__________
das Mädchen	__________	__________
Sie	__________	__________

19. Rewrite the following sentences, changing them from the present tense to the past tense.

Wer macht das Fenster auf?

____

Verstehen Sie, was ich frage?

____

Complete the given sentence with the correct form of the pronouns provided.

20. Warum geben sie __________ das Geld?

(ich) ____

(du) ____

(er) ____

(sie *s.*) ____

(wir) ____

(ihr) ____

(sie *pl.*) ____

Rewrite the following sentence twice. In the first sentence, change the indirect object to a pronoun. In the second sentence, change both the indirect object and direct object to a pronoun. For example:

Sie gab dem Lehrer ein Geschenk.

Sie gab ihm ein Geschenk.

Sie gab es ihm.

21. Die Lehrerin sandte meinen Eltern einen Brief.

____

____

Circle the letter of the word or phrase that best completes each sentence.

22. Mein Sohn ist am ____________ Mai geboren.

A. heute C. vierten
C. dreizehn D. jung

23. ____________ fährst du mit dem Zug?

A. Wer C. Wohin
B. Gestern D. Mit dem Bus

24. Der ____________ Mantel ist neu.

A. braune C. schwarz
B. alte D. groß

25. Es ____________ sehr kalt.

A. waren C. sind
B. Wetter D. wurde

Part Three

Lots More About Verbs

chapter 11

More Talking About the Past

In this chapter the present perfect tense will be introduced. In addition, the formation and use of present participles will be discussed as well as the use of dative verbs and prepositions. Some important vocabulary about geography will also be included.

CHAPTER OBJECTIVES

In this chapter you will learn about:

- Present Perfect Tense
- Present Participles
- Verbs That Take the Dative
- Prepositions That Take the Dative
- Geography

Present Perfect Tense

So far in this book, you have learned the formation of the German simple past tense. That tense is used primarily in written language. In spoken language, events in the past are expressed, for the most part, in the present perfect tense.

The English present perfect tense consists of the conjugation of *to have* plus a past participle: *I have listened, they have spoken,* and so on. The German present perfect tense is formed similarly.

The verb **haben** is conjugated in the present tense and is accompanied by a past participle. Participles of regular verbs have the following structure: **ge-** + **verb stem** + **t**. For example:

fragen:
ge + frag + t = **gefragt** er hat gefragt *he has asked*

machen:
ge + mach + t = **gemacht** er hat gemacht *he has made*

If the infinitive has a separable prefix, that prefix will precede the **ge-** prefix of the participle. For example:

zumachen:
zu + ge + mach + t = **zugemacht** er hat zugemacht *he has closed*

And if the infinitive has an inseparable prefix, that prefix replaces the **ge-** prefix of the participle. For example:

besuchen:
be + such + t = **besucht** er hat besucht *he has visited*

erwarten:
er + wart + et = **erwartet** er hat erwartet *he has expected*

If the stem of the verb ends in **-d** or **-t**, add an **-e-** before the final **-t**, as in **erwartet**.

Verbs that end with **-ieren** never have a **ge-** prefix added to the participle. For example:

studieren	er hat studiert	*he has studied*
diskutieren	er hat diskutiert	*he has discussed*

Written Practice 1

Conjugate the following regular verbs in the present perfect tense with the pronouns provided.

	lachen	**versuchen**	**vorstellen**
ich	____________	____________	____________
du	____________	____________	____________
er	____________	____________	____________
wir	____________	____________	____________
ihr	____________	____________	____________
sie	____________	____________	____________

Irregular Past Participles

German has a long list of irregular past participles. If an irregular verb has no prefix, the participle will begin with the prefix **ge-** and most often end in **-en**. If the verb has a separable prefix, that prefix will precede the **ge-** prefix of the participle. And if the verb has an inseparable prefix, that prefix replaces the **ge-** prefix of the participle. Let's look at some examples of irregular past participles.

Verbs Without a Prefix

essen	gegessen	er hat gegessen	*he has eaten*
finden	gefunden	er hat gefunden	*he has found*
geben	gegeben	er hat gegeben	*he has given*
lesen	gelesen	er hat gelesen	*he has read*
schreiben	geschrieben	er hat geschrieben	*he has written*
sehen	gesehen	er hat gesehen	*he has seen*
singen	gesungen	er hat gesungen	*he has sung*
sprechen	gesprochen	er hat gesprochen	*he has spoken*
stehlen	gestohlen	er hat gestohlen	*he has stolen*
trinken	getrunken	er hat getrunken	*he has drunk*

Notice that **essen** requires a **g** after the **ge-** prefix of the participle.

Verbs with a Separable Prefix

ansehen	*to look at*	angesehen	er hat angesehen	*he has looked at*
ausgeben	*to spend*	ausgegeben	er hat ausgegeben	*he has spent*
aussprechen	*to pronounce*	ausgesprochen	er hat ausgesprochen	*he has pronounced*
mitnehmen	*to take along*	mitgenommen	er hat mitgenommen	*he has taken along*

Verbs with an Inseparable Prefix

besitzen	*to possess*	besessen	er hat besessen	*he has possessed*
erhalten	*to receive*	erhalten	er hat erhalten	*he has received*
versprechen	*to promise*	versprochen	er hat versprochen	*he has promised*
verstehen	*to understand*	verstanden	er hat verstanden	*he has understood*

Irregular Participles Ending in *-t*

absenden	*to dispatch*	abgesandt	er hat abgesandt	*he has dispatched*
erkennen	*to recognize*	erkannt	er hat erkannt	*he has recognized*
kennen	*to be acquainted*	gekannt	er hat gekannt	*he has been acquainted*
nennen	*to name*	genannt	er hat genannt	*he has named*
senden	*to send*	gesandt	er hat gesandt	*he has sent*
wissen	*to know*	gewusst	er hat gewusst	*he has known*

Be aware that you will encounter verbs whose participles will look like their infinitives. For example:

Infinitive		**Participle**	
erhalten	*to obtain*	hat erhalten	*has obtained*
bekommen	*to receive*	hat bekommen	*has received*

Written Practice 2

Conjugate the following irregular verbs in the present perfect tense with the pronouns provided.

	sprechen	**versprechen**	**aussprechen**
ich	________	________	________
du	________	________	________
er	________	________	________
wir	________	________	________
ihr	________	________	________
sie	________	________	________

	wissen	**beschreiben (*describe*)**	**aussehen (*look like*)**
ich	________	________	________
du	________	________	________
er	________	________	________

wir ________________ ________________ ________________
ihr ________________ ________________ ________________
sie ________________ ________________ ________________

Although German verbs in the present perfect tense can be translated by the English present perfect tense, the English tendency is to use the simple past tense. For example:

Ich habe ihn besucht.	*I have visited him.* (present perfect)
	I visited him. (simple past)

Therefore, where it sounds appropriate, the English past tense will be used in this book to translate the German present perfect tense.

NOTE ***The verb haben is positioned in a present perfect sentence with the subject just as it would be in any other tense. But the past participle in the present perfect tense is always the last element of a sentence.***

Wir **haben** zwei lange Gedichte **gelernt**.	*We **learned** two long poems.*

Look at that structure in the Oral Practice that follows.

Oral Practice

 Track 59

Practice saying the following list of sentences out loud.

Haben Sie die Musik gehört?	*Did you hear the music?*
Ja, ich habe die schöne Musik gehört.	*Yes, I heard the pretty music.*
Nein, ich habe nichts gehört.	*No, I heard nothing.*
Niemand hat die Musik gehört.	*No one heard the music.*
Hast du seinen Roman gelesen?	*Did you read his novel?*
Ja, ich habe ihn gelesen.	*Yes, I read it.*
Nein, ich habe ihn noch nicht gelesen.	*No, I still have not read it.*
Was hat er gekauft?	*What did he buy?*
Er hat nichts gekauft.	*He did not buy anything.*
Karin hat ihr Fahrrad verkauft.	*Karin sold her bicycle.*

Wie lange habt ihr auf mich gewartet?	*How long have you waited for me?*
Wir haben eine Stunde auf dich gewartet.	*We waited an hour for you.*
Haben Sie noch nicht gegessen?	*Have you not eaten yet?*
Nein, ich habe noch nicht gegessen.	*No, I have not eaten yet.*
Ich bin sehr hungrig. Und ich habe Durst.	*I am very hungry. And I am thirsty.*
Die alte Frau hat krank ausgesehen.	*The old woman looked sick.*
Robert hat meine Tasche gefunden.	*Robert found my purse.*
Die Kinder haben nichts verstanden.	*The children understood nothing.*
Aber er hat langsam gesprochen.	*But he spoke slowly.*

Written Practice 3

Rewrite the following present tense sentences changing them to the present perfect tense. For example:

Er kauft einen Hut. *Er hat einen Hut gekauft.*

1. Was sagst du? ______________________?
2. Wir lernen Deutsch. ______________________.
3. Die Kinder spielen gern im Park. ______________________.
4. Sehen Sie meinen Sohn? ______________________?
5. Wir erhalten drei Briefe von ihnen. ______________________.
6. Robert wohnt in der Hauptstadt. ______________________.
7. Hört ihr die schöne Musik? ______________________?
8. Die Männer zerstören das alte Haus. ______________________.
9. Ich sende euch ein kleines Paket. ______________________.
10. Wer arrangiert die Musik? ______________________?
11. Er verspricht es. ______________________.
12. Was liest du? ______________________?
13. Gudrun nimmt mein Fahrrad. ______________________.
14. Was stiehlt der Dieb? ______________________?
15. Niemand versteht dich. ______________________.

Present Participles

English present participles are used extensively to express an action in progress or an incomplete action.

She was *combing* her hair. They were *sitting* in the dark.

Although German also has present participles, they are not used in conjugations like English present participles. German present participles are used as modifiers.

A present participle is formed quite simply by adding **-d** to an infinitive: **fahren—fahren*d*, singen—singen*d*, schlafen—schlafen*d***. When a present participle modifies a noun, it requires an adjective ending.

das schlafende Kind	*the sleeping child*
der fahrende Sänger	*the traveling (wandering) minstrel*
die singende Frau	*the singing woman*

As illustrated earlier, past participles are used in the structure of the present perfect tense. But, like present participles, they can also be used as modifiers. For example:

ein gebrochener Mensch	*a broken man*
das geschriebene Wort	*the written word*
ein gesuchter Wissenschaftler	*a much sought-after scientist*

Verbs That Take the Dative

German has a concept that does not exist in English: a category of verbs that require an object in the dative case. The translation of a sentence that has a dative verb in it appears in English to have a direct object. But in German, that object is not a direct object. It is a dative object.

Ich glaube **dem Mann** nicht. *I do not believe* ***the man***.

In the English sentence *the man* is a direct object. But **dem Mann** is in the dative case, because **glauben** is a dative verb. Other dative verbs are:

dienen	*to serve*	gehören	*to belong to*
folgen	*to follow*	helfen	*to help*
gefallen	*to please; like*	imponieren	*to impress*

The verbs **gefallen** and **gehören** are used in a special way. In the case of **gefallen**, the verb is used to express liking something. In English the structure is *subject + like + direct object*:

I + like + the book.	My mother + likes + the new car.

But the German structure is different, because the literal sentence is *something is pleasing to someone*.

Das Buch gefällt mir.	(*The book pleases me.*) *I like the book.*
Der neue Wagen gefällt meiner Mutter.	(*The new car pleases my mother.*) *My mother likes the new car.*

The verb **gehören** is also followed by the dative case. Unlike English, the preposition *to* is not needed for the meaning in German.

Das gehört mir.	*The book belongs to me.*
Der neue Wagen gehört meiner Mutter.	*The new car belongs to my mother.*

All dative verbs can be used in all the tenses. For example:

Ich glaube dem Mann nicht.	*I do not believe the man.*
Ich glaubte dem Mann nicht.	*I did not believe the man.*
Ich habe dem Mann nicht geglaubt.	*I did not believe the man.*
Wir helfen unserer Tante.	*We help our aunt.*
Wir halfen unserer Tante.	*We helped our aunt.*
Wir haben unserer Tante geholfen.	*We have helped our aunt.*

Oral Practice

 Track 60

Practice saying the following list of sentences out loud.

Hast du ihm nicht geglaubt?	*Did you not believe him?*
Nein, ich habe ihm niemals geglaubt.	*No, I have never believed him.*
Wem habt ihr geholfen?	*Whom did you help?*
Wir haben unserer Kusine geholfen.	*We helped our cousin.*
Sein Singen hat mir sehr imponiert.	*His singing really impressed me.*

Ihr Tanzen hat uns sehr imponiert.	*Her dancing really impressed us.*
Niemand hat dem König gedient.	*No one served the king.*
Wer dient der Königin?	*Who is serving the queen?*
Der Mann folgt uns.	*The man is following us.*
Nein. Niemand folgt uns.	*No. No one is following us.*
Wie gefällt dir mein Fahrrad?	*How do you like my bike?*
Es gefällt mir gut.	*I like it a lot.*
Gehört Ihnen dieser Roman?	*Does this novel belong to you?*
Nein, er gehört mir nicht.	*No, it does not belong to me.*
Dieser Roman gehört meiner Kusine.	*This novel belongs to my cousin.*

Prepositions That Take the Dative

The dative case is used for indirect objects and follows dative verbs. It is also required for objects of dative prepositions. The dative prepositions are:

aus	*out; from*	nach	*after*
außer	*except*	seit	*since*
gegenüber	*opposite; across from*	von	*from*
mit	*with*	zu	*to*
bei	*by; at* (for example, *living at someone's house*)		

The preposition **gegenüber** follows a pronoun and can follow or precede a noun. If the noun refers to a person, it tends to follow the noun.

Wir sitzen einer schönen Frau gegenüber.	*We sit across from a pretty woman.*
Wir sitzen ihr gegenüber.	*We sit across from her.*
Wir wohnen gegenüber der Bibliothek.	*We live across from the library.*

The other dative prepositions precede both nouns and pronouns. In sentences, the dative prepositions look like this:

Die Mädchen kamen aus dem Theater.	*The girls came out of the theater.*
Niemand hörte es außer meinem Freund.	*No one heard it except my friend.*
Tina hat bei ihrer Tante gewohnt.	*Tina lived at her aunt's house.*
Ich habe mit dem Hund gespielt.	*I played with the dog.*

Nach der Oper gingen wir nach Hause.	*After the opera we went home.*
Seit zwei Stunden wartet er im Flur.	*He has been waiting in the hallway for two hours.*
Ich fahre von Hamburg nach Bremen.	*I drive from Hamburg to Bremen.*
Fährt diese Straßenbahn zum Bahnhof?	*Does this streetcar go to the train station?*

When going home, or to a city, country, or continent, use **nach** to mean *to*.

Wir fahren nach Deutschland.	*We are going to Germany.*
Wir fahren nach Hause.	*We are going home.*

Use **nach** with the dative case to mean *after*.

nach dem Konzert	*after the concert*	nach einer Stunde	*after an hour*

Oral Practice

Practice saying the following list of sentences out loud.

Die Kinder kommen aus der Schule.	*The children are coming out of the school.*
Wer kommt aus der Bibliothek?	*Who is coming out of the library?*
Niemand kommt aus der Bibliothek.	*No one is coming out of the library.*
Niemand versteht mich außer Karl.	*No one understands me except Karl.*
Niemand besucht mich außer meinem Onkel.	*No one visits me except my uncle.*
Niemand hilft mir außer dir.	*No one helps me except you.*
Sie hat bei uns gewohnt.	*She lived at our house.*
Habt ihr bei euren Eltern gewohnt?	*Did you live at your parents' house?*
Nein, wir haben bei Freunden gewohnt.	*No, we lived with friends.*
Mit wem hat er getanzt?	*With whom did he dance?*
Er hat mit der schönen Studentin getanzt.	*He danced with the pretty student.*
Sie half mir nach der Arbeit.	*She helped me after work.*
Sie halfen mir nach dem Fußballspiel.	*They helped me after the soccer game.*

Ich wohne seit März in Darmstadt.	*I have been living in Darmstadt since March.*
Ich bin seit drei Wochen hier.	*I have been here for three weeks.*
Das ist ein Geschenk von der Königin.	*That is a gift from the queen.*
Ich habe es vom König erhalten.	*I received it from the king.*
Um wie viel Uhr gehst du zur Schule?	*What time do you go to school?*
Um wie viel Uhr ging er zur Arbeit?	*What time did he go to work?*

It is common to form contractions with the prepositions **von** and **zu**.

von + dem	→	**vom**
zu + dem	→	**zum**
zu + der	→	**zur**

Written Practice 4

Rewrite each sentence with the nouns or pronouns provided in parentheses. Apply the dative case appropriately.

1. Der Ausländer hat mit ______ gesprochen.

(die Kinder) ______________________________.

(meine Tante) ______________________________.

(der König) ______________________________.

(ich) ______________________________.

(wir) ______________________________.

(sie *pl.*) ______________________________.

2. Gudrun wohnt seit April bei ______.

(ihre Eltern) ______________________________.

(meine Schwester) ______________________________.

(ein Freund) ______________________________.

(er) ______________________________.

(sie *s.*) ______________________________.

(ich) ______________________________.

3. Sie bekommt einen Brief von ______.

(ihre Eltern) ______________________________.

(ein Ausländer) ______________________________.

(dein Bruder) ______________________________.

(du) ______________________________.

(ihr) ______________________________.

Geography

In this book you have already encountered several geographical regions and cities. Let's take a look at a few more.

Afrika	*Africa*	die Erdteile	*the continents*
Asien	*Asia*	Europa	*Europe*
Australien	*Australia*	Mittelamerika	*Central America*
die Antarktis	*Antartica*	Nordamerika	*North America*
die Erde	*the Earth*	Südamerika	*South America*

Oral Practice

Practice saying the following list of sentences out loud.

Wo liegt Deutschland?	*Where is Germany located?*
Deutschland liegt in Europa.	*Germany is located in Europe.*
Liegt Hamburg im Norden oder Süden?	*Is Hamburg located in the north or the south?*
Hamburg liegt im Norden.	*Hamburg is located in the north.*
Wo liegt Belgien?	*Where is Belgium located?*
Belgien liegt im Westen.	*Belgium is located in the west.*
Wo liegt Bulgarien?	*Where is Bulgaria located?*
Bulgarien liegt im Osten.	*Bulgaria is located in the east.*
Ist Griechenland im Norden?	*Is Greece in the north?*
Nein, Griechenland ist im Süden.	*No, Greece is in the south.*
Andere europäische Länder sind:	*Other European countries include:*
Estland	*Estonia*
Frankreich	*France*

Großbritannien	*Great Britain*
Irland	*Ireland*
Lettland	*Latvia*
Litauen	*Lithuania*
die Niederlande	*the Netherlands*
Norwegen	*Norway*
Portugal	*Portugal*
Rumänien	*Romania*
Russland	*Russia*
die Slowakei	*Slovakia*
Spanien	*Spain*
Tschechien	*Czech Republic*
Ukraine	*Ukraine*
Weißrussland	*White Russia*

Written Practice 5

Combine each country and capital in a sentence. Use the example sentence as your pattern. Notice the usage of a final possessive **-s** on the country name.

(Deutschland, Berlin) Die Hauptstadt Deutschlands ist Berlin.

1. (Frankreich, Paris) ______________________________.
2. (Italien, Rom) ______________________________.
3. (Russland, Moskau) ______________________________.
4. (Norwegen, Oslo) ______________________________.
5. (Polen, Warschau) ______________________________.
6. (Spanien, Madrid) ______________________________.
7. (Tschechien, Prag) ______________________________.
8. (Griechenland, Athen) ______________________________.
9. (Japan, Tokio) ______________________________.
10. (Österreich, Wien) ______________________________.

QUIZ

1. Write the present perfect tense conjugation of the following verbs with the pronouns provided.

	fragen	versuchen	vorstellen
ich	______	______	______
du	______	______	______
er	______	______	______
wir	______	______	______
ihr	______	______	______
Sie	______	______	______

2. Provide the past participle for the following verbs.

dienen ______	trinken ______
arrangieren ______	erkennen ______
gehören ______	stehlen ______
essen ______	tun ______
aussehen ______	wissen ______

3. Write the present, past, and present perfect conjugations of each of the following verbs with the pronouns provided. For example:

	fragen		
ich	*frage*	*fragte*	*habe gefragt*
du	*fragst*	*fragtest*	*hast gefragt*

	finden		
ich	______	______	______
du	______	______	______
er	______	______	______

	ausgeben		
wir	______	______	______
ihr	______	______	______
Sie	______	______	______

Using the appropriate form of the dative case, rewrite each sentence filling in the blank with the words in parentheses.

4. **Warum folgt sie ______________?**

   (die Kinder) ______________________________

   (meine Tochter) ______________________________

   (ich) ______________________________

   (du) ______________________________

5. **Der Lehrer steht ______________ gegenüber.**

   (ihr Bruder) ______________________________

   (deine Eltern) ______________________________

   (er) ______________________________

   (wir) ______________________________

6. **Das ist ein Geschenk von ______________.**

   (die Königin) ______________________________

   (unser Kind) ______________________________

   (ihr) ______________________________

   (sie *pl.*) ______________________________

Circle the letter of the word or phrase that best completes each sentence.

7. **Haben Sie die Zeitung ______________?**

   A. schreiben
   B. gelesen
   C. schrieb
   D. lasen

8. **Ich habe gestern mit ______________ gesprochen.**

   A. einem Freund
   B. du
   C. die Männer
   D. der Roman

9. Dieses Buch ______________ mir nicht.

A. gewohnt
B. geglaubt
C. die Männer
D. gefällt

10. Wie lange ______________ ihr auf mich gewartet?

A. habt
B. bekam
C. bekommen
D. hat

chapter 12

Important Details

In this chapter you will learn the special functions of the preposition **vor** and the verb **haben**. The accusative-dative propositions will be introduced as well as the use of subordinating conjunctions and the conjugation of **sein** in the present perfect tense. Some useful vocabulary regarding food and beverages will be included.

CHAPTER OBJECTIVES

In this chapter you will learn about:

- Present Perfect Tense with *Sein*
- A Special Use of *Vor*
- Expressing Hunger and Thirst with *Haben*
- Accusative-Dative Prepositions
- Other Verb Prefixes
- Subordinating Conjunctions
- Food and Beverages

Present Perfect Tense with *Sein*

German has a concept in the present perfect tense that no longer exists in English. Certain German verbs require **sein** as their auxiliary in the present perfect tense rather than **haben**. In an earlier form of English, the same thing occurred with the verb *to be*. Consider this line from the Bible: *The Lord is come*. Today, that would be said as: *The Lord has come*.

When **sein** is the auxiliary in the present perfect tense, the past participles still have the same regular and irregular formations as those with **haben**. For example:

reisen		**fahren**	
ich bin gereist	*I have traveled*	ich bin gefahren	*I have driven*
du bist gereist	*you have traveled*	du bist gefahren	*you have driven*
er ist gereist	*he has traveled*	er ist gefahren	*he has driven*
wir sind gereist	*we have traveled*	wir sind gefahren	*we have driven*
ihr seid gereist	*you have traveled*	ihr seid gefahren	*you have driven*
sie sind gereist	*they have traveled*	sie sind gefahren	*they have driven*

Of course, the question is: How do you know when to use **haben** and when to use **sein**? In general, use **haben** with verbs that are transitive, that is, verbs that take a direct object.

Er hat den Roman gelesen.	*He read the novel.* (*Novel* is the direct object.)

And use **sein** with verbs of motion, that is, verbs whose action requires movement from one place to another. For example:

Er ist nach Deutschland gefahren.	*He drove to Germany.* (Shows movement from an original location to Germany.)

It is possible to test for verbs of motion by giving a command with the verb. If the action can be carried out without moving the feet from one place to another, the verb is probably transitive and will use **haben** as its auxiliary. For example:

Sing.	Read a book.	Keep the money.

But if the feet have to move to carry out the action of the verb, the verb is probably a verb of motion and will use **sein** as its auxiliary. For example:

Run.	Go home.	Fly to Munich.

Sein is also used with verbs that show a change of physical state or a state over which a person has no direct control.

Er ist in Amerika gestorben.	*He died in America.* (Dying is a change of physical state and is one over which a person has no control.)

It is also possible to test for this usage of **sein** by giving a command with the verb. If there is no tangible action of the verb and it describes a state or condition, the verb will probably use **sein** as its auxiliary. For example:

Be nice.	Become a doctor.	Don't die.

You have already encountered many verbs in the present and past tenses that use **sein** as the auxiliary in the present perfect tense. Let's look at some conjugations in the third person singular.

Regular Verbs

folgen	er ist gefolgt	*he has followed*
marschieren	er ist marschiert	*he has marched*
reisen	er ist gereist	*he has traveled*
spazieren	er ist spaziert	*he has strolled*

Irregular Verbs

ankommen	er ist angekommen	*he has arrived*
bleiben	er ist geblieben	*he has stayed*
einsteigen	er ist eingestiegen	*he has gotten on (transportation)*
fahren	er ist gefahren	*he has driven*
fallen	er ist gefallen	*he has fallen*
fliegen	er ist geflogen	*he has flown*
gehen	er ist gegangen	*he has gone*
kommen	er ist gekommen	*he has come*
laufen	er ist gelaufen	*he has run*
mitgehen	er ist mitgegangen	*he has gone along*

rennen	er ist gerannt	*he has run*
sterben	er ist gestorben	*he has died*
umsteigen	er ist umgestiegen	*he has transferred*

NOTE ***Remember that the German present perfect tense tends to be translated into English in the simple past tense. But the example sentences above were translated into English in the present perfect tense to emphasize that* sein *means* to have *in this conjugation.***

Written Practice 1

Write the present perfect tense conjugation of the following verbs with the pronouns provided.

	spazieren	**kommen**	**umsteigen**
ich	________	________	________
du	________	________	________
er	________	________	________
wir	________	________	________
ihr	________	________	________
sie	________	________	________

	bleiben	**sterben**	**folgen**
ich	________	________	________
du	________	________	________
er	________	________	________
wir	________	________	________
ihr	________	________	________
sie	________	________	________

Oral Practice

Track 61

Practice saying the following list of sentences out loud.

Wann kommt dein Vater?	*When is your father coming?*
Er ist schon gekommen.	*He has already come.*
Wann kommen deine Eltern?	*When are your parents coming?*

Sie sind schon gekommen.	*They have already come.*
Wir sind in der Hauptstraße eingestiegen.	*We got on on Main Street.*
Wir sind am Marktplatz ausgestiegen.	*We got off at the market square.*
Wie lange seid ihr da geblieben?	*How long did you stay there?*
Wir sind den ganzen Tag da geblieben.	*We stayed there the whole day.*
Wohin ist Tina geflogen?	*Where did Tina fly?*
Sie ist nach Tokio geflogen.	*She flew to Tokyo.*
Sie ist gestern angekommen.	*She arrived yesterday.*
Lebt der Kranke noch?	*Is the patient still alive?*
Nein, er ist leider gestorben.	*No, unfortunately he died.*
Wohnen Ihre Eltern noch in Bonn?	*Do your parents still live in Bonn?*
Nein, sie sind vor einem Jahr gestorben.	*No, they died a year ago.*
Wann ist er nach Norwegen gereist?	*When did he travel to Norway?*
Er ist vor drei Tagen nach Norwegen gereist.	*He traveled to Norway three days ago.*

A Special Use of *Vor*

Use **vor** with the dative case to express how much time *ago* something occurred.

vor einer Woche	*a week ago*	vor einem Tag	*one day ago*
vor zwei Wochen	*two weeks ago*	vor zehn Tagen	*ten days ago*
vor einem Monat	*a month ago*	vor einem Jahr	*one year ago*
vor drei Monaten	*three months ago*	vor elf Jahren	*eleven years ago*

The verbs **sein** and **werden** are important verbs and must be looked at separately. They both use **sein** as their auxiliary in the present perfect tense, because these verbs describe a state: *to be* and *to become*. Their conjugations look like this in the present perfect tense:

sein		**werden**	
ich bin gewesen	*I have been*	ich bin geworden	*I have become*
du bist gewesen	*you have been*	du bist geworden	*you have become*

er ist gewesen	*he has been*	er ist geworden	*he has become*
wir sind gewesen	*we have been*	wir sind geworden	*we have become*
ihr seid gewesen	*you have been*	ihr seid geworden	*you have become*
sie sind gewesen	*they have been*	sie sind geworden	*they have become*

A third important verb to discuss is **haben**. It is a transitive verb and therefore uses **haben** in its present perfect tense conjugation.

ich habe gehabt	*I have had*	wir haben gehabt	*we have had*
du hast gehabt	*you have had*	ihr habt gehabt	*you have had*
er hat gehabt	*he has had*	sie haben gehabt	*they have had*

Use the contraction im (**in** + **dem**) with the four seasons of the year (**die vier Jahreszeiten**). All seasons are masculine.

im Winter	*in the winter*	im Sommer	*in the summer*
im Frühling	*in the spring*	im Herbst	*in the fall/autumn*

Oral Practice

Practice saying the following list of sentences out loud.

Wo sind Sie gewesen, Herr Benz?	*Where were you, Mr. Benz?*
Ich bin in Frankreich gewesen.	*I was in France.*
Ich habe meine Verwandten besucht.	*I visited my relatives.*
Es ist schon kalt geworden.	*It has already become cold.*
Ja, das Wetter im Winter ist immer kalt.	*Yes, the weather in winter is always cold.*
Haben Sie einen warmen Mantel?	*Do you have a warm coat?*
Ich habe lange in diesem Klima gelebt.	*I have lived a long time in this climate.*
Ich habe immer einen warmen Mantel gehabt.	*I have always had a warm coat.*
Ist Ihr Sohn krank gewesen?	*Was your son sick?*
Ja, er hat eine Erkältung bekommen.	*Yes, he caught a cold.*
Er ist sehr krank gewesen.	*He was very sick.*
Er ist nicht zur Schule gegangen.	*He did not go to school.*

Er ist vier Tage zu Hause geblieben.	*He stayed home four days.*
Meine Tochter ist im Sommer krank gewesen.	*My daughter was sick in the summer.*
Im Frühling ist die ganze Familie nach Belgien gereist.	*In the spring the whole family traveled to Belgium.*
Im Herbst ist die ganze Familie nach Irland geflogen.	*In the fall the whole family flew to Ireland.*

Written Practice 2

Rewrite the following present tense sentences changing them to the present perfect tense.

1. Ich bin sehr müde. ____________________.
2. Wird deine Schwester wieder gesund? ____________________?
3. Der Zug kommt um elf Uhr zehn an. ____________________.
4. Die Kinder bleiben in der Stadt. ____________________.
5. Die Touristen gehen zum Rathaus. ____________________.
6. Meine Eltern gehen im Park spazieren. ____________________.
7. Wir haben Hunger. ____________________.
8. Wohin fährst du? ____________________?
9. Die Jungen laufen zum Marktplatz. ____________________.
10. Sie haben kein Geld. ____________________.

Expressing Hunger and Thirst with *Haben*

When talking about *hunger* or *thirst*, it is possible to use the German adjectives **hungrig** and **durstig**. However, a more commonly used expression uses **haben** with the noun form of both words.

Ich habe Hunger.	*I am hungry.*
Ich habe Durst.	*I am thirsty.*

Accusative-Dative Prepositions

You have already encountered prepositions that take the accusative case and prepositions that take the dative case in this book. There is another category of prepositions that can take either the accusative case or the dative case. These prepositions are:

an	*at; to; on*	über	*over, above; about*
auf	*on*	unter	*under; among*
hinter	*behind*	vor	*before, in front of*
in	*in, into*	zwischen	*between*
neben	*next to*		

This use of two cases may seem confusing at first glance, but there is a simple explanation for it. If the preposition is used with the accusative case, it is being used to show motion to a place. If the preposition is used with the dative case, it is being used to show a location. For example:

Track 62

Showing Motion to a Place—Accusative

Ich hänge ein Bild an die Wand.	*I hang a picture on the wall.*
Ich lege das Buch auf den Tisch.	*I lay the book on the table.*
Ich laufe hinter die Tür.	*I run behind the door.*
Ich gehe in die Schule.	*I go into the school.*
Ich setze mich neben den Lehrer.	*I seat myself next to the teacher.*
Ich hänge ein Bild über den Tisch.	*I hang a picture over the table.*
Ich lege Papier unter den Stuhl.	*I lay paper under the chair.*
Ich stelle eine Stehlampe vor das Klavier.	*I place a floor lamp in front of the piano.*
Ich stelle einen Stuhl zwischen die Tische.	*I place a chair between the tables.*

Showing Location—Dative

Ein Bild hängt an der Wand.	*A picture is hanging on the wall.*
Das Buch liegt auf dem Tisch.	*The book is lying on the table.*
Ich stehe hinter der Tür.	*I stand behind the door.*
Ich bin in der Schule.	*I am in the school.*
Ich sitze neben dem Lehrer.	*I am sitting next to the teacher.*
Ein Bild hängt über dem Tisch.	*A picture is hanging over the table.*
Papier liegt unter dem Stuhl.	*Paper is lying under the chair.*

Eine Stehlampe steht vor dem Klavier.	*A floor lamp is standing in front of the piano.*
Ein Stuhl steht zwischen den Tischen.	*A chair stands between the tables.*

There is a tendency in German to use a more specific word for the English verb *to put*. If you are putting something in a horizontal position, you should use **legen** (*to lay*). If you are putting something in a vertical position, you should use **stellen** (*to place upright*). Use the accusative case with these two verbs and the accusative-dative prepositions.

Er legt das Heft auf das Bett.	*He lays the notebook on the bed.*

If you use **stellen** in this sentence instead of **legen**, it will mean that he is propping up the notebook so it can stand on one edge.

Er stellt die Vase auf das Klavier.	*He places the vase on the piano.*

If you use **legen** in this sentence instead of **stellen**, it will mean that he is laying the vase on its side.

When persons or objects are already located in a horizontal or vertical position use **liegen** (*to lie, be situated*) and **stehen** (*to stand*) respectively, with the dative case. For example:

Das Heft liegt auf dem Bett.	*The notebook is lying on the bed.*
Die Vase steht auf dem Klavier.	*The vase is standing on the piano.*

Notice that **legen** and **stellen** are regular verbs and **liegen** and **stehen** are irregular verbs. Let's look at the principal parts of their conjugations in the three tenses you know.

Present:	er legt	er stellt	er liegt	er steht
Past:	er legte	er stellte	er lag	er stand
Present Perfect:	er hat gelegt	er hat gestellt	er hat gelegen	er hat gestanden

Oral Practice

Practice saying the following list of sentences out loud.

Warum läuft der Hund an die Tür?	*Why is the dog running to the door?*
Jemand steht an der Tür und klopft.	*Someone is standing at the door and knocking.*

Ich habe mich ans Fenster gesetzt.	*I seated myself at the window.*
Ich habe mich zwischen die Jungen gesetzt.	*I seated myself between the boys.*
Ich habe die Kleider in den Schrank gehängt.	*I hung up the clothes in the wardrobe.*
Ich habe den Tisch neben das Sofa gestellt.	*I placed the table next to the sofa.*
Der Brief hat unter dem Stuhl gelegen.	*The letter lay under the chair.*
Sie hat den Brief auf den Tisch gelegt.	*She laid the letter on the table.*
Das neue Hotel ist neben dem Rathaus.	*The new hotel is next to city hall.*
Die Touristen haben vor dem Rathaus gestanden.	*The tourists stood in front of city hall.*
Wohin hat sie den Regenschirm gestellt?	*Where did she put the umbrella?*
Sie hat den Regenschirm hinter den Schrank gestellt.	*She put the umbrella behind the wardrobe.*
Karin hängt das Poster über das Bett.	*Karin hangs the poster over the bed.*
Was hängt über deinem Bett?	*What hangs above your bed?*
Über meinem Bett hängt ein Poster.	*A poster hangs above my bed.*
Frau Kamps legt das Baby aufs Bett.	*Ms. Kamps lays the baby on the bed.*
Wer schläft auf dem Bett?	*Who is sleeping on the bed?*
Das Baby schläft auf dem Bett.	*The baby is sleeping on the bed.*

Did you notice the words **ans** and **aufs** in these sentences? Certain prepositions can form contractions. You have already encountered a few. Let's add to that list. The following prepositions combine with **das** in the accusative case.

ans	(an + das)
aufs	(auf + das)
ins	(in + das)

In certain contexts the rules of movement to a place and location do not apply with these prepositions. For example, **warten auf** means *to wait for* and requires the use of the accusative case. But there is no actual movement of a person or object. With such verb and preposition combinations, the appropriate case must be memorized. Let's look at some of these verb and preposition combinations. The letter A designates the use of the accusative case, and the letter D designates the use of the dative case.

warten auf A	Ich warte auf ihn.	*I am waiting for him.*
glauben an A	Er glaubt an Gott.	*He believes in God.*
denken an A	Sie denkt an ihre Mutter.	*She thinks about her mother.*
sich verlieben in A	Ich verliebe mich in sie.	*I fall in love with her.*
sein unter D	Er war unter den Gästen.	*He was among the guests.*
reden über A	Sie redet über das Problem.	*She talks about the problem.*

When you encounter a new verb with one of the accusative-dative prepositions, check in a dictionary to determine which case to use.

The preposition **entlang** follows a noun and is used in the accusative case to indicate motion down the middle of a place or *along* a location.

Wir sind den Fluss entlang gegangen. *We went along the river.*

But when **entlang** is used in combination with **an**, the case needed is the dative case. Its meaning is then *alongside* a place.

Wir sind am Fluss entlang gegangen. *We went alongside the river.*

Written Practice 3

Rewrite each sentence filling in the blank with the words in parentheses.

Er geht an ______.

(die Tür) Er geht an die Tür.

1. Wir haben eine Stunde auf ______ gewartet.

(er) ______________________.

(du) ______________________.

(dieser Ausländer) ______________________.

(unsere Wirtin) ______________________.

(die Diplomaten) ______________________.

(ihr) ______________________.

2. Ich denke niemals an ______.

(diese Probleme) ______.

(meine Arbeit) ______.

(unser König) ______.

(sie *s.*) ______.

(Sie) ______.

(sie *pl.*) ______.

Other Verb Prefixes

You are already aware of the separable and inseparable prefixes. There are a few other prefixes that are sometimes separable and sometimes inseparable. They are:

	Separable		**Inseparable**	
durch-	dúrchfallen	*to fail*	durchfáhren	*to drive through*
hinter-	N/A		hinterlássen	*to leave behind*
über-	űberhängen	*to hang over*	übertréiben	*to exaggerate*
um-	úmkommen	*to die*	umármen	*to embrace*
unter-	únterbringen	*to put up, accommodate*	unterbréchen	*to interrupt*
voll-	vólltanken	*to fill up the tank*	vollénden	*to complete*
wider-	wíderspiegeln	*to reflect*	widerstéhen	*to resist*
wieder-	wíederkehren	*to return*	wiederhólen	*to repeat*

When the accent is on the prefix of the verb, the prefix is separable: **dúrchfallen—er fällt durch** (*he fails*). When the accent is on the stem of the verb, the prefix is inseparable: **übertréiben—er übertréibt** (*he exaggerates*).

Written Practice 4

Write the present, past, and present perfect conjugations of the following verbs with the pronouns provided. For example:

haben

er *hat hatte hat gehabt*

1. unterbrechen

ich ______________________________

du ______________________________

ihr ______________________________

2. widerspiegeln

er ______________________________

wir ______________________________

du ______________________________

Subordinating Conjunctions

Subordinating conjunctions introduce a clause that, when stated alone, does not make complete sense. For example:

Er hat gesagt, dass es spät wurde.	*He said that it was getting late.*

The subordinate clause *that it was getting late* does not make complete sense on its own. In German the subordinating conjunction (which in this sentence would be **dass** [*that*]) is the signal that there will be a word order change in the sentence: The conjugated verb will be the last element in the sentence. Notice the position of the conjugated verb in the following subordinate clauses.

Ich weiß, dass er kein Geld **hat**.	*I know that he has no money.*
Er schreibt, dass seine Mutter gestorben **ist**.	*He writes that his mother has died.*

Some of the commonly used subordinating conjunctions are:

als	*when* (past tense)	während	*while*
ob	*whether, if*	wenn	*when(ever)*
nachdem	*after*		

In sentences, they look like this:

Erik fragt, ob die Kinder Hunger haben.	*Erik asks whether the children are hungry.*
Ich besuche Martin, wenn ich in Bern bin.	*I visit Martin whenever I am in Bern.*

Als wir in Stuttgart waren, gingen wir oft ins Theater.	*When we were in Stuttgart, we often went to the theater.*
Nachdem das Baby gegessen hat, haben die Eltern Karten gespielt.	*After the baby ate, the parents played cards.*
Tina hat die Dokumente gefunden, während wir in Paris gewesen sind.	*Tina found the documents while we were in Paris.*

Written Practice 5

Complete each sentence with the clauses provided. For example:

Er schreibt, dass...

Die Kinder lernen jetzt Deutsch.

Er schreibt, dass die Kinder jetzt Deutsch lernen.

1. Sie wissen nicht, dass...

   Es ist wieder sehr kalt geworden.

   ______________________________.

   Onkel Peter ist vor zwei Tagen gestorben.

   ______________________________.

2. Niemand fragt, ob...

   Sie wohnen noch in Freiburg.

   ______________________________.

   Wir glauben ihnen.

   ______________________________.

3. Sie hat ihre Tasche verloren, während...

   Sie ist in Schweden gewesen.

   ______________________________.

   Sie hat mit den Kindern gespielt.

   ______________________________.

4. Die Königin fragt, ob...

   Der König ist noch in Frankreich.

   ______________________________.

Ihre Kinder sind schon nach Italien gereist.

____.

Die alte Frau hat Hunger gehabt.

____.

Der Wissenschaftler hat den Leuten geholfen.

____.

Food and Beverages

You already know how to use the verbs **essen** and **trinken**. Now you need some food and beverages to use them with. And remember, when you order food and beverages, use the verb **bestellen**.

das Essen	*food*	die Getränke	*beverages*
die Bratwurst	*roasted sausage*	das Pils	*lager beer*
die Erbsen	*peas*	der Wein	*wine*
der Fisch	*fish*	das Wasser	*water*
das Hähnchen	*chicken*	die Coca	*Coca-Cola*
die Kartoffeln	*potatoes*	die Cola	*Coca-Cola*
der Käse	*cheese*	der Sekt	*(German) champagne*
der Kohl	*cabbage*	der Schinken	*ham*
das Rindfleisch	*beef*	das Obst	*fruit*
das Gemüse	*vegetables*		

Oral Practice

Practice saying the following list of sentences out loud. Then restate the sentences using the vocabulary in the preceding list.

Ich esse gern Bratwurst und Käse.	*I like eating roasted sausage and cheese.*
Er trinkt gern Wein oder Sekt.	*He likes drinking wine or champagne.*
Ich habe nur Gemüse bestellt.	*I only ordered vegetables.*

QUIZ

1. Write the present perfect conjugation of the following verbs with the pronouns provided.

	gehen	marschieren	umsteigen
ich	______	______	______
du	______	______	______
er	______	______	______

	bleiben	sein	fliegen
wir	______	______	______
ihr	______	______	______
sie (*pl.*)	______	______	______

	ankommen	reisen	spazieren
ich	______	______	______
sie (*s.*)	______	______	______
Sie	______	______	______

2. In the blanks provided, write the auxiliary **haben** if the verb is transitive or write the auxiliary **sein** if the verb is intransitive or is a verb of motion.

______ gesehen	______ gelernt
______ geworden	______ gestorben
______ versprochen	______ geblieben
______ mitgegangen	______ gewesen
______ gehabt	______ geblieben
______ gegessen	______ gelaufen

3. Write the accusative and dative forms of the following pronouns and nouns in parentheses with the prepositions provided.

	Accusative	Dative
(ich)	für ______	mit ______
(du)	gegen ______	von ______
(er)	ohne ______	bei ______
(sie *s.*)	durch ______	außer ______
(wir)	um ______	zu ______

(ihr)	für ______	nach ______
(Sie)	gegen ______	mit ______
(dieser Ausländer)	ohne ______	von ______
(das Kind)	um ______	zu ______
(die Schule)	durch ______	aus ______
(viele Romane)	ohne ______	nach ______

4. Fill in the blank for the given sentence with the correct forms of the words in parentheses.

   Meine Tochter ist vor ______ geboren.

   (ein Tag) ______

   (drei Wochen) ______

   (eine Woche) ______

   (ein Jahr) ______

   (zehn Jahre) ______

5. Rewrite the sentences below with the subordinate clauses provided.

   Mein Bruder schreibt, dass...

   Seine Frau ist wieder krank geworden.

   ______

   Er ist in der Hauptstadt gewesen.

   ______

   Der Arzt fragt, ob...

   Geht es Frau Meyer besser?

   ______

   Ist Professor Benz zu Besuch gekommen?

   ______

   Ich habe meinen Mantel verloren, als...

   Ich bin in Schweden gewesen.

   ______

   Ich habe vor dem Rathaus gestanden.

   ______

Circle the letter of the word or phrase that best completes each sentence.

6. **Niemand hat ______________ bestellt.**
   A. auf dem Bett
   B. an die Tür
   C. das Rindfleisch
   D. im Flur

7. **______________ hat seinen neuen Roman gelesen.**
   A. Niemand
   B. Unseren Onkel
   C. Viele Jungen
   D. Wir

8. **Ich esse gern ______________ und Käse.**
   A. den Wein
   B. die Getränke
   C. Sekt
   D. Bratwurst

9. **Ich denke oft ______________ meine Frau.**
   A. an
   B. bis
   C. mit
   D. vor

10. **Wir haben ihn besucht, ______________ wir in Spanien waren.**
   A. während
   B. ob
   C. wider
   D. dass

chapter 13

Talking About the Future

In this chapter you will learn to use the future tense and the genitive case. In addition, negatives, adverbs, and the past perfect tense will be described. You will also encounter another pronoun type and more conjunctions.

CHAPTER OBJECTIVES

In this chapter you will learn about:

- Future Tense
- Negatives
- Adverbs of Time, Manner, and Place
- Genitive Case
- Past Perfect Tense
- Accusative Reflexive Pronouns
- More Subordinating Conjunctions
- Things Around the City

Future Tense

You have already been using a form of the future tense, because German—like English—can use a present tense conjugation to infer the future tense. This is particularly true when there is an adverb in the sentence indicating the future.

Wir gehen **morgen** in die Stadt.	*We are going to the city* ***tomorrow***.

But there is another way to express the future tense. Just as English has a future tense auxiliary (*shall, will*), German uses **werden** as its future tense auxiliary. The future tense structure is quite simple: Conjugate **werden** in the present tense and end the sentence with an infinitive. For example:

Ich werde meine Tante besuchen.	*I will visit my aunt.*
Wirst du ihm helfen?	*Will you help him?*
Sie werden in Polen bleiben.	*They will stay in Poland.*

Written Practice 1

Write the following verbs in the future tense with the pronouns provided.

	fahren	**aufmachen**	**beschreiben**
ich	______	______	______
du	______	______	______
er	______	______	______
wir	______	______	______
	haben	**sein**	**werden**
ich	______	______	______
er	______	______	______
ihr	______	______	______
sie (*pl.*)	______	______	______

Since the future tense is composed of **werden** plus an infinitive, you need not be concerned with whether a verb is regular or irregular or whether it has a prefix or not.

Regular verb:	Sie wird fragen.	*She will ask.*
Irregular verb:	Sie wird sprechen.	*She will speak.*
Separable prefix:	Sie wird zumachen.	*She will close.*
Inseparable prefix:	Sie wird bekommen.	*She will receive.*

Oral Practice

Track 63

Practice saying the following list of sentences out loud.

Werden Sie Ihrem Freund helfen?	*Will you help your friend?*
Ja, ich werde ihm helfen.	*Yes, I will help him.*
Nein, ich werde ihm nicht helfen.	*No, I will not help him.*
Wird Frau Bauer die Kinder mitnehmen?	*Will Ms. Bauer take the children along?*
Ja, sie wird die Kinder mitnehmen.	*Yes, she will take the children along.*
Nein, sie wird sie nicht mitnehmen.	*No, she will not take them along.*
Werden sie lachen oder weinen?	*Will they laugh or cry?*
Sie werden wahrscheinlich lachen.	*They will probably cry.*
Sie werden ein bisschen weinen.	*They will cry a little.*
Was wirst du tun?	*What will you do?*
Ich werde einen Job suchen.	*I will look for a job.*
Was werdet ihr tun?	*What will you do?*
Wir werden unsere Verwandten suchen.	*We will look for our relatives.*

Written Practice 2

Rewrite the future tense sentences below as present tense sentences using **morgen** to infer the future tense. For example:

Ich werde das alte Haus verkaufen.

Morgen verkaufe ich das alte Haus.

1. Sie wird ein Glas Rotwein bestellen.

   ______________________________.

2. Die Familie wird drei Briefe erhalten.

   ______________________________.

3. Der Vater wird wieder weinen.

   ______________________________.

4. Die Ausländer werden am Marktplatz umsteigen.

   ______________________________.

5. Wirst du wieder nach Portugal fliegen?

____.

6. Er wird den interessanten Roman lesen.

____.

7. Die Kinder werden unter dem Tisch spielen.

____.

Negatives

Like English, German can only have one negative in a sentence. The double negative is not an option. Let's look at some examples.

Ich verstehe **nichts**.	*I **do not** understand **anything**. (I understand **nothing**.)*
Er fuhr **nicht** in die Stadt.	*He **did not** drive to the city.*
Wir haben **keine** Zeit.	*We have **no** time.*
Niemand hat ihm geholfen.	***No one** helped him.*
Er hat mich **niemals** verstanden.	*He **never** understood me.*

NOTE ***The adverb niemals is often said as nie.***

Adverbs of Time, Manner, and Place

German has special rules for using adverbial expressions when more than one adverb will appear in a sentence. Adverbs of time will appear first, adverbs of manner second, and adverbs of place last. First, let's look at these adverbs individually.

When adverbs of time alone are used in a sentence, they follow the conjugated verb.

Ich fahre **heute** in die Stadt.	*I am driving to the city **today**.*
Sie hat **jetzt** keine Zeit.	*She has no time **now**.*

When adverbs of manner alone are used in a sentence, they follow the conjugated verb.

Ich fahre **mit dem Bus**.	*I am going **by bus**.*
Der Vater kommt **mit dem Auto**.	*The father comes **by car**.*

When adverbs of place alone are used in a sentence, they follow the conjugated verb.

Ich fahre **nach Berlin**.	*I am driving **to Berlin**.*
Der Vater kommt **ins Wohnzimmer**.	*The father comes **into the living room**.*

But when more than one adverb is used in a sentence, the adverbs must appear in the assigned order: time, manner, then place.

Wir fahren **nach Hamburg**.	*We are traveling **to Hamburg**.*
Wir fahren **morgen** nach Hamburg.	***Tomorrow** we are traveling to Hamburg.*
Wir fahren morgen **mit dem Zug** nach Hamburg.	*Tomorrow we are traveling **by train** to Hamburg.*

Written Practice 3

Rewrite each sentence, each time adding the adverbs provided in parentheses.

1. Ich komme mit der Straßenbahn.

(nach Hause) ____.

(heute) ____.

2. Wir sind mit dem Zug gereist.

(in die Schweiz) ____.

(vor einer Woche) _______________________________________.

Genitive Case

The genitive case is the last of the four German cases. Its primary function is to show possession much the way the English *'s* or the preposition *of* does.

Whose book is it?	*It is my brother's book.*
Whose father is he?	*He is the father* of *the bride.*

German achieves the possessive meaning by using the genitive case. Let's look at the genitive as it compares to the other cases.

The genitive case of nouns with the definite article:

	Masculine	Feminine	Neuter	Plural
nom	der Mann	die Frau	das Kind	die Kinder
acc	den Mann	die Frau	das Kind	die Kinder
dat	dem Mann	der Frau	dem Kind	den Kindern
gen	**des** Mannes	**der** Frau	**des** Kindes	**der** Kinder

Other determiners in the genitive case will have the same endings as the definite articles. For example:

eines Mannes	meiner Frau	dieses Kindes	ihrer Kinder
deines Mannes	seiner Frau	keines Kindes	unserer Kinder

In sentences, the genitive case looks like this:

Das Auto des Mannes ist sehr alt.	*The man's car is very old.*
Kennst du den Sohn dieser Frau?	*Do you know this woman's* son?
Der Hund meines Kindes ist braun.	*My child's dog is brown.*
Der Onkel der Kinder ist gestorben.	*The children's uncle has died.*

Notice that the possessor follows the person or object possessed.

However, when using a possessive form of a person's name or a thing, use only a final **-s** (no apostrophe, as in English), and the possessor precedes the object possessed.

Peters Wagen	*Peter's car*
Deutschlands Grenzen	*Germany's borders*

Oral Practice

 Track 64

Practice saying the following list of sentences out loud.

Wessen Handschuhe hast du?	*Whose gloves do you have?*
Ich habe die Handschuhe des Lehrers.	*I have the teacher's gloves.*
Ich habe die Handschuhe meiner Schwester.	*I have my sister's gloves.*

Ich habe die Handschuhe des Kindes.	*I have the child's gloves.*
Wessen Wagen wird er kaufen?	*Whose car will he buy?*
Er wird den Wagen der Ärztin kaufen.	*He will buy the physician's car.*
Er wird den Wagen seines Freundes kaufen.	*He will buy his friend's car.*
Er wird den Wagen einer Freundin kaufen.	*He will buy a girlfriend's car.*
Wessen Verwandten wird sie helfen?	*Whose relatives will she help?*
Sie wird den Verwandten ihres Mannes helfen.	*She will help her husband's relatives.*
Sie wird den Verwandten meiner Wirtin helfen.	*She will help my landlady's relatives.*
Sie wird den Verwandten der Gäste helfen.	*She will help the guests' relatives.*
Ist das das Fahrrad deines Bruders?	*Is that your brother's bicycle?*
Ja, das ist sein Fahrrad.	*Yes, that is his bicycle.*
Nein, das ist das Fahrrad meiner Schwester.	*No, that is my sister's bicycle.*
Ist das der Enkel deiner Nachbarin?	*Is that your neighbor's grandchild?*
Ja, das ist ihr Enkel.	*Yes, that is her grandchild.*
Nein, das ist der Enkel eines Gasts.	*No, that is a guest's grandchild.*
Die Enkelin meines Chefs ist Studentin.	*My boss's granddaughter is a student.*

Written Practice 4

Write the dative and genitive forms for the following phrases.

	Dative	**Genitive**
das Fahrrad	__________	__________
die Leute	__________	__________
mein Schrank	__________	__________

seine Nachbarin	________________	________________
unsere Gäste	________________	________________
der Handschuh	________________	________________
die Handschuhe	________________	________________
ein Roman	________________	________________
eine Bratwurst	________________	________________
der Turm	________________	________________
die Burg	________________	________________
die Kaufhäuser	________________	________________
deine Geschwister	________________	________________
der Dom	________________	________________

There is a tendency to use an **-es** ending in the genitive case of masculine and neuter singular nouns when those nouns are of one syllable.

des Kindes	*child's*	des Mannes	*man's*

But it is also correct to add only **-s**.

des Kinds	*child's*	des Manns	*man's*

Nouns that end in **s**, **ss**, **ß**, **z**, or **tz** add **-es**.

des Hauses	*house's*	des Schmerzes	*pain's*

Masculine and neuter singular nouns that have more than one syllable but do not end in **s** add only **-s**.

des Bahnhofs	*train station's*	des Lehrers	*teacher's*

Pronouns do not have a genitive form. Instead, possessive adjectives are used to show possession. You encountered these in Chapter 9.

mein	*my*	ihr	*her*	ihr	*their*
dein	*your*	unser	*our*	Ihr	*your*
sein	*his/its*	euer	*your*	wessen	*whose*

The possessive **wessen** does not show a gender or case change, unlike the other possessive adjectives.

Oral Practice

Practice saying the following list of sentences out loud.

Wird dein Bruder da arbeiten?	*Will your brother work there?*
Nein, der Bruder meines Freunds wird da arbeiten.	*No, my friend's brother will work there.*
Wird seine Tante da arbeiten?	*Will his aunt work there?*
Nein, die Tante einer Nachbarin wird da arbeiten.	*No, a neighbor's aunt will work there.*
Werden eure Geschwister da arbeiten?	*Will your brothers and sisters work there?*
Nein, die Geschwister des Chefs werden da arbeiten.	*No, the boss's brothers and sisters will work there.*
Werden Ihre Gäste mitkommen?	*Will your guests come along?*
Nein, die Gäste meines Bruders werden mitkommen.	*No, my brother's guests will come along.*
Wird ihre Kusine mitkommen?	*Will her cousin come along?*
Nein, die Kusine einer Freundin wird mitkommen.	*No, a girlfriend's cousin will come along.*
Wirst du hier aussteigen?	*Will you get off here?*
Nein, ich werde am Bahnhof aussteigen.	*No, I will get off at the train station.*
Nein, ich werde vor der Bank aussteigen.	*No, I will get off in front of the bank.*
Nein, ich werde vor dem Café aussteigen.	*No, I will get off in front of the café.*

Past Perfect Tense

In the present perfect tense, the action of the verb started in the past and ended in the present.

He has worked here all day.

In the past perfect tense, the action of the verb started in the past and ended in the past.

He had worked here until his death last year.

In German the only conjugational difference between the present perfect and the past perfect is the tense used for the auxiliaries **haben** and **sein**. In the present perfect tense, the auxiliary is conjugated in the present tense.

Present Perfect Tense

Ich habe es gesehen.	*I saw it.*	Ich bin schnell gelaufen.	*I ran fast.*
Du hast es gesehen.	*You saw it.*	Du bist schnell gelaufen.	*You ran fast.*
Er hat es gesehen.	*He saw it.*	Er ist schnell gelaufen.	*He ran fast.*
Wir haben es gesehen.	*We saw it.*	Wir sind schnell gelaufen.	*We ran fast.*
Ihr habt es gesehen.	*You saw it.*	Ihr seid schnell gelaufen.	*You ran fast.*
Sie haben es gesehen.	*They saw it.*	Sie sind schnell gelaufen.	*They ran fast.*

In the past perfect tense, the auxiliary is conjugated in the past tense.

Past Perfect Tense

Ich hatte es gesehen.	*I had seen it.*	Ich war schnell gelaufen.	*I had run fast.*
Du hattest es gesehen.	*You had seen it.*	Du warst schnell gelaufen.	*You had run fast.*
Er hatte es gesehen.	*He had seen it.*	Er war schnell gelaufen.	*He had run fast.*
Wir hatten es gesehen.	*We had seen it.*	Wir waren schnell gelaufen.	*We had run fast.*
Ihr hattet es gesehen.	*You had seen it.*	Ihr wart schnell gelaufen.	*You had run fast.*
Sie hatten es gesehen.	*They had seen it.*	Sie waren schnell gelaufen.	*They had run fast.*

The change from the present perfect tense to the past perfect tense does not influence other aspects of verb conjugations: prefixes or regularity and irregularity of conjugation.

Written Practice 5

Change the following present perfect tense sentences to the past perfect tense.

1. Robert hat mir ein Geschenk gegeben.

____.

2. Wir sind zum Park gegangen.

____.

3. Hast du mit dem kleinen Hund gespielt?

______________________________________.

4. Warum bist du so böse gewesen?

______________________________________.

5. Unsere Gäste sind in der Stadt geblieben.

______________________________________.

Accusative Reflexive Pronouns

Reflexive pronouns are those that reflect back to the subject of the sentence. In other words, they refer to the person who is the subject of the sentence. For example:

Same Person	Different Persons
Tom hurt himself.	*Tom* hurt *her*.
We bought ourselves some candy.	*We* bought *them* some candy.

The German accusative reflexive pronouns are:

Subject Pronoun	Reflexive Pronoun
ich	mich
du	dich
er	sich
sie (*s.*)	sich
es	sich
wir	uns
ihr	euch
sie (*pl.*)	sich
Sie	sich

Subject Pronoun	Reflexive Pronoun
wer	sich
was	sich
man	sich

When the direct object or the object of an accusative preposition are the same person as the subject of the sentence, use a reflexive pronoun.

Same Person

Ich frage mich, wo sie ist.	*I ask myself (wonder) where she is.*

Different Persons

Ich frage ihn, wo sie ist.	*I ask him where she is.*

Written Practice 6

Rewrite the following sentence with the new subjects provided in parentheses. Change the reflexive pronoun appropriately.

1. Er wird sich in einer Stunde rasieren.

(ich) ____.

(du) ____.

(wir) ____.

(ihr) ____.

(sie *pl.*) ____.

Some verbs require a reflexive pronoun to complete their meaning. Consider the English verb *to enjoy oneself*. You cannot say *I enjoy*. The meaning is not complete. You have to add the reflexive pronoun to make sense: *I enjoy myself*. German has similar verbs. For example:

sich beeilen	*to hurry*	sich irren	*to be mistaken*
sich freuen auf	*to look forward to*	sich verlieben in	*to be in love with*
sich freuen über	*to be happy about/with*		

When in the infinitive form, reflexive verbs are preceded by **sich**. These verbs are incomplete if the reflexive pronoun does not accompany them. Notice that **sich freuen** is used with two different prepositions. With **auf**, the verb means *to look forward to*. With **über**, the verb means *to be happy about*.

Wir freuen uns schon auf deine Party.	*We are already looking forward to your party.*
Sie freute sich über das Geschenk.	*She was happy about the gift.*

This verb can also be used without a preposition.

Ich freue mich, dass dein Mann jetzt gesund ist.	*I am happy that your husband is well now.*

Oral Practice

Practice saying the following list of sentences out loud.

Ich wasche die Kinder.	*I wash the children.*
Ich wasche mich.	*I wash myself.*
Ich setze mich an den Tisch.	*I seat myself at the table.*
Thomas setzte sich an den Tisch.	*Thomas seated himself at the table.*
Thomas rasierte sich langsam.	*Thomas shaved (himself) slowly.*
Rasierst du dich jetzt?	*Are you shaving now?*
Irrst du dich wieder?	*Are you wrong again?*
Das Kind hat sich aufs Sofa gelegt.	*The child lay down on the sofa.*
Oma wird sich aufs Sofa legen.	*Granny will lie down on the sofa.*
Wir beeilen uns.	*We hurry.*
Er hat sich beeilt.	*He hurried.*
Ich werde mich beeilen.	*I will hurry.*
Ich freue mich über das Geschenk.	*I am happy with the gift.*
Ich freue mich auf das Wochenende.	*I am looking forward to the weekend.*
Er hat sich in Tina verliebt.	*He fell in love with Tina.*
In wen hattest du dich verliebt?	*Whom had you fallen in love with?*
Er kaufte Handschuhe für ihn.	*He bought gloves for him.*
Er kaufte Handschuhe für sich.	*He bought gloves for himself.*

Written Practice 7

Make sentences by conjugating the following verb phrases in the present tense with the pronouns provided. Use the appropriate reflexive pronoun.

	sich beeilen	**sich rasieren schnell**
ich	______________.	______________.
du	______________.	______________.
er	______________.	______________.
wir	______________.	______________.
wer	______________?	______________?

	sich irren	**sich freuen über das Buch**
ich	______________.	______________.
sie (*s.*)	______________.	______________.
sie (*pl.*)	______________.	______________.
ihr	______________.	______________.
man	______________.	______________.

Written Practice 8

Change each sentence to the future tense. Replace the subjects with the words provided in parentheses. For example:

Sie schreibt einen Brief.

(du) *Du wirst einen Brief schreiben.*

1. Die Kinder waschen sich.

   (du) ______________________.

   (er) ______________________.

   (ich) ______________________.

2. Ich steige hier aus.

   (er) ______________________.

   (ihr) ______________________.

   (sie *pl.*) ______________________.

3. Er arbeitet in Bonn.

   (ich) ______________________.

   (du) ______________________.

   (wer) ______________________?

More Subordinating Conjunctions

You already know a variety of interrogative words: **wer**, **wen**, **wem**, **wessen**, **was**, **wo**, **wohin**, **woher**, **wie**, **wann**, and **warum**. These same words can function as subordinating conjunctions, which means that the conjugated verb in the subordinate clause will be the last element. Compare the following interrogative words used in both a question and a subordinate clause.

Wer ist das?	*Who is that?*
Sie fragt mich, wer das ist.	*She asks me who that is.*
Was haben sie gekauft?	*What did they buy?*

Weißt du, was sie gekauft haben?	*Do you know what they bought?*
Wo wohnt Herr Bauer?	*Where does Mr. Bauer live?*
Wir wissen, wo Herr Bauer wohnt.	*We know where Mr. Bauer lives.*
Wann hat er den Brief bekommen?	*When did he get the letter?*
Ich weiß nicht, wann er den Brief bekommen hat.	*I do not know when he got the letter.*
Wie alt ist ihre Tochter?	*How old is her daughter?*
Niemand weiß, wie alt ihre Tochter ist.	*No one knows how old her daughter is.*

You can use all interrogative words as subordinating conjunctions.

Things Around the City

When visiting a German city, you will see many of the same sights whether the city is located in the north, south, east, or west. Let's become familiar with some of things you'll see in a city.

das Kaufhaus	*department store*	der Zirkus	*circus*
das Kino	*movie theater*	der Zoo	*zoo*
das Motorrad	*motorcycle*	die Apotheke	*drugstore* (prescriptions)
das Schiff	*ship*	die Besichtigung	*tour; sightseeing*
das Stadtzentrum	*city center, downtown*	die Brücke	*bridge*
der Ausflug	*excursion*	die Burg	*castle*
der Dom	*cathedral*	die Drogerie	*drugstore* (general products)
der Flughafen	*airport*	die Hafenrundfahrt	*trip around harbor*
der Hafen	*harbor*	die Post	*post office*
der Hauptbahnhof	*main railroad station*	die Sehenswürdigkeiten	*sights*
der Laden	*shop, small store*	die Stadtmauer	*city wall*
der Turm	*tower*	die Stadtrundfahrt	*trip around the city*
der Verkehr	*traffic*	die Tour	*tour*

Let's look at a few example sentences.

Wir werden eine Stadtrundfahrt machen.	*We are going to take a trip around the city.*
Die Touristen machen morgen eine Tour.	*The tourists are going on a tour tomorrow.*
Morgen machen wir einen Ausflug.	*We are going on an excursion tomorrow.*
Die Besichtigung des Doms fängt um neun Uhr an.	*The tour of the cathedral starts at nine o'clock.*
Im Hafen sehen wir viele Schiffe aus dem Ausland.	*In the harbor we see many ships from foreign countries.*
Von der Brücke sehen wir das ganze Stadtzentrum.	*From the bridge we see the entire downtown.*
Ich fotografiere die alte Burg und den Turm.	*I photograph the old castle and the tower.*

QUIZ

Change the sentences conjugated in the present tense to the future tense with the pronouns provided. For example:

Ich bestelle ein Bier.

Er wird ein Bier bestellen.

Wir werden ein Bier bestellen.

1. **Ich komme mit.**
   Du __________
   Wir __________
   Sie (*pl.*) __________

2. **Er verspricht nichts.**
   Sie (*s.*) __________
   Ihr __________
   Man __________

3. **Write the accusative, dative, and genitive declensions for each of the following phrases.**

	Accusative	Dative	Genitive
meine Gäste	____________	____________	____________
Ihr Mantel	____________	____________	____________
seine Tochter	____________	____________	____________
das Kaufhaus	____________	____________	____________

4. **Rewrite the following sentence with the pronouns provided in parentheses. Change the reflexive pronoun appropriately.**

   Hat er sich schon gewaschen?

   (du) ____?

   (sie *s.*) ____?

   (wir) ____?

   (ihr) ____?

5. **Write new sentences by using the phrases provided and changing each question that follows to a subordinate clause.**

   Ich weiß nicht, ...

   Wo haben meine Verwandten gearbeitet?

   ____

   Wie heißen diese Männer?

   ____

   Er fragte Thomas, ...

   Warum warten die Touristen vor dem Bahnhof?

   ____

   Woher kommen diese Ausländer?

   ____

6. **Conjugate the following verbs in the present perfect tense and the past perfect tense with the pronouns provided.**

	sich beeilen	gehen	bestellen
ich	__________	__________	__________
	__________	__________	__________
sie (*s.*)	__________	__________	__________
	__________	__________	__________
wir	__________	__________	__________
	__________	__________	__________
du	__________	__________	__________
	__________	__________	__________

Circle the letter of the word or phrase that best completes each sentence.

7. **Die Touristen machen morgen eine __________.**
   A. Stadt
   B. Wochenende
   C. Tour
   D. Verwandte

8. **Unsere Gäste sind in der Stadt __________.**
   A. gearbeitet
   B. schnell rasiert
   C. gesehen
   D. geblieben

9. **Wir freuen __________ schon auf das Wochenende.**
   A. uns
   B. dich
   C. wessen
   D. Stadtmauer

10. **Sie hatten die Familie __________ besucht.**
    A. vor Ihren Verwandten
    B. auf deine Party
    C. der Besichtigung
    D. meines Freundes

chapter 14

Review of Verb Tenses

In this chapter you will learn about the differences between German and English verbs and will find the genitive prepositions introduced. In addition, dative reflexive pronouns will be discussed as well as some special forms with masculine nouns. The German modal auxiliaries will also be introduced.

CHAPTER OBJECTIVES

In this chapter you will learn about:

- Comparing German and English Verb Tenses
- Key Verbs: *Haben*, *Sein*, and *Werden*
- Genitive Prepositions
- Dative Reflexive Pronouns
- Some Special Masculine Nouns
- Modal Auxiliaries

Comparing German and English Verb Tenses

In general, we can say that German and English tenses are used in much the same way. But let's review those few differences that do exist.

Present Tense

The English present tense has three versions: the habitual, the progressive or incomplete, and the emphatic. German has one present tense form.

Die Kinder lernen Deutsch. { *The children learn German.*
The children are learning German.
The children do learn German. }

This variety of English tenses in the present occurs in the other tenses as well. In German there is only one form.

Past Tenses

When telling something that occurred in the past, German primarily uses the simple past tense in written language and the present perfect tense in spoken language. English tends to prefer the simple past tense.

Written Language:
Sie lernten Deutsch. *They learned German.*

Spoken Language:
Sie haben Deutsch gelernt. *They learned German.*

But when emphasizing what began in the past and ends in the future, use the present perfect tense.

Wir haben lange gearbeitet. *We have worked long.*

When emphasizing what began in the past and ended in the past, use the past perfect tense.

Wir hatten lange gearbeitet. *We had worked long.*

Future Tense

The German future tense resembles the English future tense in great degree. Both can use a present tense conjugation to infer the future tense, usually with an accompanying adverbial expression that indicates the future.

Wir fahren morgen nach Bremen. *We are driving to Bremen tomorrow.*

And both use an auxiliary with an infinitive to show an action in the future tense.

Ich werde in Bonn studieren. *I will study in Bonn.*

There is another future tense to consider: the future perfect tense. This identifies an action that begins and ends in the future.

Er wird es schon gelesen haben. *He will already have read it.*

This tense consists of a conjugation of **werden** followed by a past participle and either **haben** or **sein**.

Er wird es gefunden haben. *He will have found it.*
Sie wird gegangen sein. *She will have gone.*

The use of **haben** or **sein** in this tense depends upon the past participle. With transitive verbs, use **haben**. With intransitive verbs and verbs of motion, use **sein**.

Key Verbs: *Haben*, *Sein*, and *Werden*

You have undoubtedly noticed how significant these three verbs are in German conjugations. Let's review:

Haben

Haben is used as a transitive verb that means *to have*.

Ich habe neun CDs. *I have nine CDs.*

It is also used as the auxiliary of transitive verbs in the perfect tenses.

Ich habe es verstanden. *I understood it.*
Ich hatte es verkauft. *I had sold it.*
Ich werde es gelernt haben. *I will have learned it.*

Sein

Sein is used alone as an intransitive verb that means *to be*.

Sie ist meine Schwester. *She is my sister.*

It is also the auxiliary of intransitive verbs and verbs of motion in the perfect tenses.

Sie ist gestorben.	*She has died.*
Sie war Lehrerin geworden.	*She had become a teacher.*
Sie wird gefahren sein.	*She will have driven.*

Werden

Werden is used as an intransitive verb that means *to become.*

Tina wird Ärztin.	*Tina is becoming a physician.*

It is also the auxiliary of the future tense.

Tina wird Professorin werden.	*Tina will become a professor.*
Tina wird es gefunden haben.	*Tina will have found it.*

In addition, **werden** is the auxiliary of the passive voice, which will be taken up in Chapter 17.

Oral Practice

Track 65

Practice saying the following list of sentences out loud.

Ich freue mich auf ihren Besuch.	*I am looking forward to her visit.*
Wir freuten uns auf ihren Besuch.	*We looked forward to her visit.*
Hast du dich auf das Examen gefreut?	*Did you look forward to the exam?*
Er wird sich auf den Ausflug freuen.	*He will be looking forward to the excursion.*
Ich komme allein.	*I am coming alone.*
Sie kam mit einer Flasche Wein.	*She came with a bottle of wine.*
Seid ihr mit einem Freund gekommen?	*Did you come with a friend?*
Wir werden allein kommen.	*We will come alone.*
Ein Fremder ist im Garten.	*A stranger is in the garden.*
Niemand war in der Küche.	*No one was in the kitchen.*

Wer ist im Keller gewesen?	*Who was in the cellar?*
Unser Nachbar wird in den Vereinigten Staaten sein.	*Our neighbor will be in the United States.*

Written Practice 1

Conjugate the following verbs in the tenses in bold print with the pronouns provided.

		aussteigen		**versprechen**
pres	er	______________	wir	______________
past	er	______________	wir	______________
pres perf	er	______________	wir	______________
past perf	er	______________	wir	______________
fut	er	______________	wir	______________
fut perf	er	______________	wir	______________

		besuchen		**sich rasieren**
pres	du	______________	ich	______________
past	du	______________	ich	______________
pres perf	du	______________	ich	______________
past perf	du	______________	ich	______________
fut	du	______________	ich	______________
fut perf	du	______________	ich	______________

In the following conjugations use the pronoun provided for each line.

		wohnen		**verstehen**
pres	ich	______________	ich	______________
past	du	______________	du	______________
pres perf	er	______________	er	______________
past perf	wir	______________	wir	______________
fut	ihr	______________	ihr	______________
fut perf	sie (*pl.*)	______________	sie (*pl.*)	______________

Genitive Prepositions

Just like the accusative and dative cases, the genitive case has certain high-frequency prepositions.

(an)statt	*instead of*	während	*during*
trotz	*inspite of, despite*	wegen	*because of*

In sentences, these prepositions look like this:

Er kauft einen Hut (an)statt eines Hemdes.	*He buys a hat instead of a shirt.*
Trotz des Wetters fahren sie nach Bremen.	*Despite the weather they drive to Bremen.*
Während des Krieges wohnte er in London.	*During the war he lived in London.*
Sie bleibt wegen des Schnees zu Hause.	*She stays home because of the snow.*

These prepositions are sometimes used in the dative case in the colloquial language.

Oral Practice

Practice saying the following list of sentences out loud.

Statt einer Postkarte schickt er mir einen Brief.	*Instead of a postcard, he sends me a letter.*
Statt eines Briefes schickt sie mir ein Telegramm.	*Instead of a letter she sends me a telegram.*
Trotz des Regens gehen wir zum Park.	*Despite the rain we go to the park.*
Trotz des Schnees gehen wir in die Stadt.	*Despite the snow we go to the city.*
Während des Sommers fliegt sie nach Italien.	*During the summer she flies to Italy.*
Während des Frühlings fliegt er nach Norwegen.	*During the spring he flies to Norway.*

Wegen des Krieges bleiben sie zu Hause.	*Because of the war they stay at home.*
Wegen eines Gewitters bleiben sie zu Hause.	*Because of a thunderstorm they stay at home.*

Written Practice 2

Write each phrase with the genitive prepositions provided.

1. wegen

ein Examen ______________________

diese Besichtigung ______________________

die Touristen ______________________

2. während

ein Krieg ______________________

das Gewitter ______________________

der Tag ______________________

3. trotz

der Schnee ______________________

seine Geschwister ______________________

eine Nachbarin ______________________

4. anstatt

die Handschuhe ______________________

eine Küche ______________________

diese Flaschen ______________________

Dative Reflexive Pronouns

Just as there are accusative reflexive pronouns, there are also dative reflexive pronouns. Dative reflexive pronouns are used when an indirect object, an object of a dative verb, or an object of a dative preposition is the same person or thing that is the subject of the sentence. The dative reflexive pronouns are:

Subject Pronoun	**Reflexive Pronoun**
ich	mir
du	dir
er	sich
sie (*s.*)	sich
es	sich
wir	uns
ihr	euch
sie (*pl.*)	sich
Sie	sich
wer	sich
was	sich
man	sich

Here are some example sentences.

Ich kaufe mir eine Flasche Bier. — *I buy myself a bottle of beer.*
Er hilft sich so gut er kann. — *He helps himself as well as he can.*
Robert spricht mit sich selbst. — *Robert is talking to himself.*

Certain personal activities (washing, combing the hair, putting on clothes, and so on) tend to use a dative reflexive pronoun followed by a direct object in German, where in English there is only a direct object.

Wir waschen **uns die Hände**. — *We wash **our hands**.*

Notice that German uses a definite article with the direct object, where English uses a possessive pronoun.

The phrase *to break* (**sich brechen**) as in a limb or other body part is a special phrase in German. It requires a dative reflexive pronoun and a direct object.

Sie bricht **sich die Hand**. — *She breaks **her hand**.*

Oral Practice

Practice saying the following list of sentences out loud.

Wer spricht mit sich selbst? — *Who is talking to himself?*
Der alte Mann spricht mit sich selbst. — *The old man is talking to himself.*

Was tust du?	*What are you doing?*
Ich putze mir die Zähne.	*I am brushing my teeth.*
Ich kämme mir die Haare.	*I am combing my hair.*
Das Kind wäscht sich die Hände.	*The child is washing his hands.*
Sie zieht sich einen Mantel an.	*She is putting on a coat.*
Ziehst du dir eine Jacke an?	*Are you putting on a jacket?*
Nein, ich ziehe mir einen Regenmantel an.	*No, I am putting on a raincoat.*
Haben Sie sich das Bein gebrochen?	*Did you break your leg?*
Nein, ich habe mir den Arm gebrochen.	*No, I broke my arm.*
Er hat sich den Finger gebrochen.	*He broke his finger.*

Written Practice 3

Exchange the subject and the object in each sentence with the new subjects and objects provided. Make any necessary changes to the reflexive pronouns. For example:

Sie bricht sich die Hand.

(du/der Arm) Du brichst dir den Arm.

1. Er zieht sich einen Mantel an.
   (sie *s.*/die Jacke) ____________________.
   (ich/der Regenmantel) ____________________.
   (du/das Sweatshirt) ____________________.
2. Er hat sich die Fahrkarten gekauft.
   (wir/eine Flasche Wein) ____________________.
   (ihr/die Handschuhe) ____________________.
   (sie *pl.*/ein Roman) ____________________.
3. Er hat sich den Arm gebrochen.
   (ich/der Finger) ____________________.
   (sie *pl.*/die Finger) ____________________.
   (du/die Beine) ____________________.

Written Practice 4

Rewrite the following sentence with the words in parentheses. Change the reflexive pronouns appropriately. For example:

Er kauft sich ein Sweatshirt.

(ich) *Ich kaufe mir ein Sweatshirt.*

1. Ich habe mir die Hände gewaschen.

(er) ______________________.

(ihr) ______________________.

(die Männer) ______________________.

(wir) ______________________.

(du) ______________________.

Some Special Masculine Nouns

Certain masculine nouns have a special declension. These nouns are words that require an **-n** or **-en** ending in the declension. They tend to be old words, words that end in the vowel **-e**, and foreign words with the accent on the last syllable. Here are some sample words:

Old Words		**Words Ending in -e**		**Foreign Words**	
der Herr	*gentleman*	der Junge	*boy*	der Soldat	*soldier*
der Mensch	*human*	der Löwe	*lion*	der Sozialist	*socialist*
der Held	*hero*	der Knabe	*boy*	der Elefant	*elephant*
der Graf	*count, earl*	der Matrose	*sailor*	der Musikant	*musician*

When these words decline, they require an **-(e)n** ending and in the plural they end in **-(e)n** also. For example:

nom	der Mensch	der Löwe	der Elefant
acc	den Mensch**en**	den Löw**en**	den Elefant**en**
dat	dem Mensch**en**	dem Löw**en**	dem Elefant**en**
gen	des Mensch**en**	des Löw**en**	des Elefant**en**

Plural nominative: die Mensch**en**, die Löw**en**, die Elefant**en**.

Notice that the genitive case does not require an **-s** ending in this declension.

Written Practice 5

1. Decline each noun phrase in the accusative, dative, and genitive cases.

	der Held	**der Junge**	**der Soldat**
acc	________	________	________
dat	________	________	________
gen	________	________	________

2.	**der Affe** (***monkey***)	**der Prinz** (***prince***)	**der Diplomat** (***diplomat***)
acc	________	________	________
dat	________	________	________
gen	________	________	________

Modal Auxiliaries

A modal auxiliary is a conjugated verb that works together with an infinitive. When a modal auxiliary is used, the infinitive is placed at the end of the sentence. The modal auxiliaries color the meaning of the verb in the sentence by telling what obligation, permission, or ability the doer of the action has. Let's meet the modal auxiliaries.

dürfen	*may, to be allowed*	müssen	*must, to have to*
können	*can, to be able to*	sollen	*should, to be supposed to*
mögen	*to like; may*	wollen	*to want*

In the Present Tense

With most of the modal auxiliaries, there is a difference in the present tense between the verb stem in the singular conjugation and the stem in the plural conjugation.

	dürfen	**können**	**mögen**
ich	darf	kann	mag
du	darfst	kannst	magst
er	darf	kann	mag
wir	dürfen	können	mögen
ihr	dürft	könnt	mögt
sie	dürfen	können	mögen

	müssen	**sollen**	**wollen**
ich	muss	soll	will
du	musst	sollst	willst
er	muss	soll	will
wir	müssen	sollen	wollen
ihr	müsst	sollt	wollt
sie	müssen	sollen	wollen

In sentences, the modal auxiliaries look like this:

Darf ich diese Zeitung nehmen?	*May I take this newspaper?*
Niemand kann ihn verstehen.	*No one can understand him.*
Ich mag Butter nicht.	*I do not like butter.*
Wir müssen den Kindern helfen.	*We have to help the children.*
Was soll man tun?	*What should one do?*
Er will sich die Zähne putzen.	*He wants to brush his teeth.*

Oral Practice

Practice saying the sentences in the following list out loud.

Das darf man nicht tun.	*You (One) should not do that.*
Ihr dürft nicht Auto fahren.	*You are not allowed to drive a car.*
Können Sie mich hören?	*Can you hear me?*
Nein, ich kann nichts hören.	*No, I cannot hear anything.*
Das mag wohl sein.	*That may well be.*
Sie mögen mehr als zehn Jahre alt sein.	*They may be more than ten years old.*
Sie müssen heute Briefe schreiben.	*They have to write letters today.*
Der Mann muss sehr krank sein.	*The man must be very sick.*
Ihr sollt jetzt fleißig arbeiten.	*You should work diligently now.*
Der Diplomat soll schwer krank sein.	*The diplomat is supposed to be seriously ill.*
Was wollen Sie tun?	*What do you want to do?*
Ich will mir die Hände waschen.	*I want to wash my hands.*

In the Past Tense

When conjugated in the past tense, the modal auxiliaries look like regular verbs and never have an umlaut, even if there is one in the infinitive.

	dürfen	**können**	**mögen**
ich	durfte	konnte	mochte
du	durftest	konntest	mochtest
er	durfte	konnte	mochte
wir	durften	konnten	mochten
ihr	durftet	konntet	mochtet
sie	durften	konnten	mochten

	müssen	**sollen**	**wollen**
ich	musste	sollte	wollte
du	musstest	solltest	wolltest
er	musste	sollte	wollte
wir	mussten	sollten	wollten
ihr	musstet	solltet	wolltet
sie	mussten	sollten	wollten

In the Perfect Tenses

In the perfect tenses, all the modal auxiliaries use **haben** as their auxiliary. And as participles they look like regular verbs but never have an umlaut.

er hat gedurft	*he has been allowed*	er hat gemusst	*he has had to*
er hat gekonnt	*he was able to*	er hat gesollt	*he was supposed to*
er hat gemocht	*he has liked*	er hat gewollt	*he has wanted*

But the present perfect conjugation illustrated here is used only when there is no other verb in the sentence.

Mein Bruder hat es nicht gekonnt.	*My brother was not able to.*
Das habe ich nicht gewollt.	*I did not want that.*

Modal auxiliaries are intended to be used in conjunction with other infinitives. You have seen that in the present and past tenses, the second verb (an infinitive) in the sentence appears at the end of that sentence, unlike English.

Ich will eine Flasche Bier **trinken**.	*I want **to drink** a bottle of beer.*
Ich wollte eine Flasche Bier **trinken**.	*I wanted **to drink** a bottle of beer.*

In the perfect and future tenses, however, this requires a new structure: a double infinitive. When the same sentences are stated in the perfect or future tenses, the infinitive of the modal auxiliary is the last element in the sentence and forms a double-infinitive structure with the second verb. A past participle is not used in the perfect tenses.

Ich habe eine Flasche Bier **trinken wollen**.	*I **wanted to drink** a bottle of beer.*
Ich werde eine Flasche Bier **trinken wollen**.	*I will **want to drink** a bottle of beer.*

Oral Practice

 Track 66

Practice saying the following list of sentences out loud.

Was hast du tun wollen?	*What did you want to do?*
Ich habe ins Kino gehen wollen.	*I wanted to go to the movies.*
Hast du mitkommen können?	*Were you able to go along?*
Nein, ich habe arbeiten müssen.	*No, I had to work.*
Wohin habt ihr gehen sollen?	*Where were you supposed to go?*
Wir haben zum Hotel gehen sollen.	*We were supposed to go to the hotel.*
Das darfst du nicht tun.	*You may not do that.*
Ich habe das niemals tun dürfen.	*I have never been allowed to do that.*
Ich habe niemals tanzen können.	*I have never been able to dance.*

The modal auxiliary **mögen** (*to like; may*) is used frequently in another form: **möchte** (*would like*). It is a polite replacement for **wollen** (*to want*).

Ich möchte bitte eine Tasse Tee.	*I would like a cup of tea, please.*
Wir möchten nach Südamerika fliegen.	*We would like to fly to South America.*

Written Practice 6

Make complete sentences by conjugating the following phrases with the pronouns provided. Use the tenses shown in bold.

1. wollen einen Roman lesen

pres Ich ______________________________.

past Ich ______________________________.

pres perf Wir ______________________________.

fut Wir ______________________________.

2. können sehr gut Schach spielen

pres Du ______________________________.

past Du ______________________________.

pres perf Ihr ______________________________.

fut Ihr ______________________________.

3. müssen ein bisschen warten

pres Sie (*s.*) ______________________________.

past Sie (*s.*) ______________________________.

pres perf Sie (*pl.*) ______________________________.

fut Sie (*pl.*) ______________________________.

4. sollen fleißig arbeiten

pres Ich ______________________________.

past Er ______________________________.

pres perf Wir ______________________________.

fut Man ______________________________.

Written Practice 7

Rewrite the following sentences in the past and present perfect tenses.

1. Die Kinder können gut Klavier spielen.

______________________________.

______________________________.

2. Ich muss jeden Tag fleißig arbeiten.

______________________________.

______________________________.

3. Du sollst dir die Hände waschen.

______________________________.

______________________________.

4. Sie mag kein Eis.

____.

____.

5. Hier kann man umsteigen.

____.

____.

6. Ihr müsst den Nachbarn helfen.

____.

____.

QUIZ

1. **Conjugate the following verbs in the tenses shown with the pronouns provided.**

		schicken	waschen	aussteigen	bekommen
pres	ich	________	________	________	________
past	du	________	________	________	________
pres perf	er	________	________	________	________
past perf	wir	________	________	________	________
fut	ihr	________	________	________	________
fut perf	Sie	________	________	________	________

2. **In the blanks provided, write the letter that identifies the case required by each preposition: a = accusative, d = dative, a-d = accusative or dative, and g = genitive.**

mit ________	von ________
wegen ________	trotz ________
in ________	anstatt ________
während ________	durch ________
für ________	neben ________
statt ________	zu ________

Rewrite each sentence using the words in parentheses.

3. **Statt ____________ wird Herr Keller ihm helfen.**
   (meine Schwester) ________________________________
   (dieser Matrose) ________________________________
   (seine Geschwister) ________________________________

4. **Wegen ____________ musste Frau Benz in der Stadt bleiben.**
   (ihre Mutter) ________________________________
   (das Gewitter) ________________________________
   (der Regen) ________________________________

5. **Using the words in parentheses, change the subject and reflexive pronoun in the sentence. For example:**

   Ich kaufte mir einen Wagen.

   (er) *Er kaufte sich einen Wagen.*

   Ich putze mir die Zähne.
   (man) ________________________________
   (die Kinder) ________________________________
   (niemand) ________________________________
   (wir) ________________________________
   (ihr) ________________________________
   (du) ________________________________
   (Sie) ________________________________
   (mein Sohn) ________________________________

6. **Write the accusative, dative, and genitive forms of the following nouns.**

	die Kirche	**ein Held**	**Ihre Eltern**
nom	__________	__________	__________
acc	__________	__________	__________
dat	__________	__________	__________
gen	__________	__________	__________

7. Write the present and past tense conjugations of the following modal auxiliaries with the pronouns provided.

		dürfen	können	mögen
pres	ich	______	______	______
past	Sie	______	______	______

		wollen	sollen	müssen
pres	er	______	______	______
past	ihr	______	______	______

Circle the word or phrase that best completes each sentence.

8. Die Männer werden eine Flasche Bier trinken ______.

A. bekommen
B. haben
C. wollen
D. sein

9. Mein Onkel hat ______ den Arm gebrochen.

A. sich
B. ihn
C. seinen
D. wegen

10. ______ des Sommers fliegen wir nach Spanien.

A. Der Schnee
B. Während
C. Des Wetters
D. Wir freuen uns

chapter 15

Linking Ideas Together

In this chapter the German relative pronouns and relative clause formations will be introduced as well as the function of double infinitives. In addition, modal auxiliaries will be discussed again together with more about prepositions and adverbs.

CHAPTER OBJECTIVES

In this chapter you will learn about:

- Relative Pronouns
- More About Modal Auxiliaries
- Double Infinitives
- Prepositions and Inanimates
- More About Adverbs

Relative Pronouns

Relative pronouns are used to link two sentences having a common element together. For example:

The girls play soccer. The girls attend this school.

In these two sentences, the common element is, of course, *the girls*. The two sentences can be combined into one by changing one of the instances of *the girls* to a relative pronoun. In this case, the relative pronoun is *that*. *That* is used to add pertinent information about the antecedent (the word to which the relative pronoun refers). The result is:

The girls *that* attend this school play soccer.

English has more than one kind of relative pronoun. *Who* and *which* are used to provide additional but nonessential information about the antecedent.

The man, *who* happens to be my friend, lost the election.
An election, *which* is rare in these parts, will be tomorrow.

English also has an elliptical relative pronoun—that is, a relative pronoun that does not appear in a relative clause, but is understood.

The person they arrested was a drifter. (The person *that* they arrested was a drifter.)

German relative pronouns are the definite articles (**der**, **die**, **das**). They are used like subordinating conjunctions, which means that the conjugated verb is the last element in the clause. The relative pronouns must conform to the gender and number of their antecedents. For example:

der Mann, der...	*the man, who . . .*	das Kind, das...	*the child, who . . .*
die Frau, die...	*the woman, who . . .*	die Leute, die...	*the people, who . . .*

But, in addition to being the same gender and number of the antecedent, the relative pronoun can be of any case: nominative, accusative, dative, or genitive. It depends upon on how the relative pronoun is used in the relative clause: as the subject of the clause, as the direct object, as the object of a preposition, and so forth. For example:

der Mann, **der** in Bonn wohnt (subject)	*the man **that** lives in Bonn*
der Mann, **den** Tina kennt (direct object)	*the man **that** Tina knows*
der Mann, **mit dem** sie tanzt (dative prep.)	*the man **that** she dances **with*** (*the man **with whom** she dances*)

Before we look at a variety of sentences with relative clauses, let's look at the declension of the relative pronouns, paying particular attention to the few occasions in which the declension differs from the definite article.

	Masculine	**Feminine**	**Neuter**	**Plural**	
nom	der	die	das	die	*that, who, which*
acc	den	die	das	die	*that, whom, which*
dat	dem	der	dem	denen	*that, whom, which*
gen	dessen	deren	dessen	deren	*whose*

Now let's look at some example sentences. Notice how the relative pronoun conforms to the gender and number of its antecedent and is in the case needed for its function within the relative clause.

Der Lehrer, der in der Nähe wohnt, hat in England studiert.	*The teacher, who lives in the vicinity, studied in England.*
Kennen Sie die Studentin, die die Touristen fotografieren?	*Do you know the student that the tourists are photographing?*
Er findet das Buch, von dem der Professor gesprochen hat.	*He finds the book that the professor spoke about.*
Ich besuche meine Verwandten, deren Sohn im Irak ist.	*I visit my relatives whose son is in Iraq.*

Oral Practice

 Track 67

Practice saying the following list of sentences out loud.

Welches Haus hast du gekauft?	*Which house did you buy?*
Das Haus, das in der Hauptstraße steht.	*The house that is on Main Street.*

Das Haus, in dem Bach gewohnt hatte.	*The house that Bach had lived in.*
Wo ist der Politiker, den sie interviewen wollen?	*Where is the politician that they want to interview?*
Wo sind die Rockstars, mit denen sie sprechen wollen?	*Where are the rock stars with whom they want to speak?*
Wo ist die Tänzerin, über die er einen Artikel schreiben will?	*Where is the dancer that he wants to write an article about?*
Welche Gedichte willst du lernen?	*Which poems do you want to learn?*
Die Gedichte, von denen mein Lehrer sprach.	*The poems that my teacher talked about.*
Die Gedichte, die auf deutsch geschrieben sind.	*The poems that are written in German.*
Das sind die Briefmarken, die Karl mir gegeben hat.	*These are the stamps that Karl gave me.*
Das ist der Regenschirm, den Oma in Bonn gekauft hat.	*That is the umbrella that Granny bought in Bonn.*
Das ist das Wörterbuch, unter dem ich das Geld gefunden habe.	*That is the dictionary under which I found the money.*
Das ist die Dame, deren Tochter Tänzerin werden will.	*That is the lady whose daughter wants to become a dancer.*

Written Practice 1

Rewrite each sentence, changing the antecedent in bold print to the ones in parentheses and making any necessary changes.

Wo ist **das Haus**, das Erik kaufen will?

(der Hut) Wo ist der Hut, den Erik kaufen will?

1. Ich habe **die Bücher**, die du verloren hast.

   (das Heft) ____________________.

   (ein Regenschirm) ____________________.

   (die Flasche) ____________________.

   (der Artikel) ____________________.

2. Robert besucht **die Tänzerin**, deren Vater Diplomat gewesen ist.

(der Matrose) ______________________________.

(die Ausländer) ______________________________.

(eine Dame) ______________________________.

(das Mädchen) ______________________________.

3. Wo fandest du **das Geld**, nach dem der Polizist fragte?

(die Schlüssel) ______________________________?

(der Wagen) ______________________________?

(der Ausländer) ______________________________?

(das Mädchen) ______________________________?

(die Tasche) ______________________________?

4. **Das Mädchen**, das ich in Freiburg traf, wohnt jetzt in Wien.

(der Soldat) ______________________________.

(die Touristen) ______________________________.

(die Tänzerin) ______________________________.

(das Kind) ______________________________.

(der Polizist) ______________________________.

5. **Das Kind**, dessen Schwester gestorben ist, will nicht mitgehen.

(die Kinder) ______________________________.

(der Junge) ______________________________.

(die Tänzerin) ______________________________.

(das Mädchen) ______________________________.

(der Student) ______________________________.

More About Modal Auxiliaries

As you know, modal auxiliaries in the perfect and future tenses form a double-infinitive structure.

Er hat es nicht verstehen können.	*He was not able to understand it.*
Wir werden zu Hause bleiben müssen.	*We will have to stay at home.*

But when a modal auxiliary in a double-infinitive structure is used in a subordinate clause, there is a matter of word order to be considered: The conjugated auxiliary (**haben** or **werden**) of a double-infinitive structure will directly precede the double infinitive. For example:

Er sagt, dass er es nicht **hat** verstehen können.	*He says that he was not able to understand it.*
Weißt du, ob wir zu Hause **werden** bleiben müssen?	*Do you know whether we will have to stay at home?*

Written Practice 2

Complete each phrase with the sentences provided. Employ the appropriate word order.

1. Die Mutter sagt, dass...

   Sie hat die Kinder gut erziehen wollen.

   ______________________________.

   Ihr Sohn wird Soldat werden müssen.

   ______________________________.

   Die Kinder haben kein Bier trinken dürfen.

   ______________________________.

2. Ich weiß nicht, warum...

   Tina hat das Klavier nicht spielen können.

   ______________________________.

   Du wirst nach Belgien reisen sollen.

   ______________________________.

   Die Tänzerin wird in Bremen tanzen wollen.

   ______________________________.

Double Infinitives

There is a short list of other verbs that can serve as the auxiliaries of infinitives and that, in the perfect and future tenses, form a double-infinitive structure.

These verbs are: **lassen**, **sehen**, **hören**, **helfen**, and **lernen**. Let's look at some examples with one of these verbs.

Ich lasse den Wagen reparieren.	*I have the car repaired.*
Ich ließ den Wagen reparieren.	*I had the car repaired.*
Ich habe den Wagen reparieren lassen.	*I have had the car repaired.*
Ich werde den Wagen reparieren lassen.	*I will have the car repaired.*

Oral Practice

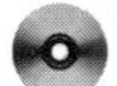

Track 68

Practice saying the following list of sentences out loud.

Haben Sie das Radio reparieren lassen?	*Did you have the radio repaired?*
Nein, ich habe es noch nicht reparieren lassen.	*No, I have not had it repaired yet.*
Hast du die Kinder im Garten spielen sehen?	*Did you see the children playing in the garden?*
Ja, ich habe sie im Garten spielen sehen.	*Yes, I saw them playing in the garden.*
Haben Sie Ihren Sohn singen hören?	*Did you hear your son singing?*
Ja, ich habe ihn schon singen hören.	*Yes, I already heard him singing.*
Wirst du deinem Bruder im Garten arbeiten helfen?	*Will you help your brother work in the garden?*
Ja, ich werde ihm im Garten arbeiten helfen.	*Yes, I will help him work in the garden.*
Sie wird schwimmen lernen.	*She will learn to swim.*
Er wird tanzen lernen.	*He will learn to dance.*
Wir werden Ski laufen lernen.	*We will learn to ski.*

Written Practice 3

Conjugate each verb phrase in the tenses shown with the pronouns provided.

		können es reparieren	**hören sie sprechen**
pres	ich	______________	______________
past	ich	______________	______________
pres perf	wir	______________	______________
fut	wir	______________	______________

		lassen ein Hemd machen	**wollen ihn interviewen**
pres	Sie	______________	______________
past	Sie	______________	______________
pres perf	er	______________	______________
fut	er	______________	______________

Prepositions and Inanimates

A preposition can be followed by most nouns or an animate pronoun.

Ich sprach mit dem Herrn.	*I spoke with the gentleman.*
Ich sprach mit ihm.	*I spoke with him.*

But when a pronoun represents an inanimate object, it forms a special structure with a preposition: a prepositional adverb. The structure of a prepositional adverb in German is **da-** plus the preposition. For example:

dafür	*for it*	damit	*with it*	davon	*from it*

When a preposition begins with a vowel, use **dar-** plus the preposition.

darauf	*on it; for it*	daraus	*from it*	darin	*in it; therein*

Let's compare a few examples with animates and inanimates.

Animate:

Er wartet auf den Matrosen.	*He is waiting for the sailor.*
Er wartet auf ihn.	*He is waiting for him.*

Inanimate:

Er wartet auf den Zug.	*He is waiting for the train.*
Er wartet darauf.	*He is waiting for it.*

Something similar occurs when asking questions with prepositions and inanimate pronouns. In this case, use **wo-** plus the preposition.

womit	*with what*	worin	*in what*	wovon	*of what*

When a preposition begins with a vowel, use **wor-** plus the preposition.

worauf	*on what*	woraus	*out of what*	worin	*in what; in which*

Let's look at some example sentences.

Animate:

Von wem sprecht ihr?	*About whom are you speaking?*
Über wen schreibt der Mann?	*About whom is the man writing?*

Inanimate:

Wovon sprecht ihr?	*About what are you speaking?*
Worüber schreibt der Mann?	*About what is the man writing?*

Oral Practice

Practice saying the following list of sentences out loud.

Von wem hast du es bekommen?	*From whom did you get it?*
Ich habe es von einem Fremden bekommen.	*I got it from a stranger.*
Wovon habt ihr gesprochen?	*What were you talking about?*
Wir haben von dem Gewitter gesprochen.	*We talked about the thunderstorm.*
Worüber freute sie sich?	*What was she happy about?*
Sie freute sich über den Artikel.	*She was happy about the article.*
Worauf freuen sich die Kinder?	*What are the children looking forward to?*
Sie freuen sich auf das Wochenende.	*They are looking forward to the weekend.*
Wofür interessiert er sich?	*What is he interested in?*
Er interessiert sich für Sport.	*He is interested in sports.*
Womit hat er kommen wollen?	*By what did he want to come?*
Er hat mit dem Bus kommen wollen.	*He wanted to come by bus.*

Written Practice 4

Rewrite each prepositional phrase twice, changing the nouns to pronouns, once as a replacement for the prepositional phrase and once as a question.

vor dem Haus	*davor*	*wovor*
an einen Freund	*an ihn*	*an wen*
1. mit seinem Chef	________	________
2. mit dem Zug	________	________
3. von der Erde	________	________
4. in seine Freundin	________	________
5. in der Stadt	________	________
6. am Tisch	________	________
7. gegen die Leute	________	________
8. gegen die Tür	________	________
9. aus dem Wohnzimmer	________	________
10. nach seiner Tante	________	________

Written Practice 5

In the blanks provided, write the letter or letters of the phrases on the right that answer the questions on the left. Not all letters will be used, and some may be used more than once.

1. Wie oft bist du in Norwegen gewesen? ________
2. Ist Ihre Tante Ärztin geworden? ________
3. Womit seid ihr gefahren? ________
4. Haben Sie heute mit Herrn Bach gesprochen? ________.
5. Wann ist der alte Musikant gestorben? ________
6. Ist der Flughafen hier in der Nähe? ________

a. Mit einem Freund.
b. Hoffentlich.
c. Ziemlich oft.
d. Leider nicht
e. Von einer Kusine.
f. Nein, eine Tänzerin.
g. In einer Stunde.
h. Wegen des Wetters.
i. Mit dem Zug.

7. Könnt ihr ihn verstehen? ______
8. Wann fängt das Konzert an? ______
9. Wird sie das Auto reparieren können? ______
10. Haben Sie das Geld gefunden? ______

j. Vor einem Jahr.
k. Ja, sehr gut.
l. Nein, noch nicht.
m. Nein, er ist weit von hier.

More About Adverbs

Adverbs modify verbs, other adverbs, and adjectives. Let's look at the types of adverbs that function in each of these cases.

Some adverbs and adverbial phrases describe frequency or time. For example:

gewöhnlich	*usually*	oft	*often*
immer	*always*	selten	*seldom*
im Sommer	*in the summer*	vor einem Jahr	*a year ago*
manchmal	*sometimes*	wieder	*again*

In a sentence these adverbs may look like this:

Wir gehen **oft** ins Kino. *We **often** go to the movies.*

Other adverbs describe a direction to a place or from a place:

dorthin *(to) there* hierher *(to) here* nach Hause *home(ward)*

For example:

Die Jungen sind **dorthin** gelaufen. *The boys ran **there**.*

Some adverbs or adverbial phrases describe the location where an action takes place:

dort (da)	*there*	oben	*above, overhead; upstairs*
draußen	*outside*	überall	*everywhere*
hier	*here*	unten	*below; downstairs*
in der Stadt	*in the city*	unter dem Tisch	*under the table*

For example:

Draußen ist es sehr kalt. *It is very cold **outside**.*

Other adverbs describe an attitude toward someone or something:

hoffentlich	*hopefully*	natürlich	*naturally*
leider	*unfortunately*	selbstverständlich	*of course, naturally*

For example:

Der Mann ist **leider** gestorben. ***Unfortunately**, the man died.*

Certain adverbs can modify other adverbs or adjectives. They tell to what degree the adverb functions. Let's look at some adverbs that can modify **langsam** (*slowly*, an adverb) or **kalt** (*cold*, an adjective).

außerordentlich kalt	*extraordinarily cold*	sehr kalt	*very cold*
außerordentlich langsam	*extraordinarily slowly*	sehr langsam	*very slowly*
relativ kalt	*relatively cold*	ziemlich kalt	*fairly cold*
relativ langsam	*relatively slowly*	ziemlich langsam	*fairly slowly*

Some adverbs are formed by adding the suffix **-erweise** to an adjective. A few such adverbs are:

Adjective	**Adverb**	
brutal	brutalerweise	*brutally*
erstaunlich	erstaunlicherweise	*astonishingly*
glücklich	glücklicherweise	*happily; fortunately*
möglich	möglicherweise	*possibly*
normal	normalerweise	*normally*

Remember that in German sentences there is a pattern of order for adverbs. They occur within sentences with time adverbs appearing first, adverbs of manner second, and adverbs of place third. For example:

Wir fahren **selten** (time) **mit dem Bus** (manner) **in die Stadt** (place). *We **seldom** go **by bus to the city**.*

See Chapter 13 for details on adverbial word order.

Written Practice 6

Rewrite each sentence adding the adverbs in parentheses. Consider how the meaning is changed by these adverbs.

1. Ihre Tochter ist ______ intelligent.
   (sehr) ____.
   (außerordentlich) ____.
   (relativ) ____.
   (ziemlich) ____.
   (erstaunlicherweise) ____.
2. ______ sehen wir viele Probleme.
   (überall) ____.
   (hier) ____.
   (dort) ____.
   (in dieser Stadt) ____.
   (in Europa) ____.
3. Unsere Familie ist ______ in Griechenland gewesen.
   (oft) ____.
   (selten) ____.
   (manchmal) ____.
   (nie) ____.
   (ziemlich oft) ____.

QUIZ

1. Write the correct forms of the relative pronouns.

	Masculine	Feminine	Neuter	Plural
nom	________	________	________	________
acc	________	________	________	________
dat	________	________	________	________
gen	________	________	________	________

2. Change the phrase in bold print to the ones in parentheses. Rewrite each sentence making the necessary changes to the relative pronouns and verbs used.

   Das Buch, das ich kaufen will, ist ziemlich alt.

   (der Wagen) ________________________

   (die Lampe) ________________________

   (die Wörterbücher) ________________________

   (das Kleid) ________________________

3. Write the following verb phrases in the four tenses shown with the pronouns provided.

		hören sie lachen	lassen das Auto reparieren
pres	er	________	________
past	wir	________	________
pres perf	ihr	________	________
fut	Sie	________	________

		lernen schwimmen	sehen sie tanzen
pres	ich	________	________
past	du	________	________
past perf	wir	________	________
fut	man	________	________

Write new sentences by completing each phrase with the sentences that follow. Make any necessary changes to the word order.

4. **Die Frauen sagen, dass...**

   Der Reporter hat den Chef interviewen wollen.

   ____

   Werner wird das Auto waschen lassen.

   ____

   Sie interessieren sich nicht für Sport.

   ____

5. **Der Student fragt, ob...**

   Werden wir den Krieg verlieren?

   ____

   Haben die Touristen dorthin reisen dürfen?

   ____

   Haben wir ihm ein Paket geschickt?

   ____

Circle the letter or the word or phrase that best completes each sentence.

6. **Ich werde _______________ arbeiten.**

   A. womit
   B. fleißig
   C. lassen
   D. von denen

7. **Der Mann, mit _______________ wir gesprochen haben, kommt aus Deutschland.**

   A. dem
   B. damit
   C. denen
   D. dessen

8. Die Tänzerin, ______________ so schön tanzt, ist meine Nichte.

A. die

B. womit

C. mit der

D. deren

9. Wir werden ______________ wohnen müssen.

A. im Ausland

B. leider

C. nach Amerika

D. zum Wohnzimmer

10. ______________ interessieren Sie sich?

A. Womit

B. Von der Erde

C. Wofür

D. Darauf

PART THREE TEST

Write the present perfect tense and the past perfect tense conjugations for the following verbs with the pronouns provided.

		Present Perfect	Past Perfect
1. helfen	ich	__________	__________
	er	__________	__________
	wir	__________	__________
2. versprechen	ich	__________	__________
	sie *s.*	__________	__________
	ihr	__________	__________
3. fliegen	du	__________	__________
	er	__________	__________
	Sie	__________	__________
4. sein	ich	__________	__________
	du	__________	__________
	wir	__________	__________

5. Provide the past participle for the following verbs with the appropriate auxiliary, **haben** or **sein**.

   fragen __________ spazieren __________

   essen __________ werden __________

   haben __________ mitgehen __________

Using the appropriate form of the dative case, complete each sentence with the words in parentheses.

6. Warum glaubst du __________ nicht?

   (mein Bruder) ____________________

   (diese Dame) ____________________

   (deine Kinder) ____________________

7. **Ich werde mit ______________ tanzen.**
   (er) ______________________________
   (sie *s.*) ______________________________
   (sie *pl.*) ______________________________

8. **Sie haben ______________ ein Paket geschickt.**
   (der Ausländer) ______________________________
   (du) ______________________________
   (wir) ______________________________

Complete each sentence, filling in the blank with the correct forms of the words in parentheses.

9. **Sie ist vor ______________ angekommen.**
   (zwei Tage) ______________________________
   (eine Woche) ______________________________
   (ein Jahr) ______________________________

10. **Er hat drei Stunden auf ______________ gewartet.**
   (ich) ______________________________
   (er) ______________________________
   (ihr) ______________________________

Write the accusative, dative, and genitive forms of the following words and phrases.

	Accusative	Dative	Genitive
11. ich	____________	____________	____________
12. du	____________	____________	____________
13. Sie	____________	____________	____________
14. meine Brüder	____________	____________	____________
15. das Kind	____________	____________	____________

Change the phrases conjugated in the present tense to the present perfect and future tenses. For example:

Ich komme mit.

Ich bin mitgekommen.

Ich werde mitkommen.

16. Wir bestellen ein Butterbrot.

____

____

17. Ihr wascht euch.

____

____

18. Wir steigen hier um.

____

____

19. Kannst du Schach spielen?

____

____

Rewrite the sentence, changing the words in bold print to the ones in parentheses. Make the appropriate changes to the relative clauses and verbs used.

20. Der Junge, dessen Vater Zahnarzt ist, wohnt in diesem großen Haus.

(die Kinder) ______________________________

(das Mädchen) ______________________________

(der Schüler) ______________________________

Rewrite the sentence to include each question that follows. Make any necessary changes to the word order.

21. **Der Reporter fragt, ob...**

    Hat der Diplomat nicht gut fahren können?

    ____

    Wird er den Helden interviewen wollen?

    ____

Circle the letter of the word or phrase that best completes each sentence.

22. **Es ist sehr heiß ______________.**

    A. gemacht   C. geworden

    B. versprochen   D. gewartet

23. **Sie irren ______________ nicht.**

    A. sich   C. schon

    B. jetzt   D. Ihnen

24. **Die Wohnung ______________ war sehr groß.**

    A. meinen Onkel   C. Ihrem Enkel

    B. unserer Nachbarin   D. trotz des Wetters

25. **______________ des Sommers bleibe ich in der Stadt.**

    A. Warum   C. Während

    B. Vor   D. Nach

Part Four

Some Fine Points

chapter 16

Comparing Things

In this chapter you will find comparative and superlative forms introduced. In addition, there will be a further discussion of relative pronouns as well as a description of several useful idioms.

CHAPTER OBJECTIVES

In this chapter you will learn about:

- More About Relative Pronouns
- A Few Common Idioms
- Comparative and Superlative of Adjectives and Adverbs
- A Little German History

More About Relative Pronouns

There is still more to know about the use of German relative pronouns.

Welcher as a Relative Pronoun

It is possible to substitute a form of **welcher** for relative pronouns that take the form of the definite article. The genitive form is the only exception to this. Compare the following declensions of relative pronouns.

	Masculine	**Feminine**	**Neuter**	**Plural**
nom	der, welcher	die, welche	das, welches	die, welche
acc	den, welchen	die, welche	das, welches	die, welche
dat	dem, welchem	der, welcher	dem, welchem	denen, welchen
gen	dessen	deren	dessen	deren

Let's look at **welcher** as it appears in sentences.

Der Soldat, welcher im Irak war, ist wieder zu Hause. — *The soldier that was in Iraq is home again.*

Der Soldat, welchen Tina kennt, ist wieder zu Hause. — *The soldier that Tina knows is home again.*

Der Soldat, von welchem alle sprechen, ist wieder zu Hause. — *The soldier that everyone is speaking about is home again.*

Der Soldat, dessen Schwester Ärztin ist, ist wieder zu Hause. — *The soldier whose sister is a physician is home again.*

Written Practice 1

Rewrite each sentence, changing the phrase in bold print to the ones provided in parentheses. Use a form of **welcher** as the relative pronoun and make any necessary changes to the sentence. For example:

Das Haus, das er kaufen will, ist alt.

(das Auto) Das Auto, welches er kaufen will, ist alt.

1. **Das Buch**, das sie gelesen hat, ist interessant.

   (der Brief) ______________________________.

   (die Zeitung) ______________________________.

(der Roman) ____.

(die Romane) ____.

2. **Das Mädchen**, mit dem Karl sprechen will, kommt aus Polen.

(die Touristen) ____.

(der Matrose) ____.

(die Tänzerin) ____.

(das Kind) ____.

Was as a Relative Pronoun

It is possible for an entire clause to be the antecedent of a relative pronoun. If this is the case, in German the relative pronoun becomes **was**. Let's look at some examples.

Er ist Zahnarzt geworden, was uns sehr erstaunte.	*He became a dentist, which astounded us very much.*
Es fing an zu regnen, was das Picknick schnell verdorben hat.	*It began to rain, which quickly spoiled the picnic.*
Es geht ihrem Mann jetzt gut, was uns sehr erfreute.	*Her husband is feeling well now, which made us very happy.*

Was also becomes the relative pronoun when the demonstrative **das** is the antecedent.

Ich verstehe das, was du sagen willst.	*I understand what you want to say.*
Verstehst du nichts von dem, was er sagt?	*Do you not understand anything of what he says?*

And **was** is the relative pronoun when the antecedent is either **alles**, **etwas**, **nichts**, **viel(es)**, or a neuter adjective used as a noun. For example:

Das ist alles, was ich geben kann.	*That is everything that I can give.*
Sie lesen etwas, was ziemlich interessant ist.	*They are reading something that is rather interesting.*
Der Lehrer versteht nichts, was das Kind schreibt.	*The teacher does not understand anything that the child writes.*
Es gibt vieles, was uns glücklich macht.	*There is much that makes us happy.*
Das war das Letzte, was er hörte.	*That was the last thing that he heard.*

Oral Practice

 Track 69

Practice saying the following list of sentences out loud.

Haben Sie etwas, was billig ist?	*Do you have something that is cheap?*
Nein, ich habe nichts, was billig ist.	*No, I have nothing that is cheap.*
Ist das alles, was Sie haben?	*Is that all that you have?*
Nein, ich habe viel mehr.	*No, I have a lot more.*
Haben Sie etwas, was nicht so teuer ist?	*Do you have something that is not so expensive?*
Ja, ich habe vieles, was nicht so teuer ist.	*Yes, I have a lot that is not so expensive.*
Karl hat den Preis gewonnen, was mich sehr erstaunte.	*Karl won the prize, which astounded me very much.*
Gudrun ist schnell gerannt, was uns sehr erstaunte.	*Gudrun ran fast, which astounded us very much.*
Erik wollte Geige spielen, was den Vater sehr erstaunte.	*Erik wanted to play the violin, which astounded the father very much.*

If a preposition is needed with **was**, a compound word with the prefix **wo-** is formed with that preposition, for example: **womit**, **wofür**. If the preposition begins with a vowel, the prefix is **wor-** is used: **worauf**, **worin**. Following are some example sentences:

Ich habe etwas, wofür du dich interessieren wirst.	*I have something that you will be interested in.*
Er schreibt nichts, worüber er nicht sprechen soll.	*He writes nothing that he should not speak about.*

Written Practice 2

Combine the first sentence with the sentences that follow. Form a relative clause with **was** or a **wo-/wor-** compound following the pattern of the example.

Ich habe nichts.

Nichts ist interessant.

Ich habe nichts, was interessant ist.

1. Ich habe etwas.

   Ich habe etwas im Park gefunden.

   ____.

   Meine Mutter hat mir etwas gegeben.

   ____.

   Du wirst dich über etwas freuen.

   ____.

   Die Kinder können mit etwas spielen.

   ____.

2. Ist das alles?

   Du kannst alles sagen.

   ____.

   Tina wollte alles kaufen.

   ____.

   Er interessiert sich für alles.

   ____.

   Sie wollen über alles sprechen.

   ____.

3. Ich lerne viel, …

   Viel steht nicht in Büchern.

   ____.

   Goethe hatte über vieles geschrieben.

   ____.

   Vieles ist interessant.

   ____.

4. Ich verstehe nichts, …

   Die alte Frau sagt nichts.

   ____.

   Du hast nichts in diesem Buch geschrieben.

   ____.

   Man lernt nichts in dieser Klasse.

   ____.

A Few Common Idioms

Idioms are special phrases or special usages of words that are accepted in a language as an understandable concept, but when translated into another language, idioms most often make little or no sense. For example, the English idiom, *eat your heart out,* would sound absolutely ridiculous if translated literally into German. The same thing occurs when translating German idioms into English.

Es gibt

German has a special idiomatic expression made up simply of the two words **es gibt**. Literally, those words mean *it gives*, but this expression is used when in English you say *there is* or *there are*: *There are a lot of toys on the floor.* (**Es gibt viele Spielzeuge auf dem Boden.**) English has both a singular and plural form of this idiom: *there is, there are*. But German has only one form for both the singular and the plural: **es gibt**.

The German idiom functions much the same way as its English counterpart, except that the object that follows **es gibt** must be in the accusative case. You should recall that this means that all masculine nouns will make a declensional change. Let's look at some example sentences.

Es gibt viele Bücher in meiner Bibliothek.	*There are a lot of books in my library.*
Heute mittag gibt es Bratwurst und Suppe.	*For lunch today there are roast sausages and soup.*
Warum gibt es keinen Wein?	*Why is there no wine?*

Oral Practice

Practice saying the following list of sentences out loud.

Was gibt es zum Abendessen?	*What is there for supper?*
Es gibt Gemüsesuppe zum Abendessen.	*There is vegetable soup for supper.*
Es gibt Rindfleisch und Kartoffeln.	*There is beef and potatoes.*
Es gibt Fisch und Reis.	*There is fish and rice.*
Was gibt es zu trinken?	*What is there to drink?*
Es gibt Kaffee oder Tee.	*There is coffee or tea.*

Es gibt Sprudel oder Mineralwasser.	*There is sparkling water or mineral water.*
Es gibt Bier oder Wein.	*There is beer or wine.*
Was gibt es zum Nachtisch?	*What is there for dessert?*
Es gibt Eis oder Pudding.	*There is ice cream or pudding.*
Es gibt einen Obstkuchen.	*There is a pie.*

Wie geht's

You learned another German idiom early in this book: **Wie geht's?** (*How are you?*) Now that you've had a thorough look at the dative case, it's time to look again at this expression. This idiom uses the pronoun **es** as its subject (**Wie geht es?**), and its objects must be in the dative case.

The question **Wie geht's**? shows the pronoun **es** as a contraction. But when an object is added, the contraction is not used. Following are some examples:

Wie geht es dir?	*How are you?*
Es geht mir gut, danke. Und dir?	*I am fine, thanks. And you?*
Wie geht es Ihnen?	*How are you?*
Es geht mir sehr gut. Und Ihnen?	*I am very well. And you?*
Ziemlich gut.	*Fairly well.*
Wie geht es Ihrem Mann?	*How is your husband?*
Nicht so gut.	*Not so well.*
Es ging ihm letzte Woche viel besser.	*He was much better last week.*
Hoffentlich geht es ihm nächste Woche wieder besser.	*I hope he will be better again next week.*
Es wird mir auch besser gehen.	*I will feel better, too.*

The pronoun **es** is the subject of other common expressions, in which some mysterious *it* is the cause of meteorological conditions.

Es regnet.	*It is raining.*
Es schneit.	*It is snowing.*

Both **regnen** and **schneien** are regular verbs and use the auxiliary **haben** in the perfect tenses.

Gern Haben

Another useful idiomatic expression is **gern haben**. Its translation is *to like* or *to be fond of*. The verb **haben** can be conjugated in any tense, and the object of that verb is then followed by **gern**. For example:

Hast du mich nicht gern?	*Don't you like me?*
Tina hatte den neuen Studenten gern.	*Tina liked the new student.*
Haben Sie sie gern gehabt?	*Did you like her?*
Ich werde diesen Mann nie gern haben.	*I will never like this man.*

Geboren

The infinitive **gebären** means *to bear (a child)*. Its conjugation in the various tenses looks like this:

Present

ich gebäre	*I bear*	sie gebärt (*or* gebiert)	*she bears*

Past

ich gebar	*I bore*	sie gebar	*she bore*

Present Perfect

ich habe geboren	*I have bore*	sie hat geboren	*she has bore*

Future

ich werde gebären	*I will bear*	sie wird gebären	*she will bear*

The expression *to be born* is a common one: *I was born in July; She was born thirty years ago*. In German that expression is composed of the conjugation of the verb **sein** and the past participle **geboren**. In sentences it looks like this:

Mein Vater ist im Jahre 1970 geboren.	*My father was born in 1970.*
Wann bist du geboren?	*When were you born?*

Use **ist** with **geboren** when talking about people who are still alive. Use **wurde** with **geboren** when talking about people who are deceased.

Mein Sohn ist vor drei Wochen geboren.	*My son was born three weeks ago.*
Goethe wurde im Jahre 1749 geboren.	*Goethe was born in 1749.*

When giving the year that someone was born, you can use the phrase **im Jahre** with the year. It is also possible to use the year alone. In that case, do not use the preposition **in**.

Er ist im Jahre 1977 geboren.	*He was born in 1977.*
Er ist 1977 geboren.	*He was born in 1977.*

Do not use **im Jahre** with a month and a date.

Er ist im Oktober 1977 geboren.	*He was born in October 1977.*
Er ist am achten Oktober 1977 geboren.	*He was born on the eighth of October, 1977.*

Oral Practice

Practice saying the following list of sentences out loud.

Wann sind Sie geboren?	*When were you born?*
Ich bin im April geboren.	*I was born in April.*
In welchem Jahr bist du geboren?	*In what year were you born?*
Ich bin im Jahre 1988 geboren.	*I was born in 1988.*
Wo seid ihr geboren?	*Where were you born?*
Wir sind in Frankreich geboren.	*We were born in France.*
Wer ist in Deutschland geboren?	*Who was born in Germany?*
Professor Benz ist in Deutschland geboren.	*Professor Benz was born in Germany.*
Mozart wurde in Österreich geboren.	*Mozart was born in Austria.*
Wurde Bach in Deutschland geboren?	*Was Bach born in Germany?*
Ja, Bach wurde in Deutschland geboren.	*Yes, Bach was born in Germany.*
Wo wurde John F. Kennedy geboren?	*Where was John F. Kennedy born?*
Er wurde in den Vereinigten Staaten geboren.	*He was born in the United States.*

Written Practice 3

Using the names and years provided, write sentences that tell when someone was born and when someone died. For example:

Benjamin Franklin 1706–1790

Benjamin Frankin wurde 1706 geboren.

Er ist 1790 gestorben.

1. Wilhelm II. 1859–1941

   ____.

   ____.

2. Otto von Bismarck 1815–1898

   ____.

   ____.

3. mein Bruder 1995–2005

   ____.

   ____.

4. Karl der Große 742–814

   ____.

   ____.

5. meine Mutter 1966–1998

   ____.

   ____.

Comparative and Superlative of Adjectives and Adverbs

The basic form of an adjective or adverb is called the positive form. But two other forms exist that play significant roles in language: the comparative and the superlative.

The comparative of an adjective or adverb makes a comparison between two persons or things.

John is *bigger* than Mary. She runs *faster* than her brother.

And like English, German forms a comparative by adding **-er** to the adjective or adverb.

klein	*small*	kleiner	*smaller*
schnell	*fast*	schneller	*faster*
weit	*far*	weiter	*farther*

Adjectives or adverbs with the vowels **a**, **o**, **u**, may require an umlaut in the comparative.

alt	*old*	älter	*older*
groß	*big*	größer	*bigger*
jung	*young*	jünger	*younger*

The word **als** (*than*) is used to identify the person or thing being compared to the subject: **Er ist älter als Erik.** (*He is older than Erik.*)

Comparatives have no ending when used as predicate adjectives or adverbs. But if the comparative is an adjective modifying a noun directly, it will have an adjective ending.

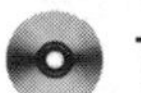 Track 70

Adverb:

Er spricht schneller.	*He speaks faster.*
Sie läuft langsamer als Tanja.	*She runs slower than Tanja.*

Predicate Adjective:

Unser Haus ist größer.	*Our house is bigger.*
Mein Sohn ist kleiner als Ihr Sohn.	*My son is smaller than your son.*

Adjective Ending:

Der kleinere Junge ist mein Sohn.	*The smaller boy is my son.*
Das jüngere Mädchen ist meine Tochter.	*The younger girl is my daughter.*

The English superlative ends in *-est*: *tallest, funniest, biggest,* and so forth. German is similar but not identical—the ending **-sten** is added. A predicate adjective or adverb in the German superlative is formed using a prepositional phrase with **an**. Many adjectives and adverbs that contain the vowels **a**, **o**, **u** may require an umlaut in the superlative.

hart	*hard*	am härtesten	*(the) hardest*
jung	*young*	am jüngsten	*(the) youngest*
klein	*small*	am kleinsten	*(the) smallest*
rot	*red*	am rötesten	*(the) reddest*
schnell	*fast*	am schnellsten	*(the) fastest*
weit	*far*	am weitesten	*(the) farthest*

As you see from **hart**, **rot**, and **weit**, when an adjective or adverb ends in **-d**, **-t**, **-s**, **-ss**, **-ß**, or **-z**, the superlative suffix will be **-esten**.

am ältesten	*(the) oldest*
am blödesten	*(the) most*
am kürzesten	*(the) shortest idiotic*

If the superlative is an adjective modifying a noun directly, it will have an adjective ending and the preposition **an** is omitted.

Track 70

Adverb:

Er spricht am schnellsten.	*He speaks the fastest.*
Sie läuft am langsamsten.	*She runs the slowest.*

Predicate Adjective:

Unser Haus ist am größten.	*Our house is the biggest.*
Mein Sohn ist am kleinsten.	*My son is the smallest.*

Adjective Ending:

Der kleinste Junge ist mein Sohn.	*The smallest boy is my son.*
Das jüngste Mädchen ist meine Tochter.	*The youngest girl is my daughter.*

Just as English has a few irregular forms in the comparative and superlative, so, too, does German.

Positive		**Comparative**		**Superlative**	
bald	*soon*	eher	*sooner*	am ehesten	*soonest*
groß	*big*	größer	*bigger*	am größten	*biggest*
gut	*good*	besser	*better*	am besten	*best*
hoch	*high*	höher	*higher*	am höchsten	*highest*
nah	*near*	näher	*nearer*	am nächsten	*nearest*

Written Practice 4

Form the comparative and superlative of the following adjectives.

	Comparative	Superlative
klein	*kleiner*	*am kleinsten*
1. kalt	__________	__________
2. interessant	__________	__________
3. gut	__________	__________
4. lang	__________	__________
5. dunkel	__________	__________
6. warm	__________	__________
7. schwarz	__________	__________
8. ruhig	__________	__________
9. weiß	__________	__________
10. arm	__________	__________

A Little German History

In the days of the Roman Empire, Tacitus wrote about the tribes of northern Europe—the Germanic tribes (**die germanischen Stämme**). They were fierce people who lived a more primitive existence than the Romans or other ethnic groups within the Roman Empire.

The Germanic people evolved over the centuries into the modern Germans who lived in a large number of small principalities. These principalities, as well as other larger states, were part of the Holy Roman Empire (**das heilige römische Reich deutscher Nation**), which in the beginning was ruled by Emperor Charlemagne (**Kaiser Karl der Große**). The word **Kaiser** is the German word for *Emperor* or *Caesar*.

The little German principalities were overseen by lesser nobles than Emperor Charlemagne in *Aix-la-Chapelle* (**Aachen**). These lesser nobles were called:

der Freiherr	*baron*	die Gräfin	*countess*
die Freifrau	*baroness*	der Herzog	*duke*
der Graf	*count*	die Herzogin	*duchess*

As Prussia (**Preußen**) grew more powerful and influential, it began to dominate the smaller principalities, and in the nineteenth century, under the leadership of Otto von Bismarck, a new united land emerged: Germany (**Deutschland**). At the same time, the Prussian king claimed the title **Kaiser** and was no longer referred to as **König**.

After World War I (**der erste Weltkrieg**), the monarchy collapsed, and Germany became a republic (**die Weimarer Republik**). In 1933 Adolf Hitler took over power and led the country with the title *leader* (**der Führer**). His political party was called the **Nazi** party, which is short for the National Socialistic German Workers' Party (**die Nationalsozialistische Deutsche Arbeiterpartei**). Soon after the end of the World War II (**der zweite Weltkrieg**), West Germany became a republic once again (**die Bundesrepublik Deutschland** or **BRD**), and East Germany became a separate republic (**die Deutsche Demokratische Republik** or **DDR**).

The new head of the West German republic was called the chancellor (**der Kanzler**) and the parliament was called the **Bundestag**. With the end of the Cold War (**der kalte Krieg**) in the late 1980s, Germany achieved the reunification (**die Wiedervereinigung**) it had sought since the end of World War II. The capital (**die Hauptstadt**) of West Germany at that time was Bonn. The capital of East Germany was East Berlin (**Ostberlin**). Today the capital of unified Germany is the historical capital, **Berlin**. Over the entrance to the parliament building in the capital city is the inscription **Dem Deutschen Volke** (*To the German people*).

Oral Practice

Practice saying the following list of sentences out loud.

Ich finde Geschichte sehr interessant.	*I find history very interesting.*
Weißt du etwas über die deutsche Geschichte?	*Do you know something about German history?*
Nein, ich weiß wenig über die deutsche Geschichte.	*No, I know little about German history.*
Der erste Kaiser des ersten Reiches war Karl der Große.	*The first emperor of the First Reich was Charlemagne.*

Der letzte Kaiser des zweiten Reiches war Wilhelm II. (der zweite).	*The last emperor of the Second Reich was Wilhelm II.*
Adolf Hitler war der Führer des dritten Reiches.	*Adolf Hitler was the leader of the Third Reich.*
Im Jahre 1989 endete der kalte Krieg.	*The Cold War ended in 1989.*
Die Mauer zwischen Ost- und Westberlin wurde abgerissen.	*The wall between East and West Berlin was pulled down.*
Deutschland ist jetzt eine Republik.	*Germany is a republic now.*
Hat Deutschland einen Kanzler oder eine Kanzlerin?	*Does Germany have a male or female chancellor?*
Was war die Hauptstadt der Bundesrepublik Deutschland?	*What was the capital of the Federal Republic of Germany?*
Die Hauptstadt der Bundesrepublik war Bonn.	*The capital of the Federal Republic was Bonn.*
Was war die Hauptstadt der DDR?	*What was the capital of the GDR?*
Die Hauptstadt der DDR war Ostberlin.	*The capital of the GDR was East Berlin.*
Was ist die heutige Hauptstadt Deutschlands?	*What is the present capital of Germany?*
Die heutige Hauptstadt ist Berlin.	*The present capital is Berlin.*
Wie heißt das deutsche Parlament?	*What is the name of the German parliament?*
Das deutsche Parlament heißt der Bundestag.	*The German parliament is called the* Bundestag.

Written Practice 5

Circle the letter of the word or phrase that best completes each sentence.

1. In welchem Jahr _______ er geboren?
   (a) wart (c) sein
   (b) wurde (d) kann

2. Alles, ______ sie sagte, war sehr interessant.
   (a) welches (c) dass
   (b) das (d) was

3. Hast du das schöne Mädchen ______?
   (a) gern (c) sehr gut
   (b) welche (d) gebären

4. Es gibt ______.
   (a) keinen Nachtisch (c) kein Wein
   (b) noch (d) wahrscheinlich

5. Unser Kind ist ______ geboren.
   (a) Dezember (c) Donnerstag
   (b) 2001 (d) der zehnte Mai

6. Der Matrose, ______ ich gesprochen habe, ist ein Held.
   (a) für wen (c) von welchem
   (b) darüber (d) über ihn

7. Wir besichtigen ______, die mehr als 500 Jahre alt ist.
   (a) ein Schiff (c) einer Stadt
   (b) eine Kirche (d) der Stadtmauer

8. Ich ______ im Januar 1980 geboren.
   (a) bin (c) konnte
   (b) wurde (d) habe

9. Wann kommt der Zug, ______ wir dorthin fahren werden?
   (a) mit welchem (c) darin
   (b) von dem (d) worauf

10. Er gab mir etwas, ______ ich lange gewartet habe.
   (a) wann (c) damit
   (b) worauf (d) welche

11. Berlin ist die ______ Deutschlands.
   (a) Mauer (c) Kaiser
   (b) Bundesrepublik (d) Hauptstadt

12. Wilhelm II. war Kaiser des zweiten ______.
    (a) Republik (c) Reiches
    (b) Weltkrieg (d) Königs

13. Meine Tochter ist in Österreich ______.
    (a) gewohnt (c) gegangen
    (b) gelebt (d) geboren

14. Zu Hause sprechen wir ______ Deutsch.
    (a) gewöhnlich (c) in einer Stunde
    (b) brutalerweise (d) es gibt

15. Es gibt ______, was uns glücklich macht.
    (a) alle (c) kein Nachtisch
    (b) vieles (d) welches

16. Mein Vater ist ______ als mein Onkel.
    (a) schön (c) älter
    (b) am schnellsten (d) arm

17. Wer kann ______ laufen?
    (a) der langsame (c) weite
    (b) am schnellsten (d) hoch

18. Erik ist der ______ Student.
    (a) klein (c) größer
    (b) am ärmsten (d) beste

19. Meine Schwester spielt das Klavier ______.
    (a) am schlechtesten (c) kälter
    (b) bessere (d) heißeste

20. Welche Stadt ist ______?
    (a) kleinere (c) älteste
    (b) näher (d) das größte

QUIZ

The definite article forms of relative pronouns are given below. Write in their **welcher** counterparts.

1. **nom** **der** ________ **die** ________ **das** ________ **die** ________
2. **acc** **den** ________ **die** ________ **das** ________ **die** ________
3. **dat** **dem** ________ **der** ________ **dem** ________ **denen** ________
4. **gen** **dessen** ________ **deren** ________ **dessen** ________ **deren** ________

Combine the first sentence with the one that follows, making each one a relative clause with a relative pronoun. Then rewrite the sentence using **welcher** as the relative pronoun. For example:

Der Seemann fuhr auf einem Schiff.

Das Schiff ging bei einer Insel unter.

Der Seemann fuhr auf einem Schiff, das bei einer Insel unterging.

Der Seemann fuhr auf einem Schiff, welches bei einer Insel unterging.

5. **Er hat ein Auto.**
   Er wird das Auto reparieren lassen.

   ____

   ____

6. **Complete the following sentences with the one that follows. Form each one as a relative clause.**
   Martin hat etwas, ...
   Du wirst dich über etwas freuen.

   ____

Ich verstehe nichts, ...

Er hat nichts gesagt.

____

Write a statement using the example as a guide.

Der Präsident wurde im Jahre 1743 geboren.

Er ist im Jahre 1826 gestorben.

7. **Goethe 1749–1832**

____

____

8. **Form the comparative and superlative forms of the adjectives provided in parentheses. For example:**

(schön)	*schöner*	*am schönsten*
(alt)	________	________
(klein)	________	________
(jung)	________	________
(gut)	________	________
(viel)	________	________
(groß)	________	________
(interessant)	________	________

Rewrite each sentence, filling in the blanks with the proper forms of the nouns or pronouns given.

9. **Warum gibt es __________?**
   (kein Wein) ____________________________
   (nur eine Flasche Milch) ________________________
   (kein Bier) ____________________________
   (kein Sekt) ____________________________

10. **Hast du ______________ gern?**

(er) ______________________________

(der Soldat) ______________________________

(sie *pl.*) ______________________________

(die Kinder) ______________________________

(das Kind) ______________________________

chapter 17

Using Commands

In this chapter you will learn about the passive voice and adjective endings. In addition, the imperative will be introduced as well as some useful vocabulary for plants and animals.

CHAPTER OBJECTIVES

In this chapter you will learn about:

- Passive Voice
- Adjective Endings with *Der-* Words
- Imperative
- Plants
- Animals

Passive Voice

Until now, you have dealt with verbs in the active voice. In the active voice, the subject is the doer of the action of the verb.

John kisses Mary.

John is the doer of the action, the one who does the kissing. But in the passive voice, the doer of the action is put in a passive position in the sentence. And the doer of the action can even be omitted from the sentence. For example:

Mary is being kissed by John.

The subject of this sentence is Mary. But she's not doing the kissing. Look at the same sentence with the doer of the action omitted.

Mary is being kissed.

The subject is still Mary, but the doer of the action isn't even mentioned. Another example:

The money was stolen from the bank.

Who took the money? A robber? The head of the bank? The doer of the action is not stated.

The German passive voice consists of a conjugation of **werden** followed by a past participle. Don't confuse this with the future tense, which is **werden** followed by an infinitive. Let's look at some examples of the German passive voice in the present tense.

das Geld wird gefunden	*the money is found*
Maria wird geküsst	*Maria is kissed*
es wird oft gesagt	*it is often said*
die Schüler werden unterrichtet	*the pupils are instructed*

The doer of the action, when added to the passive voice structure, becomes the object of the dative preposition **von**.

Das Geld wird von einem Jungen gefunden.	*The money is found by a boy.*
Was wird von ihr gesagt?	*What is said by her?*

Maria wird von Johannes geküsst.	*Maria is kissed by Johannes.*
Die Schüler werden von der Lehrerin unterrichtet.	*The pupils are instructed by the teacher.*

Naturally, a passive sentence can be stated in other tenses as well. The passive conjugation is simply the conjugation of **werden** in the various tenses with a past participle added:

Present: er wird
Past: er wurde
Present Perfect: er ist geworden
Past Perfect: er war geworden
Future: er wird werden
Future Perfect: er wird geworden sein

There is one significant difference: In the passive voice the participle **worden** is used in place of **geworden**. Let's look at some examples.

Track 71

Present:

Sie wird von ihren Eltern geliebt.	*She is loved by her parents.*

Past:

Sie wurde von ihren Eltern geliebt.	*She was loved by her parents.*

Present Perfect:

Sie ist von ihren Eltern geliebt worden.	*She was loved by her parents.*

Past Perfect:

Sie war von ihren Eltern geliebt worden.	*She had been loved by her parents.*

Future:

Sie wird von ihren Eltern geliebt werden.	*She will be loved by her parents.*

Future Perfect:

Sie wird von ihren Eltern geliebt worden sein.	*She will have been loved by her parents.*

It is possible to change an active sentence into a passive sentence quite simply. First, determine the tense of the active sentence; that will be the tense of the passive sentence.

Mein Bruder fand den Regenschirm. (past tense) — *My brother found the umbrella.*

Then change the verb of the active sentence into a past participle.

fand → **gefunden**

Change the direct object (accusative case) of the active sentence into the subject (nominative case) of the passive sentence.

den Regenschirm → **Der Regenschirm**...gefunden.

Conjugate **werden** for the new subject in the tense of the original active sentence.

Der Regenschirm **wurde**...gefunden.

Make the subject of the active sentence the object of the preposition **von** in the passive sentence.

Der Regenschirm wurde **von meinem Bruder** gefunden. — *The umbrella was found by my brother.*

Let's try that again with another active sentence.

Die Studentin hat den Brief geschrieben. — *The student wrote the letter.*

Tense: present perfect
Past participle: geschrieben
New subject: der Brief
Conjugation of *werden*: ist...worden
Object of *von*: von der Studentin

And when all the elements are put together, the passive sentence looks like this:

Der Brief ist von der Studentin geschrieben worden. — *The letter was written by the student.*

Written Practice 1

Change the following present tense active sentences to present tense passive sentences. Consider how the meanings change.

1. Der Lehrer kauft zwei Bücher.

   ______________________________.

2. Sie liest den Roman.

   ______________________________.

3. Der Bäcker bäckt das Brot.

   ______________________________.

4. Mein Vater ruft mich.

   ______________________________.

5. Die Soldaten singen viele Lieder.

   ______________________________.

Change the following past tense active sentences to past tense passive sentences.

6. Herr Bauer verkaufte das Haus.

   ______________________________.

7. Meine Mutter rief Tante Gerda an.

   ______________________________.

8. Sie tranken zwei Tassen Kaffee.

   ______________________________.

9. Er lernte diese Gedichte.

   ______________________________.

10. Die Wirtin brachte den Morgenkaffee.

    ______________________________.

Change the following present perfect tense active sentences to present perfect tense passive sentences.

11. Er hat den Roman geschrieben.

    ______________________________.

12. Die Kinder haben einen Hut gefunden.

    ______________________________.

13. Meine Schwester hat das Eis gegessen.

______________________________________.

Change the following future tense active sentences to future tense passive sentences.

14. Der Reporter wird den Artikel schreiben.

______________________________________.

15. Die Ausländer werden das Museum besuchen.

______________________________________.

Oral Practice

Practice saying the following list of sentences out loud.

Die Lampe wurde gebrochen.	*The lamp was broken.*
Die Vase wurde auch gebrochen.	*The vase was broken, too.*
Was wurde repariert?	*What was repaired?*
Der Wagen wurde repariert.	*The car was repaired.*
Ist das Radio auch repariert worden?	*Was the radio repaired, too?*
Ja, es ist von Herrn Benz repariert worden.	*Yes, it was repaired by Mr. Benz.*
Was wird von Tina gebracht werden?	*What will be brought by Tina?*
Ein Obstkuchen wird von ihr gebracht werden.	*A fruit pie will be brought by Tina.*
Eine Flasche Wein wird von Thomas gebracht werden.	*A bottle of wine will be brought by Thomas.*
Von wem werden eure Kinder unterrichtet?	*By whom are your children taught?*
Unsere Kinder werden von Frau Keller unterrichtet.	*Our children are taught by Ms. Keller.*
Der Kuchen ist von meinem Sohn gebacken worden.	*The cake was baked by my son.*
Die Lieder sind von meiner Tochter gesungen worden.	*The songs were sung by my daughter.*

Die Kunsthalle ist von ihnen besucht worden.	*The art museum was visited by them.*
Der Artikel ist von ihr geschrieben worden.	*The article was written by her.*
Was ist passiert?	*What happened?*
Der Bahhof ist zerstört worden.	*The railroad station was destroyed.*
Was ist geschehen?	*What happened?*
Mein Pass ist gestohlen worden.	*My passport has been stolen.*

Adjective Endings with *Der-* Words

The definite articles (**der**, **die**, and **das**) are called **der-** words. But there are other **der-** words as well. It is important to identify them, because they act as signals for the adjective endings required. Following is a list of **der-** words to familiarize yourself with:

alle	*(plural only) all*	jeder	*each*
derselbe	*the same*	jener	*that*
dieser	*this*	welcher	*which*

When these **der-** words are used in the nominative case, the gender signal (**-r** for masculine, **-e** for feminine, and **-s** for neuter) appears in the **der-** word itself. The ending of the adjective that follows is then always an **-e**.

Nominative Case

masc	der gute Lehrer	dieser nette Mann	jeder kleine Junge
fem	die gute Frau	jene nette Dame	welche große Lampe
neut	das gute Kind	jedes nette Mädchen	dasselbe alte Schiff

In the remaining cases (excluding the feminine and neuter accusative, which are always identical to the nominative), the ending for all adjectives is **-en**. Let's look at a chart of these adjective endings.

	Masculine	**Feminine**	**Neuter**	**Plural**
nom	der gute Mann	die gute Frau	das gute Kind	die gut**en** Kinder
acc	den gut**en** Mann	die gute Frau	das gute Kind	die gut**en** Kinder
dat	dem gut**en** Mann	der gut**en** Frau	dem gut**en** Kind	den gut**en** Kindern
gen	des gut**en** Mannes	der gut**en** Frau	des gut**en** Kindes	der gut**en** Kinder

This pattern of adjective endings can be used for any **der-** word. For example, in the masculine:

nom	der gute Mann	dieser gute Mann	jeder gute Mann
acc	den gut**en** Mann	diesen gut**en** Mann	jeden gut**en** Mann
dat	dem gut**en** Mann	diesem gut**en** Mann	jedem gut**en** Mann
gen	des gut**en** Mannes	dieses gut**en** Mannes	jedes gut**en** Mannes

Written Practice 2

Write the following phrases in the accusative, dative, and genitive cases.

nom	**jener nette Wirt**	**diese kleine Bluse**	**welches rote Auto**
acc	________________	________________	________________
dat	________________	________________	________________
gen	________________	________________	________________
nom	**derselbe alte Wagen**	**jenes neue Haus**	**alle fremden Leute**
acc	________________	________________	________________
dat	________________	________________	________________
gen	________________	________________	________________

Oral Practice

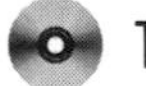 Track 72

Practice saying the following list of sentences out loud.

Kennen Sie den alten Herrn?	*Do you know the old gentleman?*
Nein, ich kenne ihn nicht.	*No, I do not know him.*
Hast du mit jener schönen Tänzerin gesprochen?	*Did you speak with that pretty dancer?*
Nein, ich habe mit dieser netten Schauspielerin gesprochen.	*No, I spoke with this nice actress.*
Ist das das Fahrrad dieses kleinen Kindes?	*Is that this little child's bike?*
Nein, das ist das Fahrrad jenes großen Jungen.	*No, that is that big boy's bike.*
Ist das der Fußball desselben großen Jungen?	*Is that the same big boy's soccer ball?*

Nein, das ist der Fußball dieses schönen Mädchens.	*No, that is this pretty girl's soccer ball.*
Hast du mit jenen interessanten Ausländern getanzt?	*Did you dance with those interesting foreigners?*
Ja, ich habe mit allen Ausländern getanzt.	*Yes, I danced with all the foreigners.*

Written Practice 3

Rewrite each sentence with the adjectives provided in parentheses. Supply the appropriate adjective endings. For example:

Kennst du die ______ Frau?

(alt) Kennst du die alte Frau?

1. Die Kinder dieses ______ Mannes lernen gut.

   (jung) ______________________________.

   (krank) ______________________________.

2. Sie hat mit demselben ______ Diplomaten gesprochen.

   (neu) ______________________________.

   (schlau) ______________________________.

3. Jede ______ Tanne ist mehr als zwanzig Jahre alt.

   (grün) ______________________________.

   (groß) ______________________________.

Imperative

An imperative is a command form of a verb. English imperatives are quite simple to form: the infinitive minus the particle *to*: *Go! Be quiet. Have a nice time.*

German has three imperative forms, because there are three forms of the word *you*: **du**, **ihr**, and **Sie**.

Du Form

To form the **du** form of the imperative of most verbs, use the stem of the verb and add **-e** (in colloquial speech the **-e** is often dropped).

Infinitive	*Du* Form of Imperative	
kommen	Komm(e)!	*Come.*
singen	Singe!	*Sing.*
fahren	Fahre!	*Drive.*

If the verb has an inseparable prefix, the imperative is not affected. But if the prefix is separable, the prefix appears at the end of the sentence as it does in the normal conjugation of the verb.

anrufen	Rufe an!	*Telephone.*
aussteigen	Steige aus!	*Get off!* (transportation)
erwarten	Erwarte!	*Expect.*
mitgehen	Gehe mit!	*Go along.*
verstehen	Verstehe!	*Understand.*
zerstören	Zerstöre!	*Destroy.*

If the verb is irregular in the present tense and has a vowel change from **-e-** to **-i-** or **-ie-**, that vowel change will also appear in the **du** form of the imperative.

Infinitive	Third Person	du Form	
ansehen	sieht an	Sieh an!	*Look at.*
helfen	hilft	Hilf!	*Help!*
stehl.en	stiehlt	Stiehl!	*Steal.*

When this kind of irregularity occurs in the **du** form of the imperative, there is no **-e** ending.

The *Ihr* Form

The **ihr** form of the imperative is the same as in the present tense.

Infinitive	Second Person Plural	ihr Form	
mitsingen	singt mit	Singt mit!	*Sing along.*
versprechen	versprecht	Versprecht!	*Promise.*
warten	wartet	Wartet!	*Wait!*

The *Sie* Form

The **Sie** form of the imperative is also the same as the present tense, but the imperative verb is followed by the pronoun **Sie**.

Infinitive	Third Person Formal	Sie Form	
ausgeben	geben aus	Geben Sie aus!	*Spend!*
kommen	kommen	Kommen Sie!	*Come!*
verstehen	verstehen	Verstehen Sie!	*Understand!*

It is important to consider the imperative forms of **haben**, **sein**, and **werden** separately. Take careful note of how these imperatives are formed.

	haben	**sein**	**werden**
du	Habe!	Sei!	Werde!
ihr	Habt!	Seid!	Werdet!
Sie	Haben Sie!	Seien Sie!	Werden Sie!

NOTE ***All imperatives are punctuated with an exclamation point (!) in German.***

Use the three forms of the imperative in the same way that you use the three pronouns that mean *you*. **Du** is informal and singular. **Ihr** is informal and plural. And **Sie** is formal and either singular or plural. For example:

Erik, steh auf! Es ist schon spät.	*Erik, get up. It is already late.*
Kinder, esst langsam!	*Children, eat slowly.*
Frau Keller, bitte warten Sie hier!	*Ms. Keller, wait here, please.*

Oral Practice

Practice saying the following list of sentences out loud.

Thomas, warte! Ich komme schon.	*Thomas, wait. I am coming.*
Bleibt an der Ecke!	*Stay on the corner.*
Stehen Sie bitte auf!	*Please stand up.*
Bleiben Sie bitte sitzen!	*Please remain seated.*
Bleiben Sie bitte stehen!	*Please remain standing.*
Tina, rauche nicht so viel!	*Tina, do not smoke so much.*
Kinder, schreit nicht so laut!	*Children, do not yell so loudly.*
Herr Bauer, kommen Sie schnell!	*Mr. Bauer, come quickly.*
Rufen Sie die Polizei an!	*Call the police.*
Bringen Sie mir ein Glas Wasser!	*Bring me a glass of water.*

Bitte setzen Sie sich!	*Please sit down.*
Jungen, spielt nicht im Garten!	*Boys, do not play in the garden.*
Hilf mir!	*Help me.*
Vergiss nicht!	*Do not forget.*
Mach schnell!	*Hurry up.*
Sprich Deutsch!	*Speak German.*
Sei ruhig!	*Be quiet.*

Written Practice 4

Form the three types of imperative with the verbs provided.

	du	**ihr**	**Sie**
verkaufen	________	________	________
versprechen	________	________	________
trinken	________	________	________
vorstellen	________	________	________
tun	________	________	________
zumachen	________	________	________
lesen	________	________	________
laufen	________	________	________
sein	________	________	________

Using *Wir*

There is another kind of imperative that is directed not only at another party but includes the speaker as well. In English this kind of imperative begins with *Let's* (*Let us*).

Let's go to the show tonight.	Let's not argue anymore.

In German this kind of imperative is formed by conjugating a verb in the first person plural (**wir**) present tense and following that verb with the pronoun **wir**.

Gehen wir nach Hause!	*Let's go home.*
Stellen wir die Gäste vor!	*Let's introduce the guests.*

Written Practice 5

With the verbs provided, form both the **du** form of the imperative and the **wir** form that includes the speaker in the command. Consider the meaning of the two forms.

	du	**wir**
sprechen	______________	______________
sagen	______________	______________
reisen	______________	______________
aufmachen	______________	______________
zerstören	______________	______________
warten	______________	______________
essen	______________	______________
erhalten	______________	______________
ausgeben	______________	______________

A similar *Let's* expression is formed with the verb **lassen** and **uns**. With this expression, use the imperative form of lassen for **du**, **ihr**, or **Sie**.

du	Lass uns gehen!	*Let's go.*
ihr	Lasst uns darüber sprechen!	*Let's talk about it.*
Sie	Lassen Sie uns mitgehen!	*Let's go along.*

Using Infinitives

There is yet another imperative form that is used primarily for official commands to groups or unspecified people. The verb form is the infinitive, and no formal or informal relationship is implied. For example:

Zurückbleiben!	*Stand back.* (Could be heard on a railway platform.)
Nicht rauchen!	*No smoking.* (Could be seen on a sign on a wall.)

Plants

The following is a list of the names of plants that you will often hear in German. Let's get acquainted with these plant words.

das Gemüse	*vegetables*	der Mais	*maize, corn*
das Gras	*grass*	der Rasen	*lawn*

das Korn	*grain*	die Beere	*berry*
das Obst	*fruit*	die Blume	*flower*
der Baum	*tree*	die Nelke	*carnation*
der Blumenstrauß	*bouquet*	die Pflanze	*plant*
der Busch	*bush*	die Tanne	*fir, pine*

Oral Practice

Practice saying the following list of sentences out loud.

In diesem Garten wachsen viele Pflanzen.	*Many plants grow in this garden.*
Hier wachsen Rosen und Nelken.	*Roses and carnations grow here.*
Hier wächst nur Gemüse.	*Only vegetables grow here.*
Hier wurden viele Bäume gepflanzt.	*Many trees were planted here.*
Der Busch wurde neben dem Haus gepflanzt.	*The bush was planted next to the house.*
Zwischen den Tannen wachsen Tulpen.	*Tulips grow between the pines.*
Die Bauern haben Korn, Mais und Beeren gepflanzt.	*The farmers planted grain, corn, and berries.*
Die Obstbäume sind kleiner.	*The fruit trees are smaller.*

Animals

The following is a list of the names of animals that you will often hear in German.

das Huhn	*chicken*	der Fuchs	*fox*
das Kaninchen	*rabbit*	der Hase	*hare*
das Nilpferd	*hippo*	der Tiger	*tiger*
das Pferd	*horse*	der Wolf	*wolf*
das Schaf	*sheep*	die Katze	*cat*
das Schwein	*pig*	die Kuh	*cow*
der Bär	*bear*	die Schlange	*snake*

Oral Practice

Practice saying the following list of sentences out loud.

Ich bin nie auf einem Pferd geritten.	*I have never ridden a horse.*
Auf dem Bauernhof leben viele Tiere.	*Many animals live on the farm.*
Auf dem Bauernhof leben Kühe, Schafe und Schweine.	*Cows, sheep, and pigs live on the farm.*
Der Bauer füttert die Hühner, Pferde und Schweine.	*The farmer feeds the chickens, horses, and pigs.*
Lebt ein Bär oder ein Wolf im Walde?	*Does a bear or a wolf live in the woods?*
Ein Fuchs ist sehr schlau.	*A fox is very sly.*
Ein Nilpferd lebt an einem Fluss.	*A hippo lives near a river.*
Die Tiger leben in Asien.	*Tigers live in Asia.*
Nicht alle Schlangen sind gefährlich.	*Not all snakes are dangerous.*
Die Löwen sind auf der Jagd.	*The lions are on the hunt.*
Habt ihr Haustiere?	*Do you have pets?*
Ja, wir haben zwei Katzen und einen Igel.	*Yes, we have two cats and a hedgehog.*
Nein, wir dürfen keine Haustiere halten.	*No, we are not allowed to have pets.*

Written Practice 6

Circle the letter of the word or phrase that best completes each sentence.

1. _______ ruhig! Ich kann nichts hören.
   (a) Bleiben   (c) Schlau
   (b) Sei   (d) Liegen

2. Die alte Dame hat ihre Tasche _______.
   (a) gefallen   (c) vergessen
   (b) aufgestanden   (d) verlieren

3. Hier darf man keine _______ halten.
   (a) Kaiser
   (b) Busch
   (c) Haustiere
   (d) Wohnungen

4. Warum musst du immer so laut _______?
   (a) schlafen
   (b) schreien
   (c) Hunger haben
   (d) gern haben

5. Im Garten _______ keine Nelken mehr.
   (a) wachsen
   (b) blieb
   (c) rufen an
   (d) angerufen

6. Wer hat die Pferde und _______ gefüttert?
   (a) Schafe
   (b) Busch
   (c) Bäume
   (d) Tulpen

7. Kinder, _______ bitte auf!
   (a) warten
   (b) steht
   (c) standen
   (d) erwartet

8. Diese grüne _______ ist sehr lang.
   (a) Schlange
   (b) Flaschen
   (c) Igel
   (d) Kuh

9. Es ist kalt und _______ wieder.
   (a) schneit
   (b) vergisst
   (c) bleibt
   (d) wächst

10. Ein Fuchs kann sehr _______ sein.
   (a) schlau
   (b) letzte
   (c) wahrscheinlich
   (d) ruhigen

11. Nilpferde und Löwen leben in _______.
   (a) Asien
   (b) Norddeutschland
   (c) Afrika
   (d) zu Hause

12. Herr Professor, _______ mich bitte an!
   (a) rufen Sie
   (b) seht
   (c) sieh
   (d) bleiben Sie

13. Der ______ hat hier viele Bäume gepflanzt.
   (a) Katze
   (b) Mais
   (c) Wolf
   (d) Bauer

14. Sein Sohn isst kein ______.
   (a) Gemüse
   (b) Nachtisch
   (c) Igel
   (d) Obstbäume

15. Hast du diesen ______ Artikel gelesen?
   (a) neue
   (b) interessanten
   (c) ruhig
   (d) schlaue

QUIZ

Rewrite each verb in the present tense passive voice with the pronoun provided. For example:

er singt *wird gesungen*

1. **er spielt** ______________________
   man arbeitet ______________________
   wir machen zu ______________________
   er verspricht ______________________
   ich nehme mit ______________________

2. **Write each of the following passive phrases in the tenses shown with the pronouns provided.**

		werden gesehen	werden besucht	werden genannt
pres	ich	________	________	________
past	du	________	________	________
pres perf	er	________	________	________
fut	Sie	________	________	________

		werden gelernt	werden gefüttert	werden aufgemacht
pres	es	______	______	______
past	er	______	______	______
past perf	sie (*s.*)	______	______	______
fut	sie (*pl.*)	______	______	______

Change the following active voice sentences to the passive voice. Retain the tenses of the active sentences.

3. Der Präsident hat die neue Kanzlerin vorgestellt.

____

4. Sie hatten die alte Kirche abgerissen.

____

5. Ich pflanzte den Busch neben dem Haus.

____

Rewrite each sentence, adding the adjective provided in parentheses. For example:

Ich besuchte ______ Frau.

(alt) *Ich besuchte eine alte Frau.*

6. Haben Sie jenen ______ Bären gesehen?

(groß) ______________________________

(braun) ______________________________

7. Diese ______ Männer werden uns helfen.

(jung) ______________________________

(alt) ______________________________

8. Wann kommt der ______ Zug?

(nächst) ______________________________

(letzt) ______________________________

Circle the letter of the word or phrase that best completes each sentence.

9. Wir dürfen keine Haustiere ________________.

A. versuchen
B. mitgenommen
C. halten
D. ausgegeben werden

10. Form the three imperatives for the verbs provided.

	du	**ihr**	**Sie**
treffen	________	________	________
pflanzen	________	________	________
schlafen	________	________	________
werden	________	________	________
sein	________	________	________
mitkommen	________	________	________
besuchen	________	________	________
geben	________	________	________
sehen	________	________	________
sprechen	________	________	________

chapter 18

Using the Passive Voice

In this chapter you will find a further discussion of the passive voice and how it functions with modal auxiliaries. Adjective endings following **ein-** words will be introduced as well as some vocabulary regarding professions.

CHAPTER OBJECTIVES

In this chapter you will learn:

- More About the Passive Voice
- Modal Auxiliaries in the Passive Voice
- *Sich Lassen* and the Passive Voice
- Adjective Endings with *Ein-* Words
- Professions

More About the Passive Voice

Learning about the passive voice is not over yet. For example, some active sentences have a dative object in them, and when such sentences are changed to the passive voice, the dative object, naturally, reappears in the passive sentence.

Direct objects, which are in the accusative case, become nominative subjects in the passive, but dative case objects do not change their case when placed in a passive sentence. Compare the following two pairs of examples:

Accusative Case Direct Object Changed to Nominative Case in the Passive Voice

Das Kind findet **den Ball**.	*The child finds **the ball**.*
Der Ball wird von dem Kind gefunden.	***The ball** is found by the child.*

Dative Case Object in the Passive Voice

Sie haben **dem Kind** geholfen.	*They helped **the child**.*
Dem Kind ist von ihnen geholfen worden.	***The child** was helped by them.*

The dative object in the passive sentence cannot be the subject of the sentence, because it is in the dative case. Subjects are in the nominative case. Let's look at a few more examples, which show an active sentence changed to a passive sentence.

Die Lehrerin dankte allen Eltern.	*The teacher thanked all the parents.*
Allen Eltern wurden von der Lehrerin gedankt.	*All the parents were thanked by the teacher.*
Niemand wird ihm glauben.	*No one will believe him.*
Ihm wird von niemandem geglaubt werden.	*He will not be believed by anyone.*

Written Practice 1

Change each of the following present tense sentences to the past, present perfect, and future tenses.

1. Mir wird von ihm geholfen.

   ______________________________.

   ______________________________.

   ______________________________.

2. Der Lehrerin wird nicht geglaubt.

   ______________________________.

   ______________________________.

   ______________________________.

3. Ihm wird dafür gedankt.

____.

____.

____.

4. Wird dem Professor imponiert?

____?

____?

____?

Sometimes the subject of a sentence that contains a dative object is the pronoun **es**, which in most instances is elliptical, that is, it is understood but not spoken or written. However, the passive voice is sometimes expressed by beginning the main clause of the sentence with the pronoun **es**—but, in this case, **es** is not really the subject. The subject occurs after the conjugated verb and determines the kind of conjugation required. Let's look at a few examples.

Es wird hier nur Deutsch gesprochen.	*Only German is spoken here.*
Es wurden viele Häuser zerstört.	*Many houses were destroyed.*
Es wurde uns dafür gedankt.	*We were thanked for it.*

Modal Auxiliaries in the Passive Voice

Just as modal auxiliaries are used in the active voice together with an infinitive (**muss...trinken**), they can be used in the passive voice with a passive infinitive. A passive infinitive is a past participle followed by **werden** (**muss...gesehen werden**). Let's compare the two uses of modal auxiliaries.

Active Voice:

Ich kann die Musik nicht **hören**.	*I cannot* ***hear*** *the music.*
Sie wollte mit Hans **tanzen**.	*She wanted* ***to dance*** *with Hans.*

Passive Voice:

Mir kann nicht **geholfen werden**.	*I cannot* ***be helped****.*
Sie wollte von allen **bewundert werden**.	*She wanted* ***to be admired*** *by everyone.*

The modal auxiliaries in passive voice sentences can be conjugated in all the tenses except the future perfect, which becomes an awkward structure and is avoided. Even the present and past perfect tend to be replaced by the simple past tense. But for the purpose of illustration, let's look at a modal auxiliary in the passive voice in all the pertinent tenses.

Present:
Etwas muss gesagt werden. *Something has to be said.*

Past:
Etwas musste gesagt werden. *Something had to be said.*

Present Perfect:
Etwas hat gesagt werden müssen. *Something had to be said.*

Past Perfect:
Etwas hatte gesagt werden müssen. *Something had had to be said.*

Future:
Etwas wird gesagt werden müssen. *Something will have to be said.*

Written Practice 2

Rewrite the following active voice sentences with the modals provided. Retain the tenses of the original sentences. For example:

Er ging zur Schule.

(müssen) Er musste zur Schule gehen.

1. Frau Schäfer wird nach Hannover fahren.
   (sollen) ______________________________.
   (wollen) ______________________________.
   (müssen) ______________________________.
2. Haben Sie Ihre Nachbarn eingeladen?
   (können) ______________________________?
   (müssen) ______________________________?
   (dürfen) ______________________________?

Follow the same directions, but notice that the original sentences are now in the passive voice.

3. Hans wird von seiner Schwester geküsst.

(wollen) ________________________________.

(müssen) ________________________________.

(sollen) ________________________________.

4. Ist der Wagen repariert worden?

(können) ________________________________?

(müssen) ________________________________?

(sollen) ________________________________?

5. Ihm wird sofort geholfen.

(sollen) ________________________________.

(können) ________________________________.

(müssen) ________________________________.

Written Practice 3

Rewrite each sentence replacing the original modal auxiliary with the ones provided in parentheses. Retain the original tense of the sentences.

1. Das Haus soll geräumt werden.

(können) ________________________________.

(müssen) ________________________________.

2. Es konnte nicht repariert werden.

(dürfen) ________________________________.

(müssen) ________________________________.

3. Das Kind wird fotografiert werden müssen.

(wollen) ________________________________.

(können) ________________________________.

Oral Practice

 Track 73

Practice saying the following list of sentences out loud.

Was muss gewaschen werden?	*What has to be washed?*
Der Wagen muss gewaschen werden.	*The car has to be washed.*
Wer kann eingeladen werden?	*Who can be invited?*
Unsere Verwandten können eingeladen werden.	*Our relatives can be invited.*
Herr Benz soll nicht eingeladen werden.	*Mr. Benz should not be invited.*
Was durfte nicht geschrieben werden?	*What was not allowed to be written?*
Diese Geschichte durfte nicht geschrieben werden.	*This story was not allowed to be written.*
Sein Lebenslauf durfte nicht geschrieben werden.	*His autobiography was not allowed to be written.*
Kann ihm nicht geholfen werden?	*Can he not be helped?*
Kann ihr nicht geglaubt werden?	*Can she not be believed?*
Kann dir nicht imponiert werden?	*Can you not be impressed?*

Written Practice 4

Rewrite each sentence with the new subjects provided in parentheses. Make any necessary changes.

1. Ist ______ abgeschleppt worden?

   (es) ________________________________?

   (sie *pl.*) ________________________________?

   (der Wagen) ________________________________?

   (die Autos) ________________________________?

   (der Bus) ________________________________?

2. ______ konnte nicht verstanden werden.

   (sein Freund) ________________________________.

   (die Kinder) ________________________________.

(ich) ____.

(du) ____.

(wir) ____.

3. ________ wird niemals geglaubt werden.

(sie *pl.*) ____.

(sie *s.*) ____.

(er) ____.

(meine Frau) ____.

(der Physiker) ____.

Sich Lassen and the Passive Voice

It is possible to avoid passive structures by using a conjugation of **sich lassen** accompanied by an infinitive (**lässt sich...machen**). This pair of words is translated as *can be*. In English that's a form of passive voice with a modal auxiliary, but in German it's a reflexive verb used in place of a passive voice conjugation. Let's look at some examples.

Das alte Radio **lässt sich** nicht reparieren.	*The old radio **cannot be** repaired.*
Diese Probleme **ließen sich** leicht lösen.	*These problems **could be** solved easily.*

When this structure is conjugated in the various tenses, you will notice that a double-infinitive structure occurs in the perfect and future tenses. For example:

Present:
Das lässt sich nicht tun. — *That cannot be done.*

Past:
Das ließ sich nicht tun. — *That could not be done.*

Present Perfect:
Das hat sich nicht tun lassen. — *That could not be done.*

Future:
Das wird sich nicht tun lassen. — *That will not be able to be done.*

Written Practice 5

Rewrite each passive sentence with **sich lassen**. Keep the tense of the original sentences. Be aware of the change of meaning that occurs. For example:

Das lange Wort wird leicht geschrieben.

Das lange Wort lässt sich leicht schreiben.

1. Der Fernsehapparat wurde nicht repariert.

   ______________________________.

2. Diese Romane sind schnell gelesen worden.

   ______________________________.

3. Die Bären wurden nicht fotografiert.

   ______________________________.

4. Das wird sehr leicht geändert.

   ______________________________.

Written Practice 6

Rewrite the following passive sentences in the tenses shown.

1. **pres** ______________________________.

   past Das ließ sich nicht verstehen.

   pres perf ______________________________.

   fut ______________________________.

2. **pres** Wird dem Gast gut gedient?

   past ______________________________?

   pres perf ______________________________?

   fut ______________________________?

3. **pres** ______________________________.

   past ______________________________.

   pres perf ______________________________.

   fut Du wirst gesehen werden.

4. **pres** ______________________________.
   past Der kranken Katze konnte nicht geholfen werden.
   pres perf ______________________________.
   fut ______________________________.
5. **pres** Nichts kann getan werden.
   past ______________________________.
   pres perf ______________________________.
   fut ______________________________.

Adjective Endings with *Ein-* Words

You have already learned about the adjective endings with **der-** words. Adjective endings with **ein-** words function slightly differently.

The **ein-** words are **ein** and **kein** plus the possessive adjectives (**mein**, **dein**, **sein**, **ihr**, **unser**, **euer**, **ihr**, **Ihr**). With **ein-** words, the identification of the gender of a noun is provided in the adjective in the nominative case. With **der-** words, gender is identified in the **der-** word itself. Let's compare the difference.

Der- **Word Plus Adjective**

Masculine	**Feminine**	**Neuter**	**Plural**
der nette Herr	**die** nette Frau	**das** nette Kind	**die** netten Frauen

Ein- **Word Plus Adjective**

Masculine	**Feminine**	**Neuter**	**Plural**
ein nett**er** Herr	eine nett**e** Frau	ein nett**es** Kind	keine nett**en** Frauen

No matter which **ein-** word is used, the adjective endings function in the same way.

ihr guter Mann	ihr junger Mann
seine kleine Schwester	seine kranke Schwester
kein schönes Mädchen	kein intelligentes Mädchen

This difference between **der-** words and **ein-** words does not exist in the plural. With either kind of determiner, the adjective ending is always **-en** in all four cases.

nom	diese roten Autos
acc	unsere deutschen Verwandeten
dat	jenen alten Leuten
gen	Ihrer netten Kinder

The feminine and neuter are always identical in both the nominative and accusative, therefore the adjective endings with **ein-** words used in the nominative will also be used in the accusative.

nom	ihre kleine Schwester	sein neues Heft
acc	ihre kleine Schwester	sein neues Heft

In all other instances the adjective ending will always be **-en**.

	Masculine	**Feminine**	**Neuter**	**Plural**
nom	ein netter Herr	eine nette Frau	ein nettes Kind	keine netten Frauen
acc	einen netten Herrn	eine nette Frau	ein nettes Kind	keine netten Frauen
dat	einem netten Herrn	einer netten Frau	einem netten Kind	keinen netten Frauen
gen	eines netten Herrn	einer netten Frau	eines netten Kindes	keiner netten Frauen

Written Practice 7

Provide the appropriate adjective endings in all four cases for the nouns provided.

	mein jung Freund	**unser alt Tante**	**ihr neu Fahrrad**
nom	______________	______________	______________
acc	______________	______________	______________
dat	______________	______________	______________
gen	______________	______________	______________

	dein klein Haus	**jed- groß Stuhl**	**dies- grau Katze**
nom	______________	______________	______________
acc	______________	______________	______________
dat	______________	______________	______________
gen	______________	______________	______________

With the following phrases, provide the missing cases.

nom	______	______
acc	*ihren kleinen Sohn*	______
dat	______	*deiner jungen Schwester*
gen	______	______
nom	______	______
acc	______	______
dat	*einer kranken Dame*	*unserem letzten Brief*
gen	______	______

Oral Practice

Practice saying the following sentences out loud.

Wer hat meinen neuen Hut gefunden?	*Who found my new hat?*
Robert hat deinen neuen Hut gefunden.	*Robert found your new hat.*
Welches Auto hat sie verkauft?	*Which car did she sell?*
Sie hat ihr schwarzes Auto verkauft.	*She sold her black car.*
Sie hat ihr altes Auto verkauft.	*She sold her old car.*
Welchen Gürtel wollte er kaufen?	*Which belt did he want to buy?*
Er wollte einen braunen Gürtel kaufen.	*He wanted to buy a brown belt.*
Er wollte Ihren neuen Gürtel kaufen.	*He wanted to buy your new belt.*
Wessen Hund ist das?	*Whose dog is that?*
Das ist der Hund eines neuen Lehrers.	*That is a new teacher's dog.*
Das ist der Hund meiner amerikanischen Kusine.	*That is my American cousin's dog.*

Written Practice 8

Rewrite each sentence with the phrases provided in parentheses, making the necessary changes to adjective endings.

1. Ist das der Bruder _______?
   (dein amerikanischer Gast) ______________________________?
   (Ihre nette Kusine) ______________________________?
   (eure jungen Freunde) ______________________________?
2. Kennen Sie _______?
   (meine neue Freundin) ______________________________?
   (sein alter Onkel) ______________________________?
   (ihr intelligenter Sohn) ______________________________?
3. Hans wollte mit _______ spielen.
   (unser kleiner Hund) ______________________________.
   (jene netten Kinder) ______________________________.
   (sein neuer Fußball) ______________________________.

Written Practice 9

Fill in the blanks with any appropriate adjective and its required ending.

1. Der ____________________ Rechtsanwalt ist ein Freund von mir.
2. Kennst du meine ____________________ Gärtnerin?
3. Thomas hat mit seinen ____________________ Geschwistern gearbeitet.
4. Gudrun will von allen ____________________ Jungen bewundert werden.
5. Ihre ____________________ Wohnung soll geräumt werden.
6. Sie haben sein ____________________ Auto abgeschleppt.
7. Habt ihr euren ____________________ Dolmetscher eingeladen?
8. Ist das ein ____________________ Gürtel?
9. Sie hatte keine ____________________ Flaschen gefunden.
10. Unser ____________________ Wohnzimmer ist dunkel.

Professions

When you inquire as to someone's profession, you ask:

Was sind Sie von Beruf?	*What is your occupation?*
Was bist du von Beruf?	*What is your occupation?*

The responses are numerous, because there are so many words that describe professions or occupations. When reading the following list, remember that the masculine version is shown. The feminine version is, in most cases, the same word but with **-in** added to the end of the word. Also, sometimes a vowel will be replaced by an umlaut vowel (**-ä-**, **-ö-**, or **-ü-**) for the feminine version.

der Arbeiter	*(blue-collar) worker*	der Mechaniker	*mechanic*
der Architekt	*architect*	der Pfleger	*(male) nurse; caretaker*
der Beamte	*government*	der Physiker	*physicist*
			employee
der Chemiker	*chemist*	der Politiker	*politician*
der Dichter	*poet*	der Rechtsanwalt	*lawyer*
der Dolmetscher	*translator*	der Schaffner	*conductor* (transportation)
der Erzieher	*nursery school teacher*	der Schriftsteller	*writer, author*
der Fotograf	*photographer*	der Sekretär	*secretary*
der Geschäftsmann (die -frau)	*businessman*	der Sportler	*athlete*
der Kaufmann (die -frau)	*merchant, businessman*	der Taxifahrer	*taxi driver*
der Maurer	*bricklayer*	der Trainer	*coach*

There are different ways to describe what you do for a profession. For example:

Ich arbeite als Pflegerin.	*I work as a nurse.*
Ich arbeite in der Firma als Dolmetscher.	*I work in the company as a translator.*

Ich bin in dieser Firma als Mechaniker beschäftigt.	*I am employed in the company as a mechanic.*
Ich bin Taxifahrer aber will Architekt werden.	*I am a taxi driver but want to become an architect.*

Written Practice 10

Circle the letter of the word or phrase that best completes each sentence.

1. Wen haben Sie _______?
   (a) abschleppen (c) gepflanzt
   (b) änderten (d) eingeladen

2. Wird _______ damit geholfen?
   (a) ihnen (c) euren Rechtsanwalt
   (b) unsere (d) keine Leute

3. Der kranke Mann _______ sofort nach Hause gebracht werden.
   (a) musste (c) hat
   (b) ist (d) gekonnt

4. Ist dein Wagen wieder _______ worden?
   (a) gewachsen (c) bewunderten
   (b) abgeschleppt (d) können

5. Die Geschäftsfrau kann nicht _______ werden.
   (a) soll (c) gefunden
   (b) hat (d) geglaubt

6. Ist deine Mutter Hausfrau oder _______?
   (a) Physikerin (c) Gärtnerinnen
   (b) Politiker (d) Erzieher

7. Werner hat ein neues _______ angezogen.
   (a) Ball (c) Affen
   (b) Pflanze (d) Hemd

8. Tanja hat _______ neues Auto.
   (a) diese (c) welches
   (b) ein (d) jenen

9. Was ist Ihr Vater von _______?
   (a) zu Hause (c) Beruf
   (b) bewundert (d) Arbeiter

10. Meine Tochter ist jetzt als Architektin _______.
   (a) gearbietet (c) eingeladen
   (b) beschäftigt (d) geändert

Oral Practice

Practice saying the following list of sentences out loud.

Was sind Sie von Beruf?	*What is your occupation?*
Ich bin Gärtner.	*I am a gardener.*
Ich arbeite als Dolmetscherin.	*I work as a translator.*
Ich bin als Maurer beschäftigt.	*I am employed as a bricklayer.*
Was ist deine Schwester von Beruf?	*What is your sister's occupation?*
Sie ist Geschäftsfrau.	*She is a businesswoman.*
Sie arbeitet als Chemikerin.	*She works as a chemist.*
Sie ist bei einer Firma als Sekretärin beschäftigt.	*She is employed in a company as a secretary.*
Mein Vater war Arbeiter.	*My father was a blue-collar worker.*
Jetzt arbeitet er als Beamter.	*Now he works as a government employee.*
Meine Mutter war Erzieherin.	*My mother was a nursery school teacher.*
Jetzt ist sie als Fotografin beschäftigt.	*Now she is employed as a photographer.*
Mein Sohn will Kaufmann werden.	*My son wants to become a merchant.*
Meine Tochter ist Sportlerin.	*My daughter is an athlete.*
Ist Ihr Onkel Rechtsanwalt?	*Is your uncle a lawyer?*
Nein, er ist Politiker.	*No, he is a politician.*
War Ihre Tante Schriftstellerin?	*Was your aunt a writer?*
Nein, sie war Dichterin.	*No, she was a poet.*
Dem Schaffner wurde gedankt.	*The conductor was thanked.*

Dem Taxifahrer konnte nicht geglaubt werden.	*The taxi driver could not be believed.*
Sein Wagen musste abgeschleppt werden.	*His car had to be towed away.*
Der neue Trainer war Mechaniker.	*The new coach was a mechanic.*

QUIZ

Rewrite the following sentences in the tenses shown.

1. **pres** ______________________________

   past *Der Wagen musste abgeschleppt werden.*

   pres perf ______________________________

   fut ______________________________

2. **pres** *Ihnen wird dafür gedankt.*

   past ______________________________

   past perf ______________________________

   fut ______________________________

3. **pres** ______________________________

   past ______________________________

   pres perf ______________________________

   fut *Es wird sich nicht leicht ändern lassen.*

Rewrite the following passive sentence with the new subjects provided in parentheses.

4. ____________ **wurde von ihnen geholfen.**

   (er) ______________________________

   (wir) ______________________________

   (der Beamte) ______________________________

   (die Dichterin) ______________________________

   (du) ______________________________

Fill in the missing cases, providing the appropriate adjective endings.

5. nom	*ein netter Mann*	______________
acc	______________	______________
dat	______________	*seiner neuen Freundin*
gen	______________	______________
6. nom	______________	*Ihre alten Stühle*
acc	*kein interessantes Buch*	______________
dat	______________	______________
gen	______________	______________

Circle the letter of the word or phrase that best completes each sentence.

7. Das ist mein ______________ Gedicht.

A. letzte
B. erstes
C. langen
D. ruhig

8. Mein Vater ______________ als Mechaniker.

A. arbeitet
B. beschäftige
C. dienen
D. sein Beruf

9. Die kranke Frau ______________ nach Hause gebracht werden.

A. ist
B. konnten
C. muss
D. werdet

10. Nein, das ______________ sich nicht tun.

A. ließ
B. können
C. werden
D. Heft

chapter 19

Using the Subjunctive Mood

In this chapter you will learn about the subjunctive mood. In addition, foreign words in German and some idioms will also be introduced.

CHAPTER OBJECTIVES

In this chapter you will learn about:

- Subjunctive Mood
- Indirect Discourse
- Foreign Words in German
- More Idioms

Subjunctive Mood

The subjunctive mood is a grammatical function that is losing ground in English. Many speakers avoid it, and some probably cannot identify it when they hear it or read it. Some examples of the English subjunctive conjugation are:

Long *live* the king!
I suggest you *be* on time tomorrow.
If only my husband *were* here.

The subjunctive mood plays a significant role in the German language, however. Let's look first at how the subjunctive conjugations are formed.

German has two subjunctive tenses: the present subjunctive (also called subjunctive I) and the past subjunctive (also called subjunctive II).

Present Subjunctive/Subjunctive I

The present subjunctive has the appearance of a present tense verb, but there are small differences between the subjunctive conjugation and the indicative (the normal present tense conjugation). This is true even of the modal auxiliaries. The conjugational endings in the present subjunctive are: **-e**, **-est**, **-e**, **-en**, **-et**, and **-en**. To conjugate in the subjunctive, remove the infinitive ending from the stem of the verb and add these endings. For example:

	kommen	**versprechen**	**zumachen**	**können**
ich	komme	verspreche	mache zu	könne
du	kommest	versprechest	machest zu	könnest
er	komme	verspreche	mache zu	könne
wir	kommen	versprechen	machen zu	können
ihr	kommet	versprechet	machet zu	könnet
sie	kommen	versprechen	machen zu	können

There are some important things to note about this conjugation:

1. The first person and third person singular (**ich** and **er**) are always identical.
2. Present tense irregularities such as adding an umlaut (**ich fahre**, **du fährst**, **er fährt**) or by making a vowel change (**ich sehe**, **du siehst**, **er sieht**) do not occur.
3. The first person singular and plural (**ich** and **wir**) and the third person plural (**sie**) are often identical to the indicative conjugation. This is occasionally true with the **ihr** form with verb stems that end in **-t** or **-d**. This fact will become important later on.
4. Prefixes are not affected by the subjunctive conjugation and continue to follow the same rules as stated previously.

Of course, it is wise to look at the present subjunctive conjugation of **haben**, **sein**, and **werden** separately. They always play a special role in the conjugation of verbs.

	haben	**sein**	**werden**
ich	habe	sei	werde
du	habest	seiest	werdest
er	habe	sei	werde
wir	haben	seien	werden
ihr	habet	seiet	werdet
sie	haben	seien	werden

Written Practice 1

Conjugate the following verbs in the present subjunctive with the pronouns provided. Place an X after the verbs that are identical to the indicative present tense conjugation.

	schlafen	**vergessen**	**mitnehmen**
ich	___________	___________	___________
du	___________	___________	___________
er	___________	___________	___________
wir	___________	___________	___________
ihr	___________	___________	___________
sie	___________	___________	___________

	fragen	**aussehen**	**sein**
ich	___________	___________	___________
du	___________	___________	___________
er	___________	___________	___________
wir	___________	___________	___________
ihr	___________	___________	___________
sie	___________	___________	___________

Past Subjunctive/Subjunctive II

The past subjunctive is formed from the past tense conjugation of verbs. If a verb is regular in the indicative past tense, it will have the same conjugation in the past subjunctive. Let's look at the past subjunctive of a few regular verbs.

	fragen	**aufmachen**	**besuchen**
ich	fragte	machte auf	besuchte
du	fragtest	machtest auf	besuchtest
er	fragte	machte auf	besuchte
wir	fragten	machten auf	besuchten
ihr	fragtet	machtet auf	besuchtet
sie	fragten	machten auf	besuchten

Irregular verbs are another story. The irregular past tense stem is used in the subjunctive conjugation, and the endings **-e**, **-est**, **-e**, **-en**, **-et**, and **-en** are added. You may have noticed that these are the same endings used in the present subjunctive. Also, irregular past tense verbs that have an **a**, **o**, **u** will add an umlaut in this conjugation. Some examples follow:

	verlieren	**sprechen**	**beschreiben**
ich	verlöre	spräche	beschriebe
du	verlörest	sprächest	beschriebest
er	verlöre	spräche	beschriebe
wir	verlören	sprächen	beschrieben
ihr	verlöret	sprächet	beschriebet
sie	verlören	sprächen	beschrieben

	mitgehen	**bleiben**	**fahren**
ich	ginge mit	bliebe	führe
du	gingest mit	bliebest	führest
er	ginge mit	bliebe	führe
wir	gingen mit	blieben	führen
ihr	ginget mit	bliebet	führet
sie	gingen mit	blieben	führen

And, of course, we have to isolate **haben**, **sein**, and **werden** for a special look.

	haben	**sein**	**werden**
ich	hätte	wäre	würde
du	hättest	wärest	würdest
er	hätte	wäre	würde
wir	hätten	wären	würden
ihr	hättet	wäret	würdet
sie	hätten	wären	würden

The modal auxiliaries in the past subjunctive look very much like their indicative past tense conjugations. However, those modals that have an umlaut in the infinitive add one in the past subjunctive.

	könnnen	**wollen**	**dürfen**
ich	könnte	wollte	dürfte
du	könntest	wolltest	dürftest
er	könnte	wollte	dürfte
wir	könnten	wollten	dürften
ihr	könntet	wolltet	dürftet
sie	könnten	wollten	dürften

Most irregular verbs that have a **-te** ending in the past tense do something special in the past subjunctive: The past tense vowel **-a-** is changed to **-e-**. Let's compare the past indicative with the past subjunctive of this category of verbs.

Past Indicative

	kennen	**senden**	**nennen**
ich	kannte	sandte	nannte
du	kanntest	sandtest	nanntest
er	kannte	sandte	nannte
wir	kannten	sandten	nannten
ihr	kanntet	sandtet	nanntet
sie	kannten	sandten	nannten

Past Subjunctive

	kennen	**senden**	**nennen**
ich	kennte	sendete	nennte
du	kenntest	sendetest	nenntest
er	kennte	sendete	nennte
wir	kennten	sendeten	nennten
ihr	kenntet	sendetet	nenntet
sie	kennten	sendeten	nennten

The verb **wissen**, which usually conforms to the conjugation type just illustrated (it adds the **-te** ending), does not use the vowel **-e-** in the past subjunctive. Let's compare this verb in both the present subjunctive and the past subjunctive.

	Present Subjunctive	Past Subjunctive
ich	wisse	wüsste
du	wissest	wüsstest
er	wisse	wüsste
wir	wissen	wüssten
ihr	wisset	wüsstet
sie	wissen	wüssten

Just as in the present subjunctive, the first and third person singular conjugations (**ich** and **er**) are always the same in the past subjunctive.

ich fragte	er fragte (*regular verb*)
ich käme	er käme (*irregular verb with umlaut*)
ich ginge	er ginge (*irregular verb*)
ich dürfte	er dürfte (*modal auxiliary*)

Indirect Discourse

Direct discourse is a direct quote of what someone has said: John said, "I like to drink black coffee." Indirect discourse is the retelling of what someone has said.

John said that he likes to drink black coffee.

German also has direct and indirect discourse. Direct quotes are handled the same as in English.

Johann sagte, „Ich trinke gern schwarzen Kaffee."

But indirect discourse is another matter. A German statement in indirect discourse requires the conjugated verb to be in the present subjunctive.

Johann sagte, dass er gern schwarzen Kaffee **trinke**.

The use of **dass** (*that*) can also be omitted in indirect discourse.

Johann sagte, er **trinke** gern schwarzen Kaffee.

It is not only the verb **sagen** that introduces a statement in indirect discourse. There are many others that do the same thing.

antworten	*to answer*	glauben	*to believe*
berichten	*to report*	meinen	*to think, to have the opinion, to mean*
denken	*to think*	mitteilen	*to inform*
erzählen	*to tell, relate*	schreiben	*to write*
fragen	*to ask*		

These verbs are in the past tense when used with indirect discourse.

Karl **antwortete**, er habe heute keine Zeit.	*Karl answered that he has no time today.*
Meine Tante **erzählte**, dass ein Unglück geschehen sei.	*My aunt told (us) that an accident happened.*

Written Practice 2

Change the direct quotes to indirect discourse using the phrases provided. For example:

Er sagte, dass…

„Karl ist krank gewesen."

Er sagte, dass Karl krank gewesen sei.

1. Er sagte, dass…

   „Zwei Autos sind abgeschleppt worden."

   ______________________________.

   „Die Regierung wird den armen Menschen helfen."

   ______________________________.

   „Er geht nur selten ins Theater."

   ______________________________.

2. Ein Freund schrieb uns, dass…

   „Er kann nächste Woche kommen."

   ______________________________.

   „Sein Bruder ist in Gudrun verliebt."

   ______________________________.

   „Seine Familie hat das Geld noch nicht erhalten."

   ______________________________.

Oral Practice

 Track 74

Practice saying the following list of sentences out loud.

Er sagte, dass das Wetter schlecht sei.	*He said that the weather is bad.*
Er sagte, dass er wenig Zeit habe.	*He said that he has little time.*
Sie sagte, Frau Benz sei wieder schwanger.	*She said Ms. Benz is pregnant again.*
Sie sagte, Erik wolle Sportler werden.	*She said Erik wants to become an athlete.*
Er berichtete, dass der Politiker gut angekommen sei.	*He reported that the politician arrived safely.*
Er berichtete, die Kanzlerin reise morgen ab.	*He reported the chancellor is departing tomorrow.*
Sie teilte uns mit, dass der alte Dichter sterbe.	*She informed us that the old poet is dying.*
Sie teilte uns mit, der Fluss habe das Dorf überschwemmt.	*She informed us that the river flooded the village.*

Consider the following examples carefully. They illustrate how the various tenses in direct discourse appear in indirect discourse. The simple past, the present perfect, and the past perfect all have the same form in indirect discourse.

Present:
„Er hat kein Geld." — Er sagte, dass er kein Geld habe.

Past:
„Er hatte kein Geld." — Er sagte, dass er kein Geld gehabt habe.

Present Perfect:
„Er hat kein Geld gehabt." — Er sagte, dass er kein Geld gehabt habe.

Past Perfect:
„Er hatte kein Geld gehabt." — Er sagte, dass er kein Geld gehabt habe.

Future:
„Er wird kein Geld haben." — Er sagte, dass er kein Geld haben werde.

Written Practice 3

Rewrite the following direct quotes as indirect discourse using the phrases provided. Use the appropriate present subjunctive tense form.

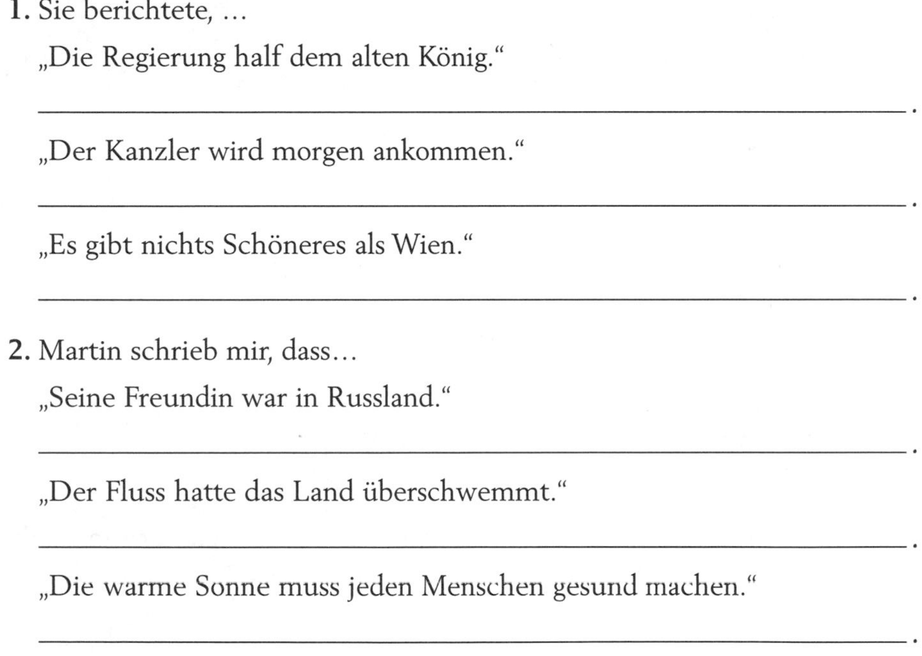

1. Sie berichtete, …

   „Die Regierung half dem alten König."

   ______________________________.

   „Der Kanzler wird morgen ankommen."

   ______________________________.

   „Es gibt nichts Schöneres als Wien."

   ______________________________.

2. Martin schrieb mir, dass…

   „Seine Freundin war in Russland."

   ______________________________.

   „Der Fluss hatte das Land überschwemmt."

   ______________________________.

   „Die warme Sonne muss jeden Menschen gesund machen."

   ______________________________.

Indirect Questions

An indirect question functions in the same way as indirect discourse. But indirect questions are introduced by the verb **fragen**. If there is no interrogative word (**was**, **warum**, **wo**, and so on) in the question, the conjunction **ob** (*whether*) begins the clause. For example:

Sie fragte, ob Hans noch krank sei.	*She asked whether Hans is still sick.*
Sie fragte, wohin der Gärtner jetzt gehe.	*She asked where the gardener is going now.*
Sie fragte, was der Schriftsteller berichtet habe.	*She asked what the writer reported.*

Written Practice 4

Change the following direct questions to indirect questions using the phrases provided. Use the conjunction **ob** where there is no interrogative word.

1. Mein Mann fragte, …

„Wo ist mein neuer Pullover?"

____.

„Kann Erik den Wagen reparieren?"

____.

„Wessen Tasche hat der Dieb gestohlen?"

____.

„Waren sie schon in der Hauptstadt?"

____.

„Wie viel wird Herr Bauer dafür ausgeben?"

____.

So far, you have been using the present subjunctive conjugation only in indirect discourse and indirect questions. But the past subjunctive plays a role here as well. When the indicative present tense and the present subjunctive are identical, use the past subjunctive. For example:

„Sie haben kein Geld."	*They have no money.*

The verb is the same in the present indicative (**haben**) as it is in the present subjunctive (**haben**). Therefore, the past subjunctive is used when this sentence is stated in indirect discourse.

Herr Bauer erzählte, dass sie kein Geld **hätten**.	*Mr. Bauer said that they have no money.*

Let's look at a few more examples.

„Die Kinder sollen zu Hause bleiben."	*The children should stay home.*
Herr Bauer erzählte, dass die Kinder zu Hause bleiben **sollten**.	*Mr. Bauer said that the children should stay at home.*

„Ihr werdet alles in der Küche finden."	*You will find everything in the kitchen.*
Herr Bauer erzählte, dass ihr alles in der Küche finden **würdet**.	*Mr. Bauer said that you will find everything in the kitchen.*
„Sie verkaufen das große Haus."	*They sell the large house.*
Herr Bauer erzählte, dass sie das große Hause **verkauften**.	*Mr. Bauer said that they are selling the large house.*

There is a tendency in the spoken language to avoid the present subjunctive conjugation and to use the past subjunctive exclusively. Compare the following examples:

Spoken German:

Sie sagte, dass ihr Mann wieder gesund **wäre**.	*She said that her husband* ***is*** *well again.*
Sie sagte, dass ihr Mann in England gearbeitet **hätte**.	*She said that her husband* ***had*** *worked in England.*

Written German:

Sie sagte, dass ihr Mann wieder gesund **sei**.	*She said that her husband is well again.*
Sie sagte, dass ihr Mann in England gearbeitet **habe**.	*She said that her husband had worked in England.*

Oral Practice

Practice saying the following list of sentences out loud.

Thomas sagte, dass Tina beim Arzt wäre.	*Thomas said that Tina is at the doctor's office.*
Er sagte, dass Tina beim Arzt gewesen wäre.	*He said that Tina was at the doctor's office.*
Er sagte, dass Tina nicht arbeiten könnte.	*He said that Tina cannot work.*
Er sagte, dass sie zu Hause bleiben müsste.	*He said that she has to stay home.*
Er sagte, dass sie sich den Arm gebrochen hätte.	*He said that she had broken her arm.*

Er sagte, dass sie nicht nach Bonn fahren würde.	*He said that she would not travel to Bonn.*
Sie fragte, ob Erik in Berlin arbeiten wollte.	*She asked whether Erik wants to work in Berlin.*
Sie fragte, ob Erik Jura studiert hätte.	*She asked whether Erik had studied law.*
Sie fragte, wo er früher gewohnt hätte.	*She asked where he had lived previously.*
Sie fragte, warum er nicht verheirat wäre.	*She asked why he is not married.*
Sie fragte, wie viel er in Berlin verdienen könnte.	*She asked how much he can earn in Berlin.*

Foreign Words in German

German is much like English in its willingness to adopt foreign words to enrich the language. There is a large category of German verbs of foreign origin that end in **-ieren**. You have already encountered several of them. The following list will familiarize you with a few more high-frequency verbs of this type.

delegieren	*to send as a delegate; to delegate*		
demonstrieren	*to demonstrate*	notieren	*to make a note of something*
faszinieren	*to fascinate*	produzieren	*to produce*
kontrollieren	*to control*	programmieren	*to program*
kopieren	*to copy*	protestieren	*to protest*
manifestieren	*to manifest*	restaurieren	*to restore*

These are only a few examples. This is a large category of verbs, and as you gain experience with German, you will encounter many more.

German has borrowed vocabulary from a variety of foreign sources including English. Here are a few of these words to consider.

anklicken	*to click* (*on an icon*)	die Farce	*farce*
chatten	*to chat* (*in a chat room*)	die Gala	*gala*
das Derby	*derby* (*horse race*)	die Hardware	*hardware* (*computer*)

das Design	*design*	die Software	*software*
das Happening	*happening*	faxen	*to fax*
das Internet	*Internet*	intuitiv	*intuitive*
das Motocross	*motocross*	invalid	*invalid (handicapped)*
der Browser	*browser*	nonchalant	*nonchalant*
der Computer	*computer*	posten	*to post*
der Favorit	*favorite*	surfen	*to surf*
der Manager	*manager*	updated	*updated*

Though this list of words and their definitions may seem obvious, it is always wise to consult a dictionary to find the precise meaning of a foreign word in German. There are often nuances of meaning or usages of the word that are not always immediately apparent.

The verb **fixieren**, for example, is an **-ieren** verb, which says that it most likely comes from a foreign source. And the stem **fix-** suggests that the verb means *to fix*. This is quite true, but the verb does not mean *to repair*. This verb means *to fix one's gaze* on someone or something. Rely on a dictionary for precision.

More Idioms

Idioms require a special explanation. Just as in English, German has a variety of idioms that cannot always be translated literally. Consider this English phrase: *Get a load of her*. Each of the words can be found separately in a dictionary, but the meaning (*Look at her*) will not be discovered that way.

Let's look at a few useful German idioms and special phrases with their English translations.

Das kommt darauf an.	*That depends.*
Du nimmst mich auf dem Arm.	*You are pulling my leg.*
Er erzählte mir ein Ammenmärchen.	*He told me a cock-and-bull story.*
Er hat schon lange ins Gras gebissen.	*He kicked the bucket long ago.*
Er kam vom Regen in die Traufe.	*He got out of the frying pan and into the fire.*
Er trägt sein Herz auf der Zunge.	*He wears his heart on his sleeve.*

Es tut mir leid.	*I am sorry.*
Gott sei Dank!	*Thank goodness!*
Hau ab!	*Get out! Knock it off!*
Ich brach das Schweigen, indem ich ihn zuerst anredete.	*I broke the ice by speaking to him first.*
Ich habe ein Hühnchen mit dir zu rupfen.	*I have a bone to pick with you.*
Stell dir mal vor!	*Just imagine.*
Was ist los?	*What is the matter?*
Wir wollen darum losen. Kopf oder Zahl?	*Let's flip for it. Heads or tails?*

QUIZ

Write the present and past subjunctive conjugations with the pronouns provided for each of the following verbs.

1.	**Present versuchen**	**Past**	**Present kommen**	**Past**
ich	________	________	________	________
du	________	________	________	________
wir	________	________	________	________

2.	**Present fahren**	**Past**	**Present gehen**	**Past**
du	________	________	________	________
er	________	________	________	________
ihr	________	________	________	________

3.	**Present brauchen**	**Past**	**Present aussehen**	**Past**
ich	________	________	________	________
sie (*s.*)	________	________	________	________
Sie	________	________	________	________

4.	**Present werden**	**Past**	**Present sein**	**Past**
ich	________	________	________	________
du	________	________	________	________
sie (*pl.*)	________	________	________	________

Change each direct quote to indirect discourse, using the phrases provided. For example:

Erik sagte, dass...

„Seine Mutter ist sehr krank."

Erik sagte, dass seine Mutter sehr krank sei.

5. Erik sagte, dass ...

„Seine Freundin will in Darmstadt arbeiten."

____

„Niemand hat ihm etwas über den Film erzählt."

____

„Martin wird ein Buch für seine Frau kaufen."

____

„Unsere Freunde wollen einen neuen VW kaufen."

____

Die Lehrerin fragte, ob...

„Ist Herr Schneider bei euch zu Gast?"

____

„Hat Felix einen Bleistift gefunden?"

____

„Lernten die Schüler lesen und schreiben?"

____

„Wird die warme Sonne den Kranken gesund machen?"

____

Circle the letter of the word or phrase that best completes each sentence.

6. **Er sagte, dass ihre Eltern ein Kind adoptieren ____________.**
   A. wollten
   B. mussten
   C. werde
   D. hätten

7. **Die Zeitung ____________, dass die Dichterin gestorben sei.**
   A. konnte
   B. sagt
   C. berichtete
   D. könnte

8. **Niemand hat ihn gefragt, ____________ er unsere Verwandten kenne.**
   A. dass
   B. weil
   C. müsste
   D. ob

9. **Ich sagte zu der Wirtin, dass mein Zimmer zu klein ____________.**
   A. wäre
   B. hätte
   C. seien
   D. habe

10. **Sie fragte Frau Benz, ____________ sie sich die Hände waschen könnten.**
    A. dass
    B. wo
    C. denn
    D. für wen

chapter 20

Expressing Wishes and Conditions

In this chapter you will find a further discussion of the subjunctive mood and its uses. In addition, infinitive clauses will be introduced.

CHAPTER OBJECTIVES

In this chapter you will learn about:

- Expressing Wishes with the Subjunctive
- Subjunctive with *Als Ob*
- Expressing Conditions with the Subjunctive
- Irregular Verbs in the Subjunctive
- Being Polite in the Subjunctive
- Infinitive Clauses

Expressing Wishes with the Subjunctive

The past subjunctive is used in more ways than just in indirect discourse. It is the conjugational form needed to express wishes. In such expressions it is often accompanied by the conjunction **wenn** (*if*). But a wish statement is still correct if **wenn** is omitted. Consider the following examples:

Wenn ich nur noch jung wäre! Wäre ich nur noch jung!	*If only I were still young.*
Wenn wir nur mehr Geld hätten! Hätten wir nur mehr Geld!	*If only we had more money.*

Oral Practice

Practice saying the following list of sentences out loud.

Wären wir doch in unserer Heimat! Wenn wir doch in unserer Heimat wären!	*If we were just back in our homeland.*
Hätte sie doch ihren Mann nie verlassen! Wenn sie doch ihren Mann nie velassen hätte!	*If she had just never left her husband.*
Hätte er doch mehr Mut! Wenn er doch mehr Mut hätte!	*If he had just had more courage.*
Könnte ich ihm doch helfen! Wenn ich ihm doch helfen könnte!	*If I could just help him.*
Wäret ihr nur bei mir! Wenn ihr nur bei mir wäret!	*If only you were with me.*
Wäre das Kind nur wieder gesund! Wenn das Kind nur wieder gesund wäre!	*If only the child were well again.*
Hätten wir doch mehr Glück gehabt! Wenn wir doch mehr Glück gehabt hätten!	*If we had just had more luck.*
Wäre er nur früher gekommen! Wenn er nur früher gekommen wäre!	*If only he had come earlier.*

You will notice that there are two tenses inferred by wishes like those just illustrated: a present tense wish and a past tense wish. For example:

Wenn er doch mehr Mut hätte!	*If he just had more courage.*
Wenn er doch mehr Mut gehabt hätte!	*If he had just had more courage.*

Wish expressions occur only in those two forms. Naturally, if the past tense wish uses a verb of motion or an intransitive verb, the auxiliary **sein** must be used.

Käme sie nur früher!	*If only she came earlier.*
Wäre sie nur früher gekommen!	*If only she had come earlier.*

Subjunctive with *Als Ob*

The conjunction **als ob** (*as if*) (sometimes stated as **als wenn**) introduces a subordinate clause that requires a verb in the past subjunctive. Since the clause is a subor-dinate clause, the conjugated verb is the last element in the clause.

Er tut so, als ob er alles wüsste.	*He acted as if he knew everything.*
Sie sprach, als ob sie viel intelligenter wäre.	*She spoke as if she were much more intelligent.*

Written Practice 1

Complete each phrase with the sentences provided.

1. Erik tat so, als ob...

Er ist sehr klug. (**klug** = *smart*)

____.

Er ist plötzlich reich geworden.

____.

Er kann diese Probleme lösen.

____.

Er hat den Kanzler schon kennen gelernt.

____.

2. Sie schrie, als ob...

Sie hat ein Ungeheuer gesehen. (**das Ungeheuer** = *monster*)

____.

Sie muss sterben.

____.

Sie ist wahnsinnig. (**wahnsinnig** = *insane*)

____.

Sie kann nicht schwimmen.

____.

Expressing Conditions with the Subjunctive

The conjunction **wenn** is used to express a condition (the conditional subjunctive). It states that if a certain condition is met, a certain result will occur. For example:

Condition: →	**Result:**
Wenn Bonn nicht so weit wäre,	führen wir dorthin.
Condition: *If Bonn were not so far.*	Result: *We'd drive there.*

In the clause that shows the result (the non-**wenn** clause), it is common to use **würde** plus an infinitive in place of the past subjunctive verb. In such an instance, the previous example will look like this:

Wenn Bonn nicht so weit wäre, **würden** wir dorthin **fahren**. — *If Bonn were not so far, we would drive there.*

The structure of **würde** plus an infinitive is widely used in the non-**wenn** clause. However, if the tense of the verb is a perfect tense or if the conjugated verb is a modal, the **würde**-plus-infinitive structure can be avoided. For example:

A Single Verb: brauchen

Wenn ich gesund wäre, würde ich den Arzt nicht brauchen. — *If I were well, I would not need the doctor.*

Future Tense:

Wenn ich gesund wäre, würde ich morgen nach Spanien reisen. — *If I were well, I would travel to Spain tomorrow.*

Modal Auxiliary:

Wenn ich gesund wäre, könnte ich ins Kino gehen. — *If I were well, I could go to the movies.*

A Perfect Tense:

Wenn ich gesund gewesen wäre, hätte ich meinen Onkel in Bonn besucht.	*If I had been well, I would have visited my uncle in Bonn.*

Written Practice 2

Using **wenn** in the first clause, combine the following pairs of sentences. For example:

Wir haben mehr Zeit. Wir gehen ins Kino.

Wenn wir mehr Zeit hätten, würden wir ins Kino gehen.

1. Ich verstehe Deutsch. Ich lese diese Bücher.

   ______________________________.

2. Wir können ihm helfen. Er ist glücklich.

   ______________________________.

3. Sie haben ihm mehr Geld gegeben. Er hat das neue Haus gekauft.

   ______________________________.

4. Ich habe im Lotto gewonnen. Ich bin nach Amerika geflogen.

   ______________________________.

5. Der Schüler ist fleißiger gewesen. Er hat das Gedicht auswendig gelernt.

   ______________________________.

Irregular Verbs in the Subjunctive

A few verbs do not form the past subjunctive in the regular manner. Examine the list that follows and take note of these exceptions of past subjunctive forms.

Infinitive		**Past Subjunctive**
empfehlen	*to recommend*	empföhle
gelten	*to be valid; worth*	gölte *or* gälte
helfen	*to help*	hülfe
schwimmen	*to swim*	schwömme
schwören	*to swear, curse*	schwüre
stehen	*to stand*	stünde *or* stände

sterben	*to die*	stürbe
verderben	*to ruin, spoil*	verdürbe
verstehen	*to understand*	verstünde *or* verstände
werben	*to recruit; court*	würbe
werfen	*to throw, hurl*	würfe

Oral Practice

 Track 75

Practice saying the following list of sentences out loud.

Wenn ich älter wäre, würde ich in Frankreich arbeiten.	*If I were older, I would work in France.*
Wenn ich älter wäre, könnte ich in Berlin studieren.	*If I were older, I could study in Berlin.*
Wenn ich älter wäre, würde ich bei meinem Onkel wohnen.	*If I were older, I would live at my uncle's house.*
Wenn ich älter wäre, müsste ich meinen eigenen Wagen kaufen.	*If I were older, I would have to buy my own car.*
Sie hätte mir geholfen, wenn sie mehr Zeit gehabt hätte.	*She would have helped me, if she had had more time.*
Sie hätte mir geholfen, wenn sie in der Nähe gewohnt hätte.	*She would have helped me, if she had lived in the area.*
Sie hätte mir geholfen, wenn sie nicht so krank gewesen wäre.	*She would have helped me, if she had not been so sick.*
Sie hätte mir geholfen, wenn ihr Wagen repariert worden wäre.	*She would have helped me, if her car had been repaired.*

Being Polite in the Subjunctive

In order to sound more polite, it is common to use the past subjunctive **möchte** (*would like*) in place of **wollen** (*to want*).

Ich will ein Stück Kuchen.	*I want a piece of cake.*
Ich **möchte** ein Stück Kuchen.	*I **would like** a piece of cake.*
Was wollen Sie essen?	*What do you want to eat?*
Was **möchten** Sie essen?	*What **would** you **like** to eat?*

Infinitive Clauses

There are times in German when **zu** is added to an infinitive. That combination is called an infinitive clause. Infinitive clauses are frequently used following **viel(es)**, **etwas**, and **nichts**. For example:

Es gibt viel zu tun.	*There is a lot to do.*
Ich habe etwas zu sagen.	*I have something to say.*
Gibt es nichts zu trinken?	*Is there nothing to drink?*

If an infinitive has a inseparable prefix (**be-**, **emp-**, **ent-**, **er-**, **ge-**, **ver-**, or **zer-**), **zu** in an infinitive phrase will precede the verb.

Er hatte etwas zu verkaufen.	*He had something to sell.*

If the infinitive has a separable prefix (**an-**, **ein-**, **durch-**, **mit-**, **vor-**, or **zu-**), **zu** will stand between the prefix and the infinitive, and the phrase will be written as one word.

Er findet etwas anzuziehen.	*He finds something to put on.*

You must also use an infinitive phrase after **etwas** and **nichts** when they are followed by an adjective used as a noun.

Der Soldat hat nichts **Neues** zu berichten.	*The soldier has nothing* ***new*** *to report.*
Der Künstler fand etwas **Interessantes** zu malen.	*The artist found something* ***interesting*** *to paint.*

Es as a Signal for an Infinitive Clause

Sentences that use the pronoun **es** as their subject can signal the need for an infinitive clause.

Es ist wichtig sich jeden Tag zu duschen.	*It is important to shower every day.*
Es war schwer mit dem alten Mann zu reden.	*It was hard to talk with the old man.*
Es fiel mir nicht ein, Geld von ihm zu borgen.	*It did not occur to me to borrow money from him.*

Written Practice 3

Change the sentences in parentheses to infinitive clauses, attaching them to the sentence provided. For example:

Es war schwer...

(Sie tanzt mit Erik.)

Es war schwer mit Erik zu tanzen.

1. Es ist sehr wichtig...

   (Die Kinder trinken genug Milch.)

   ______________________________.

   (Er arbeitet fleißig.)

   ______________________________.

   (Wir kommen pünktlich an.)

   ______________________________.

   (Sie helfen alten Menschen.)

   ______________________________.

   (Sie hat gute Freunde.)

   ______________________________.

   (Wir sind höflich. [**höflich** = *polite*])

   ______________________________.

Phrases That Require an Infinitive Clause

There are some specific phrases that always require an infinitive clause. They begin with a preposition and end with the infinitive clause.

anstatt...zu *instead of* ohne...zu *without (doing something)* um...zu *in order to*

Clauses formed with these three structures can precede or follow the main clause of the sentence.

Helga borgte Geld, anstatt Arbeit zu suchen.	*Helga borrowed money instead of looking for work.*
Er fuhr nach Hause, ohne uns zu helfen.	*He went home without helping us.*

Um Geld zu verdienen, musste Erik nach Leipzig ziehen. — *In order to earn money, Erik had to move to Leipzig.*

Written Practice 4

Change the sentences in parentheses to infinitive clauses, attaching them to the sentences provided. For example:

Er kam in die Küche, ohne...

(Er wäscht sich die Hände.)

Er kam in die Küche, ohne sich die Hände zu waschen.

1. Er kam in die Küche, ohne...

   (Er grüsst seine Mutter.)

   ______________________________.

   (Er hilft seiner Mutter.)

   ______________________________.

   (Er macht die Tür zu.)

   ______________________________.

2. Karin arbeitet in Berlin, um...

   (Sie verdient mehr Geld.)

   ______________________________.

   (Sie wohnt bei einer Tante.)

   ______________________________.

   (Sie besucht die großen Museen.)

   ______________________________.

3. Die Kinder stehen an der Ecke, anstatt...

   (Sie gehen zur Schule.)

   ______________________________.

   (Sie besuchen ihren kranken Onkel.)

   ______________________________.

   (Sie beeilen sich nach Hause zu kommen.)

   ______________________________.

Other Verbal Structures with Infinitive Clauses

Thus far, you have dealt with infinitive clauses that consist of **zu** and a single verb: **zu gehen**, **anzuziehen**, **zu besuchen**, and so forth. But other verbal structures can also occur in infinitive clauses.

Modals:

Er **kann** seinen Onkel **besuchen**.	*He **can visit** his uncle.*
Er spart sein Geld, um seinen Onkel **besuchen zu können**.	*He saves his money in order **to be able to visit** his uncle.*

Perfect Tense:

Er **hat** einen Schatz **gefunden**.	*He **found** a treasure.*
Er glaubt einen Schatz **gefunden zu haben**.	*He believes **to have found** a treasure.*
Er **ist** in die Hauptstadt **geflogen**.	*He **flew** to the capital.*
Er behauptet in die Hauptstadt **geflogen zu sein.**	*He claims **to have flown** to the capital.*

Passive:

Er **wird** von einem Freund **besucht**.	*He **is visited** by a friend.*
Er behauptet von einem Freund **besucht zu werden**.	*He claims **to be visited** by a friend.*
Er **ist verhaftet worden**.	*He **was arrested**.*
Er schämte sich **verhaftet worden zu sein**.	*He was ashamed **to have been arrested**.*

In each of the previous examples, the conjugated verb of the first sentence becomes the infinitive preceded by **zu** in the infinitive clause. This occurs whether the conjugated verb is a modal auxiliary, the auxiliary in a perfect tense, or the auxiliary of a passive structure.

kann besuchen	→	*besuchen zu können*
hat gefunden	→	*gefunden zu haben*
ist geflogen	→	*geflogen zu sein*
wird besucht	→	*besucht zu werden*
ist besucht worden	→	*besucht worden zu sein*

Written Practice 5

Rewrite each of the following verb phrases as an infinitive clause with **zu**. Consider what each infinitive clause means.

1. muss arbeiten ______________________________
2. soll vergessen ______________________________
3. will sprechen ______________________________
4. hat gelernt ______________________________
5. hat verstanden ______________________________
6. ist gewesen ______________________________
7. ist mitgegangen ______________________________
8. wird zerstört ______________________________
9. wurde aufgemacht ______________________________
10. ist bewundert worden ______________________________

Written Practice 6

Circle the letter of the word or phrase that best completes each sentence.

1. Das Kind schrie, ________ es ein Ungeheuer gesehen hätte.
   (a) wenn (c) ob
   (b) wohin (d) als ob

2. Karl hilft Karin, ________ uns zu helfen.
   (a) anstatt (c) von ihm
   (b) als wenn (d) von ihnen

3. Der Dieb wäre glücklich gewesen, wenn ihn niemand ________.
   (a) geblieben wäre (c) gesehen hätte
   (b) ankommen würde (d) geglaubt würde

4. ________ du mir glaubtest, könnte ich dir damit helfen.
   (a) Als ob (c) Anstatt
   (b) Wenn (d) Ohne zu

5. Thomas ging zur Schule, _______ sich die Haare zu kämmen.
   (a) ohne (c) wenn
   (b) als ob (d) denn

6. Wenn er dich kennte, _______ er dich einladen.
   (a) soll (c) würde
   (b) möchten (d) hätte

7. _______ mein Mann nur hier!
   (a) Wäre (c) Möchte
   (b) Könnte (d) Hätte

8. Wenn der alte Mann _______, würde seine Frau weinen.
   (a) verstand (c) gehabt habe
   (b) müsste (d) stürbe

9. Die Schauspielerin lächelte, als ob ich etwas Dummes _______.
   (a) gesagt hätte (c) verkaufen werde
   (b) geflogen wäre (d) bewundert worden wäre

10. Wenn ich doch bei meinen Eltern _______!
   (a) hülfe (c) müsste
   (b) wäre (d) möchte

11. Wenn ich plötzlich reich würde, dann _______ ich viele neue Freunde.
   (a) fände (c) gegeben hätte
   (b) gäbe (d) gefunden worden wäre

12. Felix _______, als ob er nicht verstanden hätte.
   (a) machte zu (c) tat so
   (b) sprecht (d) glaubte

13. Gudrun redete, als ob sie alles _______.
   (a) wüsste (c) geschrieben würde
   (b) erwartet (d) fahren möchte

14. Es ist wichtig gut fahren _______ können.
   (a) hätte (c) ob
   (b) wäre (d) zu

15. Wenn ich das Geld gefunden hätte, hätte ich es Ihnen ________.
    (a) verloren (c) geben können
    (b) verhaftet worden (d) vorgestellt

QUIZ

Write the past subjunctive and the present conditional of the following verbs in the third person singular. For example:

gehen	*ginge*	*würde gehen*
1. tragen	________	________
bringen	________	________
versuchen	________	________
werden	________	________
sein	________	________
lassen	________	________
aussehen	________	________
helfen	________	________
verstehen	________	________
wissen	________	________

Rewrite each sentence to include the phrases in parentheses, making them the result of a conditional statement. For example:

Wenn er hier wäre, ________________.

(Er hilft mir.)

Wenn er hier wäre, würde er mir helfen.

2. Wenn er hier wäre, ________________.

(Er spricht mit Onkel Peter.)

____

(Ich kann ihm ein Geschenk geben.)

____

(Er muss auf dem Sofa schlafen.)

____

3. **Wenn das Wetter besser gewesen wäre, ______________.**
   (Die Kinder haben im Garten gespielt.)

   ____

   (Der Wagen ist repariert worden.)

   ____

   (Ich bin früher nach Hause gegangen.)

   ____

4. **Wenn ______________, würde sie uns Eis kaufen.**
   (Sie hat mehr Geld.)

   ____

   (Die jüngeren Kinder sind hier.)

   ____

   (Es wird sehr heiß.)

   ____

Rewrite each sentence to include the phrases in parentheses. For example:

Er lacht, als ob...

(Die Geschichte ist dumm.)

Er lacht, als ob die Geschichte dumm wäre.

5. **Sie tat so, als ob...**
   (Sie kann alles verstehen.)

   ____

   (Sie ist so klug.)

   ____

(Wir werden ihr damit helfen.)

____

Rewrite each sentence by forming infinitive clauses from the sentences in parentheses. For example:

Es ist wichtig...

(Wir verstehen das Problem.)

Es ist wichtig das Problem zu verstehen.

6. **Es ist oft schwer...**
   (Wir glauben einem Dieb.)

   ____

   (Ich finde interessante Bücher.)

   ____

   (Sie bleiben im Hotel, wenn das Wetter schön ist.)

   ____

7. **Er ist nach Wien gereist, um...**
   (Er sucht Arbeit.)

   ____

   (Er kann an der Universität studieren)

   ____

   (Er geht in die Oper.)

   ____

8. **Er hat immer behauptet...**
   (Er ist ein Freund von mir.)

   ____

(Er kann vier Sprachen sprechen.)

____

(Er hat die Kanzlerin kennen gelernt.)

____

9. Die Kinder kamen nach Hause, ohne...
(Sie waschen sich die Hände.)

____

(Sie haben Brot und Milch gekauft.)

____

(Sie haben ihre Freunde mitgebacht.)

____

10. Martin wollte bis zehn Uhr schlafen, anstatt...
(Er fährt in die Stadt.)

____

(Er lässt den alten Wagen reparieren.)

____

(Er hilft seinem Vater.)

____

Still Struggling

German declensions require being aware of the signals that determine which case to use, and prepositions are important signals of this type. Be sure to refer to Appendix B: Prepositions and Their Required Cases at the end of this book.

PART FOUR TEST

Combine each first sentence with the one that follows, so each sentence has a relative clause with a definite article relative pronoun. Then rewrite the new sentences using **welcher** as the relative pronoun. For example:

Er hat ein Auto.

Er wird das Auto reparieren lassen.

Er hat ein Auto, das er wird reparieren lassen.

Er hat ein Auto, welches er wird reparieren lassen.

1. **Die Männer haben wenig Freizeit.**
   Ich arbeite mit den Männern in einer Fabrik.

   ___

   ___

2. **Sie haben das Dorf besichtigt.**
   Meine Tante ist in dem Dorf geboren.

   ___

   ___

Complete the following sentence with the one that follows, forming it as a relative clause.

3. **Die Kinder finden alles, ...**
   Ihre Eltern haben alles versteckt.

   ___

   ___

Write each of the following passive phrases in the tenses shown with the pronouns provided.

4. **werden vorgestellt**

   pres **ich** ______________________

   past **du** ______________________

   pres perf **er** ______________________

   fut **wir** ______________________

5. **muss verhaftet werden**

   pres **ich** ______________________

   past **du** ______________________

   pres perf **ihr** ______________________

   fut **Sie** ______________________

Rewrite the following active voice sentences in the passive voice. Retain the tenses of the active voice sentences.

6. **Die Lehrer haben das Examen diskutiert.**

   ____

7. **Wir werden ein neues Haus kaufen.**

   ____

8. **Die Wirtin stellt den neuen Mieter vor.**

   ____

Rewrite each sentence, adding the adjectives provided in parentheses. For example:

Ich besuche eine ______________ Frau.

(alt) *Ich besuche eine alte Frau.*

9. **Habt ihr einen ______________ Bären gesehen?**

   (groß) ______________________________________

10. **Die Töchter dieser __________ Frau arbeiten in Kiel.**
(alt) ______________________________

11. **Alle __________ Kinder müssen an der Ecke warten.**
(jünger) ______________________________

Form the three imperatives for the verbs provided.

12.

	du	ihr	Sie
treffen	________	________	________
aufmachen	________	________	________
sehen	________	________	________
sein	________	________	________
werden	________	________	________

Provide the appropriate adjective endings for each blank in the cases provided.

13.

nom	*ein guter Mann*	________
acc	________	*seine letzte Frage*
dat	________	________
acc	*dieses kleine Haus*	________
dat	________	________
gen	________	*meiner alten Handschuhe*

Write the present and past subjunctive conjugations with the pronouns provided for each of the following verbs.

	Present Subj.	Past Subj.
14. vorstellen		
ich	________	________
du	________	________
er	________	________
15. werden		
wir	________	________
ihr	________	________
Sie	________	________

16. **sein**

ich	______	______
sie (*s.*)	______	______
sie (*pl.*)	______	______

Rewrite each sentence with the direct quotes provided, forming a statement in indirect discourse. For example:

Erik sagte, dass...

„Seine Mutter ist sehr krank."

Erik sagte, dass seine Mutter sehr krank sei.

17. **Frau Schneider sagte, dass...**
    „Ihr Bruder will in der Hauptstadt wohnen."

    ____

    „Niemand wird ihr darüber erzählen."

    ____

    „Die Touristen werden sich morgen mit der Kanzlerin treffen."

    ____

    Der Beamte fragte, ob...
    „Ist das ihr Koffer?"

    ____

    „Ist der Wagen repariert worden?"

    ____

    „Haben die Ausländer ihre Fahrkarten bekommen?"

    ____

Complete each sentence with the phrases in parentheses, using them as the result of a conditional statement. For example:

Wenn er hier wäre, ...

(Er hilft mir.)

Wenn er hier wäre, würde er mir helfen.

18. Wenn er hier wäre, ...
(Tina kann mit ihm sprechen.)

____

(Wir fahren mit ihm in die Stadt.)

____

19. Wenn das Wetter besser gewesen wäre, ...
(Ich bin in die Berge gefahren.)

____

(Sie haben zum Stadtpark gehen können.)

____

Complete each sentence with the phrases in parentheses. For example:

Er lacht, als ob...

(Die Geschichte ist dumm.)

Er lacht, als ob die Geschichte dumm wäre.

20. Er tat so, als ob...
(Er hat alles verstanden.)

____

(Er kann sein Geld nicht finden.)

____

(Er hat mich gar nicht gesehen.)

____

Der Student spricht, als ob...
(Er ist sehr klug.)

____

(Wir wollen ihm nicht helfen.)

____

(Er kennt mich nicht.)

____

Complete the following sentence by forming infinitive clauses from the sentences in parentheses. For example:

Es ist wichtig...

(Wir verstehen das Problem.)

Es ist wichtig das Problem zu verstehen.

21. **Sie fahren in die Schweiz, um...**
(Sie besuchen Freunde.)

____

(Sie kaufen ein kleines Haus in den Bergen.

____

(Sie fotografieren die alten Dörfer.)

____

Circle the letter of the word or phrases that best completes each sentence.

22. **Martin hat die neue Schülerin ______________.**

A. gefallen
C. gern
B. würde sehen
D. besuchen

23. Tina, ______________ mich bitte an!

A. ruf

B. kommt

C. bleiben Sie

D. aussehen

24. Mein Sohn will sein braunes ______________ anziehen.

A. Leute

B. Hemd

C. Schuhe

D. Handschuh

25. Der alte Mann fragt uns, ______________ der nächste Zug kommen wird.

A. wenn

B. haben gewusst

C. wie viel

D. um wie viel Uhr

Final Exam

Circle the letter of the word or phrase that best completes each sentence.

1. ______________ ist das?
   A. Frau Schneider B. Name C. Was D. Nicht

2. Der Student ______________ Martin.
   A. heißt B. wie C. Herr D. Frau

3. ______________ ist das Konzert?
   A. Wann B. Gestern C. Ja D. Wer

4. Ist die Frau Ihre Mutter ______________ Ihre Tante?
   A. oder B. trotz C. wenn D. sehr

5. Wie ______________ CDs hast du?
   A. keine B. lange C. viele D. mehr

6. ______________ wird heiß.
   A. Diese Uhr B. Der Ofen C. Seine Briefe D. Unsere Blumen

7. Mein Sohn ______________ seine Lehrerin.
   A. sieht B. besuchen C. bekamt D. wurden

8. Das Kind nimmt ein ______________ Milch.
   A. groß B. kleine C. Dorf D. Glas

9. **Wir ______________ sie, wo das neue Restaurant ist.**
   A. fragen B. spielen C. werden D. haben

10. **______________ fahrt ihr morgen?**
    A. Heute B. Wohin C. Wer D. Zu Hause

11. **Wir wohnen ______________ in der Hauptstadt.**
    A. sehr B. neu C. spät D. jetzt

12. **Die ______________ ist nicht sehr groß.**
    A. Brief B. Schule C. Haus D. Kinder

13. **Die Touristen sind ______________ gefahren.**
    A. zu Fuß B. mit dem Zug C. zu Hause D. nächste Woche

14. **Kennen Sie ______________ Bruder?**
    A. meinen B. euer C. Ihre D. unserem

15. **Meine Freundin kommt ______________ spät zur Party.**
    A. warum B. wie viel C. sehr D. kein

16. **Der alte Mann ______________ ein neues Hemd.**
    A. brauchten B. trägt C. wollt D. gekauft

17. **Ich ______________ nicht, wer da wohnt.**
    A. weiß B. habe C. kennen D. sagen

18. **Sie können ______________ Freitag warten.**
    A. bis B. ans C. an D. mit

19. **Ihre Kinder ______________ kein Brot.**
    A. hatte B. gingen mit C. aßen D. verstanden

20. **Sie hatten nur sechs ______________.**
    A. Affe B. Wohnung C. Bleistifte D. Schwester

21. **Bist du vom Theater ______________ Bahnhof gegangen?**
    A. im B. zum C. ohne D. wider

22. **Wir haben mehr als eine Stunde ______________ euch gewartet.**
A. heute B. vom C. getan D. auf

23. **Hast du diesen Roman ______________?**
A. ohne einen Freund B. gelesen C. schreibst D. zu deinen Eltern

24. **Die junge Dame hat mit meinem Kind ______________.**
A. gespielt B. aufgemacht C. verstanden D. erkannt

25. **Der neue Schüler hat ______________ gespielt.**
A. besser B. schlechten C. gute D. keiner

26. **Ihre Großmutter ______________ sehr krank ausgesehen.**
A. hat B. nach C. noch D. war

27. **Die neue Wohnung ______________ ist sehr klein.**
A. unserer Nachbarin B. meinem Enkel C. diese Ausländer D. der Zeit

28. **Er hatte ein Geschenk für ______________.**
A. diesem Herrn B. seinen Sohn C. ihr D. dir

29. **______________ Brille hat er gefunden?**
A. Wessen B. Unserer C. Mein D. Etwas

30. **Morgen fliegen wir ______________ München.**
A. im B. ohne C. in D. nach

31. **Meine Tochter studiert ______________ einer Universität in Deutschland.**
A. vor B. vom C. durch D. an

32. **Deutschland liegt in ______________.**
A. Europa B. April C. Winter D. Berlin

33. **Die ______________ Italiens ist Rom.**
A. Leute B. Hauptstadt C. Länder D. Osten

34. **Ich kann dir nicht ______________.**
A. helfen B. finden C. sehen D. gehabt

35. **Wann ____________ Tina nach Hause kommen?**
A. können B. würde C. wird D. ist

36. **Meine Schwester ist ____________ als mein Bruder.**
A. älter B. klein C. am schnellsten D. junge

37. **Während des ____________ wohnten sie in London.**
A. Haus B. Krieges C. Sommer D. Wagens

38. **Ich ziehe ____________ eine blaue Bluse an.**
A. unser B. dich C. mir D. sich

39. **Die Männer, ____________ in einer Fabrik arbeiten, sind meine Freunde.**
A. der B. die C. denen D. deren

40. **Wir fahren nach Paris, ____________ Freunde zu besuchen.**
A. ob B. um C. wegen D. trotz

41. **Der Kanzler hat etwas ____________ zu sagen.**
A. wichtiges B. nichts C. neu D. intelligent

42. **Die Fenster sind aufgemacht ____________.**
A. geworden B. haben C. worden D. gehabt

43. **Sie erzählte, dass der alte Mann kein Geld ____________.**
A. bekommt B. habe C. wollen D. gegeben

44. **Wenn ich in Bonn wäre, ____________ ich bei meiner Tante wohnen.**
A. kann B. könne C. würde D. worden

45. **Martin fragte, ____________ Helga bei euch zu Gast wäre.**
A. ob B. als ob C. dass D. wessen

46. **____________ er mehr Geld hätte, könnte er eine Afrikareise machen.**
A. Als B. Weil C. Als ob D. Wenn

47. **Die Tochter des Lehrers tanzte ____________.**
A. schlechte B. am besten C. konnte D. längere

48. **Der Film fängt um ______________ Uhr an.**

A. neunzehn B. einundzwanzigste C. zweiundzwanzigsten D. spät

49. **Die Schauspielerin ist ______________ 1941 gestorben.**

A. Hauptstadt B. geboren C. im Jahre D. jünger

50. **Martin hat die neue Studentin ______________.**

A. gewesen B. etwas C. studieren D. gern

Appendix A

Principal Parts of Irregular Verbs

The second person singular and third person singular are shown in the present tense throughout the list below. In the past tense and subjunctive imperfect, only the third person singular is illustrated. You will see, however, that in the present tense conjugations of **sein** and **tun**, all persons are illustrated.

Indicative Infinitive	**Present**	**Past**	**Past Participle**	**Subjunctive Imperfect**
backen	bäckst bäckt	buk *or* backte	gebacken	büke *or* backte
befehlen	befiehlst befiehlt	befahl	befohlen	beföhle
beginnen	beginnst beginnt	begann	begonnen	begönne
beißen	beißt beißt	biss	gebissen	bisse
bergen	birgst birgt	barg	geborgen	bürge

Indicative Infinitive	Present	Past	Past Participle	Subjunctive Imperfect
bersten	birst birst	barst	geborsten	börste
betrügen	betrügst betrügt	betrog	betrogen	betröge
bewegen	bewegst bewegt	bewog	bewogen	bewöge
biegen	biegst biegt	bog	gebogen	böge
bieten	bietest bietet	bot	geboten	böte
binden	bindest bindet	band	gebunden	bände
bitten	bittest bittet	bat	gebeten	bäte
blasen	bläst bläst	blies	geblasen	bliese
bleiben	bleibst bleibt	blieb	geblieben	bliebe
bleichen	bleichst bleicht	blich	geblichen	bliche
braten	brätst brät	briet	gebraten	briete
brechen	brichst bricht	brach	gebrochen	bräche
brennen	brennst brennt	brannte	gebrannt	brennte
bringen	bringst bringt	brachte	gebracht	brächte
denken	denkst denkt	dachte	gedacht	dächte
dingen	dingst dingt	dingte *or* dang	gedungen	dingte
dreschen	drischst drischt	drosch	gedroschen	drösche
dringen	dringst dringt	drang	gedrungen	dränge

Indicative Infinitive	Present	Past	Past Participle	Subjunctive Imperfect
dürfen	darfst darf	durfte	gedurft	dürfte
empfangen	empfängst empfängt	empfing	empfangen	empfinge
empfehlen	empfiehlst empfiehlt	empfahl	empfohlen	empföhle
empfinden	empfindest empfindet	empfand	empfunden	empfände
erlöschen	erlischst erlischt	erlosch	erloschen	erlösche
erschrecken	erschrickst erschrickt	erschrak	erschrocken	erschäke
erwägen	erwägst erwägt	erwog	erwogen	erwöge
essen	isst isst	aß	gegessen	ässe
fahren	fährst fährt	fuhr	gefahren	führe
fallen	fällst fällt	fiel	gefallen	fiele
fangen	fängst fängt	fing	gefangen	finge
fechten	fichtest ficht	focht	gefochten	föchte
finden	findest findet	fand	gefunden	fände
flechten	flichtst flicht	flocht	geflochten	flöchte
fliegen	fliegst fliegt	flog	geflogen	flöge
fliehen	fliehst flieht	floh	geflohen	flöhe
fließen	fließt fließt	floss	geflossen	flösse
fressen	frisst frisst	fraß	gefressen	frässe

Indicative Infinitive	Present	Past	Past Participle	Subjunctive Imperfect
frieren	frierst friert	fror	gefroren	fröre
gären	gärst gärt	gor	gegoren	göre
gebären	gebierst gebiert	gebar	geboren	gebäre
geben	gibst gibt	gab	gegeben	gäbe
gedeihen	gedeihst gedeiht	gedieh	gediehen	gediehe
gehen	gehst geht	ging	gegangen	ginge
gelten	giltst gilt	galt	gegolten	gälte *or* gölte
genesen	genest genest	genas	genesen	genäse
genießen	genießt genießt	genoss	genossen	genösse
geraten	gerätst gerät	geriet	geraten	geriete
gewinnen	gewinnst gewinnt	gewann	gewonnen	gewänne *or* gewönne
gießen	gießt gießt	goss	gegossen	gösse
gleichen	gleichst gleicht	glich	geglichen	gliche
gleiten	gleitest gleitet	glitt	geglitten	glitte
glimmen	glimmst glimmt	glomm *or* glimmte	geglommen *or* geglimmt	glömme
graben	gräbst gräbt	grub	gegraben	grübe
greifen	greifst greift	griff	gegriffen	griffe
haben	hast hat	hatte	gehabt	hätte

Indicative Infinitive	Present	Past	Past Participle	Subjunctive Imperfect
halten	hältst hält	hielt	gehalten	hielte
hängen	hängst hängt	hing	gehangen	hinge
hauen	haust haut	hieb	gehauen	hiebe
heben	hebst hebt	hob	gehoben	höbe
heißen	heißt heißt	hieß	geheißen	hieße
helfen	hilfst hilft	half	geholfen	hülfe
kennen	kennst kennt	kannte	gekannt	kennte
klimmen	klimmst klimmt	klomm *or* klimmte	geklommen *or* geklimmt	klömme
klingen	klingst klingt	klang	geklungen	klänge
kneifen	kneifst kneift	kniff	gekniffen	kniffe
kommen	kommst kommt	kam	gekommen	käme
können	kannst kann	konnte	gekonnt	könnte
kriechen	kriechst kriecht	kroch	gekrochen	kröche
laden	lädst *or* ladest lädt *or* ladet	lud *or* ladete	geladen *or* geladet	lüde *or* ladete
lassen	lässt lässt	ließ	gelassen	ließe
laufen	läufst läuft	lief	gelaufen	liefe
leiden	leidest leidet	litt	gelitten	litte
leihen	leihst leiht	lieh	geliehen	liehe

Indicative Infinitive	Present	Past	Past Participle	Subjunctive Imperfect
lesen	liest liest	las	gelesen	läse
liegen	liegst liegt	lag	gelegen	läge
lügen	lügst lügt	log	gelogen	löge
mahlen	mahlst mahlt	mahlte	gemahlen	mahlte
meiden	meidest meidet	mied	gemieden	miede
melken	melkst melkt	melkte	gemelkt *or* gemolken (*adj.*)	mölke
messen	misst misst	maß	gemessen	mässe
mögen	magst mag	mochte	gemocht	möchte
müssen	musst muss	musste	gemusst	müsste
nehmen	nimmst nimmt	nahm	genommen	nähme
nennen	nennst nennt	nannte	genannt	nennte
pfeifen	pfeifst pfeift	pfiff	gepfiffen	pfiffe
pflegen	pflegst pflegt	pflegte *or* pflog	gepflegt *or* gepflogen	pflegte *or* pflöge
preisen	preist preist	pries	gepriesen	priese
quellen	quillst quillt	quoll	gequollen	quölle
raten	rätst rät	riet	geraten	riete
reiben	reibst reibt	rieb	gerieben	riebe
reißen	reißt reißt	riss	gerissen	risse

Indicative Infinitive	Present	Past	Past Participle	Subjunctive Imperfect
reiten	reitest reitet	ritt	geritten	ritte
rennen	rennst rennt	rannte	gerannt	rennte
riechen	riechst riecht	roch	gerochen	röche
ringen	ringst ringt	rang	gerungen	ränge
rinnen	rinnst rinnt	rann	geronnen	rönne
rufen	rufst ruft	rief	gerufen	riefe
salzen	salzst salzt	salzte	gesalzt *or* gesalzen (*fig.*)	salzte
saufen	säufst säuft	soff	gesoffen	söffe
saugen	saugst saugt	sog	gesogen	söge
schaffen	schaffst schafft	schuf	geschaffen	schüfe
schallen	schallst schallt	scholl	geschallt	schölle
scheiden	scheidest scheidet	schied	geschieden	schiede
scheinen	scheinst scheint	schien	geschienen	schiene
schelten	schiltst schilt	schalt	gescholten	schölte
scheren	schierst schiert	schor	geschoren	schöre
schieben	schiebst schiebt	schob	geschoben	schöbe
schießen	schießt schießt	schoss	geschossen	schösse
schinden	schindest schindet	schund	geschunden	schünde

Indicative Infinitive	Present	Past	Past Participle	Subjunctive Imperfect
schlafen	schläfst schläft	schlief	geschlafen	schliefe
schlagen	schlägst schlägt	schlug	geschlagen	schlüge
schleichen	schleichst schleicht	schlich	geschlichen	schliche
schleifen	schleifst schleift	schliff	geschliffen	schliffe
schleißen	schleißt schleißt	schliss	geschlissen	schlisse
schliefen	schliefst schlieft	schloff	geschloffen	schlöffe
schließen	schließt schließt	schloss	geschlossen	schlösse
schlingen	schlingst schlingt	schlang	geschlungen	schlänge
schmeißen	schmeißt schmeißt	schmiss	geschmissen	schmisse
schmelzen	schmilzt schmilzt	schmolz	geschmolzen	schmölze
schneiden	schneidest schneidet	schnitt	geschnitten	schnitte
schrecken	schrickst schrickt	schrak	geschrocken	schräke
schreiben	schreibst schreibt	schrieb	geschrieben	schriebe
schreien	schreist schreit	schrie	geschrien	schriee
schreiten	schreitest schreitet	schritt	geschritten	schritte
schweigen	schweigst schweigt	schwieg	geschwiegen	schwiege
schwellen	schwillst schwillt	schwoll	geschwollen	schwölle
schwimmen	schwimmst schwimmt	schwamm	geschwommen	schwömme

Indicative Infinitive	Present	Past	Past Participle	Subjunctive Imperfect
schwinden	schwindest schwindet	schwand	geschwunden	schwände
schwingen	schwingst schwingt	schwang	geschwungen	schwänge
schwören	schwörst schwört	schwur	geschworen	schwüre
sehen	siehst sieht	sah	gesehen	sähe
sein	bin bist ist sind seid sind	war	gewesen	wäre
senden	sendest sendet	sandte *or* sendete	gesandt *or* gesendet	sendete
sieden	siedest siedet	sott *or* siedete	gesotten	sötte *or* siedete
singen	singst singt	sang	gesungen	sänge
sinken	sinkst sinkt	sank	gesunken	sänke
sinnen	sinnst sinnt	sann	gesonnen	sänne
sitzen	sitzt sitzt	saß	gesessen	säße
sollen	sollst soll	sollte	gesollt	sollte
spalten	spaltest spaltet	spaltete	gespalten *or* gespaltet	spaltete
speien	speist speit	spie	gespien	spie
spinnen	spinnst spinnt	spann	gesponnen	spönne
spleißen	spleißt spleißt	spliss	gesplissen	splisse
sprechen	sprichst spricht	sprach	gesprochen	spräche
sprießen	sprießt sprießt	spross	gesprossen	sprösse

Indicative Infinitive	Present	Past	Past Participle	Subjunctive Imperfect
springen	springst springt	sprang	gesprungen	spränge
stechen	stichst sticht	stach	gestochen	stäche
stecken	steckst steckt	steckte *or* stak	gesteckt	steckte *or* stäke
stehen	stehst steht	stand	gestanden	stünde *or* stände
stehlen	stiehlst stiehlt	stahl	gestohlen	stöhle *or* stähle
steigen	steigst steigt	stieg	gestiegen	stiege
sterben	stirbst stirbt	starb	gestorben	stürbe
stieben	stiebst stiebt	stob *or* stiebte	gestoben *or* gestiebt	stöbe *or* stiebte
stinken	stinkst stinkt	stank	gestunken	stänke
stoßen	stößt stößt	stieß	gestoßen	stieße
streichen	streichst streicht	strich	gestrichen	striche
streiten	streitest streitet	stritt	gestritten	stritte
tragen	trägst trägt	trug	getragen	trüge
treffen	triffst trifft	traf	getroffen	träfe
treiben	treibst treibt	trieb	getrieben	triebe
treten	trittst tritt	trat	getreten	träte
triefen	triefst trieft	troff	getrieft *or* getroffen	tröffe
trinken	trinkst trinkt	trank	getrunken	tränke

Indicative Infinitive	Present	Past	Past Participle	Subjunctive Imperfect
tun	tue tust tut tun tut tun	tat	getan	täte
verderben	verdirbst verdirbt	verdarb	verdorben	verdürbe
verdrießen	verdrießt verdrießt	verdross	verdrossen	verdrösse
vergessen	vergisst vergisst	vergaß	vergessen	vergäße
verhehlen	verhehlst verhehlt	verhehlte	verhehlt *or* verhohlen	verhehlte
verlieren	verlierst verliert	verlor	verloren	verlöre
verwirren	verwirrst verwirrt	verwirrte	verwirrt *or* verworren (*adj.*)	verwirrte
wachsen	wächst wächst	wuchs	gewachsen	wüchse
wägen	wägst wägt	wog *or* wägte	gewogen	wöge *or* wägte
waschen	wäschst wäscht	wusch	gewaschen	wüsche
weichen	weichst weicht	wich	gewichen	wiche
weisen	weist weist	wies	gewiesen	wiese
wenden	wendest wendet	wandte *or* wendete	gewandt *or* gewendet	wendete
werben	wirbst wirbt	warb	geworben	würbe
werden	wirst wird	wurde	geworden	würde
werfen	wirfst wirft	warf	geworfen	würfe
wiegen	wiegst wiegt	wog	gewogen	wöge
winden	windest windet	wand	gewunden	wände

Indicative Infinitive	Present	Past	Past Participle	Subjunctive Imperfect
wissen	weißt	wusste	gewusst	wüsste
	weiß			
wollen	willst	wollte	gewollt	wollte
	will			
zeihen	zeihst	zieh	geziehen	ziehe
	zeiht			
ziehen	ziehst	zog	gezogen	zöge
	zieht			
zwingen	zwingst	zwang	gezwungen	zwänge
	zwingt			

Some irregular verbs are used in impersonal expressions and are conjugated only in the third person singular.

Indicative Infinitive	Present	Past	Past Participle	Subjunctive Imperfect
dünken	dünkt	dünkte *or*	gedünkt *or*	dünkte *or*
	deucht	deuchte	gedeucht	deuchte
gelingen	gelingt	gelang	gelungen	gelänge
geschehen	geschieht	geschah	geschehen	geschähe
misslingen	misslingt	misslang	misslungen	misslänge

Appendix B

Prepositions and Their Required Cases

Accusative	Dative	Accusative-Dative	Genitive
bis	aus	an	(an)statt
durch	außer	auf	angesichts
für	bei	hinter	anlässlich
gegen	gegenüber	in	außerhalb
ohne	mit	neben	beiderseits
um	nach	über	bezüglich
wider	seit	unter	diesseits
	trotz	vor	hinsichtlich
	von	zwischen	jenseits
	wegen		trotz
	zu		unterhalb
			während
			wegen

English-German Dictionary

a, an ein, eine
address Adresse (*f.*)
to admire bewundern
to adopt adoptieren
after nach
afterward nachdem
against gegen
against wider
airplane Flugzeug (*n.*)
airport Flughafen (*m.*)
all alle
alone allein
along entlang
Alps Alpen (*pl.*)
already schon
always immer
America Amerika
American Amerikaner (*m.*)
and und
angry, mad böse
to annoy, irritate reizen
to answer antworten
apartment Wohnung (*f.*)
apothecary Apotheke (*f.*)
April April (*m.*)
Arabic arabisch
architect Architekt (*m.*)
arm Arm (*m.*)
around um
to arrange arrangieren
to arrest verhaften
to arrive ankommen
as als
to ask fragen
to astound erstaunen
at an
at home zu Hause
athlete Sportler (*m.*)
attractive attraktiv
August August (*m.*)
aunt Tante (*f.*)
Australia Australien
Austria Österreich
autumn Herbst (*m.*)
bad schlecht
to bake backen
baker Bäcker (*m.*)
ball Ball (*m.*)
ballpoint pen Kuli (*m.*)
bank Bank (*f.*)
baron Freiherr (*m.*)
baroness Freifrau (*f.*)
to be sein
to be acquainted with kennen

to be called, named heißen
to be pleased, glad sich freuen
to be valid, worth gelten
to be wrong sich irren
to bear (a child) gebären
bear Bär (*m.*)
because denn, weil
because of wegen
to become, get; shall/will werden
bed Bett (*n.*)
beef Rindfleisch (*n.*)
beer Bier (*n.*)
before, in front of vor
behind hinter
to believe glauben
to belong to gehören
belt Gürtel (*m.*)
berry Beere (*f.*)
between zwischen
beverage Getränk (*n.*)
bicycle Fahrrad (*n.*)
big groß
billion Milliarde (*f.*)
black schwarz
blind blind
blouse Bluse (*f.*)
book Buch (*n.*)
boss Chef (*m.*)
bottle Flasche (*f.*)
bouquet Blumenstrauß (*m.*)
boy Junge (*m.*)
bread Brot (*n.*)
to break brechen
bricklayer Maurer (*m.*)
bridge Brücke (*f.*)
bright hell
to bring bringen
brother Bruder (*m.*)
brown braun
bus Bus (*m.*)
bush Busch (*m.*)
businessman Geschäftsmann (*m.*)
businesswoman Geschäftsfrau (*f.*)
but aber
butcher Metzger (*m.*)
to buy kaufen
by bei
by heart auswendig
cabbage Kohl (*m.*)
to call up, telephone anrufen
calm, quiet ruhig
Canada Kanada
capital city Hauptstadt (*f.*)
capitalist Kapitalist (*m.*)
car Auto (*n.*)
car Wagen (*m.*)
carnation Nelke (*f.*)
carpet Teppich (*m.*)
castle Burg (*f.*)
cat Katze (*f.*)
cathedral Dom (*m.*)
CD CD (*f.*)
chair Stuhl (*m.*)
chalk Kreide (*f.*)
chancellor Kanzler (*m.*)
to change ändern
cheap billig
cheese Käse (*m.*)
chemist Chemiker (*m.*)
chess Schach (*n.*)
chicken Hühnchen (*n.*)
chicken Huhn (*n.*)
child Kind (*n.*)
church Kirche (*f.*)
circus Zirkus (*m.*)
city center, downtown Stadtzentrum (*n.*)
city excursion Stadtrundfahrt (*f.*)
city hall Rathaus (*n.*)
city Stadt (*f.*)
city wall Stadtmauer (*f.*)
to clear away, vacate räumen
climate Klima (*n.*)
clock; hour; watch Uhr (*f.*)
to close zumachen
clothes Kleider (*pl.*)
coach (athletic), trainer Trainer (*m.*)
coat Mantel (*m.*)
cock-and-bull story Ammenmärchen (*n.*)
coffee Kaffee (*m.*)
coke (Coca-Cola) Coca (*f.*), Cola (*f.*)
cold Erkältung (*f.*)
cold kalt

to collect sammeln
Cologne Köln
to come kommen
communist Kommunist (*m.*)
computer Computer (*m.*)
concert Konzert (*n.*)
conductor (transportation) Schaffner (*m.*)
conflict Konflikt (*m.*)
constitution Konstitution (*f.*)
continent Erdteil (*m.*)
to control kontrollieren
cool kühl
to copy kopieren
corn Mais (*m.*)
corner Ecke (*f.*)
count Graf (*m.*)
cow Kuh (*f.*)
to cry weinen
cupboard Schrank (*m.*)
to cut schneiden
to dance tanzen
dangerous gefährlich
dark dunkel
daughter Tochter (*f.*)
day Tag (*m.*)
death Tod (*m.*)
December Dezember (*m.*)
to delegate, send as a delegate delegieren
to demonstrate demonstrieren
Denmark Dänemark
dentist Zahnarzt (*m.*)
department store Kaufhaus (*n.*)
to describe beschreiben
desk Schreibtisch (*m.*)
dessert Nachtisch (*m.*)
to destroy zerstören
dialect Dialekt (*m.*)
dictionary Wörterbuch (*n.*)
difficult schwer
diligent fleißig
diplomat Diplomat (*m.*)
to dispatch absenden
to do tun
to do handicrafts basteln
door Tür (*f.*)
to drink trinken
to drive, travel fahren
drugstore Drogerie (*f.*)
duke Herzog (*m.*)
during während
each jeder
early früh
earth, Earth Erde (*f.*)
east Osten (*m.*)
easy leicht
eat essen
eat (used for animals) fressen
effective effektiv
eight acht
eighteen achtzehn
eighty achtzig
eleven elf
emperor Kaiser (*m.*)
empire Reich (*n.*)
entire, whole ganz
evening Abend (*m.*)
examination Examen (*n.*)
except außer
to expect, await erwarten
expensive teuer
to fall fallen
to fall in love sich verlieben
family Familie (*f.*)
far weit
farmer Bauer (*m.*)
to fascinate faszinieren
fast schnell
father Vater (*m.*)
February Februar (*m.*)
federal parliament Bundestag (*m.*)
to feel empfinden
to feel fühlen
fifteen fünfzehn
fifty fünfzig
to find finden
fir, pine tree Tanne (*f.*)
fish Fisch (*m.*)
to fit passen
five fünf
to flood überschwemmen
floor Boden (*m.*)
floor lamp Stehlampe (*f.*)

flower Blume (*f.*)
to fly fliegen
to follow folgen
fondly gern
food Essen (*n.*)
for für
foreigner Ausländer (*m.*)
to forget vergessen
forty vierzig
four vier
fourteen vierzehn
fox Fuchs (*m.*)
Friday Freitag (*m.*)
friend Freund (*m.*)
from, of von
from where woher
fruit Obst (*n.*)
fruit pie Obstkuchen (*m.*)
funny komisch
to gather, collect sammeln
German Deutsche (*m./f.*)
German champagne Sekt (*m.*)
Germanic germanisch
Germany Deutschland
get off (transportation) aussteigen
get on (transportation) einsteigen
gift Geschenk (*n.*)
girl Mädchen (*n.*)
girlfriend Freundin (*f.*)
to give geben
glass Glas (*n.*)
glove Handschuh (*m.*)
to go gehen
to go along mitgehen
to go cycling Rad fahren
to go in for, pursue; participate in; drive treiben
go skiing Ski laufen
God Gott (*m.*)
good gut
good-bye auf Wiederschauen, auf Wiedersehen
good day, hello guten Tag
good evening guten Abend
good morning guten Morgen
good night gute Nacht
government Regierung (*f.*)
grain Korn (*n.*)
grandchild Enkel (*m.*)
grandfather Großvater (*m.*)
grandmother Großmutter (*f.*)
grass Gras (*n.*)
gray grau
green grün
to greet grüssen
to grow wachsen
guest Gast (*m.*)
half halb
hallway Flur (*m.*)
ham Schinken (*m.*)
to hang hängen
to happen geschehen
to happen passieren
happy, lucky glücklich
harbor Hafen (*m.*)
harbor excursion Hafenrundfahrt (*f.*)
hare Hase (*m.*)
hat Hut (*m.*)
to have haben
to have the opinion, mean meinen
heads or tails Kopf oder Zahl
healthy gesund
to hear hören
heart Herz (*n.*)
heavy schwer
hedgehog Igel (*m.*)
hell Hölle (*f.*)
to help helfen
her ihr
here hier
high hoch
to hike, wander wandern
hippo Nilpferd (*n.*)
his sein
history Geschichte (*f.*)
hockey Eishockey (*n.*)
to hold halten
holy heilig
home(ward) nach Hause
to horrify entsetzen
horse Pferd (*n.*)
hospital Krankenhaus (*n.*)
hot heiß

hour Stunde (*f.*)
house Haus (*n.*)
how, as wie
human, person Mensch (*m.*)
hundred hundert
hungry hungrig
hunt Jagd (*f.*)
hurry sich beeilen
ice, ice cream Eis (*n.*)
if wenn
to imagine sich vorstellen
to imitate imitieren
to immigrate immigrieren
to impress imponieren
in in
to inform, notify mitteilen
insane wahnsinnig
inspite of trotz
instead of anstatt (statt)
to instruct, teach unterrichten
interesting interessant
to interrupt unterbrechen
to introduce vorstellen
to invite einladen
Italy Italien
jacket Jacke (*f.*)
January Januar (*m.*)
job Job (*m.*)
July Juli (*m.*)
June Juni (*m.*)
key Schlüssel (*m.*)
to kick, shove stoßen
king König (*m.*)
to kiss küssen
kitchen Küche (*f.*)
to knock klopfen
to know, be acquainted with kennen
to know wissen
lady Dame (*f.*)
lager beer Pils (*n.*)
lamp Lampe (*f.*)
landlady Wirtin (*f.*)
last letzte
late spät
to laugh lachen
law Jura (*n./pl.*)
lawn Rasen (*m.*)
lawyer Rechtsanwalt (*m.*)
to lay legen
leader Führer (*m.*)
to learn lernen
left link
less; minus weniger
to let lassen
library Bibliothek (*f.*)
to lie, recline lügen
to lie (omit the truth) lügen
light, easy leicht
light Licht (*n.*)
to like, please gefallen
little, small klein
little, few wenig
little bit bisschen
living room Wohnzimmer (*n.*)
long lang
to look at ansehen
to look for suchen
to look like aussehen
to lose verlieren
loud laut
to love lieben
main railroad station Hauptbahnhof (*m.*)
male nurse Pfleger (*m.*)
to manifest manifestieren
many, much viel(e)
to march marschieren
March März (*m.*)
market square Marktplatz (*m.*)
married verheiratet
May Mai (*m.*)
meat Fleisch (*n.*)
mechanic Mechaniker (*m.*)
merchant Kaufmann (*m.*)
milk Milch (*f.*)
million Million (*f.*)
mineral water Mineralwasser (*n.*)
minus minus
Monday Montag (*m.*)
monster Ungeheuer (*n.*)
month Monat (*m.*)
more mehr
morning Morgen (*m.*)

mother Mutter (*f.*)
motorcycle Motorrad (*n.*)
movie Film (*m.*)
movie theater Kino (*n.*)
Munich München
music Musik (*f.*)
my mein
name Name (*m.*)
to name nennen
nation Nation (*f.*)
near nah
to need brauchen
neighbor Nachbar (*m.*)
never nie
new neu
newspaper Zeitung (*f.*)
next to, near neben
nice nett
night Nacht (*f.*)
nine neun
nineteen neunzehn
ninety neunzig
no one niemand
north Norden (*m.*)
North America Nordamerika
not nicht
not any, none kein
to note, make a note of something notieren
notebook Heft (*n.*)
nothing nichts
novel Roman (*m.*)
November November (*m.*)
now jetzt
nurse Krankenschwester (*f.*)
nursery school teacher Erzieher (*m.*)
October Oktober (*m.*)
official, government employee Beamte (*m.*)
often oft
old alt
on auf
on foot zu Fuß
one eins
one man
to open aufmachen
opposite gegenüber
or oder
to order bestellen
to organize organisieren
our unser
out aus
outing Ausflug (*m.*)
oven Ofen (*m.*)
over, above über
package Paket (*n.*)
pain Schmerz (*m.*)
parents Eltern (*pl.*)
park Park (*m.*)
parliament Parlament (*n.*)
party Party (*f.*)
party (political) Partei (*f.*)
passport Pass (*m.*)
patient Kranke (*m.*)
peas Erbsen (*pl.*)
pencil Bleistift (*m.*)
people Leute (*pl.*)
people, nation Volk (*n.*)
person Mensch (*m.*)
pessimist Pessimist (*m.*)
pet Haustier (*n.*)
to photograph fotografieren
photographer Fotograf (*m.*)
physician Arzt (*m.*)
physicist Physiker (*m.*)
piano Klavier (*n.*)
picnic Picknick (*n.*)
picture Bild (*n.*)
picture postcard Ansichtskarte (*f.*)
pig Schwein (*n.*)
pilot Pilot (*m.*)
pink rosa
plant Pflanze (*f.*)
to plant pflanzen
to play spielen
please bitte
to please, make happy erfreuen
to pluck rupfen
plus plus
pocket Tasche (*f.*)
poet Dichter (*m.*)
police Polizei (*f.*)
polite höflich
politician Politiker (*m.*)

poor arm
position Position (*f.*)
to possess, own besitzen
postcard Postkarte (*f.*)
post office Post (*f.*)
postage stamp Briefmarke (*f.*)
poster Poster (*n.*)
potato Kartoffel (*f.*)
pregnant schwanger
prep school Gymnasium (*n.*)
president Präsident (*m.*)
pretty schön
probably wahrscheinlich
problem Problem (*n.*)
to produce produzieren
professor Professor (*m.*)
to program programmieren
to promise versprechen
to pronounce aussprechen
to protect schützen
to protest protestieren
to push schieben
to put, place stellen
quarter Viertel (*n.*)
queen Königin (*f.*)
rabbit Kaninchen (*n.*)
radio Radio (*n.*)
railroad station Bahnhof (*m.*)
rain Regen (*m.*)
to rain regnen
to read lesen
to receive bekommen
to recommend empfehlen
to recruit werben
red rot
to reflect widerspiegeln
to relate erzählen
relative Verwandte (*m.*)
to report berichten
republic Republik (*f.*)
to request bitten
to restore restaurieren
reunification Wiedervereinigung (*f.*)
rice Reis (*m.*)
to ride reiten
right recht
to rinse spülen
river Fluss (*m.*)
roast sausage Bratwurst (*f.*)
Roman römisch
room Zimmer (*n.*)
rose Rose (*f.*)
to run laufen, rennen
to run away weglaufen
Russian russisch
same derselbe
sandwich Butterbrot (*n.*)
Saturday Samstag, Sonnabend (*m.*)
to say sagen
schedule Fahrplan (*m.*)
school Schule (*f.*)
scientist Wissenschaftler (*m.*)
to scratch kratzen
season Jahreszeit (*f.*)
to seat oneself sich setzen
second zweite
secretary Sekretär (*m.*)
to see sehen
to sell verkaufen
to send schicken
to send senden
September September (*m.*)
to serve dienen
to set setzen
seven sieben
seventeen siebzehn
seventy siebzig
shall, will werden
to shave rasieren
sheep Schaf (*n.*)
ship Schiff (*n.*)
shop, store Laden (*m.*)
short kurz
to shout schreien
siblings Geschwister (*pl.*)
sick krank
sights Sehenswürdigkeiten (*pl.*)
sightseeing tour Besichtigung (*f.*)
since seit
to sing singen
singer Sänger (*m.*)
sister Schwester (*f.*)

to sit sitzen
six sechs
sixteen sechzehn
sixty sechzig
sky Himmel (*m.*)
to sleep schlafen
slow langsam
smart klug
to smoke rauchen
snake Schlange (*f.*)
snow Schnee (*m.*)
to snow schneien
soccer Fußball (*m.*)
soccer player Fußballspieler (*m.*)
sofa Sofa (*n.*)
someone jemand
son Sohn (*m.*)
song Lied (*n.*)
Sunday Sonntag (*m.*)
soon bald
south Süden (*m.*)
South America Südamerika
sparkling water Sprudel (*m.*)
sparkling wine Sekt (*m.*)
to speak sprechen
to speak to anreden
to spend ausgeben
to spoil, rot verderben
sport (form of) Sportart (*f.*)
spring Frühling (*m.*)
to stand stehen
to stand back, remain behind zurückbleiben
to start, begin anfangen
to stay, remain bleiben
to steal stehlen
stairs, staircase Treppe (*f.*)
still noch
story, history Geschichte (*f.*)
street Straße (*f.*)
streetcar Straßenbahn (*f.*)
to stroll spazieren
to study studieren
summer Sommer (*m.*)
Sunday Sonntag (*m.*)
supper Abendessen (*n.*)
to swear schwören
sweater Pullover (*m.*)
sweatshirt Sweatshirt (*n.*)
Sweden Schweden
to swim schwimmen
table Tisch (*m.*)
table tennis Tischtennis (*m.*)
to take along/with mitnehmen
to talk reden
taxi driver Taxifahrer (*m.*)
tea Tee (*m.*)
teacher Lehrer (*m.*)
telegram Telegramm (*n.*)
ten zehn
to thank danken
that dass (*conj.*)
that jener
there da, dort
there is/are es gibt
thief Dieb (*m.*)
to think denken
third dritte
thirst Durst (*m.*)
thirteen dreizehn
thirty dreißig
this dieser
thousand tausend
three drei
through durch
Thursday Donnerstag (*m.*)
ticket Fahrkarte (*f.*)
tiger Tiger (*m.*)
time Zeit (*f.*)
tired müde
to zu
today heute
today's (*adj.*) heutig
tomorrow morgen
tongue Zunge (*f.*)
too zu
tour Tour (*f.*)
tourist Tourist (*m.*)
to tow away abschleppen
traffic Verkehr (*m.*)
train Zug (*m.*)
to transfer umsteigen
to travel reisen

tree Baum (*m.*)
tribe Stamm (*m.*)
trillion Billion (*f.*)
trip Reise (*f.*)
to try probieren
Tuesday Dienstag (*m.*)
tulip Tulpe (*f.*)
tunnel Tunnel (*m.*)
twelve zwölf
twenty zwanzig
twins Zwillinge (*pl.*)
two zwei
umbrella Regenschirm (*m.*)
uncle Onkel (*m.*)
under unter
to understand verstehen
unfortunately leider
university Universität (*f.*)
until, as far as bis
vase Vase (*f.*)
vegetable soup Gemüsesuppe (*f.*)
vegetables Gemüse (*n.*)
very sehr
vicinity Nähe (*f.*)
Vienna Wien
village Dorf (*n.*)
violin Geige (*f.*)
to visit besuchen
to wait warten
wall Wand (*f.*)
war Krieg (*m.*)
warm warm
to wash waschen
water Wasser (*n.*)
to wear tragen
weather Wetter (*n.*)
Wednesday Mittwoch (*m.*)
week Woche (*f.*)
weekend Wochenende (*n.*)
west Westen (*m.*)
what was
when wann
whenever wenn
where wo
where to wohin
whether ob
which welcher
white weiß
who wer
whose wessen
why warum
wife, woman Frau (*f.*)
to win, gain gewinnen
window Fenster (*n.*)
wine Wein (*m.*)
wing Flügel (*m.*)
winter Winter (*m.*)
with mit
without ohne
wolf Wolf (*m.*)
woman, wife Frau (*f.*)
word Wort (*n.*)
to work arbeiten
worker Arbeiter (*m.*)
world war Weltkrieg (*m.*)
to write schreiben
writer Schriftsteller (*m.*)
year Jahr (*n.*)
yellow gelb
yesterday gestern
you du, ihr, Sie
young jung
your dein, euer, Ihr
zoo Zoo (*m.*)

German-English Dictionary

Abend (*m.*) evening
Abendessen (*n.*) dinner, supper
aber but
abschleppen to tow away
absenden to dispatch, send off
acht eight
achtzehn eighteen
achtzig eighty
adoptieren to adopt
Adresse (*f.*) address
alle all, everyone
allein alone
Alpen (*pl.*) Alps
als as, when
alt old
Amerika America
Amerikaner (*m.*) American
Ammenmärchen (*n.*) cock-and-bull story
an at
ändern to change
anfangen to start
ankommen to arrive
anreden to address, speak to
anrufen to call up, telephone
ansehen to look at
Ansichtskarte (*f.*) picture postcard
anstatt (statt) instead of
antworten to answer
Apotheke (*f.*) drugstore, apothecary
April (*m.*) April
arabisch Arabic
arbeiten to work
Arbeiter (*m.*) worker
Architekt (*m.*) architect
arm poor
Arm (*m.*) arm
arrangieren to arrange
Arzt (*m.*) physician
attraktiv attractive
auf on
auf Wiederschauen good-bye
auf Wiedersehen good-bye
aufmachen to open
August (*m.*) August
aus out
Ausflug (*m.*) outing
ausgeben to spend
Ausländer (*m.*) foreigner
aussehen to look like
außer except
aussprechen to pronounce
aussteigen to get off (transportation)
Australien Australia
auswendig by heart

Auto (*n.*) car
backen to bake
Bäcker (*m.*) baker
Bahnhof (*m.*) railroad station
bald soon
Ball (*m.*) ball
Bank (*f.*) bank
Bär (*m.*) bear
basteln to do handicrafts
Bauer (*m.*) farmer
Baum (*m.*) tree
Beamte (*m.*) official, government employee
sich beeilen hurry
Beere (*f.*) berry
bei by, at
bekommen to receive, get
berichten to report
beschreiben to describe
Besichtigung (*f.*) sightseeing tour
besitzen to possess, own
bestellen to order
besuchen to visit
Bett (*n.*) bed
bewundern to admire
Bibliothek (*f.*) library
Bier (*n.*) beer
Bild (*n.*) picture
billig cheap
Billion (*f.*) trillion
bis until, as far as
bisschen little bit
bitte please
bitten to request
bleiben to remain, stay
Bleistift (*m.*) pencil
blind blind
Blume (*f.*) flower
Blumenstrauß (*m.*) bouquet
Bluse (*f.*) blouse
Boden (*m.*) floor
böse angry, mad
Bratwurst (*f.*) roast sausage
brauchen to need
braun brown
brechen to break
Briefmarke (*f.*) postage stamp
bringen to bring
Brot (*n.*) bread
Brücke (*f.*) bridge
Bruder (*m.*) brother
Buch (*n.*) book
Bundestag (*m.*) federal parliament
Burg (*f.*) castle
Bus (*m.*) bus
Busch (*m.*) bush
Butterbrot (*n.*) sandwich
CD (*f.*) CD
Chef (*m.*) boss
Chemiker (*m.*) chemist
Coca (*f.*) Coca-Cola
Cola (*f.*) Coca-Cola
Computer (*m.*) computer
da there
Dame (*f.*) lady
Dänemark Denmark
danken to thank
dass that (*conj.*)
dein your
delegieren to delegate, send as a delegate
demonstrieren to demonstrate
denken to think
denn because
derselbe same
Deutsche (*m./f.*) German
Deutschland Germany
Dezember (*m.*) December
Dialekt (*m.*) dialect
Dichter (*m.*) poet
Dieb (*m.*) thief
dienen to serve
Dienstag (*m.*) Tuesday
dieser this
Diplomat (*m.*) diplomat
Dom (*m.*) cathedral
Donnerstag (*m.*) Thursday
Dorf (*n.*) village
dort there
drei three
dreißig thirty
dreizehn thirteen
dritte third
Drogerie (*f.*) drugstore

dunkel dark
durch through
Durst (*m.*) thirst
Ecke (*f.*) corner
effektiv effective
einladen to invite
eins one
einsteigen to get on (transportation)
Eis (*n.*) ice, ice cream
Eishockey (*n.*) hockey
elf eleven
Eltern (*pl.*) parents
empfehlen to recommend
empfinden to feel
Enkel (*m.*) grandchild
entlang along
entsetzen to horrify
Erbsen (*pl.*) peas
Erde (*f.*) earth, Earth
Erdteil (*m.*) continent
erfreuen to please, make happy
Erkältung (*f.*) cold
erstaunen to astound
erwarten to expect, await
erzählen to relate, tell
Erzieher (*m.*) nursery school teacher
es gibt there is/are
essen to eat
Essen (*n.*) food
euer your
Examen (*n.*) examination
fahren to drive, travel
Fahrkarte (*f.*) ticket
Fahrplan (*m.*) schedule
Fahrrad (*n.*) bicycle
fallen to fall
Familie (*f.*) family
faszinieren to fascinate
Februar (*m.*) February
Fenster (*n.*) window
Film (*m.*) film, movie
finden to find
Fisch (*m.*) fish
Flasche (*f.*) bottle
Fleisch (*n.*) meat
fleißig diligent
fliegen to fly
Flügel (*m.*) wing
Flughafen (*m.*) airport
Flugzeug (*n.*) airplane
Flur (*m.*) hallway
Fluss (*m.*) river
folgen to follow
Fotograf (*m.*) photographer
fotografieren to photograph
fragen to ask
Frau (*f.*) woman, wife
Freifrau (*f.*) baroness
Freiherr (*m.*) baron
Freitag (*m.*) Friday
fressen to eat (used for animals)
sich freuen to be glad, pleased
Freund (*m.*) friend
Freundin (*f.*) girlfriend
früh early
Frühling (*m.*) spring
Fuchs (*m.*) fox
fühlen to feel
Führer (*m.*) leader
fünf five
fünfzehn fifteen
fünfzig fifty
für for
Fußball (*m.*) soccer
Fußballspieler (*m.*) soccer player
ganz whole, entire
Gast (*m.*) guest
gebären to bear (a child)
geben to give
gefährlich dangerous
gefallen to like, please
gegen against
gegenüber opposite
gehen to go
gehören to belong to
Geige (*f.*) violin
gelb yellow
gelten to be valid, worth
Gemüse (*n.*) vegetables
Gemüsesuppe (*f.*) vegetable soup
germanisch Germanic
gern fondly

Geschäftsfrau (*f.*) businesswoman
Geschäftsmann (*m.*) businessman
geschehen to happen
Geschenk (*n.*) gift
Geschichte (*f.*) history, story
Geschwister (*pl.*) siblings
gestern yesterday
gesund healthy
Getränk (*n.*) beverage
gewinnen to win, gain
Glas (*n.*) glass
glauben to believe
glücklich happy, lucky
Gott (*m.*) God
Graf (*m.*) count
Gras (*n.*) grass
grau gray
groß big
Großmutter (*f.*) grandmother
Großvater (*m.*) grandfather
grün green
grüssen to greet
Gürtel (*m.*) belt
gut good
gute Nacht good night
guten Abend good evening
guten Morgen good morning
guten Tag good day, hello
Gymnasium (*n.*) prep school
haben to have
Hafen (*m.*) harbor
Hafenrundfahrt (*f.*) harbor excursion
halb half
halten to hold
Handschuh (*m.*) glove
hängen to hang
Hase (*m.*) hare
Hauptbahnhof (*m.*) main railroad station
Hauptstadt (*f.*) capital city
Haus (*n.*) house
Haustier (*n.*) pet
Heft (*n.*) notebook
heilig holy
heiß hot
heißen to be called, named
helfen to help
hell bright
Herbst (*m.*) fall, autumn
Herz (*n.*) heart
Herzog (*m.*) duke
heute today
heutig today's (*adj.*)
hier here
Himmel (*m.*) sky
hinter behind
hoch high
höflich polite
Hölle (*f.*) hell
hören to hear
Huhn (*n.*) chicken
Hühnchen (*n.*) chicken
hundert hundred
hungrig hungry
Hut (*m.*) hat
Igel (*m.*) hedgehog
ihr you, her, their
Ihr your
imitieren to imitate
immer always
immigrieren to immigrate
imponieren to impress
in in
interessant interesting
sich irren to be wrong
Italien Italy
Jacke (*f.*) jacket
Jagd (*f.*) hunt
Jahr (*n.*) year
Jahreszeit (*f.*) season
Januar (*m.*) January
jeder each
jemand someone
jener that
jetzt now
Job (*m.*) job
Juli (*m.*) July
jung young
Junge (*m.*) boy
Juni (*m.*) June
Jura (*pl.*) law
Kaffee (*m.*) coffee
Kaiser (*m.*) emperor

kalt cold
Kanada Canada
Kaninchen (*n.*) rabbit
Kanzler (*m.*) chancellor
Kapitalist (*m.*) capitalist
Kartoffel (*f.*) potato
Käse (*m.*) cheese
Katze (*f.*) cat
kaufen to buy
Kaufhaus (*n.*) department store
Kaufmann (*m.*) merchant
kein none, not any
kennen to know, be acquainted with
Kind (*n.*) child
Kino (*n.*) movie theater
Kirche (*f.*) church
Klavier (*n.*) piano
Kleider (*pl.*) clothes
klein little
Klima (*n.*) climate
klopfen to knock
klug smart
Kohl (*m.*) cabbage
Köln Cologne
komisch funny
kommen to come
Kommunist (*m.*) communist
Konflikt (*m.*) conflict
König (*m.*) king
Königin (*f.*) queen
Konstitution (*f.*) constitution
kontrollieren to control
Konzert (*n.*) concert
Kopf oder Zahl heads or tails
kopieren to copy
Korn (*n.*) grain
krank sick
Kranke (*m.*) patient
Krankenhaus (*n.*) hospital
Krankenschwester (*f.*) nurse
kratzen to scratch
Kreide (*f.*) chalk
Krieg (*m.*) war
Küche (*f.*) kitchen
Kuh (*f.*) cow
kühl cool
Kuli (*m.*) ballpoint pen
kurz short
küssen to kiss
lachen to laugh
Laden (*m.*) store, shop
Lampe (*f.*) lamp
lang long
langsam slow
lassen to let
laufen to run
laut loud
legen to lay
Lehrer (*m.*) teacher
leicht light, easy
leider unfortunately
lernen to learn
lesen to read
letzte last
Leute (*pl.*) people
Licht (*n.*) light
lieben to love
Lied (*n.*) song
liegen to lie, recline
link left
lügen to lie (omit the truth)
Mädchen (*n.*) girl
Mai (*m.*) May
Mais (*m.*) corn
man one
manifestieren to manifest
Mantel (*m.*) coat
Marktplatz (*m.*) market square
marschieren to march
März (*m.*) March
Maurer (*m.*) bricklayer
Mechaniker (*m.*) mechanic
mehr more
mein my
meinen to have the opinion, mean
Mensch (*m.*) person, human
Metzger (*m.*) butcher
Milch (*f.*) milk
Milliarde (*f.*) billion
Million (*f.*) million
Mineralwasser (*n.*) mineral water
minus minus

mit with
mitgehen to go along/with
mitnehmen to take along/with
mitteilen to inform
Mittwoch (*m.*) Wednesday
Monat (*m.*) month
Montag (*m.*) Monday
morgen tomorrow
Morgen (*m.*) morning
Motorrad (*n.*) motorcycle
müde tired
München Munich
Musik (*f.*) music
Mutter (*f.*) mother
nach after
nach Hause home(ward)
Nachbar (*m.*) neighbor
nachdem afterward
Nachtisch (*m.*) dessert
nah near
Nähe (*f.*) vicinity
Name (*m.*) name
Nation (*f.*) nation
neben near, next to
Nelke (*f.*) carnation
nennen to name
nett nice
neu new
neun nine
neunzehn nineteen
neunzig ninety
nicht not
nichts nothing
nie never
niemand no one
Nilpferd (*n.*) hippo
noch still
Nordamerika North America
Norden north
notieren to note, make a note of something
November (*m.*) November
ob whether
Obst (*n.*) fruit
Obstkuchen (*m.*) fruit pie
oder or
Ofen (*m.*) oven
oft often
ohne without
Oktober (*m.*) October
Onkel (*m.*) uncle
organisieren to organize
Osten east
Österreich Austria
Paket (*n.*) package
Park (*m.*) park
Parlament (*n.*) parliament
Partei (*f.*) party (political)
Party (*f.*) party
Pass (*m.*) passport
passen to fit
passieren to happen
Pessimist (*m.*) pessimist
Pferd (*n.*) horse
Pflanze (*f.*) plant
pflanzen to plant
Pfleger (*m.*) male nurse
Physiker (*m.*) physicist
Picknick (*n.*) picnic
Pilot (*m.*) pilot
Pils (*n.*) lager beer
plus plus
Politiker (*m.*) politician
Polizei (*f.*) police
Position (*f.*) position
Post (*f.*) post office
Poster (*n.*) poster
Postkarte (*f.*) postcard
Präsident (*m.*) president
probieren to try, taste
Problem (*n.*) problem
produzieren to produce
Professor (*m.*) professor
programmieren to program
protestieren to protest
Pullover (*m.*) sweater
Rad fahren to go cycling
Radio (*n.*) radio
Rasen (*m.*) lawn
rasieren to shave
Rathaus (*n.*) city hall
rauchen to smoke
räumen to clear away

recht right
Rechtsanwalt (*m.*) lawyer
reden to talk
Regen (*m.*) rain
Regenschirm (*m.*) umbrella
Regierung (*f.*) government
regnen to rain
Reich (*n.*) empire
Reis (*m.*) rice
Reise (*f.*) trip
reisen to travel
reiten to ride
reizen to annoy, irritate
rennen to run
Republik (*f.*) republic
restaurieren to restore
Rindfleisch (*n.*) beef
Roman (*m.*) novel
römisch Roman
rosa pink
Rose (*f.*) rose
rot red
ruhig quiet, calm
rupfen to pluck
russisch Russian
sagen to say
sammeln to gather, collect
Samstag (*m.*) Saturday
Sänger (*m.*) singer
Schach (*n.*) chess
Schaf (*n.*) sheep
Schaffner (*m.*) conductor (transportation)
schicken to send
schieben to push
Schiff (*n.*) ship
Schinken (*m.*) ham
schlafen to sleep
Schlange (*f.*) snake
schlecht bad
Schlüssel (*m.*) key
Schmerz (*m.*) pain
Schnee (*m.*) snow
schneiden to cut
schneien to snow
schnell fast
schon already
schön pretty
Schrank (*m.*) cupboard
schreiben to write
Schreibtisch (*m.*) desk
schreien to shout
Schriftsteller (*m.*) writer
Schule (*f.*) school
schützen to protect
schwanger pregnant
schwarz black
Schweden Sweden
Schwein (*n.*) pig
schwer heavy, difficult
Schwester (*f.*) sister
schwimmen to swim
schwören to swear
sechs six
sechzehn sixteen
sechzig sixty
sehen to see
Sehenswürdigkeiten (*pl.*) sights
sehr very
sein his
sein to be
seit since
Sekretär (*m.*) secretary
Sekt (*m.*) sparkling wine, German champagne
senden to send
September (*m.*) September
setzen to set
sich setzen to sit down
sieben seven
siebzehn seventeen
siebzig seventy
singen to sing
sitzen to sit
Ski laufen to go skiing
Sofa (*n.*) sofa
Sohn (*m.*) son
Sommer (*m.*) summer
Sonnabend (*m.*) Saturday
Sonntag (*m.*) Sunday
spät late
spazieren to stroll
spielen to play
Sportart (*f.*) (form of) sport

Sportler (*m.*) athlete
sprechen to speak
Sprudel (*m.*) sparkling water
spülen to rinse
Stadt (*f.*) city
Stadtmauer (*f.*) city wall
Stadtrundfahrt (*f.*) city excursion
Stadtzentrum (*n.*) city center
Stamm (*m.*) tribe
stehen to stand
Stehlampe (*f.*) floor lamp
stehlen to steal
stellen to put, place
stoßen to kick, shove
Straße (*f.*) street
Straßenbahn (*f.*) streetcar
studieren to study
Stuhl (*m.*) chair
Stunde (*f.*) hour
suchen to seek, look for
Südamerika South America
Süden south
Sweatshirt (*n.*) sweatshirt
Tag (*m.*) day
Tanne (*f.*) fir, pine tree
Tante (*f.*) aunt
tanzen to dance
Tasche (*f.*) pocket
tausend thousand
Taxifahrer (*m.*) taxi driver
Tee (*m.*) tea
Telegramm (*n.*) telegram
Teppich (*m.*) carpet
teuer expensive
Tiger (*m.*) tiger
Tisch (*m.*) table
Tischtennis (*m.*) table tennis
Tochter (*f.*) daughter
Tod (*m.*) death
Tour (*f.*) tour
Tourist (*m.*) tourist
tragen to wear
Trainer (*m.*) trainer, coach
treiben to drive; go in for; pursue; participate in
Treppe (*f.*) stairs, staircase
trinken to drink
trotz inspite of
Tulpe (*f.*) tulip
tun to do
Tunnel (*m.*) tunnel
Tür (*f.*) door
über over, above
überschwemmen to flood
Uhr (*f.*) clock; hour; watch
um around
umsteigen to transfer
und and
Ungeheuer (*n.*) monster
Universität (*f.*) university
unser our
unter under
unterbrechen to interrupt
unterrichten to teach, instruct
Vase (*f.*) vase
Vater (*m.*) father
verderben to spoil, rot
vergessen to forget
verhaften to arrest
verheiratet married
verkaufen to sell
Verkehr (*m.*) traffic
sich verlieben to fall in love
verlieren to lose
versprechen to promise
verstehen to understand
Verwandte (*m.*) relative
viel(e) much, many
vier four
Viertel (*n.*) quarter
vierzehn fourteen
vierzig forty
Volk (*n.*) people, nation
von from, of
vor before, in front of
vorstellen to introduce
sich vorstellen to imagine
wachsen to grow
Wagen (*m.*) car
wahnsinnig insane
während during
wahrscheinlich probably
Wand (*f.*) wall

wandern to hike, wander
wann when
warm warm
warten to wait
warum why
was what
waschen to wash
Wasser (*n.*) water
wegen because of
weglaufen to run away
Wein (*m.*) wine
weinen to cry
weiß white
weit far
welcher which
Weltkrieg (*m.*) world war
wenig little, few
weniger less; minus
wenn whenever, if
wer who
werben to recruit
werden to become, get; shall/will
wessen whose
Westen west
Wetter (*n.*) weather
wider against
widerspiegeln to reflect
wie how, as
Wiedervereinigung (*f.*) reunification
Winter (*m.*) winter
Wirtin (*f.*) landlady
wissen to know
Wissenschaftler (*m.*) scientist
wo where
Woche (*f.*) week
Wochenende (*n.*) weekend
woher from where
wohin where to
Wohnung (*f.*) apartment
Wohnzimmer (*n.*) living room
Wolf (*m.*) wolf
Wort (*n.*) word
Wörterbuch (*n.*) dictionary
Zahnarzt (*m.*) dentist
zehn ten
Zeit (*f.*) time
Zeitung (*f.*) newspaper
zerstören to destroy
Zimmer (*n.*) room
Zirkus (*m.*) circus
Zoo (*m.*) zoo
zu to, too
zu Fuß on foot
zu Hause at home
Zug (*m.*) train
zumachen to close
Zunge (*f.*) tongue
zurückbleiben to stand back, remain behind
zwanzig twenty
zwei two
zweite second
Zwillinge (*pl.*) twins
zwischen between
zwölf twelve

Answer Key

CHAPTER 1

QUIZ

1. F 2. A 3. J 4. B 5. I 6. D 7. E 8. H 9. G 10. C

CHAPTER 2

Written Practice 1

1. Ich heiße Martin. / Mein Name ist Martin. 2. Ich heiße Tina. / Mein Name ist Tina. 3. Ich heiße Herr Schäfer. / Mein Name ist Herr Schäfer. 4. Ich heiße Frau Kamps. / Mein Name ist Frau Kamps. 5. Ich heiße Boris Becker. / Mein Name ist Boris Becker. 6. Ich heiße Maria Schell. / Mein Name ist Maria Schell. 7. Ich heiße Professor Bach. / Mein Name ist Professor Bach. 8. Ich heiße Doktor Berg. / Mein Name ist Doktor Berg. 9. Ich heiße Iris. / Mein Name ist Iris. 10. Ich heiße ________. / Mein Name ist ________.

Written Practice 2

1. die Diplomatin 2. die Studentin 3. die Artistin 4. die Kommunistin 5. die Mechanikerin 6. die Optimistin 7. die Pilotin 8. die Managerin

Written Practice 3

1. Wie heißen Sie? / Ich heiße Angela. 2. Wie heißen Sie? / Ich heiße Herr Bauer. 3. Wie heißen Sie? / Ich heiße Thomas. 4. Wie heißen Sie? / Ich heiße Frau Kamps. 5. Wie heißen Sie? / Ich heiße Gudrun Klein.

Written Practice 4

1. Wo ist das Kind? / Das Kind ist hier. 2. Wo ist mein Vater? / Mein Vater ist dort. 3. Wo ist Erik? / Erik ist in Deutschland. 4. Wo ist Thomas? / Thomas ist da. 5. Wo ist Iris? / Iris ist in München.

Written Practice 5

1. Guten Morgen, Onkel Peter. 2. Guten Abend, Herr Schneider. 3. Guten Tag, Frau Keller. 4. Gute Nacht, Martin.

Written Practice 6

1. Guten Tag, Helga. / Wie geht's? 2. Guten Morgen, Thomas. / Wie geht's? 3. Guten Abend, Tanja. / Wie geht's? 4. Guten Tag, Herr Bach. / Wie geht's? 5. Guten Morgen, Rita. / Wie geht's? 6. Guten Abend, Frau Kamps. / Wie geht's?

QUIZ

1. die Mechanikerin 2. die Lehrerin 3. Mein Name ist Werner. Ich heiße Werner. 4. Mein Name ist Tanja. Ich heiße Tanja. 5. Wer ist das? Das ist Tina. 6. Wer ist das? Das ist Herr Keller. 7. Wo ist Frau Schneider? Frau Schneider ist in Berlin. 8. Wo ist der Lehrer? Der Lehrer ist in Deutschland. 9. C 10. D

CHAPTER 3

Written Practice 1

1. Nein, Werner ist nicht in der Schweiz. 2. Nein, der Junge ist nicht mein Bruder. 3. Nein, das Mädchen ist nicht meine Schwester. 4. Nein, die Bibliothek ist nicht hier. 5. Nein, der Park ist nicht weit von hier.

Written Practice 2

1. Ist das ein Professor oder ein Lehrer? / Das ist ein Professor/Lehrer. 2. Ist das der Vater oder der Großvater? / Das ist der Vater/Großvater. 3. Ist das eine Lampe oder eine Vase? / Das ist eine Lampe/Vase. 4. Ist das Frau Bauer oder Frau Schäfer? / Das ist Frau Bauer/Frau Schäfer.

Written Practice 3

1. Wer ist das? 2. Wer ist das? 3. Was ist das? 4. Wer ist das? 5. Wo ist München?

Written Practice 4

1. Ist Ihre Schwester hier? 2. Ist Ihr Vater hier? 3. Ist Ihre Tante hier? 4. Ist Ihr Wagen hier? 5. Ist Ihre Schule hier?

Written Practice 5

Sample answers are given. 1. Ist das ein Museum oder eine Bibliothek? 2. Wo ist Ihr Vater? 3. Der Mann ist mein Onkel. 4. Was ist das? 5. Ist die Frau Ihre Mutter oder Ihre Tante? 6. Die Dame ist eine Lehrerin. 7. Mein Bruder ist in der Schweiz. 8. Der Park ist nicht weit von hier. 9. Der Herr heißt Professor Schmidt. 10. Ist das Ihre Tochter?

QUIZ

1. ein Wagen, mein Wagen, Ihr Wagen 2. eine Schule, meine Schule, Ihre Schule 3. ein Heft, mein Heft, Ihr Heft 4. Ja, die Lehrerin ist in Berlin. Nein, die Lehrerin ist nicht in Berlin. 5. Ja, mein Vater ist Amerikaner. Nein, mein Vater ist kein Amerikaner. 6. Wo ist Ihre Tante? 7. Was ist das? 8. Wer ist in Deutschland? 9. D 10. A

CHAPTER 4

Written Practice 1

1. bin 2. sind 3. bist 4. ist 5. seid 6. ist 7. ist 8. ist 9. ist 10. sind

Written Practice 2

1. Er ist hier. 2. Ist sie da? 3. Es ist weit von hier. 4. Wo ist es? 5. Sie sind zu Hause. 6. Wo ist sie? 7. sie 8. es 9. er 10. er 11. er 12. sie *s.* 13. es 14. es 15. sie *pl.*

Written Practice 3

1. Ist Ihr Vater jung? / Ist Ihr Vater krank? / Ist Ihr Vater gesund? 2. Das Buch ist interessant. / Das Buch ist neu. / Das Buch ist schwarz. 3. Wir sind klein. / Wir sind groß. / Wir sind krank.

Written Practice 4

1. neu / alt 2. krank / gesund 3. schlecht / gut 4. kurz / lang 5. jung / alt 6. groß / klein 7. weiß / schwarz 8. gesund / krank 9. lang / kurz 10. klein / groß

Written Practice 5

1. Wann ist das Examen? 2. Wer ist in der Schweiz? 3. Wann ist die Party? 4. Warum sind Thomas und Helga in Bonn 5. Warum ist Ihr Großvater zu Hause? 6. Wer ist morgen in Deutschland? 7. Wann sind wir in Leipzig? 8. Wer ist gesund? 9. Wann ist das Examen? 10. Warum ist das Kind zu Hause?

Written Practice 6

1. Tanja und Maria sind in Berlin, denn sie sind krank. 2. Das Examen ist nächste Woche. 3. Ich bin zu Hause, denn ich bin krank. 4. Das Konzert ist am Montag.

Written Practice 7

1. Vier und/plus fünf ist neun. 2. Wie viel ist acht minus/weniger sechs? 3. Zehn minus/weniger drei ist sieben.

QUIZ

1. heiße, bin 2. heißt, bist 3. heißt, ist 4. heißen, sind 5. heißt, seid 6. sie 7. es 8. er 9. D 10. C

CHAPTER 5

Written Practice 1

1. haben 2. hat 3. haben 4. habt 5. hat 6. hast 7. haben 8. haben 9. hat 10. hat

Written Practice 2

1. Hast du die CDs? / Hast du das Geld? / Hast du ein Heft? 2. Ich habe die Fahrkarten. / Ich habe den Fahrplan. / Ich habe das Brot.

Written Practice 3

1. Was hast du? 2. Was hast du? 3. Was habt ihr? 4. Was haben Sie? 5. Was hast du? 6. Was haben Sie?

Written Practice 4

1. Doktor Keller, ist das Ihr Schreibtisch? 2. Tanja, ist das dein Schreibtisch? 3. Tante Gerda, ist das dein Schreibtisch? 4. Albert und Tina, ist das euer Schreibtisch? 5. Frau Schäfer, ist das Ihr Schreibtisch?

Written Practice 5

1. dein / euer / Ihr 2. deine / eure / Ihre 3. dein / euer / Ihr 4. deine / eure / Ihre 5. dein / euer / Ihr

Written Practice 6

1. Wie viel Milch habt ihr? / Wir haben viel Milch. 2. Wie viele CDs habt ihr? / Wir haben viele CDs. 3. Wie viel Geld habt ihr? / Wir haben viel Geld. 4. Wie viele Fahrkarten habt ihr? / Wir haben viele Fahrkarten. 5. Wie viele Schlüssel habt ihr? / Wir haben viele Schlüssel.

Written Practice 7

1. Wer hat mein Geld? / Wer hat viel Geld? / Wer hat kein Geld? 2. Martin hat eure Schlüssel. / Martin hat viele Schlüssel. / Martin hat keine Schlüssel. 3. Wo ist deine Freundin? / Wo is Ihre Freundin? / Wo ist eure Freundin?

Written Practice 8

1. Nein, wir haben kein Brot. 2. Nein, Frau Keller hat keine Schlüssel. 3. Nein, ich habe kein Geld. 4. Nein, das Kind hat keine Milch. 5. Nein, meine Schwester hat keine Bluse. 6. Nein, wir haben keine Zimmer. 7. Nein, Robert hat keine CDs. 8. Nein, mein Vater hat kein Bier.

Written Practice 9

1. Wo ist das Sofa? / Wo sind der Stuhl und der Schreibtisch? 2. Die Zimmer haben ein Fenster. / Die Zimmer haben kein Fenster. 3. Der Tisch ist sehr klein. / Die Zimmer sind sehr klein.

QUIZ

1. haben, habe 2. hat, hast 3. dein, euer, Ihr, kein, sing. 4. deine, eure, Ihre, keine, plur. 5. deine, eure, Ihre, keine, sing. 6. Nein, ich habe kein Sofa. 7. Nein, Frau Benz hat keine Schwester. 8. Nein, ich habe kein Bild. 9. C 10. C

PART ONE TEST

1. E, A, D, C, B 2. heiße, heißt, heißt, heißen, heißt 3. bin, bist, ist, seid, sind 4. Was ist das? 5. Wo ist Ihr/dein Vater? 6. Warum ist er zu Hause? 7. Wer ist sehr alt? 8. Wann ist die Party? 9. eine, Ihre, keine 10. ein, Ihr, kein 11. Nein, das Fenster ist nicht klein. 12. Nein, Karl und Gudrun sind nicht zu Hause. 13. er 14. sie *pl.* 15. es 16. sie *s.* 17. groß, klein 18. neu, alt 19. Nein, ich habe keine Schlüssel. 20. Nein, wir haben kein Brot. 21. B 22. A 23. C 24. D 25. A

CHAPTER 6

Written Practice 1

1. Deine Tochter wird Lehrerin. / Meine Schwester wird auch Lehrerin. 2. Erik wird Zahnarzt. / Sie werden auch Zahnarzt. 3. Die Kinder werden Fußballspieler. / Er wird auch Fußballspieler.

Written Practice 2

1. c 2. a 3. j 4. e 5. g 6. i 7. f 8. d 9. b 10. h

Written Practice 3

1. Es wird wieder kalt. 2. Es wird wieder kühl. 3. Es wird wieder hell. 4. Es wird wieder dunkel. 5. Es wird wieder heiß.

Written Practice 4

horen: ich höre / du hörst / er hört / wir hören / ihr hört / sie hören / Tina hört; **suchen:** ich suche / du suchst / er sucht / wir suchen / ihr sucht / sie suchen / Tina sucht; **fragen:** ich frage / du fragst / er fragt / wir fragen / ihr fragt / sie fragen / Tina fragt

Written Practice 5

1. Fährst du mit dem Bus oder mit dem Zug? 2. Fährt sie mit dem Bus oder mit dem Zug? 3. Fahren Sie mit dem Bus oder mit dem Zug? 4. Fährt Herr Weber mit dem Bus oder mit dem Zug? 5. Fahren sie mit dem Bus oder mit dem Zug? 6. Fährt er mit dem Bus oder mit dem Zug? 7. Fahren die Kinder mit dem Bus oder mit dem Zug?

Written Practice 6

1. Ja, Herr Mann schreibt ein Buch. 2. Ja, wir hören die Musik. 3. Ja, ich trage einen Hut. 4. Ja, wir sind in Österreich. / Nein, wir sind nicht in Österreich. 5. Ja, ich fahre mit dem Bus. / Nein, ich fahre nicht mit dem Bus. 6. Ja, Onkel Peter schläft im Park. / Nein, Onkel Peter schläft nicht im Park. 7. Ja, die Kinder fallen ins Bett. / Nein, die Kinder fallen nicht ins Bett. 8. Ja, wir kommen nach Hause. / Nein, wir kommen nicht nach Hause.

Written Practice 7

1. Die Kinder sind dreizehn Jahre alt. 2. Das Museum ist fünfzehn Jahre alt. 3. Du bist zwanzig Jahre alt.

QUIZ

1. ich werde, komme, lerne / du wirst, kommst, lernst / er wird, kommt, lernt / wir werden, kommen, lernen / ihr werdet, kommt, lernt / Sie werden, kommen, lernen / Karl und Tina werden, kommen, lernen 2. Meine Schwester wird Ärztin. Du wirst Krankenschwester. 3. Sie werden Mechaniker. Er wird Zahnarzt. 4. ich fahre, falle, schlafe / du fährst, fällst, schläfst / er fährt, fällt, schläft / wir fahren, fallen, schlafen / ihr fahrt, fallt, schlaft / Sie fahren, fallen, schlafen / die Kinder fahren, fallen, schlafen 5. Ich habe sechs Schlüssel. 6. Erik hat zehn Fahrkarten. 7. Mein Sohn ist achtzehn Jahre alt. 8. Meine Tochter ist fünfzehn Jahre alt. 9. B 10. A

CHAPTER 7

Written Practice 1

sprechen: ich spreche / du sprichst / er spricht / wir sprechen / ihr sprecht / sie sprechen;
sehen: ich sehe / du siehst / er sieht / wir sehen / ihr seht / sie sehen

Written Practice 2

1. Er besucht meine Freundin. / Er erwartet meine Freundin. / Er versteht meine Freundin. / Er findet meine Freundin. 2. Eric sieht die Schlüssel. / Eric sucht die Schlüssel. / Eric stiehlt die Schlüssel. / Eric verkauft die Schlüssel.

Written Practice 3

1. kleine 2. weiße 3. dunkel 4. jung 5. neue 6. graue 7. deutsche

Written Practice 4

1. c 2. e 3. h 4. j 5. l 6. g 7. f 8. k 9. d 10. b

Written Practice 5

Sample answers are given. 1. Meine Mutter liest eine Zeitung. 2. Die Kinder spielen im Park. 3. Der alte Mann spricht Englisch und Deutsch. 4. Ich habe kein Geld. Ich kann es nicht kaufen. 5. Der Dieb stiehlt meine Tasche. 6. Ist der Kaffee heiß oder kalt? 7. Es ist dunkel. Wo ist die Lampe? 8. Siehst du die Bibliothek? 9. Guten Abend, Frau Doktor. 10. Der braune Hut ist sehr alt. 11. Ist euer Vater wieder gesund? 12. Ist der neue Wagen braun oder rot? 13. Ich finde meine Schlüssel. 14. Martin bestellt ein Butterbrot und ein Glas Milch. 15. Die Schlüssel gehören Tina.

Written Practice 6

1. Wer besucht eine Freundin in Berlin? 2. Wohin fährt dein/Ihr Vater? 3. Was finden die Kinder? 4. Warum trägt sie ein Sweatshirt? 5. Wie alt ist deine Tochter? 6. Wann gehst du in die Stadt? 7. Wo spielen zwei Jungen Tennis? 8. Wie viele Schlüssel hat der Professor? 9. Wohin fährt er mit dem Bus? 10. Was liest Karin? 11. Wer wartet im Park? 12. Wie viel Geld hat Erik? 13. Was versteht Sonja? 14. Warum liest du das Buch? 15. Was trägt Onkel Heinz?

QUIZ

1. ich sehe, spreche, verstehe, reise / du siehst, sprichst, verstehst, reist / er sieht, spricht, versteht, reist / wir sehen, sprechen, verstehen, reisen / ihr seht, sprecht, versteht, reist / Sie sehen, sprechen, verstehen, reisen 2. Er sucht einen Brief. / Er liest einen Brief. / Er sieht einen Brief. / Er hat einen Brief. / 3. Andrea kauft ein Buch. / Andrea verkauft ein Buch. / Andrea liest ein Buch. / Andrea stiehlt ein Buch. / 4. Die Kinder verstehen Deutsch. / Die Kinder sprechen Deutsch. / 5. Ich nehme eine Tasse Tee. / Ich bestelle eine Tasse Tee. 6. B 7. D 8. A 9. A 10. C

CHAPTER 8

Written Practice 1

1. Warum fährt man mit der Straßenbahn? 2. Wie kommt man vom Rathaus zum Bahnhof? 3. Weiß man, wohin Gudrun reist? 4. Hier spricht man Deutsch.

Written Practice 2

kommen: ich komme / wir kommen / du kommst / ihr kommt / er kommt / sie kommen / man kommt / dieser Herr kommt / die Kinder kommen / diese Dame kommt

Written Practice 3

1. Herr Braun/Er kommt aus London. 2. Der Amerikaner/Er kommt aus New York. 3. Die Österreicherin/Sie kommt aus Wien. 4. Frau Benz/Sie kommt aus Deutschland. 5. Diese Dame/Sie kommt aus Italien.

Written Practice 4

1. Morgen reisen die Touristen nach Italien. 2. Im Park sehen wir viele Kinder. 3. Im Restaurant bestelle ich ein Glas Bier. 4. Vom Rathaus zur Schule fahren sie mit dem Auto. 5. Heute fliegt mein Vater nach Australien.

Written Practice 5

1. Meine Eltern wohnen jetzt in Freiburg. 2. Lebt Ihre Großmutter noch? 3. Wir kennen den Mann nicht. Wie heißt er? 4. Er fährt mit dem Zug nach Rom. 5. Herr Benz wohnt in der Schillerstraße. 6. Wohin fährst/gehst du? 7. Wissen Sie, wo Frau Schneider wohnt? 8. Ich gehe zum Rathaus. Es ist nicht weit von hier. 9. Warum geht ihr zu Fuß? 10. Kennen Sie meine Eltern nicht?

Written Practice 6

1. Wir fotografieren das Rathaus. 2. Martin verliert das Geld. 3. Ich studiere Deutsch und Russisch. 4. Die Kinder probieren den Pudding. 5. Diese Leute spazieren im Park.

Written Practice 7

ankommen: ich komme an / du kommst an / er kommt an / wir kommen an / ihr kommt an / sie kommen an; **einsteigen:** ich steige ein / du steigst ein / er steigt ein/ wir steigen ein / ihr steigt ein / sie steigen ein; **vorstellen:** ich stelle vor / du stellst vor / er stellt vor / wir stellen vor / ihr stellt vor / sie stellen vor

Written Practice 8

1. Kennen Sie meinen Onkel? / Kennen Sie diese Dame? / Kennen Sie den Professor? / Kennen Sie das Mädchen? 2. Dieser Mann kauft einen Wagen. / Dieser Mann kauft mein Haus. / Dieser Mann kauft Ihre CDs. / Dieser Mann kauft den Teppich.

Written Practice 9

1. Wer verkauft meinen Wagen? / Wer verkauft einen Hut? / Wer verkauft die Fahrkarten? / Wer verkauft das Auto? / Wer verkauft es? 2. Kennt ihr meine Eltern? / Kennt ihr den Lehrer? / Kennt ihr die Leute? / Kennt ihr meinen Freund? / Kennt ihr ihn?

QUIZ

1. Wo sind Ihre/deine Eltern? 2. Wohin gehen die Touristen? 3. Woher kommen Erik und Tina? 4. Der alte Mann kennt meinen Vater nicht. / Der alte Mann kennt diese Frau nicht. / Der alte Mann kennt den Lehrer nicht. / Der alte Mann kennt diese Leute nicht. / Der alte Mann kennt ihn nicht. 5. die Kinder, mich, dich, meinen Freund, ihn, sie, einen Hut, uns, euch, Sie 6. sie, ihn, sie 7. A 8. B 9. C 10. A

CHAPTER 9

Written Practice 1

1. Ich finde seine Kleider. 2. Ich kenne ihre Freundin. 3. Wir kaufen euren Wagen. 4. Ich sehe mein Kind. 5. Er nimmt deine Milch. 6. Ihre Eltern wohnen in Leipzig. 7. Unser Chef weiß nichts.

Written Practice 2

1. Ich besuche Ihre Eltern in München. / Ich besuche eure Eltern in München. / Ich besuche unsere Eltern in München. 2. Wer findet meinen Bleistift? / Wer findet seinen Bleistift? / Wer findet unseren Bleistift?

Written Practice 3

fragen: ich fragte / du fragtest / er fragte / wir fragten / ihr fragtet / sie fragten / wer fragte; **gehören:** ich gehörte / du gehörtest / er gehörte / wir gehörten / ihr gehörtet / sie gehörten / wer gehörte; **vorstellen:** ich stellte vor / du stelltest vor / er stellte vor / wir stellten vor / ihr stelltet vor / sie stellten vor / wer stellte vor

Written Practice 4

1. **fahren:** ich fuhr / du fuhrst / er fuhr / wir fuhren / ihr fuhrt / sie fuhren / dieser Mann fuhr; **kommen:** ich kam / du kamst / er kam / wir kamen / ihr kamt / sie kamen / dieser Mann kam; **fliegen:** ich flog / du flogst / er flog / wir flogen / ihr flogt / sie flogen / dieser Mann flog

Written Practice 5

essen: aß; **lesen:** las; **sagen:** sagte; **sprechen:** sprach; **bleiben:** blieb; **heißen:** hieß; **haben:** hatte; **gehen:** ging; **sein:** war; **warten:** wartete; **arbeiten:** arbeitete; **werden:** wurde; **finden:** fand; **wissen:** wusste; **verstehen:** verstand; **ankommen:** kam an

Written Practice 6

1. Ich kam mit dem Bus. 2. Es wurde heute sehr kalt. 3. Warum aßt ihr im Wohnzimmer? 4. Meine Tochter studierte an einer Universität in Amerika. 5. Wo stiegen wir um? 6. Die Männer zerstörten das alte Haus. 7. Wen sahst du im Wohnzimmer? 8. Der Chef diskutierte die Probleme. 9. Ich war immer krank. 10. Wusstest du, wer die Bücher verkaufte?

Written Practice 7

1. Ich fand eine neue Lampe für dich. / Ich fand eine neue Lampe für meinen Freund. / Ich fand eine neue Lampe für sie. / Ich fand eine neue Lampe für Ihren Chef. 2. Diese Frau hatte nichts gegen mich. / Diese Frau hatte nichts gegen uns. / Diese Frau hatte nichts gegen Ihre Chefin. / Diese Frau hatte nichts gegen Sie. 3. Robert kam ohne das Geld. / Robert kam ohne ihn. / Robert kam ohne sie. / Robert kam ohne seinen Vater. 4. Er ging ohne seinen Freund zum Park. / Er ging ohne dich zum Park. / Er ging ohne uns zum Park. / Er ging ohne ihren Onkel zum Park. / Er ging ohne euch zum Park. / Er ging ohne seine Kinder zum Park. 5. Die Amerikaner fuhren bis Hamburg. / Die Amerikaner fuhren bis München. / Die Amerikaner fuhren bis Polen. / Die Amerikaner fuhren bis gestern Abend. / Die Amerikaner fuhren bis elf Uhr.

Written Practice 8

1. die Bücher 2. die Arme 3. die Väter 4. die Schwestern 5. die Böden 6. die Rathäuser 7. die Himmel 8. die Ärztinnen 9. die Kleider 10. die Tanten 11. die Brüder 12. die Hefte 13. die Zeitungen 14. die Tische 15. die Teppiche 16. die Lampen

QUIZ

1. Ich habe seine Schlüssel./Ich habe seinen Schlüssel. 2. Erik las mein Buch. 3. Werner besuchte unsere Eltern. 4. Frau Keller verliert meinen Hut. / Frau Keller verliert deinen Hut. 5. Ich besuchte seinen Onkel. / Ich besuchte unseren Onkel. 6. ich war, gab aus, hatte / du warst, gabst aus, hattest / er war, gab aus, hatte / wir waren, gaben aus, hatten / ihr wart, gabt aus, hattet / sie waren, gaben aus, hatten / die Leute waren, gaben aus, hatten 7. Verkaufte er seinen Wagen? / Verstanden Sie, was er sagte? 8. Frau Schneider hatte einen Brief für mich. / Frau Schneider hatte einen Brief für ihn. / Frau Schneider hatte einen Brief für meinen Onkel. / Der Mann sprach gegen Ihren Sohn. / Der Mann sprach gegen sie. / Der Mann sprach gegen uns. 9. C 10. A

CHAPTER 10

Written Practice 1

denken: ich denke / du denkst / er denkt; **anfangen:** ich fange an / du fängst an / er fängt an; **helfen:** ich helfe / du hilfst / er hilft; **brechen:** du brichst / er bricht / wir brechen; **fallen:** du fällst / er fällt / wir fallen; **vergessen:** du vergisst / er vergisst / wir vergessen; **fallen:** ich fiel / er fiel / wir fielen; **bringen:** ich brachte / er brachte / wir brachten; **stehen:** ich stand / er stand / wir standen; **rennen:** ich rannte / du ranntest / ihr ranntet; **anrufen:** ich rief an / du riefst an / ihr rieft an; **schneiden:** ich schnitt / du schnittest / ihr schnittet

Written Practice 2

der Metzger: **ihr**em Metzger / **mein**em Metzger / **dies**em Metzger; **die Wohnung:** **ihr**er Wohnung / **mein**er Wohnung / **dies**er Wohnung; **das Land:** **ihr**em Land / **mein**em Land / **dies**em Land; **die Bücher:** **ihr**en Büchern / **mein**en Büchern / **dies**en Büchern; **die Uhr:** **ihr**er Uhr / **mein**er Uhr / **dies**er Uhr

Written Practice 3

1. Der Metzger gab mir ein Geschenk. / Der Metzger gab dir ein Geschenk. / Der Metzger gab ihnen ein Geschenk. / Der Metzger gab meinem Sohn ein Geschenk. / Der Metzger gab meinen Söhnen ein Geschenk. / Der Metzger gab der Ausländerin ein Geschenk. 2. Wer schreibt ihr einen Brief? / Wer schreibt uns einen Brief? / Wer schreibt Ihnen einen Brief? / Wer schreibt euch einen Brief? / Wer schreibt der Polizei einen Brief? / Wer schreibt Ihren Kindern einen Brief? 3. Was sendet er uns? / Was sendet er ihnen? / Was sendet er euch? / Was sendet er Ihnen? / Was sendet er mir?

Written Practice 4

1. Robert schrieb ihr einen Brief. / Robert schrieb ihn ihr. 2. Ich kaufte ihm ein Auto. / Ich kaufte es ihm. 3. Senden Sie ihnen neue Bücher? / Senden Sie sie ihnen? 4. Gudrun brachte ihr ein Heft. / Gudrun brachte es ihr. 5. Wir verkauften ihnen die Kleider. / Wir verkauften sie ihnen.

Written Practice 5

1. halb 2. fünfunddreißig 3. eins 4. Viertel 5. zwölf 6. fünfundvierzig 7. vor / vier

Written Practice 6

1. Er besuchte uns am ersten März. / Er besuchte uns am dritten März. / Er besuchte uns am neunten März. / Er besuchte uns am fünfzehnten März. / Er besuchte uns am siebenundzwanzigsten März. 2. Ihr

Sohn ist am dreißigsten Juli geboren. / Ihr Sohn ist am einunddreißigsten Juli geboren. / Ihr Sohn ist am zweiten Juli geboren. / Ihr Sohn ist am siebten Juli geboren. / Ihr Sohn ist am zwölften Juli geboren.

Written Practice 7

1. Ich spiele gern Schach. 2. Ich wandere gern. 3. Ich schwimme gern. 4. Ich spiele gern Golf. 5. Ich fahre gern Rad. 6. Ich laufe gern Ski. 7. Ich lese gern.

QUIZ

1. ich aß, sah, lief / du aßt, sahst, liefst / er aß, sah, lief / ich brachte, rief an, vergass / du brachtest, riefst an, vergasst / er brachte, rief an, vergass 2. unserem Rad, seinem Rad, diesem Rad / unserem Brief, seinem Brief, diesem Brief / unserer Postkarte, seiner Postkarte, dieser Postkarte / unseren Kindern, seinen Kindern, diesen Kindern 3. Der Lehrer gab mir einen Kuli. / Der Lehrer gab dir einen Kuli. / Der Lehrer gab ihm einen Kuli. / Der Lehrer gab ihr einen Kuli. / Der Lehrer gab Ihnen einen Kuli. 4. Sie brachte ihr die Kleider. / Sie brachte sie ihr. / Ich kaufte ihnen einen neuen Ball. / Ich kaufte ihn ihnen. 5. Es ist halb elf. Es ist zehn Uhr dreißig. 6. Es ist Viertel vor fünf. Es ist vier Uhr fünfundvierzig. 7. Es ist Viertel nach acht. Es ist acht Uhr fünfzehn. 8. Mein Sohn ist am ersten März geboren. / Mein Sohn ist am dritten März geboren. / Mein Sohn ist am sechzehnten März geboren. / Mein Sohn ist am zweiundzwanzigsten März geboren. / Mein Sohn ist am dreißigsten März geboren. 9. C 10. D

PART TWO TEST

1. ich werde, du wirst, er wird, wir werden 2. ich sehe, du siehst, er sieht, ihr seht 3. ich fahre, du fährst, er fährt, Sie fahren 4. ich gehe mit, du gehst mit, er geht mit, wir gehen mit 5. ich besuche, besuchte / du besuchst, besuchtest / er besucht, besuchte / ihr besucht, besuchtet 6. ich helfe, half / du hilfst, halfst / er hilft, half / Sie helfen, halfen 7. ich bin, war / du bist, warst / er ist, war / wir sind, waren 8. ich habe, hatte / du hast, hattest / er hat, hatte / ihr habt, hattet 9. Wem gab meine Schwester einen Bleistift? 10. Was lesen die Kinder? 11. Wen besucht Herr Benz in Hamburg? 12. Wer ist im Park? 13. Wohin fuhr Tina mit dem Zug? 14. Wann fängt das Konzert an? 15. Wo sind die Jungen? 16. kenne, gehen, weiß, fahren 17. einen Hut, diese Bluse, deinen Lehrer, ihn 18. meine Mutter, meiner Mutter / dein Auto, deinem Auto / den Zahnarzt, dem Zahnarzt / das Mädchen, dem Mädchen / Sie, Ihnen 19. Wer machte das Fenster auf? / Verstanden Sie, was ich fragte? 20. mir, dir, ihm, ihr, uns, euch, ihnen 21. Die Lehrerin sandte ihnen einen Brief. / Die Lehrerin sandte ihn ihnen. 22. C 23. C 24. A 25. D

CHAPTER 11

Written Practice 1

lachen: ich habe gelacht / du hast gelacht / er hat gelacht / wir haben gelacht / ihr habt gelacht / sie haben gelacht; **versuchen:** ich habe versucht / du hast versucht / er hat versucht / wir haben versucht / ihr habt versucht / sie haben versucht; **vorstellen:** ich habe vorgestellt / du hast vorgestellt / er hat vorgestellt / wir haben vorgestellt / ihr habt vorgestellt / sie haben vorgestellt

Written Practice 2

sprechen: ich habe gesprochen / du hast gesprochen / er hat gesprochen / wir haben gesprochen / ihr habt gesprochen / sie haben gesprochen; **versprechen:** ich habe versprochen / du hast versprochen / er hat versprochen / wir haben versprochen / ihr habt versprochen / sie haben versprochen; **aussprechen:** ich habe ausgesprochen / du hast ausgesprochen / er hat ausgesprochen / wir haben ausgesprochen / ihr habt ausgesprochen / sie haben ausgesprochen; **wissen:** ich habe gewusst / du hast gewusst / er hat gewusst / wir haben gewusst / ihr habt gewusst / sie haben gewusst; **beschreiben:** ich habe beschrieben / du hast beschrieben / er hat beschrieben / wir haben beschrieben / ihr habt beschrieben / sie haben beschrieben; **aussehen:** ich habe ausgesehen / du hast ausgesehen / er hat ausgesehen / wir haben ausgesehen / ihr habt ausgesehen / sie haben ausgesehen

Written Practice 3

1. Was hast du gesagt? 2. Wir haben Deutsch gelernt. 3. Die Kinder haben gern im Park gespielt. 4. Haben Sie meinen Sohn gesehen? 5. Wir haben drei Briefe von ihnen erhalten. 6. Robert hat in der Hauptstadt gewohnt. 7. Habt ihr die schöne Musik gehört? 8. Die Männer haben das alte Haus zerstört. 9. Ich habe euch ein kleines Paket gesandt. 10. Wer hat die Musik arrangiert? 11. Er hat es versprochen. 12. Was hast du gelesen? 13. Gudrun hat mein Fahrrad genommen. 14. Was hat der Dieb gestohlen? 15. Niemand hat dich verstanden.

Written Practice 4

1. Der Ausländer hat mit den Kindern gesprochen. / Der Ausländer hat mit meiner Tante gesprochen. / Der Ausländer hat mit dem König gesprochen. / Der Ausländer hat mit mir gesprochen. / Der Ausländer hat mit uns gesprochen. / Der Ausländer hat mit ihnen gesprochen. 2. Gudrun wohnt seit April bei ihren Eltern. / Gudrun wohnt seit April bei meiner Schwester. / Gudrun wohnt seit April bei einem Freund. / Gudrun wohnt seit April bei ihm. / Gudrun wohnt seit April bei ihr. / Gudrun wohnt seit April bei mir. 3. Sie bekommt einen Brief von ihren Eltern. / Sie bekommt einen Brief von einem Ausländer. / Sie bekommt einen Brief von deinem Bruder. / Sie bekommt einen Brief von dir. / Sie bekommt einen Brief von euch.

Written Practice 5

1. Die Hauptstadt Frankreichs ist Paris. 2. Die Hauptstadt Italiens ist Rom. 3. Die Hauptstadt Russlands ist Moskau. 4. Die Hauptstadt Norwegens ist Oslo. 5. Die Hauptstadt Polens ist Warschau. 6. Die Hauptstadt Spaniens ist Madrid. 7. Die Hauptstadt Tschechiens ist Prag. 8. Die Hauptstadt Griechenlands ist Athen. 9. Die Hauptstadt Japans ist Tokio. 10. Die Hauptstadt Österreichs ist Wien.

QUIZ

1. ich habe gefragt, habe versucht, habe vorgestellt / du hast gefragt, hast versucht, hast vorgestellt / er hat gefragt, hat versucht, hat vorgestellt / wir haben gefragt, haben versucht, haben vorgestellt / ihr habt gefragt, habt versucht, habt vorgestellt / Sie haben gefragt, haben versucht, haben vorgestellt 2. gedient, getrunken / arrangiert, erkannt / gehört, gestohlen / gegessen, getan / ausgesehen, gewusst 3. ich finde, fand, habe gefunden / du findest, fandest, hast gefunden / er findet, fand, hat gefunden / wir geben aus, gaben aus, haben ausgegeben / ihr gebt aus, gabt aus, habt ausgegeben / Sie geben aus, gaben aus, haben ausgegeben 4. Warum folgt sie den Kindern? / Warum folgt sie meiner Tochter? / Warum folgt sie mir? / Warum folgt sie dir? 5. Der Lehrer steht ihrem Bruder gegenüber. / Der Lehrer steht deinen Eltern gegenüber. / Der Lehrer steht ihm gegenüber. / Der Lehrer steht uns gegenüber. 6. Das ist ein Geschenk von der Königin. / Das ist ein Geschenk von unserem Kind. / Das ist ein Geschenk von euch. / Das ist ein Geschenk von ihnen. 7. B 8. A 9. D 10. A

CHAPTER 12

Written Practice 1

spazieren: ich bin spaziert / du bist spaziert / er ist spaziert / wir sind spaziert / ihr seid spaziert / sie sind spaziert; **kommen:** ich bin gekommen / du bist gekommen / er ist gekommen / wir sind gekommen / ihr seid gekommen / sie sind gekommen; **umsteigen:** ich bin umgestiegen / du bist umgestiegen / er ist umgestiegen / wir sind umgestiegen / ihr seid umgestiegen / sie sind umgestiegen; **bleiben:** ich bin geblieben / du bist geblieben / er ist geblieben / wir sind geblieben / ihr seid geblieben / sie sind geblieben; **sterben:** ich bin gestorben / du bist gestorben / er ist gestorben / wir sind gestorben / ihr seid gestorben / sie sind gestorben; **folgen:** ich bin gefolgt / du bist gefolgt / er ist gefolgt / wir sind gefolgt / ihr seid gefolgt / sie sind gefolgt

Written Practice 2

1. Ich bin sehr müde gewesen. 2. Ist deine Schwester wieder gesund geworden? 3. Der Zug ist um elf Uhr zehn angekommen. 4. Die Kinder sind in der Stadt geblieben. 5. Die Touristen sind zum Rathaus gegangen. 6. Meine Eltern sind im Park spazieren gegangen. 7. Wir haben Hunger gehabt. 8. Wohin bist du gefahren? 9. Die Jungen sind zum Marktplatz gelaufen. 10. Sie haben kein Geld gehabt.

Written Practice 3

1. Wir haben eine Stunde auf ihn gewartet. / Wir haben eine Stunde auf dich gewartet. / Wir haben eine Stunde auf diesen Ausländer gewartet. / Wir haben eine Stunde auf unsere Wirtin gewartet. / Wir haben eine Stunde auf die Diplomaten gewartet. / Wir haben eine Stunde auf euch gewartet. 2. Ich denke niemals an diese Probleme. / Ich denke niemals an meine Arbeit. / Ich denke niemals an unseren König. / Ich denke niemals an sie. / Ich denke niemals an Sie. / Ich denke niemals an sie.

Written Practice 4

1. **unterbrechen:** ich unterbreche / ich unterbrach / ich habe unterbrochen; du unterbrichst / du unterbrachst / du hast unterbrochen; ihr unterbrecht / ihr unterbracht / ihr habt unterbrochen
2. **widerspiegeln:** er spiegelt wider / er spiegelte wider / er hat widergespiegelt; wir spiegeln wider / wir spiegelten wider / wir haben widergespiegelt; du spiegelst wider / du spiegeltest wider / du hast widergespiegelt

Written Practice 5

1. Sie wissen nicht, dass es wieder sehr kalt geworden ist. / Sie wissen nicht, dass Onkel Peter vor zwei Tagen gestorben ist. 2. Niemand fragt, ob sie noch in Freiburg wohnen. / Niemand fragt, ob wir ihnen glauben. 3. Sie hat ihre Tasche verloren, während sie in Schweden gewesen ist. / Sie hat ihre Tasche verloren, während sie mit den Kindern gespielt hat. 4. Die Königin fragt, ob der König noch in Frankreich ist. / Die Königin fragt, ob ihre Kinder schon nach Italien gereist sind. / Die Königin fragt, ob die alte Frau Hunger gehabt hat. / Die Königin fragt, ob der Wissenschaftler den Leuten geholfen hat.

QUIZ

1. ich bin gegangen, bin marschiert, bin umgestiegen / du bist gegangen, bist marschiert, bist umgestiegen / er ist gegangen, ist marschiert, ist umgestiegen / wir sind geblieben, sind gewesen, sind geflogen / ihr seid geblieben, seid gewesen, seid geflogen / sie sind geblieben, sind gewesen, sind geflogen / ich bin

angekommen, bin gereist, bin spaziert / sie ist angekommen, ist gereist, ist spaziert / Sie sind angekommen, sind gereist, sind spaziert 2. haben gesehen, haben gelernt / sein geworden, sein gestorben / haben versprochen, sein geblieben / sein mitgegangen, sein gewesen / haben gehabt, sein geblieben / haben gegessen, sein gelaufen 3. für mich, mit mir / gegen dich, von dir / ohne ihn, bei ihm / durch sie, außer ihr / um uns, zu uns / für euch, nach euch / gegen Sie, mit Ihnen / ohne diesen Ausländer, von diesem Ausländer / um das Kind, zu dem Kind / durch die Schule, aus der Schule / ohne viele Romane, nach vielen Romanen 4. einem Tag, drei Wochen, einer Woche, einem Jahr, zehn Jahren 5. Mein Bruder schreibt, dass seine Frau wieder krank geworden ist. / Mein Bruder schreibt, dass er in der Hauptstadt gewesen ist. / Der Artzt fragt, ob es Frau Meyer besser geht. / Der Artzt fragt, ob Professor Benz zu Besuch gekommen ist. / Ich habe meinen Mantel verloren, als ich in Schweden gewesen bin. / Ich habe meinen Mantel verloren, als ich vor dem Rathaus gestanden habe. 6. C 7. A 8. D 9. A 10. A

CHAPTER 13

Written Practice 1

fahren: ich werde fahren / du wirst fahren / er wird fahren / wir werden fahren; **aufmachen:** ich werde aufmachen / du wirst aufmachen / er wird aufmachen / wir werden aufmachen; **beschreiben:** ich werde beschreiben / du wirst beschreiben / er wird beschreiben / wir werden beschreiben; **haben:** ich werde haben / er wird haben / ihr werdet haben / sie werden haben; **sein:** ich werde sein / er wird sein / ihr werdet sein / sie werden sein; **werden:** ich werde werden / er wird werden / ihr werdet werden / sie werden werden

Written Practice 2

1. Morgen bestellt sie ein Glas Rotwein. 2. Morgen erhält die Familie drei Briefe. 3. Morgen weint der Vater wieder. 4. Morgen steigen die Ausländer am Marktplatz um. 5. Morgen fliegst du wieder nach Portugal? 6. Morgen liest er den interessanten Roman. 7. Morgen spielen die Kinder unter dem Tisch.

Written Practice 3

1. Ich komme mit der Straßenbahn nach Hause. / Ich komme heute mit der Straßenbahn nach Hause.
2. Wir sind mit dem Zug in die Schweiz gereist. / Wir sind vor einer Woche mit dem Zug in die Schweiz gereist.

Written Practice 4

dat: dem Fahrrad / den Leuten / meinem Schrank / seiner Nachbarin / unseren Gästen / dem Handschuh / den Handschuhen / einem Roman / einer Bratwurst / dem Turm / der Burg / den Kaufhäusern / deinen Geschwistern / dem Dom; **gen:** des Fahrrads / der Leute / meines Schranks / seiner Nachbarin / unserer Gäste / des Handschuhs / der Handschuhe / eines Romans / einer Bratwurst / des Turms / der Burg / der Kaufhäuser / deiner Geschwister / des Doms

Written Practice 5

1. Robert hatte mir ein Geschenk gegeben. 2. Wir waren zum Park gegangen. 3. Hattest du mit dem kleinen Hund gespielt? 4. Warum warst du so böse gewesen? 5. Unsere Gäste waren in der Stadt geblieben.

Written Practice 6

1. Ich werde mich in einer Stunde rasieren. / Du wirst dich in einer Stunde rasieren. / Wir werden uns in einer Stunde rasieren. / Ihr werdet euch in einer Stunde rasieren. / Sie werden sich in einer Stunde rasieren.

Written Practice 7

sich beeilen: Ich beeile mich. / Du beeilst dich. / Er beeilt sich. / Wir beeilen uns. / Wer beeilt sich? **sich rasieren schnell:** Ich rasiere mich schnell. / Du rasierst dich schnell. / Er rasiert sich schnell. / Wir rasieren uns schnell. / Wer rasiert sich schnell? **sich irren:** Ich irre mich. / Sie irrt sich. / Sie irren sich. / Ihr irrt euch. / Man irrt sich. **sich freuen über das Buch:** Ich freue mich über das Buch. / Sie freut sich über das Buch. / Sie freuen sich über das Buch. / Ihr freut euch über das Buch. / Man freut sich über das Buch.

Written Practice 8

1. Du wirst dich waschen. / Er wird sich waschen. / Ich werde mich waschen. 2. Er wird hier aussteigen. / Ihr werdet hier aussteigen. / Sie werden hier aussteigen. 3. Ich werde in Bonn arbeiten. / Du wirst in Bonn arbeiten. / Wer wird in Bonn arbeiten?

QUIZ

1. Du wirst mitkommen. / Wir werden mitkommen. / Sie werden mitkommen. 2. Sie wird nichts versprechen. / Ihr werdet nichts versprechen. / Man wird nichts versprechen. 3. meine Gäste, meinen Gästen, meiner Gäste / Ihren Mantel, Ihrem Mantel, Ihres Mantels / seine Tochter, seiner Tochter, seiner Tochter / das Kaufhaus, dem Kaufhaus, des Kaufhauses 4. Hast du dich schon gewaschen? / Hat sie sich schon gewaschen? / Haben wir uns schon gewaschen? / Habt ihr euch schon gewaschen? 5. Ich weiß nicht, wo meine Verwandten gearbeitet haben. / Ich weiß nicht, wie diese Männer heißen. / Er fragte Thomas, warum die Touristen vor dem Bahnhof warten. / Er fragte Thomas, woher diese Ausländer kommen. 6. ich habe mich beeilt, bin gegangen, habe bestellt / ich hatte mich beeilt, war gegangen, hatte bestellt / sie hat sich beeilt, ist gegangen, hat bestellt / sie hatte sich beeilt, war gegangen, hatte bestellt / wir haben uns beeilt, sind gegangen, haben bestellt / wir hatten uns beeilt, waren gegangen, hatten bestellt / du hast dich beeilt, bist gegangen, hast bestellt / du hattest dich beeilt, warst gegangen, hattest bestellt 7. C 8. D 9. A 10. D

CHAPTER 14

Written Practice 1

aussteigen: pres er steigt aus / **past** er stieg aus / **pres perf** er ist ausgestiegen / **past perf** er war ausgestiegen / **fut** er wird aussteigen / **fut perf** er wird ausgestiegen sein; **versprechen: pres** wir versprechen / **past** wir versprachen / **pres perf** wir haben versprochen / **past perf** wir hatten versprochen / **fut** wir werden versprechen / **fut perf** wir werden versprochen haben; **besuchen: pres** du besuchst / **past** du besuchtest / **pres perf** du hast besucht / **past perf** du hattest besucht / **fut** du wirst besuchen / **fut perf** du wirst besucht haben; **sich rasieren: pres** ich rasiere mich / **past** ich rasierte mich / **pres perf** ich habe mich rasiert / **past perf** ich hatte mich rasiert / **fut** ich werde mich rasieren / **fut perf** ich werde mich rasiert haben; **wohnen: pres** ich wohne / **past** du wohntest / **pres perf** er hat gewohnt / **past perf** wir hatten gewohnt / **fut** ihr werdet wohnen / **fut perf** sie werden gewohnt haben; **verstehen: pres** ich verstehe / **past** du verstandest / **pres perf** er hat verstanden / **past perf** wir hatten verstanden / **fut** ihr werdet verstehen / **fut perf** sie werden verstanden haben

Written Practice 2

1. wegen des Examens / wegen dieser Besichtigung / wegen der Touristen
2. während eines Krieges / während des Gewitters / während des Tages
3. trotz des Schnees / trotz seiner Geschwister / trotz einer Nachbarin
4. anstatt der Handschuhe / anstatt einer Küche / anstatt dieser Flaschen

Written Practice 3

1. Sie zieht sich die Jacke an. / Ich ziehe mir den Regenmantel an. / Du ziehst dir das Sweatshirt an. 2. Wir haben uns eine Flasche Wein gekauft. / Ihr habt euch die Handschuhe gekauft. / Sie haben sich einen Roman gekauft. 3. Ich habe mir den Finger gebrochen. / Sie haben sich die Finger gebrochen. / Du hast dir die Beine gebrochen.

Written Practice 4

1. Er hat sich die Hände gewaschen. / Ihr habt euch die Hände gewaschen. / Die Männer haben sich die Hände gewaschen. / Wir haben uns die Hände gewaschen. / Du hast dir die Hände gewaschen.

Written Practice 5

1. **acc:** den Helden / den Jungen / den Soldaten; **dat:** dem Helden / dem Jungen / dem Soldaten; **gen:** des Helden / des Jungen / des Soldaten 2. **acc:** den Affen / den Prinzen / den Diplomaten; **dat:** dem Affen / dem Prinzen / dem Diplomaten; **gen:** des Affen / des Prinzen / des Diplomaten

Written Practice 6

1. Ich will einen Roman lesen. / Ich wollte einen Roman lesen. / Wir haben einen Roman lesen wollen. / Wir werden einen Roman lesen wollen. 2. Du kannst sehr gut Schach spielen. / Du konntest sehr gut Schach spielen. / Ihr habt sehr gut Schach spielen können. / Ihr werdet sehr gut Schach spielen können. 3. Sie muss ein bisschen warten. / Sie musste ein bisschen warten. / Sie haben ein bisschen warten müssen. / Sie werden ein bisschen warten müssen. 4. Ich soll fleißig arbeiten. / Er sollte fleißig arbeiten. / Wir haben fleißig arbeiten sollen. / Man wird fleißig arbeiten sollen.

Written Practice 7

1. Die Kinder konnten gut Klavier spielen. / Die Kinder haben gut Klavier spielen können. 2. Ich musste jeden Tag fleißig arbeiten. / Ich habe jeden Tag fleißig arbeiten müssen. 3. Du solltest dir die Hände waschen. / Du hast dir die Hände waschen sollen. 4. Sie mochte kein Eis. / Sie hat kein Eis gemocht. 5. Hier konnte man umsteigen. / Hier hat man umsteigen können. 6. Ihr musstet den Nachbarn helfen. / Ihr habt den Nachbarn helfen müssen.

QUIZ

1. ich schicke, wasche, steige aus, bekomme / du schicktest, wuschst, stiegst aus, bekamst / er hat geschickt, hat gewaschen, ist ausgestiegen, hat bekommen / wir hatten geschickt, hatten gewaschen, waren ausgestiegen, hatten bekommen / ihr werdet schicken, werdet waschen, werdet aussteigen, werdet bekommen / Sie werden geschickt haben, werden gewaschen haben, werden ausgestiegen sein, werden bekommen haben 2. mit d, von d / wegen g, trotz g / in a-d, anstatt g / während g, durch a / für a, neben a-d / statt g, zu d 3. Statt meiner Schwester wird Herr Keller ihm helfen. / Statt dieses Matrosen wird Herr Keller ihm helfen. / Statt seiner Geschwister wird Herr Keller ihm helfen. 4. Wegen ihrer Mutter musste Frau Benz in der Stadt bleiben. / Wegen des Gewitters musste Frau Benz in der Stadt bleiben. /

Wegen des Regens musste Frau Benz in der Stadt bleiben. 5. Man putzt sich die Zähne. / Die Kinder putzen sich die Zähne. / Niemand putzt sich die Zähne. / Wir putzen uns die Zähne. / Ihr putzt euch die Zähne. / Du putzt dir die Zähne. / Sie putzen sich die Zähne. / Mein Sohn putzt sich die Zähne. 6. die Kirche, ein Held, Ihre Eltern / die Kirche, einen Helden, Ihre Eltern / der Kirche, einem Helden, Ihren Eltern / er Kirche, eines Helden, Ihrer Eltern 7. ich darf, kann, mag / Sie durften, konnten, mochten / er will, soll, muss / ihr wolltet, solltet, musstet 8. C 9. A 10. B

CHAPTER 15

Written Practice 1

1. Ich habe das Heft, das du verloren hast. / Ich habe einen Regenschirm, den du verloren hast. / Ich habe die Flasche, die du verloren hast. / Ich habe den Artikel, den du verloren hast. 2. Robert besucht den Matrosen, dessen Vater Diplomat gewesen ist. / Robert besucht die Ausländer, deren Vater Diplomat gewesen ist. / Robert besucht eine Dame, deren Vater Diplomat gewesen ist. / Robert besucht das Mädchen, dessen Vater Diplomat gewesen ist. 3. Wo fandest du die Schlüssel, nach denen der Polizist fragte? / Wo fandest du den Wagen, nach dem der Polizist fragte? / Wo fandest du den Ausländer, nach dem der Polizist fragte? / Wo fandest du das Mädchen, nach dem der Polizist fragte? / Wo fandest du die Tasche, nach der der Polizist fragte? 4. Der Soldat, den ich in Freiburg traf, wohnt jetzt in Wien. / Die Touristen, die ich in Freiburg traf, wohnen jetzt in Wien. / Die Tänzerin, die ich in Freiburg traf, wohnt jetzt in Wien. / Das Kind, das ich in Freiburg traf, wohnt jetzt in Wien. / Der Polizist, den ich in Freiburg traf, wohnt jetzt in Wien. 5. Die Kinder, deren Schwester gestorben ist, wollen nicht mitgehen. / Der Junge, dessen Schwester gestorben ist, will nicht mitgehen. / Die Tänzerin, deren Schwester gestorben ist, will nicht mitgehen. / Das Mädchen, dessen Schwester gestorben ist, will nicht mitgehen. / Der Student, dessen Schwester gestorben ist, will nicht mitgehen.

Written Practice 2

1. Die Mutter sagt, dass sie die Kinder gut hat erziehen wollen. / Die Mutter sagt, dass ihr Sohn Soldat wird werden müssen. / Die Mutter sagt, dass die Kinder kein Bier haben trinken dürfen. 2. Ich weiß nicht, warum Tina das Klavier nicht hat spielen können. / Ich weiß nicht, warum du nach Belgien wirst reisen sollen. / Ich weiß nicht, warum die Tänzerin in Bremen wird tanzen wollen.

Written Practice 3

können es reparieren: pres ich kann es reparieren / **past** ich konnte es reparieren / **pres perf** wir haben es reparieren können / **fut** wir werden es reparieren können; **hören sie sprechen: pres** ich höre sie sprechen / **past** ich hörte sie sprechen / **pres perf** wir haben sie sprechen hören / **fut** wir werden sie sprechen hören; **lassen ein Hemd machen: pres** Sie lassen ein Hemd machen / **past** Sie ließen ein Hemd machen / **pres perf** er hat ein Hemd machen lassen / **fut** er wird ein Hemd machen lassen; **wollen ihn interviewen: pres** Sie wollen ihn interviewen / **past** Sie wollten ihn interviewen / **pres perf** er hat ihn interviewen wollen / **fut** er wird ihn interviewen wollen

Written Practice 4

1. mit ihm / mit wem 2. damit / womit 3. davon / wovon 4. in sie / in wen 5. darin / worin 6. daran / woran 7. gegen sie / gegen wen 8. dagegen / wogegen 9. daraus / woraus 10. nach ihr / nach wem

Written Practice 5

1. c 2. b, d, f, l 3. i 4. d, l 5. j 6. b, d, m 7. d, k 8. g 9. b, d, l 10. d, l

Written Practice 6

1. Ihre Tochter ist sehr intelligent. / Ihre Tochter ist außerordentlich intelligent. / Ihre Tochter ist relativ intelligent. / Ihre Tochter ist ziemlich intelligent. / Ihre Tochter ist erstaunlicherweise intelligent. 2. Überall sehen wir viele Probleme. / Hier sehen wir viele Probleme. / Dort sehen wir viele Probleme. / In dieser Stadt sehen wir viele Probleme. / In Europa sehen wir viele Probleme. 3. Unsere Familie ist oft in Griechenland gewesen. / Unsere Familie ist selten in Griechenland gewesen. / Unsere Familie ist manchmal in Griechenland gewesen. / Unsere Familie ist nie in Griechenland gewesen. / Unsere Familie ist ziemlich oft in Griechenland gewesen.

QUIZ

1. nom der, die, das, die / acc den, die, das, die / dat dem, der, dem, denen / gen dessen, deren, dessen, deren 2. Der Wagen, den ich kaufen will, ist ziemlich alt. / Die Lampe, die ich kaufen will, ist ziemlich alt. / Die Wörterbücher, die ich kaufen will, sind ziemlich alt. / Das Kleid, das ich kaufen will, ist ziemlich alt. 3. er hört sie lachen, lässt das Auto reparieren / wir hörten sie lachen, ließen das Auto reparieren / ihr habt sie lachen hören, habt das Auto reparieren lassen / Sie werden sie lachen hören, werden das Auto reparieren lassen / ich lerne schwimmen, sehe sie tanzen / du lerntest schwimmen, sahst sie tanzen / wir hatten schwimmen lernen, hatten sie tanzen sehen / man wird schwimmen lernen, wird sie tanzen sehen 4. Die Frauen sagen, dass der Reporter den Chef hat interviewen wollen. / Die Frauen sagen, dass Werner das Auto wird waschen lassen. / Die Frauen sagen, dass sie sich nicht für Sport interessieren. 5. Der Student fragt, ob wir den Krieg verlieren werden. / Der Student fragt, ob die Touristen dorthin haben reisen dürfen. / Der Student fragt, ob wir ihm ein Paket geschickt haben. 6. B 7. A 8. A 9. A 10. C

PART THREE TEST

1. ich habe geholfen, hatte geholfen / er hat geholfen, hatte geholfen / wir haben geholfen, hatten geholfen 2. ich habe versprochen, hatte versprochen / sie hat versprochen, hatte versprochen / ihr habt versprochen, hattet versprochen 3. du bist geflogen, warst geflogen / er ist geflogen, war geflogen / Sie sind geflogen, waren geflogen 4. ich bin gewesen, war gewesen / du bist gewesen, warst gewesen / wir sind gewesen, waren gewesen 5. haben gefragt, sein spaziert / haben gegessen, sein geworden / haben gehabt, sein mitgegangen 6. meinem Bruder, dieser Dame, deinen Kindern 7. ihm, ihr, ihnen 8. dem Ausländer, dir, uns 9. zwei Tagen, einer Woche, einem Jahr 10. mich, ihn, euch 11. mich, mir, mein 12. dich, dir, dein 13. Sie, Ihnen, Ihr 14. meine Brüder, meinen Brüdern, meiner Brüder 15. das Kind, dem Kind, des Kindes 16. Wir haben ein Butterbrot bestellt. / Wir werden ein Butterbrot bestellen. 17. Ihr habt euch gewaschen. / Ihr werdet euch waschen. 18. Wir sind hier umgestiegen. / Wir werden hier umsteigen. 19. Hast du Schach spielen können? / Wirst du Schach spielen können? 20. Die Kinder, deren Vater Zahnarzt ist, wohnen in diesem großen Haus. / Das Mädchen, dessen Vater Zahnarzt ist, wohnt in diesem großen Haus. / Der Schüler, dessen Vater Zahnarzt ist, wohnt in diesem großen Haus. 21. Der Reporter fragt, ob der Diplomat nicht gut hat fahren können. / Der Reporter fragt, ob er den Helden wird interviewen wollen. 22. C 23. A 24. B 25. C

CHAPTER 16

Written Practice 1

1. Der Brief, welchen sie gelesen hat, ist interessant. / Die Zeitung, welche sie gelesen hat, ist interessant. / Der Roman, welchen sie gelesen hat, ist interessant. / Die Romane, welche sie gelesen hat, sind interessant. 2. Die Touristen, mit welchen Karl sprechen will, kommen aus Polen. / Der Matrose, mit welchem Karl sprechen will, kommt aus Polen. / Die Tänzerin, mit welcher Karl sprechen will, kommt aus Polen. / Das Kind, mit welchem Karl sprechen will, kommt aus Polen.

Written Practice 2

1. Ich habe etwas, was ich im Park gefunden habe. / Ich habe etwas, was meine Mutter mir gegeben hat. / Ich habe etwas, worüber du dich freuen wirst. / Ich habe etwas, womit die Kinder spielen können. 2. Ist das alles, was du sagen kannst? / Ist das alles, was Tina kaufen wollte? / Ist das alles, wofür er sich interessiert? / Ist das alles, worüber Sie sprechen wollen? 3. Ich lerne viel, was nicht in Büchern steht. / Ich lerne viel, worüber Goethe geschrieben hatte. / Ich lerne viel, was interessant ist. 4. Ich verstehe nichts, was die alte Frau sagt. / Ich verstehe nichts, was du in diesem Buch geschrieben hast. / Ich verstehe nichts, was man in dieser Klasse lernt.

Written Practice 3

1. Wilhelm II. wurde 1859 geboren. / Er ist 1941 gestorben. 2. Otto von Bismarck wurde 1815 geboren. / Er ist 1898 gestorben. 3. Mein Bruder wurde 1995 geboren. / Er ist 2005 gestorben. 4. Karl der Große wurde 742 geboren. / Er ist 814 gestorben. 5. Meine Mutter wurde 1966 geboren. / Sie ist 1998 gestorben.

Written Practice 4

1. kälter / am kältesten 2. interessanter / am interessantesten 3. besser / am besten 4. länger / am längsten 5. dunkler / am dunkelsten 6. wärmer / am wärmsten 7. schwärzer / am schwärzesten 8. ruhiger / am ruhigsten 9. weißer / am weißesten 10. ärmer / am ärmsten

Written Practice 5

1. b 2. d 3. a 4. a 5. b 6. c 7. b 8. a 9. a 10. b 11. d 12. c 13. d 14. a 15. b 16. c 17. b 18. d 19. a 20. b

QUIZ

1. welcher, welche, welches, welche 2. welchen, welche, welches, welche 3. welchem, welcher, welchem, welchen 4. dessen, deren, dessen, deren 5. Er hat ein Auto, das er wird reparieren lassen. / Er hat ein Auto, welches er wird reparieren lassen. 6. Martin hat etwas, wrüber du dich freuen wirst. / Ich verstehe nichts, was er gesagt hat. 7. Goethe wurde im Jahre 1749 geboren. / Er ist im Jahre 1832 gestorben. 8. älter, am ältesten / kleiner, am kleinsten / jünger, am jüngsten / besser, am besten / mehr, am meisten / größer, am größten / interessanter, am interessantesten 9. Warum gibt es keinen Wein? / Warum gibt es nur eine Flasche Milch? / Warum gibt es kein Bier? / Warum gibt es keinen Sekt? 10. Hast du ihn gern? / Hast du den Soldaten gern? / Hast du sie gern? / Hast du die Kinder gern? / Hast du das Kind gern?

CHAPTER 17

Written Practice 1

1. Zwei Bücher werden von dem Lehrer gekauft. 2. Der Roman wird von ihr gelesen. 3. Das Brot wird von dem Bäcker gebacken. 4. Ich werde von meinem Vater gerufen. 5. Viele Lieder werden von den Soldaten gesungen. 6. Das Haus wurde von Herrn Bauer verkauft. 7. Tante Gerda wurde von meiner Mutter angerufen. 8. Zwei Tassen Kaffee wurden von ihnen getrunken. 9. Diese Gedichte wurden von ihm gelernt. 10. Der Morgenkaffee wurde von der Wirtin gebracht. 11. Der Roman ist von ihm geschrieben worden. 12. Ein Hut ist von den Kindern gefunden worden. 13. Das Eis ist von meiner Schwester gegessen worden. 14. Der Artikel wird von dem Reporter geschrieben werden. 15. Das Museum wird von den Ausländern besucht werden.

Written Practice 2

acc: jenen netten Wirt / diese kleine Bluse / welches rote Auto; **dat:** jenem netten Wirt / dieser kleinen Bluse / welchem roten Auto; **gen:** jenes netten Wirts / dieser kleinen Bluse / welches roten Autos; **acc:** denselben alten Wagen / jenes neue Haus / alle fremden Leute; **dat:** demselben alten Wagen / jenem neuen Haus / allen fremden Leuten; **gen:** desselben alten Wagens / jenes neuen Hauses / aller fremden Leute

Written Practice 3

1. Die Kinder dieses jungen Mannes lernen gut. / Die Kinder dieses kranken Mannes lernen gut. 2. Sie hat mit demselben neuen Diplomaten gesprochen. / Sie hat mit demselben schlauen Diplomaten gesprochen. 3. Jede grüne Tanne is mehr als zwanzig Jahre alt. / Jede große Tanne is mehr als zwanzig Jahre alt.

Written Practice 4

verkaufen: Verkaufe! / Verkauft! / Verkaufen Sie! **versprechen:** Versprich! / Versprecht! / Versprechen Sie! **trinken:** Trinke! / Trinkt! / Trinken Sie! **vorstellen:** Stelle vor! / Stellt vor! / Stellen Sie vor! **tun:** Tue! / Tut! / Tun Sie! **zumachen:** Mache zu! / Macht zu! / Machen Sie zu! **lesen:** Lies! / Lest! / Lesen Sie! **laufen:** Laufe! / Lauft! / Laufen Sie! **sein:** Sei! / Seid! / Seien Sie!

Written Practice 5

sprechen: Sprich! / Sprechen wir! **sagen:** Sage! / Sagen wir! **reisen:** Reise! / Reisen wir! **aufmachen:** Mache auf! / Machen wir auf! **zerstören:** Zerstöre! / Zerstören wir! **warten:** Warte! / Warten wir! **essen:** Iss! Essen wir! **erhalten:** Erhalte! / Erhalten wir! **ausgeben:** Gib aus! / Geben wir aus!

Written Practice 6

1. b 2. c 3. c 4. b 5. a 6. a 7. b 8. a 9. a 10. a 11. c 12. a 13. d 14. a 15. b

QUIZ

1. wird gespielt, wird gearbeitet, werden zugemacht, wird versprochen, werde mitgenommen 2. ich werde gesehen, werde besucht, werde genannt / du wurdest gesehen, wurdest besucht, wurdest genannt / er ist gesehen worden, ist besucht worden, ist genannt worden / Sie werden gesehen werden, werden besucht werden, werden genannt werden / es wird gelernt, wird gefüttert, wird aufgemacht / er wurde

gelernt, wurde gefüttert, wurde aufgemacht / sie war gelernt worden, war gefuttert worden, war aufgemacht worden / sie werden gelernt werden, werden gefüttert werden, werden aufgemacht werden 3. Die neue Kanzlerin ist von dem Präsidenten vorgestellt worden. 4. Die alte Kirche war von ihnen abgerissen worden. 5. Der Busch wurde von mir neben dem Haus gepflanzt. 6. Haben Sie jenen großen Bären gesehen? / Haben Sie jenen braunen Bären gesehen? 7. Diese jungen Männer werden uns helfen. / Diese alten Männer werden uns helfen. 8. Wann kommt der nächste Zug? / Wann kommt der letzte Zug? 9. C 10. Triff! Trefft! Treffen Sie! / Pflanze! Pflanzt! Pflanzen Sie! / Schlafe! Schlaft! Schlafen Sie! / Werde! Werdet! Werden Sie! / Sei! Seid! Seien Sie! / Komme mit! Kommt mit! Kommen Sie mit! / Besuche! Besucht! Besuchen Sie! / Gib! Gebt! Geben Sie! / Sieh! Seht! Sehen Sie! / Sprich! Sprecht! Sprechen Sie!

CHAPTER 18

Written Practice 1

1. Mir wurde von ihm geholfen. / Mir ist von ihm geholfen worden. / Mir wird von ihm geholfen werden. 2. Der Lehrerin wurde nicht geglaubt. / Der Lehrerin ist nicht geglaubt worden. / Der Lehrerin wird nicht geglaubt werden. 3. Ihm wurde dafür gedankt. / Ihm ist dafür gedankt worden. / Ihm wird dafür gedankt werden. 4. Wurde dem Professor imponiert? / Ist dem Professor imponiert worden? / Wird dem Professor imponiert werden?

Written Practice 2

1. Frau Schäfer wird nach Hannover fahren sollen. / Frau Schäfer wird nach Hannover fahren wollen. / Frau Schäfer wird nach Hannover fahren müssen. 2. Haben Sie Ihre Nachbarn einladen können? / Haben Sie Ihre Nachbarn einladen müssen? / Haben Sie Ihre Nachbarn einladen dürfen? 3. Hans wird von seiner Schwester geküsst werden wollen. / Hans wird von seiner Schwester geküsst werden müssen. / Hans wird von seiner Schwester geküsst werden sollen. 4. Hat der Wagen repariert werden können? / Hat der Wagen repariert werden müssen? / Hat der Wagen repariert werden sollen? 5. Ihm soll sofort geholfen werden. / Ihm kann sofort geholfen werden. / Ihm muss sofort geholfen werden.

Written Practice 3

1. Das Haus kann geräumt werden. / Das Haus muss geräumt werden. 2. Es durfte nicht repariert werden. / Es musste nicht repariert werden. 3. Das Kind wird fotografiert werden wollen. / Das Kind wird fotografiert werden können.

Written Practice 4

1. Ist es abgeschleppt worden? / Sind sie abgeschleppt worden? / Ist der Wagen abgeschleppt worden? / Sind die Autos abgeschleppt worden? / Ist der Bus abgeschleppt worden? 2. Sein Freund konnte nicht verstanden werden. / Die Kinder konnten nicht verstanden werden. / Ich konnte nicht verstanden werden. / Du konntest nicht verstanden werden. / Wir konnten nicht verstanden werden. 3. Ihnen wird niemals geglaubt werden. / Ihr wird niemals geglaubt werden. / Ihm wird niemals geglaubt werden. / Meiner Frau wird niemals geglaubt werden. / Dem Physiker wird niemals geglaubt werden.

Written Practice 5

1. Der Fernsehapparat ließ sich nicht reparieren. 2. Diese Romane haben sich schnell lesen lassen. 3. Die Bären ließen sich nicht fotografieren. 4. Das lässt sich sehr leicht ändern.

Written Practice 6

1. **pres** Das lässt sich nicht verstehen. / **pres perf** Das hat sich nicht verstehen lassen. / **fut** Das wird sich nicht verstehen lassen. 2. **past** Wurde dem Gast gut gedient? / **pres perf** Ist dem Gast gut gedient worden? / **fut** Wird dem Gast gut gedient werden? 3. **pres** Du wirst gesehen. / **past** Du wurdest gesehen. / **pres perf** Du bist gesehen worden. 4. **pres** Der kranken Katze kann nicht geholfen werden. / **pres perf** Der kranken Katze hat nicht geholfen werden können. / **fut** Der kranken Katze wird nicht geholfen werden können. 5. **past** Nichts konnte getan werden. / **pres perf** Nichts hat getan werden können. / **fut** Nichts wird getan werden können.

Written Practice 7

nom: mein junger Freund / unsere alte Tante / ihr neues Fahrrad; **acc:** meinen jungen Freund / unsere alte Tante / ihr neues Fahrrad; **dat:** meinem jungen Freund / unserer alten Tante / ihrem neuen Fahrrad; **gen:** meines jungen Freundes / unserer alten Tante / ihres neuen Fahrrads; **nom:** dein kleines Haus / jeder große Stuhl / diese graue Katze; **acc:** dein kleines Haus / jeden großen Stuhl / diese graue Katze; **dat:** deinem kleinen Haus / jedem großen Stuhl / dieser grauen Katze; **gen:** deines kleinen Hauses / jedes großen Stuhls / dieser grauen Katze; **nom:** ihr kleiner Sohn / deine junge Schwester; **acc:** deine junge Schwester; **dat:** ihrem kleinen Sohn; **gen:** ihres kleinen Sohns / deiner jungen Schwester; **nom:** eine kranke Dame / unser letzter Brief; **acc:** eine kranke Dame / unseren letzten Brief; **gen:** einer kranken Dame / unseres letzten Briefes

Written Practice 8

1. Ist das der Bruder deines amerikanischen Gasts? / Ist das der Bruder Ihrer netten Kusine? / Ist das der Bruder eurer jungen Freunde? 2. Kennen Sie meine neue Freundin? / Kennen Sie seinen alten Onkel? / Kennen Sie ihren intelligenten Sohn? 3. Hans wollte mit unserem kleinen Hund spielen. / Hans wollte mit jenen netten Kindern spielen. / Hans wollte mit seinem neuen Fußball spielen.

Written Practice 9

Sample answers are given. 1. alte 2. neue 3. jüngeren 4. hübschen 5. neue 6. kaputtes 7. deutschen 8. brauner 9. reinen 10. kleines

Written Practice 10

1. d 2. a 3. a 4. b 5. d 6. a 7. d 8. b 9. c 10. b

QUIZ

1. Der Wagen muss abgeschleppt werden. / Der Wagen hat abgeschleppt werden müssen. / Der Wagen wird abgeschleppt werden müssen. 2. Ihnen wurde dafür gedankt. / Ihnen war dafür gedankt worden. / Ihnen wird dafür gedankt werden. 3. Es lässt sich nicht leicht ändern. / Es ließ sich nicht leicht ändern. / Es hat sich nicht leicht ändern lassen. 4. Ihm wurde von ihnen geholfen. / Uns wurde von ihnen geholfen. / Dem Beamten wurde von ihnen geholfen. / Der Dichterin wurde von ihnen geholfen. / Dir wurde von ihnen geholfen. 5. seine neue Freundin / einen netten Mann, seine neue Freundin / einem netten Mann / eines netten Mannes, seiner neuen Freundin 6. kein interessantes Buch / Ihre alten Stühle / keinem interessanten Buch, Ihren alten Stühlen / keines interessanten Buches, Ihrer alten Stühle 7. B 8. A 9. C 10. A

CHAPTER 19

Written Practice 1

schlafen: ich schlafe X / du schlafest / er schlafe / wir schlafen X / ihr schlafet / sie schlafen X; **vergessen:** ich vergesse X / du vergessest / er vergesse / wir vergessen X / ihr vergesset / sie vergessen X; **mitnehmen:** ich nehme mit X / du nehmest mit / er nehme mit / wir nehmen mit X / ihr nehmet mit / sie nehmen mit X; **fragen:** ich frage X / du fragest / er frage / wir fragen X / ihr fraget / sie fragen X; **aussehen:** ich sehe aus X / du sehest aus / er sehe aus / wir sehen aus X / ihr sehet aus / sie sehen aus X; **sein:** ich sei / du seiest / er sei / wir seien / ihr seiet / sie seien

Written Practice 2

1. Er sagte, dass zwei Autos abgeschleppt worden seien. / Er sagte, dass die Regierung den armen Menschen helfen werde. / Er sagte, dass er nur selten ins Theater gehe. 2. Ein Freund schrieb uns, dass er nächste Woche kommen könne. / Ein Freund schrieb uns, dass sein Bruder in Gudrun verliebt sei. / Ein Freund schrieb uns, dass seine Familie das Geld noch nicht erhalten habe.

Written Practice 3

1. Sie berichtete, die Regierung habe dem alten König geholfen. / Sie berichtete, der Kanzler werde morgen ankommen. / Sie berichtete, es gebe nichts Schöneres als Wien. 2. Martin schrieb mir, dass seine Freundin in Russland gewesen sei. / Martin schrieb mir, dass der Fluss das Land überschwemmt habe. / Martin schrieb mir, dass die warme Sonne jeden Menschen gesund machen müsse.

Written Practice 4

1. Mein Mann fragte, wo sein neuer Pullover sei. / Mein Mann fragte, ob Erik den Wagen reparieren könne. / Mein Mann fragte, wessen Tasche der Dieb gestohlen habe. / Mein Mann fragte, ob sie schon in der Hauptstadt gewesen seien. / Mein Mann fragte, wie viel Herr Bauer dafür ausgeben werde.

QUIZ

1. ich versuche, versuchte, komme, käme / du versuchest, versuchtest, kommest, kämest / wir versuchen, versuchten, kommen, kämen 2. du fahrest, führest, gehest, gingest / er fahre, führe, gehe, ginge / ihr fahret, führet, gehet, ginget 3. ich brauche, brauchte, sehe aus, sähe aus / sie brauche, brauchte, sehe aus, sähe aus / Sie brauchen, brauchten, sehen aus, sähen aus 4. ich werde, würde, sei, wäre / du werdest, würdest, seiest, wärest / sie werden, würden, seien, wären 5. Erik sagte, dass seine Freundin in Darmstadt arbeiten wolle. / Erik sagte, dass niemand ihm etwas über den Film erzählt habe. / Erik sagte, dass Martin ein Buch für seine Frau kaufen werde. / Erik sagte, dass unsere Freunde einen neuen VW kaufen wollten. / Die Lehrerin fragte, ob Herr Schneider bei euch zu Gast sei. / Die Lehrerin fragte, ob Felix einen Bleistift gefunden habe. / Die Lehrerin fragte, ob die Schüler lesen und schreiben lernten. / Die Lehrerin fragte, ob die warme Sonne den Kranken gesund machen werde. 6. A 7. C 8. D 9. A 10. B

CHAPTER 20

Written Practice 1

1. Erik tat so, als ob er sehr klug wäre. / Erik tat so, als ob er plötzlich reich geworden wäre. / Erik tat so, als ob er diese Probleme lösen könnte. / Erik tat so, als ob er den Kanzler schon kennen gelernt hätte. 2. Sie

schrie, als ob sie ein Ungeheuer gesehen hätte. / Sie schrie, als ob sie sterben müsste. / Sie schrie, als ob sie wahnsinnig wäre. / Sie schrie, als ob sie nicht schwimmen könnte.

Written Practice 2

1. Wenn ich Deutsch verstünde, würde ich diese Bücher lesen. 2. Wenn wir ihm helfen könnten, würde er glücklich sein. 3. Wenn sie ihm mehr Geld gegeben hätten, hätte er das neue Haus gekauft. 4. Wenn ich im Lotto gewonnen hätte, wäre ich nach Amerika geflogen. 5. Wenn der Schüler fleißiger gewesen wäre, hätte er das Gedicht auswendig gelernt.

Written Practice 3

1. Es ist sehr wichtig genug Milch zu trinken. / Es ist sehr wichtig fleißig zu arbeiten. / Es ist sehr wichtig pünktlich anzukommen. / Es ist sehr wichtig alten Menschen zu helfen. / Es ist sehr wichtig gute Freunde zu haben. / Es ist sehr wichtig höflich zu sein.

Written Practice 4

1. Er kam in die Küche, ohne seine Mutter zu grüssen. / Er kam in die Küche, ohne seiner Mutter zu helfen. / Er kam in die Küche, ohne die Tür zuzumachen. 2. Karin arbeitet in Berlin, um mehr Geld zu verdienen. / Karin arbeitet in Berlin, um bei einer Tante zu wohnen. / Karin arbeitet in Berlin, um die großen Museen zu besuchen. 3. Die Kinder stehen an der Ecke, anstatt zur Schule zu gehen. / Die Kinder stehen an der Ecke, anstatt ihren kranken Onkel zu besuchen. / Die Kinder stehen an der Ecke, anstatt sich zu beeilen nach Hause zu kommen.

Written Practice 5

1. arbeiten zu müssen 2. vergessen zu sollen 3. sprechen zu wollen 4. gelernt zu haben 5. verstanden zu haben 6. gewesen zu sein 7. mitgegangen zu sein 8. zerstört zu werden 9. aufgemacht zu werden 10. bewundert worden zu sein

Written Practice 6

1. d 2. a 3. c 4. b 5. a 6. c 7. a 8. d 9. a 10. b 11. a 12. c 13. a 14. d 15. c

QUIZ

1. trüge, würde tragen / brächte, würde bringen / versuchte, würde versuchen / würde, würde werden / wäre, würde sein / ließe, würde lassen / sähe aus, würde aussehen / hülfe, würde helfen / verstünde, würde verstehen / wüsste, würde wissen 2. Wenn er hier wäre, würde er mit Onkel Peter sprechen. / Wenn er hier wäre, würde ich ihm ein Geschenk geben. / Wenn er hier wäre, müsste er auf dem Sofa schlafen. 3. Wenn das Wetter besser gewesen wäre, hätten die Kinder im Garten gespielt. / Wenn das Wetter besser gewesen wäre, wäre der Wagen repariert worden. / Wenn das Wetter besser gewesen wäre, wäre ich früher nach Hause gegangen. 4. Wenn sie mehr Geld hätte, würde sie uns Eis kaufen. / Wenn die jüngeren Kinder hier wären, würde sie uns Eis kaufen. / Wenn es sehr heiß würde, würde sie uns Eis kaufen. 5. Sie tat so, als ob sie alles verstehen könnte. / Sie tat so, als ob sie so klug wäre. / Sie tat so, als ob wir ihr damit helfen würden. 6. Es ist oft schwer einem Dieb zu glauben. / Es ist oft schwer interessante Bücher zu finden. / Es ist oft schwer im Hotel zu bleiben, wenn das Wetter schön ist. 7. Er ist nach Wien gereist, um Arbeit zu suchen. / Er ist nach Wien gereist, um an der Universität studieren zu können. / Er ist nach Wien gereist, um in die Oper zu gehen. 8. Er hat immer behauptet ein Freund von mir zu sein. / Er hat immer behauptet vier Sprachen sprechen zu können. / Er hat immer behauptet die Kanzlerin kennen gelernt

zu haben. 9. Die Kinder kamen nach Hause, ohne sich die Hände zu waschen. / Die Kinder kamen nach Hause, ohne Brot und Milch gekauft zu haben. / Die Kinder kamen nach Hause, ohne ihre Freunde mitgebracht zu haben. 10. Martin wollte bis zehn Uhr schlafen, anstatt in die Stadt zu fahren. / Martin wollte bis zehn Uhr schlafen, anstatt den alten Wagen reparieren zu lassen. / Martin wollte bis zehn Uhr schlafen, anstatt seinem Vater zu helfen.

PART FOUR TEST

1. Die Männer, mit denen ich in einer Fabrik arbeite, haben wenig Freizeit. / Die Männer, mit welchen ich in einer Fabrik arbeite, haben wenig Freizeit. 2. Sie haben das Dorf, in dem meine Tante geboren ist, besichtigt. / Sie haben das Dorf, in welchem meine Tante geboren ist, besichtigt. 3. Die Kinder finden alles, was ihre Eltern versteckt haben. 4. ich werde vorgestellt / du wurdest vorgestellt / er ist vorgestellt worden / wir werden vorgestellt werden 5. ich muss verhaftet werden / du musstest verhaftet werden / ihr hattet verhaftet werden müssen / Sie werden verhaftet werden müssen 6. Das Examen ist von den Lehrern diskutiert worden. 7. Ein neues Haus wird von uns gekauft werden. 8. Der neue Mieter wird von der Wirtin vorgestellt. 9. Habt ihr einen großen Bären gesehen? 10. Die Töchter dieser alten Frau arbeiten in Kiel. 11. Alle jüngeren Kinder müssen an der Ecke warten. 12. triff!, trefft!, treffen Sie! / mach auf!, macht auf!, machen Sie auf! / sieh!, seht!, sehen Sie! / sei!, seid!, seien Sie! / werde!, werdet!, werden Sie! 13. seine letzte Frage / einen guten Mann / einem guten Mann, seiner letzten Frage / meine alten Handschuhe / diesem kleinen Haus, meinen alten Handschuhen / dieses kleinen Hauses 14. ich stelle vor, stellte vor / du stellest vor, stelltest vor / er stelle vor, stellte vor 15. wir werden, würden / ihr werdet, würdet / Sie werden, würden 16. ich sei, wäre / sie sei, wäre / sie seien, wären / 17. Frau Schneider sagte, dass ihr Bruder in der Hauptstadt wohnen wolle. / Frau Schneider sagte, dass niemand ihr darüber erzählen werde. / Frau Schneider sagte, dass die Touristen sich morgen mit der Kanzlerin treffen würden. / Der Beamte fragte, ob das ihr Koffer sei. / Der Beamte fragte, ob der Wagen repariert worden sei. / Der Beamte fragte, ob die Ausländer ihre Fahrkarten bekommen hätten. 18. Wenn er hier wäre, könnte Tina mit ihm sprechen. / Wenn er hier wäre, würden wir mit ihm in die Stadt fahren. 19. Wenn das Wetter besser gewesen wäre, wäre ich in die Berge gefahren. / Wenn das Wetter besser gewesen wäre, hätten sie zum Stadtpark gehen können. 20. Er tat so, als ob er alles verstanden hätte. / Er tat so, als ob er sein Geld nicht finden könnte. / Er tat so, als ob er mich gar nicht gesehen hätte. / Der Student spricht, als ob er sehr klug wäre. / Der Student spricht, als ob wir ihm nicht helfen wollten. / Der Student spricht, als ob er mich nicht kennte. 21. Sie fahren in die Schweiz, um Freunde zu besuchen. / Sie fahren in die Schweiz, um ein kleines Haus in den Bergen zu kaufen. / Sie fahren in die Schweiz, um die alten Dörfer zu fotografieren. 22. C 23. A 24. B 25. D

FINAL EXAM

1. C 2. A 3. A 4. A 5. C 6. B 7. A 8. D 9. A 10. B 11. D 12. B 13. B 14. A 15. C 16. B 17. A 18. A 19. C 20. C 21. B 22. D 23. B 24. A 25. A 26. A 27. A 28. B 29. A 30. D 31. D 32. A 33. B 34. A 35. C 36. A 37. B 38. C 39. B 40. B 41. A 42. C 43. B 44. C 45. A 46. D 47. B 48. A 49. C 50. D

Index